Walled Life

Walled Life
Concrete, Cinema, Art

JENNY STÜMER

BLOOMSBURY ACADEMIC
NEW YORK • LONDON • OXFORD • NEW DELHI • SYDNEY

BLOOMSBURY ACADEMIC
Bloomsbury Publishing Inc
1385 Broadway, New York, NY 10018, USA
50 Bedford Square, London, WC1B 3DP, UK
29 Earlsfort Terrace, Dublin 2, Ireland

BLOOMSBURY, BLOOMSBURY ACADEMIC and the Diana logo are
trademarks of Bloomsbury Publishing Plc

First published in the United States of America 2022
Paperback edition published 2023

Copyright © Jenny Stümer, 2022

For legal purposes the Acknowledgments on p. viii constitute an extension
of this copyright page.

Cover design: Eleanor Rose
Cover images © Getty Images

All rights reserved. No part of this publication may be reproduced or transmitted
in any form or by any means, electronic or mechanical, including photocopying,
recording, or any information storage or retrieval system, without prior
permission in writing from the publishers.

Bloomsbury Publishing Inc does not have any control over, or responsibility for, any
third-party websites referred to or in this book. All internet addresses given in this
book were correct at the time of going to press. The author and publisher
regret any inconvenience caused if addresses have changed or sites have
ceased to exist, but can accept no responsibility for any such changes.

Library of Congress Cataloging-in-Publication Data
Names: Stümer, Jenny, author.
Title: Walled life : concrete, cinema, art / Jenny Stümer.
Description: New York : Bloomsbury Academic, 2022. |
Includes bibliographical references and index. |
Summary: "Examining political walls as screened media and media screens
through the artworks and films they inspire, Walled life lends an urgent
focus to the effective negotiations that govern political space in an
increasingly divided world"– Provided by publisher.
Identifiers: LCCN 2021047870 (print) | LCCN 2021047871 (ebook) | ISBN 9781501380365
(hardback) | ISBN 9781501380372 (epub) | ISBN 9781501380389 (adobe pdf)
Subjects: LCSH: Walls–Political aspects. | Boundaries–Political aspects. |
Mass media–Political aspects. | Arts–Political aspects.
Classification: LCC JC323 .S858 2022 (print) | LCC JC323 (ebook) |
DDC 320.1/2–dc23/eng/20211202
LC record available at https://lccn.loc.gov/2021047870
LC ebook record available at https://lccn.loc.gov/2021047871

ISBN:	HB:	978-1-5013-8036-5
	PB:	978-1-5013-8040-2
	ePDF:	978-1-5013-8038-9
	eBook:	978-1-5013-8037-2

Typeset by Integra Software Services Pvt. Ltd.

To find out more about our authors and books visit www.bloomsbury.com
and sign up for our newsletters.

For Marlo

Contents

Acknowledgments viii
Note on Text Translations x

1 Introduction 1
2 Berlin: No Wall in Sight 21
3 Looking to the Other Side: The Walls between Us 49
4 Palestine: Dreams of Walls and Undead Lives 79
5 Mirror, Mirror, on the Wall: Ambiguous Projections 107
6 Mexico: Colonial Ghosts, Walled Minds 135
7 To Trump Them All: The Most Beautiful Wall 161
8 Leap into Freedom: Concluding Remarks 187

Notes 198
Bibliography 234
Index 250

Acknowledgments

This book would not have been possible without the wonderful support and encouragement of Misha Kavka. Her long-standing intellectual guidance, generosity, and friendship have shaped this project in innumerable ways and have taught me more than these pages can reflect. Misha has modeled for me a rare form of academic mentorship and I am beyond grateful for her insight, direction, and compassion. I also want to thank Stephen Turner for his reassurance and curiosity as well as for the countless thought-provoking conversations we had. Allan Cameron and Irene Lee who have been nothing but encouraging and whose academic interests and good humored support have kept me going. Special thanks are due to Neal Curtis, who suggested the title for this book and who has supported me in more ways than I can count over the years. His generosity, thoughtfulness, friendship, and interest in the project have been inspiring and helped me stay motivated during challenging times. Thanks also to my colleagues in Media and Communication at Auckland University and especially to Larry May for his enthusiasm and support as well as Jennifer Kirby and Joe Lim for the solidarity and laughter. My appreciation also goes to Katie Gallof at Bloomsbury for all the effort and for giving me the opportunity to share my thoughts in this book. Along the way I have been lucky to have had the support of friends and family. There are too many to name, but a special mention goes to Emma Blackett, who has cheered me on throughout and whose brilliant insights and deep care have been inspirational. Lillian Hanly and Farzad Zamani, for their warmth and friendship, for pushing me in the best ways, and for always having an open ear. Alena Kavka, for her big-hearted thoughtfulness and generous reassurance. Thanks also to Anisha Sankar, for her kindness and encouragement, particularly in the final stages of this book. Finally, I want to thank my partner Toivo James for his incredible support, patience, and love, for picking me up and keeping me grounded all the way through and for always believing in me and this project.

An earlier version of the section on *The Invisible Frame* and *Rabbit à la Berlin* in Chapter 3 was published as a chapter in *East West and The Center: Reframing Post-1989 European Cinema*, edited by Michael Gott and Todd Herzog, 23–36. Edinburgh: Edinburgh University Press, 2015. It reappears here with the kind permission of the publisher.

ACKNOWLEDGMENTS

Some of the ideas and points I raise throughout the book previously appeared in an article entitled "Imperial Whiteness: Fantasy, Colonialism and New Walls" in *New Global Studies* 13, no. 3 (2019): 301–20. I thank the publisher (De Gruyter) for granting me permission to reestablish them here and to reprint some of that material.

Note on Text Translations

For Chapter 2, original German comments can be found in the endnotes and have been translated by the author.

1

Introduction

We create borders, build walls, and fences, divide, classify and make hierarchies. We try to exclude—from humanity itself—those who have been degraded, those who we look down on or who do not look like us, those with whom we imagine never being able to get along.

But there is only one world. We are all part of it, and we all have a right to it.

ACHILLE MBEMBE

Those who build walls are their own prisoners

URSULA K. LE GUIN

Is that it?

DEREK LANDY

What can a wall tell us about the world, a nation, or a person? How do fences, barriers, and walls affect those who build them and those who live in their shadows? In *Walled Life* I take the wall as a starting point in order to think about the cultural imaginaries, affective histories, and collective fantasies that shape political division. I understand the wall not simply as a soulless obstruction or a dead pile of bricks, but as something that creates atmospheres and worlds—a structure that generates feelings and impressions, cultivating the imagination and disrupting intimacies, unsettling relations, and also bringing them into zones of contact. I think of the wall as a canvas or a screen, capable of telling stories or foreclosing them, creating meaning and desolation, all at the same time. By focusing on the ways in which political walls are tied to emotions, stories, and fantasies about invading others that find expression in film, photography, graffiti, performances, and other media, I highlight the critical role of cinema and art in contesting exclusionary politics. In this book, I am interested in the narratives and images that supplement political walls and articulate ongoing legacies of domination, fantasies of protection, routines of boredom, visceral responses, silent crises, and other messy attachments. I also explore how filmmakers, artists, and activists utilize the wall to challenge divisive culture. In short, I am thinking about the ways in which political walls are thoroughly mediated and work as media in their own right, chronicling affective encounters that reveal something about the state of the world.

Growing up in Berlin, my starting point for unpacking these questions and concerns has always been the city's infamous wall. Of course, today, the Berlin Wall is old and tired. The once massive structure dividing a continent, a country, and a city is now a mere shadow of its former self, carefully refurbished and retired, complete with authentic cracks and holes, scars and lines. An icon of the past, the Berlin Wall seems almost absurd in the space of the present: it has become a symbol of hyperbolic freedom, a tacky tourist attraction, and a gallery for art. Tamed and preserved, it lingers as a colorful history lesson—painted over, decorated, taxidermized. And yet, the wall still tells us stories that resonate with the present: These stories speak of separated families, violent persecution, and ruthless apathy. They reflect on fantasies of security and intimate prisons, human aspiration, and, of course, despair. Ultimately, these stories document the wall's own vulnerability and the fallibility of its creators, but they also rejoice in the resilience of those who endured division (or continue to live with barriers today). Paying witness to its inevitable demise, the stories the wall can tell us are themselves occupied by those who challenge barriers, artistically or practically, together and alone. In other words, the wall I want to tell you about reaches far beyond Berlin. The wall I am concerned with is haunting the world. It has solidified countless times throughout history, shifting, rebuilding, falling, and reappearing again. It resurfaces as a slogan, materializes where camps are built and refugees must be kept out. It lingers where stones meet tanks. It endures in hearts and minds. The wall that inspired this book has always been more than a political barrier: It is a concept, a feeling, a memory, a promise, a prison, a ghost, a shield, a screen, a medium.

Foundations

Despite the rhetoric of a unified world, we increasingly face the violence of separation: our world espouses itself as being walled in the physical, metaphorical, and political sense. Alain Badiou suggests post-1989 that there is in fact such a thing as "the world's wall,"[1] which serves as a reference point for ever newer modes of division, effacement, and conflict. He explains that "the overwhelming majority of the population have at best restricted access to this world. They are locked out, often literally so."[2] Acutely, such modes of division are reflected in global anxieties surrounding the figure of the migrant; they are palpable in images of caged children in the United States or those that show them swept up on the shores of Europe. They resonate with refugee tents in Idomeni, checkpoints in Gaza, and fences across Sinai; but they also contour the divisive lines of our post-Brexit, pandemic-stricken, fake news world, in which synagogues and mosques are viciously attacked, women still demand the right to be heard, indigenous peoples are once more arrested for protecting their lands, and Black people still have to assert that their lives matter. I suggest these divides can be understood as the manifestation of a persistent circle of violence, within which walls, fences, and barriers present themselves as effects of historical forces that create modes of toxic protection and privilege at the cost of physical and psychological impediment.

Indeed, political walls (in their material manifestation) have made a stunning re-appearance on the face of the world. Élisabeth Vallet, who has tracked the emergence of border walls since the end of the Second World War, counts no less than eighty-one such barriers in 2021.[3] From Donald Trump's campaign to build a wall at the US-Mexican border to Israel's progressing separation barrier in the West Bank and Europe's re-erection of walls and fences in the face of its refugee "crisis," political walls are a symptom of our time and a testimony to the divisive and polarized politics of the twenty-first century. It seems that the more we imagine ourselves as part of an increasingly open, free, and transnational community, the more we are confronted with the occupying, partitioning, barricading, and walling-off of cities, territories, and nations. After the fall of the Berlin Wall, such barriers have continuously reminded the world, from Palestine to Europe to Mexico, that political division is a recurring motif in the writing and rewriting of global maps and identities.

Thinkers like Alain Badiou and Étienne Balibar have long analyzed these developments in the wake of the Berlin Wall's demise.[4] Both have suggested that the "end of history," as the end of grand narratives, has neatly survived its own epitaph, with the myth of global unity subverted by increased fortification. More recently, Wendy Brown revived this discussion, investigating the resurgence of walls as a reaction to the waning sovereignty of nation-states in the twenty-first century.[5] Her analysis exposes the emergent walls in Israel-Palestine and at the US-Mexican border as having similarities with the crumbled Berlin Wall—in fact all three seek to fix an equally vulnerable ideological narrative. Linking emerging border walls to the fears that energized the global War on Terror, Reece Jones has further shown that twenty-first-century walls expand and consolidate sovereign power by homogenizing populations in opposition to an uncivilized elsewhere.[6] Intimating the ways in which historical walls likewise condition contemporary political structures with reference to colonial legacies, Achille Mbembe has additionally explained that the organization of political life has always been invested in "procedures of differentiation, classification and hierarchization aimed at exclusion"[7] and that these "fierce colonial desires"[8] are now translated into the will to "impose a regime of separation"[9]—one which is based on the necropolitical premise that selected segments of population are literally considered disposable[10] (in resonance with Judith Butler "ungrievable"[11]) or what Mbembe identifies as a "superfluous humanity"[12] locked out behind walls.

Collectively, these lines of thought attest to an imaginary substantiation of the global politics of walls. The walls of the world exclude the other as they create the other by exclusion. At first glance, political walls function to omit "the other," whose status as "intruder" does not so much threaten, but actually maintains, the rigid political imaginary of a nation in fear. The Israeli West Bank barrier exemplifies this "separation as a philosophy"[13] meant to protect a community from an impending threat while creating a boundary to support collective identification. Complemented by the increasing fortification of its counterpart in Mexico and the new walls appearing all around Europe, the barrier envisions the emergence of the modern walled state, where collectives are stabilized and protected against the backdrop of an imaginary other, which is equally feared and disdained. In this way, the new walls resonate with the memory of the demolished Berlin Wall, as they reintroduce means of exclusion and control into contemporary political landscapes. Political walls demarcate a highly controlled space at the same time as they produce (and foreclose) confined modes of community.

Highlighting the affective tissues that bind and separate groups of people, Lauren Berlant and Sara Ahmed have expanded discussions of political investments by drawing attention to the role of emotion and fantasy. Both authors provide insight into the psycho-affective formations that mobilize attentive relations to a world in crisis. As Ahmed puts it "emotions are a form of cultural politics,"[14] producing attachments to "affect worlds," as Berlant would add.[15] Seen from this perspective, walls are (also) a site of affective staging that register and potentially energize collective experience as a form of worldmaking. Circulating political feeling, such "affective economies," to use Ahmed's indispensable term, do not locate emotions in either subject or object, but reproduce them as the effect of encounter.[16] In other words, emotions produce and undo the boundaries that sustain walled states and minds, creating the affective parameters of inside and outside. "The nation's borders and defenses are like skin,"[17] in Ahmed's words, as such, they mediate relations between external and internal, us and them, here and there, through sensory experiences of pain, fear, disgust, boredom, anger, hate, or love. Political walls hence need to be viewed in the full context of the visceral intimacies they provoke and disable.

What I want to draw attention to in this book, then, is the way in which the walled space is saturated by cultural narratives, emotional investments, and psychological undercurrents that reproduce the political boundary on an imaginary and affective level and thereby assist in the construction of a walled identity. This way of being in the shadows of political walls—or what I call "walled life"—delimits the unconscious settings, silent barriers, and emotional legacies that are internalized and reproduced within and between individuals as part of a walled existence. Walled life unfolds in resonance with the way that Sigmund Freud, Cathy Caruth, Kaja Silverman, and Jacqueline Rose have analyzed the workings of trauma,[18] Renata Salecl examines the politics of fantasy[19] and Lauren Berlant unfolds the crisis of the ordinary "in stories about navigating what's overwhelming."[20] Drawing on these discussions, I explore the way in which psychic division and emotional barricades are informed by political formations (and vice versa). Hence, what is interesting about the visual statement of a concrete wall made of solid, impenetrable surfaces is how these façades, as symptoms of cultural alienation, make visible the psychological and emotional foundation of political space. Political walls carry with them (and on them) collective fantasies and historical narratives, re-enacting, but also potentially subverting, the power divisions they are meant to support. Put simply, *political walls are media*.

Drawing on the example of the former Berlin Wall as the wall of the past, Israel's separation barrier as the wall of the present, and the impending wall at the US-Mexican border as the wall of the future, the book examines the psychological and affective settings of political division as materialized in political boundaries. I consider the reinforcement and subversion of border fortifications primarily through film and art practices that turn walls into screens in order to think through different expressions of the "walled life" that is experienced in these political landscapes. I maintain that if we read political walls as forms of media, they become legible not simply as shields, impositions, or monuments, but as a projection surface (in the technological and psychological sense) by which the psycho-politics of walls intimate "a historical present that becomes apprehensible as an affective urgency"[21] as Berlant might put it. My analysis hence goes beyond the discussion of political architecture and expands insights into political mediation. While I draw on the political setting of the walled state,[22] I am primarily interested in the ways in which psychological and affective barriers interact with political structures as mediated by cinema, art, and, of course, the wall itself.

I work from the premise that the wall is the concretization of a sensory trace, informing and performing human divisions (and revision) as linked to past, present, and future. As a screen the wall thereby exposes the affective makeup of political space, because it is the point where political conflicts and shared atmospheres are either blocked from consciousness or made available for a process of encounter. In this regard, as a construct, the wall does not simply evoke, but is central to the very logic of trauma. Barriers are formed to protect the psyche, and isolated segments of feelings, like isolated people, become alienated, split off, and ultimately imprisoned.[23] Invariably, these segments act "like a foreign body"[24] or something other within the most intimate territory of the self, despite and because of these protective measures. Taking the resonance between trauma and wall as a way into understanding the affective trajectories of a walled life, I demonstrate how the wall acts as a psycho-political structure that, if viewed as a medium, opens up new forms and fantasy constructions through which alternative political discourses can be formed.

My argument is situated at the intersections between the political and the psychological. I work from the spatial organization of what Hannah Arendt, Carl Schmitt, Giorgio Agamben, and Robert Cover have aptly described as the nomos[25] to theorize the spatial, legal, and normative realization of a specific political formation in order to move this discussion to the emotional barricading of the mind in the Freudian unconscious, the collective attachments invoked by Lauren Berlant and Sara Ahmed, and the fantasies of the political as discussed by Renata Salecl, Jacqueline Rose, and Ghassan Hage.[26] I argue that while political walls work as ideological screens concerned with the erasure of the other (side), mirroring or shielding a national identity, they can also be read as media screens that project the politics on which they rest and the personal intersections they produce, thereby enabling encounters across two "sides." The psychological projections inherent to the wall must therefore be brought to the forefront of perception, by recognizing the barrier's function as a screen and by examining the ways in which the wall remediates psychological conflicts and unconscious separations. In particular, I investigate the ways in which political walls are underwritten by a post-socialist, post-colonial, and post-holocaust imaginary.

As media screens political walls either serve as backdrops for constructing and examining political realities or supply surfaces onto which political commentary can be projected. The experiences of walled life are envisioned through documentary and fictional films that often engage the silent and invisible structures that political impositions cement. Similarly, the wall's rewritable materiality negotiates a walled existence through graffiti, murals, photography, and installations. Each wall is caught up in a complex dynamic of visibility and invisibility, absence and presence that various artists have brought to the surface/screen. Each wall attests to the separation of people(s) and also to the silent barriers we erect from within. By screening the affective sensorium of divisive politics, I propose, these walls can be read with and against each other in order to demonstrate that the conceptual wall is remediated in different contexts and times to "tell us about itself." I maintain that by bringing to the surface the conflicts at the physical and psychological faultlines of human communities, political walls allow us to rethink, rewrite, and reclaim the meaning of these structures, enabling a re-vision of their politics.

Nomos, Law, Wall

In order to unpack the ways in which the political is underwritten by the personal, it is useful to begin the conceptualization of political walls with a discussion of the Western nomos. Invoking how the political order is legally and spatially realized by means of enclosures, norms, and laws, the nomos provides insight into the ways in which walls have always served the biopolitical realization of sovereignty through territorial demarcation. Etymologically the Greek word "nomos" refers to the law that is established as part of a political assemblage by means of distribution, possession, and dwelling.[27] The nomos hence evokes the political through the division of land viewed as property. In other words, giving form to the structure of the political, the nomos relies on acts of zoning, controlling, walling, and owning a space, so as to then establish the law of its order. Political walls, in other words, resonate with the way Western philosophy understands the establishment of the political order primarily as spatial and bounded, while also exposing how such politics rest on modes of exclusion and occupation.

Tellingly, to Hannah Arendt the nomos demarcates "quite literally a wall,"[28] by which the boundary between the self and others is made clear as the condition of Western politics. Arendt explains that originally the wall/nomos defined the "boundaries between one household and the other"[29] delimiting a private sphere; however, the wall also established how "the law of the city-state"[30] was distributed and contained. Within this logic, the political order was brought into existence via spatial demarcation, because "only the inclosure was political";[31] and yet, in order to "be political," one also had to harbor "a private place of one's own."[32] This interplay between the inside and the outside, the public and the private, self and other, as mediated by a political boundary, conditions the Western nomos from the outset, positioning the wall as the raison d'etre for a political order and its community.

Indeed, it appears that "the western archive is premised on the crystallization of the idea of a border,"[33] as Mbembe has aptly put it; as such we may read the wall as its most constitutive tool. Accordingly, Carl Schmitt describes the nomos as "the first measure of all subsequent measures,"[34] the "first land-appropriation, understood as the first partition and classification of space."[35] Schmitt's analysis exposes a will to grab power by means of seizing a territory, reminding us that the violence of political walls has always been associated with the crimes of Western modernity. (Consider the barbarism of National Socialism and colonialism, both of which share disturbing links grounded in modernity's genocidal expansionism, according to Patrick Wolfe[36]). Echoing these histories, the Schmittian nomos seeks "to divide" or "to pasture"[37] the earth as a way to provide the "order and orientation" for the political, and delimiting a "force-field"[38] by which a people "becomes historically situated."[39] To Schmitt, too, the nomos can "be described as a wall,"[40] in whose presence "the political and social order of a people becomes spatially visible."[41] Schmitt's analysis, like Arendt's, hence, posits the premise of (spatial) division at the heart of the political. Seen in this light the wall appears as the antithesis to relationality (between territories and people); and yet, at closer glance, the wall also works as an inevitable connection between its "two sides."

Indeed, the wall cannot disavow its outside: it manifests as a literal indistinction between "us" and "them." Echoing this logic, Giorgio Agamben theorizes political sovereignty in relation to a "state of exception," which "does not limit itself to distinguishing what is inside from what is outside but instead traces a threshold... between the two."[42] Like the wall, the sovereign exception puts the inside and the outside into "a complex topological relation that makes the validity of the juridical order possible."[43] In this way, Western politics is constituted by "an exclusion which is simultaneously an inclusion,"[44] an idea which is physically mediated in the appearance of political walls and the way in which they establish hierarchies of precarity. More acutely, according to Agamben, the state of exception is "a zone of indistinction,"[45] and "a line that constantly needs to be redrawn."[46] Serving as the foundation of sovereign power, the wall suggests that regimes of exclusion substantiate political power. Crucially, Agamben's argument rests on the premise that the exception "has become the rule,"[47] "increasingly appearing as a technique of government rather than an exceptional matter."[48] His sentiment is reinforced by the rampant emergence of barriers and fences all over the world as a way to secure not simply nations, but the privileges they maintain (at all costs); simultaneously, these barriers change the face of democracies and contradict the values they uphold.

To this end, political walls have an unsettling resonance with the histories of authoritarianism and occupation, tarnishing contemporary democracies in their attempts to wall-in their values, their identities, their way of life and foretelling a disquieting future. It is vital to recall that Agamben's threshold (or wall) appears as "indeterminacy between democracy and absolutism"[49] and as such it reminds us that political walls compromise humanity before all else. To Agamben the state of exception finds its most troubling expression in the appearance of the Nazi concentration camp as "a pure, absolute, and impossible biopolitical space."[50] He cautions that the camp "will appear as hidden paradigm of the political space of modernity"[51] and advises that "we learn to recognize" its "metamorphoses and disguise."[52] I suggest that we read political walls in resonance with Agamben's warning. The more we barricade nations, fence-off others, and wall-in ourselves, the more we enable the vicious fantasy of political exceptionality to manifest itself, compromising the other's and our own humanity in the process.

Walled World

Today, the politics of walls only highlight Badiou's observation that "in human terms—the 'unified' world of globalization is a sham,"[53] and that the walls of the past have "merely shifted." Adding to this observation, Balibar explains that, although contemporary processes of globalization have weakened the force of borders, such boundaries also attain new meaning(s).[54] Balibar explains as early as 2004 that globalization facilitates the permeability of boundaries primarily in terms of economics and communication. However, the resulting formation "needs borders more than ever to segregate, at least in tendency, wealth and poverty in distinct territorial zones."[55] Because of this, Balibar maintains that "less than ever is the contemporary world a 'world without borders.'"[56] The emergence of systematic forms of exclusion renders borders, walls, and fences essential to "the constitution of social condition on a global scale,"[57] a phenomenon which Balibar describes more precisely as a process of "global apartheid."[58]

In this sense, the local significance of the boundary may be diminished, but globally, more than ever, it serves the partitioning of political and cultural structures into "us" and "them," enabling, yet again, the hierarchization of some lives against others and legitimizing "exceptional" forms of violence. The wall hence marks a local projection of global distributions of authority, surveillance, and power. However, Balibar also points out that the clash between notions of apartheid and the imagined "'democratic' and 'social' forms of the modern national state"[59] evoke too stark a contrast. Balibar is hopeful that this may lead to the emergence of transnational over purely national forms of belonging,[60] thereby drawing attention to the imaginary inconsistencies that confront the walled state in a globalized world.

Applying the inherent potentialities of these imaginary inconsistencies to challenge the fortification of the nation-state, Wendy Brown later suggests that we examine the nation-state in terms of its vulnerabilities. Brown posits that the waning sovereignty of the nation-state in the face of the global imagination leads to a forceful reappearance of walls. In *Walled States: Waning Sovereignty*, Brown explains that these new walls, analogous to the vanished Berlin Wall, respond to a felt decomposition of the nation, seeking to protect the imagined community on which it rests. For Brown the new walls function as spectacles of state power and materialize the ideology of the community, thereby assisting the collective's imaginary coherence while essentially mediating its unity. Brown reads this as revealing the vulnerability of the nation-state, or, as she puts it, "rather than resurgent expression of nation-state sovereignty, the new walls are icons of its erosion."[61]

Conversely, Junita Sundberg points out that Brown's focus on the revelation of the state's instability overlooks the fact that the new walls attest to the "increasing power of states."[62] Sundberg claims that walls instead denote the erosion of the law, leading to the "walling up" of not just people but of democracy,[63] much in the way that Agamben describes the state of exception. Although Sundberg's point is an important nod to the escalating surveillance exercised by the walled state, her analysis does not necessarily contradict Brown's argument. Instead, it should be pointed out that Brown's discussion moves beyond the political setting of walls, as she raises questions about the "mental organization of space"[64] and the imaginary constitution of national identities in walled states. Hence, Brown draws attention to ways in which walls "fictively restore a national imaginary,"[65] addressing *feelings* of vulnerability in a crisis-ridden world and provoking a refortification of established settings of privilege and power. Despite laying the focus on different aspects, both authors share an interest in the way in which walls constitute the collective within their boundaries, assembling imaginary and political forms of togetherness/separation.

Walled Lives

While the wall negotiates communities, it is also a means (or medium) by which politics come to be experienced. Such forms of mediation are directly linked to the registers of the mind and the sensory experience of the body, demanding that we shift the perspective from the political formation to the visceral responses and fantasmatic in/coherences they produce. Put simply, we need to examine the ways in which the political boundary shapes, creates, and threatens the minds and hearts that reside in its shadow; in short, we need to investigate walled life. Essentially, the politics of walls are highly reliant on the creation and maintenance of collective imaginaries and feelings, despite contradicting these fantasies and attachments in practice. Such inconsistencies suggest that the psychological formation of the wall conceals its tangible inadequacies and unruly connections. Indeed, the politics of walls are supported by the creation and maintenance of ideological imaginations and narratives in relation to the wall. For example, Brown suggests that we pay attention to the psychic defenses gratified by physical walls, and the way in which political walls perform a desire "to resolve the vulnerability and helplessness produced by myriad global forces."[66] Conversely, we also need to acknowledge the vulnerabilities the wall creates. Attempts at challenging and confronting political walls hence need to consider physical and political division in relation to the conceptual, affective, and psychological constitution of barriers and the communities they produce.

In other words, in order to discuss its politics, the affective sensorium of the wall needs to be brought to the forefront of the investigation. This means that we have to extend the critical discussion of political walls by (also) engaging them in a psychoanalytical discourse. Such an analysis may help to "grasp what the new walls psychically address or assuage, even when they cannot deliver on their material promise,"[67] and shed light on the difficult legacies and affective investments that shape them. By turning the view to feeling and fantasy, we can understand the ways in which the politics and communities envisioned by Arendt, Agamben, or Badiou are psychologically maintained and diversified. This draws attention to the ways in which the collective psychological effects of the wall are progressively realized through the experiences it generates and the intersubjective relations it expresses. Ultimately, like any relation between self and other, the relations negotiated by the wall are primarily intimate, ambivalent, and potentially messy.

Jacqueline Rose, Slavoj Žižek, and Renata Salecl have stressed that "fantasy should be at the heart of our political vocabulary,"[68] implying that collectives are characterized by, and rely on, fantasy structures at the core of their experience (and the ways in which they organize the experience of the individual). Similarly, Freud investigates fantasy as the way in which the individual understands what it cannot grasp in order to cope with reality[69] and Lauren Berlant explains that fantasy is both "an opening and a defense."[70] In each case, fantasy becomes a way of ascribing and inscribing meaning and is therefore central to the investigation of individual and collective experiences of walled life. To uncover the relation between fantasy and wall is then to look at collective crisis as more than a metaphorical extension of the individual and to engage with layers of meaning in political experience. This suggests a shift away from traumatic exceptionality to a careful unveiling of the "dominant fictions,"[71] as Silverman might say, that enclose historical experiences. In this regard, political contexts are always already characterized by a fantasy structure that is equal parts crisis and culture, continuously implying each other.

It is through these intersections between political settings and the emotional legacies they incorporate that the nomos of politics attains an intimate realization in the appearance of walled life. Politics, in other words, do not simply become "spatially visible"[72] by means of a wall, but the nomos itself marks a lived encounter that plays out within and between its inhabitants (both included and excluded), creating resistant or "intimate publics"[73] as well as invoking negative attachments, in Berlant's sense, toward neat separations and promises of security. Though not explicitly concerned with such affects, Robert Cover hints at the politics of experience, when he states that the nomos is not simply a spatial configuration, but also functions as a "normative universe."[74] Explaining that the nomos rests on the "narratives that locate it and give it meaning,"[75] Cover's analysis paves the way for a reading of political walls beyond their practical function, acknowledging that such walls are not just concrete structures, but, to a significant degree, rest on the grand narratives of the political, its fantasies, images, and affects. Hence, the wall does not simply delimit, it crucially creates "our world"[76] and fills it with meanings, emotions, and imaginaries.

The wall creates and subjugates a particular life within its limits, onto which the intimacies of the walled state are projected. At first glance walled life is often marked by absence and invisibility. Walled spaces are desolate spaces, closing out sociabilities and personal encounters. To this end, walled life is prison life (for both those who endure walls and those who build them) and it is often absent from immediate recognition (on both sides). On the other hand, walled life can hardly be "contained" in this way. Like affect, it hums and mingles, seeping through barriers and engulfing relations. Walled life thereby manifests the hidden sensorium of the political setting, because walled spaces become political precisely through the relationships they enable or foreclose. As people negotiate a walled existence, the ruptures of the political are brought to the surface and played out between friends, neighbors, families, and communities. In other words, the wall does not simply impede the people on both sides, but it also serves as a projection surface or setting, a "Schauplatz" as Freud would say, in which political affects, fantasies, and narratives become visible, palpable, and otherwise articulated.

Screens

Discovering each wall through the films and artworks it has inspired, *Walled Life* treats political walls as affective surfaces, or screened media and media screens, capable of uncovering and disrupting the politics on which they are built and thereby enabling encounters across two "sides." The wall-as-screen is protective and projective, providing insights into the fantasmatic constitution of the political, social, and imaginary everyday as shaped by walls, fences, and barriers. Such a screen does not simply shield (the view), concealing what is evaded on the other(ed) side, the screen is also always exposing, in the sense that it reveals (again and again) this point of erasure. The screen, in other words, envisions the wall's psychical reinforcement, its affective trajectories, and traumatic implications. It acknowledges the psyche "as visual model,"[77] as Kaja Silverman asserts, in which inner conflicts find expression through images and scenes produced in fantasy. This suggests that in order for walled life to be articulated, a surface or media screen is needed onto which the feelings and fantasies of individuals and collectives can be projected and subsequently engaged with. If the wall itself can provide such a screen—as numerous films and aesthetic projects attest—then the political and psychological undercurrents of its formation can be made visible in this way.

Looking at the wall as screened media and media screen elucidates the affective components of walled life. The screen proves capable of revealing the metrics for understanding how a particular "intimate public"[78] emerges in the presence of the wall, precisely because the screen offers a reflexive surface, in the figurative and literal sense, against which walled experiences can be probed. As Berlant explains, alongside Brian Massumi and Teresa Brennan, "bodies are continuously busy judging their environments and responding to the atmospheres in which they find themselves."[79] Affect is hence "a site of elucidation" that can "register the conditions of life that move across persons and worlds"[80] and communicate the moments when politics become visceral, or too close, too intimate, too immediate to contain. Returning to Ahmed's analogy between border and skin, such feelings can produce boundaries or break right through them, treading the conditions under which individuals and collectives become invested in political structures. Conversely, the wall as an aesthetic provides opportunity to give expression to the affective components of its impact. In each case, the wall remediates the finer points of the lives it shadows, while simultaneously feeding back into these experiences. Creating a reel-projection of the walled life it fosters, the wall-as-screen thereby provides the settings for its own disruption.

In other words, the process of meaning production that links the wall to the media screen lies in its ability to invoke and remediate the psychical screen. This screen must be read in its double function as both a barrier and a receptive surface, drawing attention to the way in which the wall itself is manifested as an impeding obstacle and also a projective medium. Essentially, while the wall's physical representation may work to hide an underlying psychological design, this construction has no choice but to also reveal its unconscious undercurrents. In its physical being, the wall reveals an identity established on the basis of exclusion, and hence produces forms of collectivity which are cut off and isolated. Simultaneously, the wall also communicates the inconsistent imaginaries it seeks to stabilize, precisely because it is a symptom of divisive politics and thereby provides a screen for the material it mediates. However, although this ambivalence is undeniably exhibited in the wall's very structure, it is arguably the barrier's overwhelming visibility which also works to hide these meanings. The projections inherent to the wall must hence be brought to the forefront of perception, by recognizing the barrier's function as a screen and by examining the ways in which the wall remediates psychological conflicts and unconscious separations.

Crucially, the notion of a projection surface is already inherent to the workings of our inner lives. It is conceptualized by Freud in the form of a psychical screen that binds (and separates) the unconscious and the conscious and assists in the production "of the preliminary stages of an image."[81] Freud, hence, conceptualizes the psyche like an inner cinema through which we engage with the pictorial abstractions of the unconscious—our fantasies. However, Freud quotes Hildebrandt, maintaining that "the most intimate relationship"[82] that links the different registers of the psyche, and thereby plays out on the inner screen, also "goes hand in hand with seclusion and separation."[83] From the outset, Freud's screen can, in other words, be regarded as both a barrier and a medium, which not only resonates with the mechanism of the cinema, but also evokes the image of the wall.

Indeed, for Freud, the notions of medium and barrier (cinema and wall) coincide at the intersection between unconscious and conscious.[84] More radically, the Freudian screen may provide insight into the ways in which the inner wall finds expression (and repression) in the physical world, illustrating the relation between a psychological enclosure and a political one. Hence, the concept of the inner screen raises questions about how the psychological is informed by, and articulated through, collective forms of projection in the material landscape of the political. Conversely, this also demands an engagement with the way in which these projections allow us to (re)negotiate the affective structure of the political via the screens they inhabit. In other words, understanding the workings of the inner screen of the psyche may provide insight into the dynamics that determine political walls and their remediation as aesthetic formations and ideological screens.

Expanding this idea, to Lacan, the screen, while essentially opaque, posits an "imaginary mapping"[85] akin to the workings of the mirror stage. As such both the screen and the mirror play a crucial role in the constitution of identities. Returning to the divisive structure that undergirds walled life, the wall-as-screen hence projects both, an image of the self in the form of the ego-ideal encountered in the self-absorbing reflections of the mirror stage, and an imaginary of the other side, which is read through the lens of the ideological and psychological formation of the wall and thereby "has no choice but to assume the shape predetermined by the screen,"[86] as Kaja Silverman might put it. In this sense, the screen constructs and enlarges the identities and ideologies inscribed in the wall, but it also exposes these figurative building bricks to be primarily imaged or imagined. Constructing and revealing the political and psychological parameters of walled life, such a screen works both internally and externally; it is always already a means of projection.

The screen allows us to think about walls and films as forms of collective projections that reveal and conceal social processes of meaning production. Such screenings organize the fantasmatic investments that sustain the structures of the political, but they also exteriorize the psychological processes that inform these settings and thereby open them up to contestation. Read as devices, screens work to enlarge and display the psychological designs of the political. To engage with political walls as screens in this way is to interrupt their invisibility, intervening in the rigid constitution of the walled state and bringing to the surface the barricaded existence of walled life. The screen is a barrier, akin to the notion of a shield, a mirror or a filter, but it is also a medium, in the form of a receptive surface or a projection screen. Since the logic of the screen functions both within and beyond the psyche, psycho-emotional considerations acknowledge the ways in which the wall is internalized and plays a crucial role in the political situating of the personal. Of course, this process is (re)mediated through, for example, cinematic forms that imagine the individual within social formations. Both film screens and concrete surfaces hence organize the affective and ideological economies in which individual trajectories play out. More radically, a wall may be read as a medium of text and image that provides the means for its own critique. It is often used as a canvas, stage, or backdrop for political performance, attracting artistic commentary and other expressive responses, such as graffiti, murals, photo-projections, or installations. Hence, as visual devices, both wall and cinema encourage collective forms of looking and thereby function as public screens that remediate walled lives through the interpretive lens of film and art.

Berlin, Palestine, Mexico

Examining the wall and the walled life it projects through the particular settings in Berlin, Israel, and Mexico I want to engage the wall's function as a screen in order to think about a larger structure of segregation. As I have suggested, the politics of division are concretized in bricks and mortar, but essentially these walls also work as metaphors for barriers of the mind. In this way, the walls from Berlin to Palestine and Mexico maintain an existing separation while covering over the aggressive social and political attitudes they reinforce. The new walls are hence built on old concepts, effectively generating and securing a narrative of "us and them," while performing an insistent denial of the underlying relationship between the two sides. On the one hand, each wall stands embedded in particular circumstances, pitching itself as filter, shield, and screen in response. On the other hand, the various walls reference one another and reveal a common trace. Put simply, the particularities each wall reveals lend meaning to the other(s), while reworking the intricacies of walling as a global force.

The wall in Berlin stands out, not simply because it is often quoted as the blueprint for the new walls, but also because it is now absent from the political landscape it has so profoundly inscribed. As the wall of the past, the Berlin Wall can tell us about the invisible impressions and enduring psychological traces that support the physical monument. Shifting the view from the visible wall to the invisible structure that sustains it, Joseph Beuys drew attention to this dynamic as early as 1964. Beuys challenged the Berlin Wall by interrupting its (aesthetic) perception, when he demanded that the Berlin Wall be raised by 5 cm. When asked to justify his demand, Beuys explained that "the wall is an image and should be seen as an image."[87] Beuys's absurd demand intimates the possibility of overcoming the wall, precisely because it shifts the view to a metaphorical wall (of narrative, ideology, and ultimately thought) that works to sustain the concrete wall, which is exposed as an expression of these symbolic parameters.[88] The first two chapters of this book build on Beuys' intuition, exploring the Berlin Wall as a present absence, whose enduring affectivity is mediated by art and film.

Investigating efforts to imagine the now-absent wall through artistic practices that range from photography to installation art as well as acts of commemoration, Chapter 2 "Berlin: No Wall in Sight" discusses the ways in which the Berlin Wall has been artistically projected before and after its iconic fall. The chapter proposes that the Berlin Wall is (and always has been) characterized by an architectural, social, and imaginary form of absence, positing the wall's psychological effectiveness as something that precedes its concretization and that persists long after the wall's physical demise in the form of a mental barrier. The internal wall echoes the dynamics of trauma as repeated, aestheticized, and challenged through art, but it also provides the foundation for the recent reappearance of walls all over Europe.

Similarly, Chapter 3 "Looking to the Other Side: The Walls between Us" suggests that the persistence of the Berlin Wall's psychological imposition is linked to the way in which it works as a traumatic memory, neither erasable nor present in the full sense. Looking at the wall's afterlife on the cinema screen, the chapter explores how film facilitates what Freud has coined the "dreamwork" as a way to engage with the depths of individual and national psyches. Filmic mediations of the Berlin Wall demonstrate that the cinema screen brings to the surface the contours of walled life as caught up in the ambiguous relations between past and present, historical perception, and national identities, utilizing inherently unstable perspectives on and from the East to open the discussion to present walls in the world.

The West Bank separation barrier is the iconic wall of the present, offering a contemporary study of modern forms of walling and attempting to distinguish itself from the imprisoning means of the wall in Berlin. However, despite being located in a different political and cultural context, it, too, reveals a reliance on psychological effectiveness based in invisibility. The West Bank separation barrier aggressively promotes a national fantasy, while blending out the competing realities of Israel's formation. Thereby, the West Bank separation barrier offers insight into the fantasmatic undercurrents of the Israel-Palestine conflict, and articulates the wall's imaginary function in this context.

Chapter 4 "Palestine: Dreams of Walls and Undead Lives" introduces the wall in Palestine and conceptualizes it as a screen for Israel's national imaginary as primarily concerned with a (psychological) erasure of Palestine. Identifying the West Bank separation barrier as a shield that serves to secure a traumatic vulnerability, the chapter theorizes the wall with regard to the construction of political and psychological landscapes that are maintained through fantasy projections. Utilizing the cinema screen to counter invisibility and erasure, the films under discussion document the complicated relationships obliterated by the wall. Engaging the "undead" status of Palestine and challenging the twofold erasure of being invisible or visible only as terrorists and threat, the cinema interrogates the affective choreography of walled life under occupation, screening the political unconscious of Israel-Palestine.

Developing the argument that the West Bank separation barrier primarily works as a psychological barrier (rather than simply a physical protection), Chapter 5 "Mirror, Mirror, on the Wall: Ambiguous Projections" examines the wall as a graffiti mirror, artistic stage, and media screen. Renegotiating the political field which the wall projects, art utilizing the material surface of the barrier is capable of resisting the political structure and thereby redefines the possibilities of the walled space. On the other hand, such artistic encounters are always implicated in a potential affirmation of the wall and thereby in danger of supporting its structure. The projection of political landscapes on and through the wall hence contests political identities and narratives of walled life; however, it also brings the two sides face to face by mediating moments of recognition and mirroring.

Shifting the view to the third wall of the discussion, the impending wall of the future, the US-Mexican border, exemplifies the ferocity of the wall's fantasy structure. Although it has not (quite) materialized in concrete segments, this wall has become a forceful rhetorical device in US politics, working as an affective screen for divisive politics and nationalist fantasies. As such the wall in Mexico combines the authoritarian connotations of the Berlin Wall and the neo-colonial partitions in Palestine. Evoking unsettling resonances with a violent past, the mirage of a US-Mexican border wall is only partially realized but nevertheless fully projects the cultural imaginary of manifest whiteness. While all three walls reveal as they conceal the dynamics of their political and psychological effectiveness, in the case of US-Mexico relations these building blocks are just in the process of taking new forms.

Chapter 6 "Mexico: Colonial Ghosts, Walled Minds" explores the way in which the US-Mexican border has always relied on the fantasy of walls long before Donald Trump campaigned them into the political consciousness of our time. Working from the traumatic grounding of the wall's stubborn imaginary, the chapter traces the wall as "an imperial structure,"[89] investigating a politics of haunting and the colonial histories that underwrite the border's formation while also exploring the borderlands as a stage for examining cultural otherness and transnational simultaneity. Utilizing the notion of crossing, the chapter locates Mexico's borderland in the reflexive space of the actual and conceptual inbetween, precisely because it is never quite a wall yet, while persistently materializing a settler colonial, post-holocaust imaginary, as reflected through cinema and art.

Finally, Chapter 7 "To Trump Them All: The Most Beautiful Wall" applies the anxieties and desires discussed throughout the book in order to shed light on the popular appeals of Donald Trump's insidious promise to build a wall between the United States and Mexico. Trump's wall works as an enormous screen that is needed to project the hetero-patriarchal ego-ideal that mirrors Trump's regressive attempt to return the grand narratives of paranoid nostalgia and nationalism to (American) greatness. In this regard, Trump's politics reflect a reworking of gendered and racialized privileges as the means for securing the fantasy nation of an unspecified past. Hence, the wall of the future works as a projective screen for Trump's divisive politics, fueling the affects and fantasies central to both, Trump's appeal and the strong resistance he provokes.

Ultimately, I want to show that walled life is particular and takes shape differently in each political setting; however, it also proposes an affective transference from one wall to the other. Experiences of the wall may materialize a frustrating ignorance or private suffering as in the case of Berlin, epitomize the aggressive boredom of traumatic occupation as exemplified in Palestine, or negotiate physical and psychological crossings in Mexico. In each case, the walled life discussed in this book traces a trajectory of the wall as medium. What this proposes is not so much that the situations and narratives of each wall can be equated, but that these walls lend meaning to each other through the affective exchanges, encounters, and ruptures they evoke. The book demonstrates that political walls do not simply hide the various ideas and attitudes they have come to materialize, but they are also capable of conveying and even challenging the implications of their own appearance. Hence, political walls are capable of critically interrupting themselves. Such an interruption is precisely an interruption of the spectacle of invisibility necessary to a wall's effectiveness. In conceptualizing the way in which the wall does not merely exemplify division but can be read as a medium of the collective imaginary it secures, counter-hegemonic actions can address and challenge the politics of invisibility and demarcation. The wall of the past, the wall of the present, and the wall of the future may then work as prisms or screens for retelling a shared narrative of walling, reworking the affects, memories, and experiences that create walled life.

2

Berlin: No Wall in Sight

The Berlin Wall is one of *the* dramatic images of the political iconography of the twentieth century. So much so, it is paradoxically easy to "overlook" that the political and cultural efficacy of this wall overtly relies on the exercise of spectacular invisibility. In fact, because the Berlin Wall is remembered as the iconic manifestation of Cold War binaries, it goes habitually unnoticed that its most outstanding characteristic has been that of "absence." By "absence" I mean in part the way a barrier typically works as a means of erasing the other (side) while reinforcing an enclosed perspective. However, these mediations of disappearance, invisibility, and avoidance appear to gain particular momentum in the instance of Berlin, where the notion of "absence" is also carefully inscribed in the city's geographical and imaginary setting, impacting the city's affective architecture and producing ways of seeing and experiencing the city, as can still be felt today, more than thirty years after the wall's physical demise. It seems that in Berlin, the wall has not simply vanished after the end of the Cold War; rather, it was in the first instance, and continues to be, absent.

Even while it stood as the most visible materialization of the Iron Curtain, the Berlin Wall worked to project a spectacular invisibility (its own and that of the other side). Whether we consider the concrete slabs that were infamously covered by graffiti in the West or the "clean screen"[1] that underlined the blankness of the East, post-1961 life turned away from the wall and thereby silently accepted (and perhaps supported) its lethal implications. At the same time, the other side of the wall was erased, as far as possible, from the city's perception and everyday cognizance. Tellingly, maps of East Berlin depicted the West as empty space, just as the East disappeared from the weather charts on Western television.[2] The other side became a virtual "nothing" beyond the wall: vanished, vague, ambivalent. The world, it seemed, ended at the concrete divide that cuts through the middle of Berlin.

Of course, at the same time, the famous city wall separating the East and West of Berlin at a length of 45.9 kilometers has always acted as an overtly visual political statement or image. However, this image also worked to disguise the architectural complexity of the wall, successfully evoking a consistent militarization of absence. While the colorful partition in the West became world famous, the part of the wall effectively working to imprison people, the East, was largely kept hidden from view. This notion of imprisonment (rather than anti-fascist protection) became particularly obvious after the Four Power Agreement about Berlin. From 1972 the inhabitants of West Berlin could access the Eastern part of the city by acquiring a short-term visa, whereas such crossings were nearly impossible for the inhabitants on the Eastern side.[3] Yet, the concept of the Berlin Wall has become largely associated with the graffiti imagery on the Western side. A canvas for political commentary mounting the view to the East, the Berlin Wall is inscribed in public memory as the colorful edge framing a view on socialist life. Hence, it is precisely the wall's operative side that remains absent from a global (and distinctly Western) imagination about the wall.

Essentially, the Berlin Wall also reached much further than the 155 kilometers surrounding West Berlin. It separated the country along a 1,393-kilometer inner border system, designed to keep the actual wall invisible and thereby pervasive enough to seamlessly integrate itself into the everyday life of East Germany (and of course its consequences reached far into Eastern Europe). Large parts of the GDR border were not "walled," in the sense of a concrete imposition, but were often disguised by lakes and forests, which were kept under strict surveillance. Most notably the Berlin Wall was made up of two walls—the 3.6 m high concrete slab facing the Western side of the city and the so-called interior wall facing the East. The two walls were separated by the no man's land of the "death strip," which kept the Berlin Wall on the Western side out of view from the East, at the same time as it was meant to omit the various escape attempts from the East out of Western perception. The Eastern side of the wall was hence not simply markedly absent from the public field of vision, but it was also encouraged to remain absent from thought. The concrete barrier thereby characteristically evoked what Olaf Briese has called an "aesthetic of absence."[4] Arguably, this "absence" of the Eastern wall essentially marks the Berlin Wall's main characteristic and stubbornly outlives its demise.

Today this notion of absence is important to recall, precisely because the Berlin Wall has physically disappeared but persists as a global imaginary that seeks to be (re)mediated in various ways. The physical demolition of the wall began immediately during the night of November 9, 1989, when hundreds of people took to the concrete to work off the emotional tensions and conflicts perpetuated by twenty-eight years of division. People all over the city began to hack the wall to pieces, demolishing it into absence at the same time as beginning a complicated process of preserving. These so-called wall-peckers sold the pieces, sent them off to international friends, or kept them as personal memorabilia. The wall, it seemed, offered the first instance of profitable objects for the consumptions of the socialist past. A seemingly endless supply of wall pieces has since been exchanged and sold all over the world, ironically turning this icon of communist stagnation into a capitalist enterprise. Whether these pieces can still claim authenticity some thirty years later seems to be beside the point. Rather, the ongoing exchange testifies to the circulation of (Western) imaginations about the wall, in absence of the actual concrete.

The GDR famously also started to sell off large pieces of the (painted) wall through the state-owned import-export company Limex, reassuring critics that the profits would be donated to health services and public restorations.[5] While a few segments of the Berlin Wall have been preserved in other parts of the world (mainly in the United States), most of the Berlin Wall has been destroyed. Berlin still exhibits pieces at Potsdamer Platz and the 1.4-kilometer-long Berlin Wall memorial along Bernauer Strasse. Here, tourists can still get a feel of the wall, including the opportunity to visit a "preserved" section of the death strip, complete with a watchtower and barbed wire. Yet, Briese maintains that "the goal was and is not preservation, (which is impossible anyway because the original is gone) but contemporary reconstruction."[6] Rather than maintaining the actual wall, these objects of memory help testify to and simultaneously cover over an aesthetic of absence as inherent to the wall. Exceptional in this regard is the Eastside Gallery (which will be discussed in more detail) because it marks the interior wall of the East, although it imagines it in terms of the graffiti iconography of the West. Altogether these memorials affirm an effort to imagine the wall and to mediate it, despite its absence. They thereby make clear that the wall is primarily a function of psychological barriers, an affective remnant or sticky memory. The wall's status as concrete cementation, protected by soldiers or capitalist endeavor hacked to pieces, is secondary to this task. Standing in for a psychological division, the Berlin Wall invokes a visceral, affective presence that exceeds its materiality. In this way the wall persists as an invisible structure on the face of Berlin and continues to evoke an "aesthetic of absence."

The aesthetic of absence was crucial to the wall's operation as a political imposition, but it also adhered to an invisible composition of meaning that maintained (and perhaps evoked) the wall while securing its psychological effectivity. In this context, people from Berlin often speak about a "mental" wall which has outlived the demise of the actual wall. The shifting grounds between absence and presence as well as visibility and invisibility, hence, affectively charge the barrier, sustaining the wall as a physical and psychological obstacle. This interplay, it seems, was well understood by the East German authorities, who strictly prohibited the wall's depiction and thereby any form of mediation on and of the wall. The law was meant to prevent potential escapees from gaining a detailed understanding of the border system, but inadvertently it also worked to highlight the felt presence of the wall and reinforce its psychological effectiveness. Lars Kristensen refers to an internalization of Berlin's Cold War space as "self-evident and definite,"[7] suggesting a sense of pervasiveness that led people to believe that the wall would simply always be there.

In this way, the GDR literally created a political order of (in)visibility that was not only reflected in the institutionalized "absence" of the wall, but also in a thorough control of the GDR's cultural production, later leading to the assumption that subversive engagement with the wall could only be conducted in the West.[8] However, it has become clear that the wall's logic, and the politics it stood for, could be, and were, artistically challenged in both the East and the West, either by outright opposition to the prohibition to depict the wall or through a more subtle engagement with its dynamic of absence and invisibility.

Crucially, many of those who lived with the wall often became so immersed in its structure and appearance that they could no longer notice it or reflect on its presence. This immersion, enabled by the wall's aesthetic of absence, nevertheless constitutes a significant form of emotional imposition, by which the wall's invisible presence is easily internalized as part of a walled life. The "mental" wall paradoxically draws its full presence from this kind of absence, eliciting a systematic crisis of the ordinary, as Berlant might put it[9] or a kind of insidious convergence between historical forces and lived experience that demand practical readjustments and emotional adaptations to the everyday. In resonance with this dynamic, the wall can be read as performing the dialectics of political power and emotional labor, in order to exercise its affective command. This sense of adhesive ambivalence posits the wall as that which can never be adequately accessed and yet plays out as an inner conflict. Encouraging the formation of an "intimate public" that seeks to express the informal tragedies and collective comforts prompted by the wall, this "impasse,"[10] or moment of arrested tension, stirs "collective mediations"[11] that, in one way or another, enable a metric for engaging with the wall's imposition, often by projecting the messy intimacies and changing distances it provokes.

In this way, expression of and on the wall can become a means of understanding experience[12]—an experience which, in the case of the Berlin Wall, is largely sustained by feelings of absence. The ability to mediate absence and what is made absent hence functions as a resistance to the political order of (in)visibility and the negative attachments this provokes. The act of mediating the wall constitutes a form of subverting the political imperatives and dealing with the psychological imposition in so far as such acts address the wall's affectivity, reinstating it in its full in/visibility. In other words, artistic engagement with the wall and the walled life it produces make visible the wall's affective weight. Putting into view what the spectacle of the monument seeks to efface, mediation, in this sense, counters absence by renouncing a routinized forgetting of the wall and thereby encourages a (re)making of absent history.

Once upon a Time in the East

Since the GDR government sought to prevent any form of mediation of the wall, artistic encounters were largely absent from the surface; of course, they nevertheless thrived below it. Engaging with the aesthetic of absence worked to overcome invisibility by asserting the self in relation to a highly politicized space that sought to hide its own effectiveness. It was also a way to affectively address the hidden and forbidden. In the East such acts were predominantly addressed through the medium of photography, due to its capacity to individuate and authenticate the unseen realities of the everyday. Of course, photography is also extraordinarily sensitized to the affective qualities of the objects it captures, ideally seizing what Roland Barthes has famously called the "punctum," that "sting, speck, cut"[13] or little wound that touches the viewer from afar and folds her into the affective sensorium of the image. Both amateur snapshots and professional photography have provided this kind of affective documentation of the wall, immortalizing particular experiences of and beyond the wall and paying witness to the walled life in its shadows. In this sense photography responds to the way in which politicized space is socially and affectively produced, often reorganizing and remapping its set-up by highlighting individuated views on and of the wall.

Detlef Matthes's amateur photographs of the Berlin Wall provide an example of challenging the "absent" Berlin Wall as orchestrated by the East German authorities by refusing to simply internalize its presence. Blatantly opposing the prohibition of depiction at the age of eighteen, Matthes created a rare documentation of the emptiness and absence that constitute a walled life in the form of black-and-white shots of blank concrete and a vast no-man's land.[14] The photos capture the sense of isolation experienced by the photographer, which is utilized as the defining means of a very personal encounter with the wall, perhaps making an attempt at understanding the space, while unavoidably interrogating it politically. Matthes notoriously photographed the wall from hide-outs, as a form of (risky) personal negotiation with imprisonment. Chasing a view of the West, he experienced every photograph (altogether 180)[15] as a form of triumph, reclaiming the space that essentially erased him from the other's sight, but also indulging in a kind of rebellious thrill, pushing boundaries and exercising a sense of control over what he was essentially controlled by. Put simply, the photos allowed Matthes to investigate a forbidden view, but they now also work as intimate cartographies of a largely absent view of the wall from an Eastern perspective.[16] Matthes' grainy photographs are devoid of people or any signs of social life, adding to the impression that the wall was indeed faceless or "absent" from East German everyday life on the one hand and created a form of permanent absence (of sociability) on the other. Overall, the photos depict the obscene normality of imprisonment and the peculiar absence of engagement with the wall. A "parking lot at the end of the world,"[17] as one journalist described a photograph years later, cut-off streets, and train lines as well as complex border systems reinforce a sense of endless enclosure, limitation, and loneliness.

These photos are personal investigations of an imposed environment and perhaps attempts at resisting this space while enabling meaning retrospectively. Matthes lost the photos in 1987 when the State Security (Stasi) coincidently discovered the collection, after Matthes was arrested at the notorious Pfingstkrawalle.[18] Matthes was accused of espionage and imprisoned for six weeks, until it was established that the photos were politically "harmless." Ironically, this dismissal was precisely what gave these photos political leverage in the future and further preserved them from the void of forgetting. Years after the wall's demise, Matthes found the long-forgotten photos in his Stasi file and subsequently made them accessible to the public in exhibitions.[19] Now reframed by the present, the photographs which were once the trophies of a personal dare have gained political and historical significance. Today Matthes's photos serve to document a history of isolation as experienced by an eighteen-year-old at the time, and thereby testify to the intersection between the private and the political as the cornerstones of a walled life.

Whereas Matthes's photos testified to a private and secret encounter with the wall, the works of professional GDR photographers were officially able to make appear what was hidden and hence excluded from the formal "inventory" of political discourse. Some of the most successful artistic subversions of authorized GDR culture were accomplished by reinterpreting an official practice while still following it. As Matthew Shaul and Nicola Freeman have explained, photography had the simple advantage that it was not considered a form of art in the GDR,[20] a stigma which even after reunification haunted

Eastern photography, now accused of submitting to the official social realism credo, and therefore incapable of genuine artistic creation.[21] Such arguments ignore the crossovers between confirming and subverting the official political principle of social realism, because as Paul Betts puts it, "such realism retained its critical edge in documenting a social experience" that often did not correspond to the state's official image.[22]

Indeed, art under socialism would often utilize the system against itself. Despite the official claim of depicting the reality of the working class, social realism was underscored by an insistent glorification of successful socialist progress. Where "reality," particularly that of the working class, departed from such formulas, the socialist setting was revealed to be made up of competing realities, potentially challenging the official discourse of unified contentment. Photography in this regard could show an un-orchestrated (and by extension unauthorized) life in the East, while capturing and hence reinstating the individual faces in the otherwise faceless collectivity of the GDR. Photography thereby challenged the absence of the (private) subject; or, as Susan Sontag put it, "just to show something, anything, in the photographic view is to show that it is hidden."[23] Such crossovers were often reflected in photographs of private life in the GDR, which were at once highly welcomed, as they suggested a certain (socialist) way of life, and could also gain a subversive potential, if utilized to reinstate the unseen intimacies beyond the socialist script.

In this way, artists could use an official credo to draw out the hidden affective lives of the walled existence. As Paul Betts has shown, from the 1960s various GDR photographers began photographing families in their living rooms in order to document "real existing socialism" within the domestic walls of GDR citizens.[24] These photos most prominently showed the family arranged for a portrait in the living room, frequently positioned around the coffee table, presenting the "tidy worker domicile."[25] In the mid-1980s Gundula Schulze Eldowy drew on this tradition of the domestic in her photo series *Nude*, but utilized the space in a way that exposed the socialist living room photos as highly scripted by individuating the subject beyond this script. The people in her photographs are particularized, belonging to a community located in Berlin-Mitte, of which the photographer was an intimate member.[26] They are often shown naked, or "stripped of clothes as markers of status and nation."[27] Facing the camera directly these subjects intimate a kind of disarming vulnerability as their woeful, direct eyes evade all pretense and address the viewer emotionally. Reframing the official narrative of progress, these people, hidden behind the private and political wall of socialist life, communicate a different story about the historical moment in view.

Schulze Eldowy's photographs are saturated with melancholic affect that strips the scene of any facade, instead providing a candid portrait of life in the East. While often depicted as secluded and solemn, the people in the photographs nevertheless appear unguarded and open, creating a sense of raw emotionality and fierce dignity that circumvent the obscene avoidance invoked by the wall. Many of the faces reappear throughout Schulze Eldowy's different series and thereby reinstate the intimacy and familiarity between subject and photographer. This trust enables the photographer to show her subjects in private, unwary, and without inhibition, echoing Sontag, who writes that "to take a photograph is to participate in another person's mortality, vulnerability, mutability."[28] The private space in Schulze Eldowy's series is often unarranged and uncertain, foregrounding the naked, "uncovered" individual. A lot of the photos transmit a sense of isolation and perishability, in contrast to the collective euphoria staged by official state photography. Furthermore, the images expose two different spheres of privacy in the GDR: an officially scripted way of being a family, as well as a hidden "naked" privacy of individuals which suggests an aura of despair and transience.

The notion of transience not only counters the cementation and permanence communicated by walls; it also challenges the GDR's official future orientation by foregrounding a sense of decay. Despite our tendency to associate communism with the past, following a progressive logic, Boris Groys points out that communist-ruled societies have always followed the "banner of some universal future,"[29] aggressively asserting "the credo of progress."[30] In this sense communism was "utterly modern,"[31] a modernity which was above all "a way of politically organizing time,"[32] away from a compromised and frozen past toward a "future within the present."[33] Subverting the particular temporality of communism, GDR photography could hence undermine the system's ideological directions and statutes. Schulze Eldowy's series *Berlin in a Dog's Night* lays a focus on the unseen margin of the ever "progressive" society. Rather than testifying to the anticipated future of socialist advancement, the series documents people who are anchored in a grievable past. The photos tell of a struggling, declining society and an infrastructure about to collapse. The people depicted are firmly integrated into the decaying city space, which does not reflect the projected modernity of the GDR system, but instead re-reads the walled presence with references to a war-torn past. Schulze Eldowy's photos hence unveil absence by drawing attention to the image of the "lost city,"[34] capturing the affective afterlife of a troubled history, which simultaneously anticipated the fall of the wall.

In this sense, Schulze Eldowy's images, in true socialist manner, await "the future"; however, at the same time the images foreshadow the regime's demise by looking to the past. Breaking with the East's lethargic arrangement of surveillance and futurity, Schulze Eldowy documents the affective candor of the moment as a way to pay witness to the multiple temporalities (futures and pasts) at work. As the photographer puts it in an interview in 2009: "It's not like all of a sudden, with the 9th of November, and because of Mr. Schabowski, the borders were opened. You can see it in my pictures, where the agony is already visible."[35] Showing a sense of misery, poverty, and social isolation, Schulze Eldowy engages with an informal affective culture that draws attention to the corporeal impact of the moment and which is largely felt but otherwise kept invisible, individuating the economic and societal decline of a future-oriented GDR. The photographer, herself living for more than thirteen years in the midst of the community she depicted, conveys sentiments of walled life, using stark lighting contrasts that foreground the darkness of the space and simultaneously creates a haunting emptiness. In the audio track that accompanies the exhibition of these photographs on her website,[36] Schulze Eldowy explains that she wanted to save these faces from being forgotten. To her these images utilize stories—stories of ordinary people that need to be protected from disappearance and that belong to the city of Berlin.[37] At the same time, the photographer attempted to portray a particular moment in time and an affective milieu that had been forgotten even while it still existed. In this way the people shown in Schulze Eldowy's work give a face to the history inscribed in the spatial memory of Berlin and (like all portraits) they allow for a moment of history looking back at us.

Schulze Eldowy captured moments that authenticate an absent East Berlin normality in which, as she puts it, "the splitting of Berlin is the splitting of its inhabitants."[38] These snapshots of everyday life were hidden not only from the view of the GDR authorities, but also from Western culture. The captured moments were, in other words, characterized by absence in terms of both the past they referenced and the present they created. Drawing on Walter Benjamin and Hannah Arendt, Britta Duelke explains that "the transmissibility of the past relates to its capacity to be cited in the present."[39] Hence, photographs such as Schulze Eldowy's can only depict the past if they are granted this authority. In this context Schulze Eldowy was capable of exhibiting her photography in the GDR, but it took twenty years after reunification before they provoked a second wave of appreciation. The 2007 British exhibition *Do Not Refreeze: Photography behind the Iron Curtain* exemplifies the way in which these works are retrospectively incorporated into a corpus that rewrites East German history as the testimony of a "completed" European history. Featuring Schulze Eldowy and other GDR photographers, the exhibition advertised the photos as "an extraordinary contribution to European photography"[40] which, up until this point, had "been frozen out by the Cold War."[41] Similarly, the German exhibition *Look Back Forward*[42] provided another "deferred" setting for the hidden faces of and behind the wall to appear in a unified Germany. Ironically, the photos are thereby utilized to reformulate a notion of "undivided" European history, but they also prove capable of subverting (and perhaps rewriting) GDR history, by illuminating the faces of unscripted East German private life that were otherwise hidden by and filtered through the ideological screen of the wall.

Shattered Mirrors in the West: The Wall as Screen

While critical images from the East were largely intent on an interrogation of the wall's invisible (ideological) structure, the critical response in the West could take a more physical form. The difference in power relations between the system and the artist affords a kind of affective reversal according to which the melancholy of the East can be translated into cynical humor in the West. This focus on melancholy or crisis of the ordinary in the East suggests a productive resistance to resolution and overcoming, which in the Western setting is somewhat reversed to take the shape of a more overt attempt to work through what is perceived as a traumatic moment. Testifying to an understanding of the wall's invisibility and function as a traumatic screen of Germany's political unconscious, West German artist Peter Unsicker investigated the conflicted space of the wall through art installations. Engaging with a visual articulation of the wall's absurd imposition in the last three years of its existence, his work preconfigures (often humorously) the notion of the invisible or "mental wall,"[43] as he put it, in an effort to work on and through the wall as a traumatic presence.

On November 9, 1986 (an uncanny historic echo) Unsicker, a sculptor from Heidelberg, opened his *Wallstreet Gallery* at Zimmerstrasse in West Berlin, which he still operates today. In 1986 the gallery's back door directly faced the wall with a space of merely 6 meters between the window and the wall. Although the artist's primary medium is wood and, at this point, he was "absolutely not interested in wall art,"[44] as practiced by Thierry Noir and Christophe Bouchet, he encountered the affective presence of the wall within a matter of days, feeling "totally confronted with the wall."[45] The daily question "Do I stand before or behind the wall?"[46] became what he describes as a "very personal consternation,"[47] finally prompting him to accept the wall as a task. He developed a need to work with it and on it, or arguably, *through* it by reinscribing the wall's affective bearing into the visual. Unsicker's investment of this politically and viscerally charged space resulted in a need to disrupt the wall's unbearable stagnation, but also works as a creative testimony to the anxieties informing walled life.

A week after arriving at Zimmerstrasse, Unsicker started his project in which he utilized the wall as a medium and extension of his gallery. *The Work* on Ruination (Die Arbeit am Verdorbenen), as he called it, evoked both an act of ruining and a sense of being ruined by the imposition of the wall. Ruination in Unsicker's understanding is the result of ignorance and idleness, both of which have resulted in the stagnation materialized by the wall, which he sought to overcome. In this way, Unsicker understood the space as a personal challenge to counter the aggressive invisibility of the wall, acknowledging the need to bring the wall into people's consciousness, because, as he put it, "as long as I can see the wall in front of me I know it is not running through my mind."[48] The Work on Ruination, in other words, investigated the psychological effectivity and sensory affectivity of the wall prior to (and after) its physical disappearance and engaged with its visual capacity as a surface and a (multimedia) screen by posting a series of images and installations on the wall.

Unsicker's work layers the physical appearance of the wall with its fantasmatic and affective function as an ideological projection. Engaging the wall as a (Lacanian) screen, Unsicker's art recognizes the way in which experience is constituted by an "'imaginary' mapping,"[49] as Silverman puts it, that determines how we perceive ourselves and others. The wall's fantasmatic screen functions "like a mask,"[50] but also allows for a playing with the projections of the ideological screen which is, literally, brought to the surface by Unsicker's installation. Playing with the images ostensibly hidden and/or downright imposed by the ideological screen of the political order, Unsicker's images "assume a critical importance, opening up (...) an arena for political contestation,"[51] as Lacan would have it, by literally playing with the "face" of the wall and creating a counter-image to the monument. Unsicker's work thereby drew out the Berlin Wall's absurdity by attending to the mechanism of its invisibility and traumatic imposition.

Unsicker's art can be read as working with and through the traumatic experience of Germany's division, understanding the wall's operation as a repressive shield that prevents and expresses a (shared) Second World War past. It is vital to remember that, as a political monument, the Berlin Wall provided a testimony to a German inability to engage with the horrors of the Second World War, reinstating the political and psychological dimensions of grief, guilt, and trauma. As if to shield the traumatic experience behind the screen of the pre-conscious, as Freud explains the dynamic of repression, each side of the two Germanys tended to displace the responsibility for the country's national socialist past by "frequently pass[ing it] over the border to the 'other' Germany"[52] on the other side of the wall. Whereas the West framed the GDR as a continuation of the totalitarian Nazi regime (a discourse which is still common today), the GDR blatantly legitimized itself on an "antifascist foundation myth," which went as far as officially terming the wall "the antifascist protection rampart."[53]

In contrast, Unsicker re-read the wall not so much as a point of separation or repression, but as the pivotal déjà vu inevitably putting the two Germanys into contact, physically and psychologically, with a view to a shared historical agony. Unsicker understood the wall as a plaster adhering to a wound cutting through Germany. While the wall was meant to stop the GDR from "bleeding out"[54] (or losing its people), in this very attempt it echoed the logic of trauma and the psychic forming of barriers and split-off entities. Engaging with these layered connotations allowed Unsicker to reinstate the wall's presence and to renegotiate its meaning. His first installation was hence called *Wound Plaster* and initiated the confrontation of and with the wall as part of a dialectics between harm and healing. Unsicker attached a giant plaster made of paper mâché and textile onto the wall. The plaster stretched up the 3.6 m height of the wall and was signified by a red cross and a crack through which (painted) blood was still escaping. The bandage thereby reinstated the wall as an injury cutting through Germany's political, historical, and psychological landscapes.

At the center of the red cross, Unsicker displayed a mask, the plaster mold of an eight-year-old boy, presenting the face of Germany as that of a wounded or diseased child. The face individuated the suffering induced by division, but it also indicated (and foreshadowed) the possibility of ONE German face. It is not clear which side the face belonged to as it was attached to the Western side but could also be read as pressing through the wall from the East. However, such ambivalences allow for a reading of the wall as a traumatic wound affecting the people on both sides of the barrier. In this context Unsicker understands art as a form of working through, or as he put it "a healing process in regard to the psychological hardening in this wall-wounded city."[55] The wall, to Unsicker, thereby testified to the "materialization of a diseased state of being"[56] and thereby can be read as an image of persistent crisis and trauma.

The evocation of an image of trauma and hence a sense of not simply working on but also through ruination (what is rotten inside) is based on two themes that run through Unsicker's work. First, the images he creates work through modes of literalization and, second, literal figures of speech are turned into images. Unsicker's work thereby follows the logic of confronting different (im)materialities with each other. In this case, one image (the wall as the image of trauma) is countered by another (the image created by art) to produce a scene that turns the wall's unconscious undercurrents into literalized images (rather than words), and thereby visualizes the trauma underpinning the wall. The significance of literality for trauma has been widely discussed in the field of psychoanalysis. Freud applies this notion in his engagement with the "surfacing" of the unconscious in *The Interpretation of Dreams,* which later leads Cathy Caruth to assert that trauma is in fact constituted by the insistent return of the literal.[57] However, literality and visuality relate precisely because the unconscious communicates through images that translate into words and words that are articulated by the image. Hence, Unsicker's work can be read as both literal yet visual statements that return as a response to his traumatic encounter with the wall.

The visualization of trauma echoes the will to literally attach what Caruth calls "associative chains"[58] of meaning to the trauma imposed by the wall. The installations may hence be read as a form of working through by means of the visual rather than a talking cure, producing a "screening through" while drawing attention to the structure of trauma encoded in the wall. Rancière similarly explains that "speech institutes a certain visibility,"[59] an idea literally put to work in Unsicker's project. To Unsicker the installations provide a sense of immediate coherence, "stimmig"[60] as he calls it, alluding to a sense of sanity and balance that intimates a notion of catharsis. The images he creates rearticulate something that otherwise remains "unsaid" about the wall and reaffirm the meaning of the wall as traumatic or disturbing in the Western context, rather than invisibly pervasive.

For example, Unsicker's installation *The Ice Cold War* covered a segment of the wall in ice and thereby literally froze the wall to express the "cooling down of relationships" between the two sides and perhaps the "frozen" perspective of the politics of walls. *Wood against Concrete* positions Unsicker's wood-work in opposition to the wall by leaning a large number of decomposing wood blocks against the concrete of the wall in order to create a contrast between the "organic" wood and the "dead" wall.[61] This reinstates the wall's rigidity but also suggests a working through of "dead" materiality in order to decompose the imposition. Unsicker's work hence "puts something back into the picture" that is otherwise not articulated on the surface. His images can be read as addressing the wall's invisible presence and, similar to the process of working through traumatic experience, they seek to bring these "hidden" meanings to the surface, once and for all.

Despite this drive toward resolution and healing, however, Unsicker comes to understand the notion of "work" as on-going engagement. Working on ruination intimates a form of emotional and creative labor that has to be exercised continuously as a way of confronting the wall in order to work through it, perhaps literally so. Unsicker's work thereby (perhaps unwillingly) reiterates the endurance of traumatic imposition, reading the wall, present or absent, as an ongoing project or task. In this context, Unsicker also turned the wall into the *MuSehum fuer Unbewaeltigtes*—a wordplay which in English translates as "MuSEEum for that which has not been worked through." In this sense Unsicker's work offers moments of engagement, but ultimately does not aim to provide answers; instead, he opens up possibilities of thinking through the wall's affective imposition and political absurdity. In other words, the images he creates are a form of thinking in images or image-thinking, which echoes Walter Benjamin's insightful neologism, the thought-image.

To Benjamin the thought-image is a form of writing that reinstates the image as a central part of thought. It is a constellation "in which the dialectic of thought and image is unfolded and becomes visible."[62] The dynamic can be understood as a form of writing that re-enacts the constitution of meaning in the image rather than offering only a thought product. Everything becomes literally "transformed into writing."[63] Benjamin's most famous example would be the angel of history,[64] a visual description of a perpetual looking back on a catastrophic past. Thought-images cannot be translated into conceptual language[65] or as Adorno explains it, thought-images are "picture puzzles (...) of something that cannot be said in words."[66] This alludes to the notion of trauma theory in the sense that the thought-image indeed marks "the verbalization of something that is obviously not verbal,"[67] as Freud conceptualizes the process of working through. Unsicker can be said to draw on a similar method by engaging the thought-image in reverse, turning a textual snapshot akin to Benjamin's written thought-image into a visual statement which firstly invites reflexivity and then radiates meaning in several directions, provoking a working through of the image.

For example, Unsicker's *Crack in the Mirror* installation utilizes the notion of literal reflexivity by turning the wall into a mirror that throws the gaze back at itself and thereby ironically "cracks" the Lacanian mirror. In 1989 Unsicker plastered the wall with a large number of uneven mirror pieces in order to reflect on the tension in the space and to address the "imaginary' mapping"[68] it enforced. The kaleidoscopic mirror assemblage reflected the image of the wall as indefinitely shattered, splitting individuals and landscapes, indicating that the reality thrown back at the passerby is broken or breaking. This promoted a strong sense of self-reflexivity, and a very literal transformation from optical reflection to intellectual reflection, from image to thought and back again. Unsicker's literal attachment of the mirror pieces was thereby meant to project social and human processes back into the space which sought to hide them. He explained that "the present tension at the wall is dispersed by the social power of art—transformed into light and reflection,"[69] in the sense that the wall actually disappeared on the one hand and was made obvious on the other. This brought the wall's dialectic of absence and presence to the forefront of perception in that the mirrors were used to make the wall's presence absent and thereby simultaneously made its peculiar absence present. The mirror mosaic prevented "thinking beyond the space" and demanded a potentially conflictual encounter with the self in relation to the wall. This disruptive reflexivity, the falling apart of an established sense of self provided an opportunity for a new way of "putting the pieces together."

It enabled a new perspective in which the spectator's reflection was literally inscribed onto the surface of the wall and thereby entwined with the other side through a notion of doubling (another me on the other side; another Germany).

Furthermore, the installation generated Western media attention, which was also broadcast to the artist community on the Eastern side. In other words, the ideological screen of the wall was taken up by the ideological screen of TV and thereby circumvented the barrier, defeating the imposition temporarily. Later, Unsicker recalled this small victory as generating a large number of drinks offered to him upon visiting an East Berlin bar, as he often did to mingle with artists in the East.[70] In this way the installation challenged the wall as "ordinary" and tacit but also suggested a possible reconfiguration of the space of division into a space of encounter.

Unsicker exposes both the inner wall and the historical wall as a form of projection or psychical defense in need of externalizing an inner conflict. Despite the subjectivization of perspective, however, the visitor can enter the artistic space only from a Western point of view. The wall as an ideological screen, and ultimately as a perspective, hence, continues to haunt the installations and adheres to the ideological screen as an internal mechanism. In other words, Unsicker's Wall Street Gallery brings to life a conflictual historical imaginary and simultaneously allows for an encounter with an otherwise invisible inhibition foregrounding the psychological and virtual space the wall creates. His installations do not simply simulate a historical imaginary but also stimulate the need to deal with the wall's absence. Ultimately, Unsicker's work exemplifies that the Berlin Wall makes for an extraordinary projection surface, both in the form of an ideological screen and as a canvas. The wall is tethered to forms of projection, whether in the political and psychological realm or as testified by the various graffiti works on its Western side.

Besides Unsicker's emphatic work, it is well known that the Western side of the wall attracted many more international artists such as Keith Haring, Christophe Bouchet (Thierry Noir's partner in crime), and Lev Nussberg. Their countless murals shaped the global image of the Berlin Wall as a setting for challenging the political and visual imposition on the city. The West thereby reclaimed the wall as a colorful image despite the "grey" East's official ownership of the monument. In this way the wall, as immortalized in the global imaginary, evoked a statement of Western resistance, capable of reflecting back to the West the image of its own idealized "free" self. The dynamic highlights that artistic engagement shapes political narratives; however, it needs to be acknowledged that such creativity is always bound to questions of who has the means to interrupt, critique, and engage with a given situation and who is excluded from this possibility. In the Eastern part, where the wall was a taboo, engaging with the surface in this way was nearly impossible and (for the duration of the GDR) remained invisible. When paintings on the Eastern side were finally realized in the aftermath of the wall's demise, they not only suggested a defiance of the restrictive authorities,[71] but also worked to re-map the wall by foregrounding it as a piece of art, and as a medium.

Negative Attachments in the Present: The Wall Must Stay!

While the Berlin Wall fell spectacularly in 1989, it never lost its enigmatic magnetism for art. Reveling in the once celebrated visual pleasure of this Cold War emblem, contemporary artists have utilized remainders of the wall to express affective knowledge about walls all over the world and with recourse to the Western graffiti imaginary that made the Berlin Wall world-famous. Preserved and frequently renewed, most notably along Berlin's famous Eastside Gallery, many of these paintings express an affective engagement with the wall's persistent flickering between absence and presence, even today, often serving to project memories of walled life and simultaneously helping to articulate a (national and international) perception of "a historical present that becomes apprehensible as an affective urgency."[72] On the one hand, the Eastside Gallery thereby works as a reminder that the wall is incessantly remediated in the present; on the other, it negotiates an ambivalent politics of attributing meaning to a walled existence retrospectively, often by reproducing atmospheres of historical belonging and generating more informal affective cultures. As a memorial the Eastside Galley hence exceeds the crises of melancholy and trauma in East and West it was meant to immortalize. Rather, this monument provides insight into the wall's capacity to hold, unfold, and sometimes rewrite a great variety of conflicting and ambiguous affects that saturate a walled life, long after the barrier's physical demise.

At last utilizing the empty grey interior wall of the East as a poignant canvas, the 1.3 kilometer Eastside Gallery strip was first painted by over 120 artists (including Thierry Noir) in 1990. Today it still stands as an artistic triumph over the blank invisibility once enforced from the Eastern side and has become an enduring hallmark of the creative euphoria energizing the wall's fall in 1989. Nevertheless, Olaf Briese laments the painting over of the blank wall of the East as "a total loss for the city,"[73] precisely because "this bleak interior wall... documented the bleakness of its designers almost perfectly."[74] Briese reads the art as merely "confronting the horror vacui and fear of the construction's naked practicality."[75] On the other hand, the gallery claims to have created an "expression of a unique point in time,"[76] which testifies to the affective charge of the wall's demise by "giving the wall a new face in a new time."[77] Images such as the famous *Brotherkiss* between Leonid Breshnev and Erich Honecker by Dimitrij Vrubel or Birgit Kinder's *Test the Rest* Trabant driving through the wall have become iconic and attest to the exhilaration the wall's demise evoked in early 1990, thereby ironically preserving it for affective reflection. The Eastside Gallery hence can be read as a temporal snapshot which does not constitute memory per se, but rather *enables* memory, providing a relation to the past by suggesting an affective anchor for the dematerialized wall.

Saturated with sentimentality, this memory work facilitated by the Eastside Gallery allows for a return to the historical situation of the wall, without necessarily restoring the past. Rather, sentimentality here works in Berlant's sense as "a main historical artery for making affect worlds,"[78] which captures a variety of felt encounters with the past, of which the wall has become a symbol. Such affect worlds are "organized by the unsaid" which "suffuse and destabilize the ordinary to make new social arrangements,"[79] and thereby potentially reorganize an intimate public in the present. In other words, the wall as a memory object is emotionally charged, because it provides a pathway for investigating historical legacies, contemporary politics, and personal trajectories all at once, and thereby evokes a sense of shared, if sentimental, authenticity "that enables identification and solidarity among strangers."[80] The Eastside Gallery welcomes this sense of sentimentality, since it also allows for retrospective investments and modes of relationality. Sentimentality thereby redefines the wall as a conduit to the past, ironically evoking emotional bonds to the once hated object and suggesting that historic landmarks, such as the Eastside Gallery, are in fact "placeholders" that allow for multiple ambivalent relations and retrospective attachments.

Attesting to the gallery's remarkable capacity to converge the affective sensoria of past and present, such investments in the wall were brought to the surface when the city tried to remove parts of the gallery on March 1, 2013, in order to rebuild a bridge that had been destroyed during the Second World War to construct a luxury apartment complex.[81] The plan generated a mass protest of about 6,000 activists and citizens who formed a "human wall" to protect the actual wall, passionately demanding that "the wall must stand."[82] Of course, the images of people protecting the wall from demise turned the historic meaning of the monument on its head, testifying to the way in which meaning changes retrospectively and affectively. At first glance observers hence felt they were witnessing a kind of historical Stockholm syndrome, suggesting that the protesters were emotionally held hostage by a malicious past (an assumption which is still often waged to admonish expressions of sentimentality or wistful reminiscence in relation to the East). In this sense the protest can be read as a form of expressing a negative attachment which, reverberating with Berlant's discussion of cruel optimism, affectively bound the protesters to a harmful object which at the same time, so it seemed, was experienced as "profoundly confirming."[83]

It is then not surprising that although the dismantling of the wall was temporarily stopped, the events sparked an intense debate about the historic meaning of the gallery. The protesters accused the city of erasing its history and selling it off. The supporters of the project accused the protesters of hypocrisy and misguided nostalgia, while arguing for the legitimacy of the process in strictly legal terms. Of course, such arguments fail to acknowledge the affective investments that propelled the protesters in the first place, and which exceed a negative attachment to the past. According to Berlant, sentimentality does not necessarily need to be cruel by default; rather, it can also work as "a mode of relationality in which people take emotions to express something authentic about themselves that they think the world should welcome and respect."[84] Seen in this light, the process revealed a larger problem about the privatization of public space and about the legitimacy of public monuments as constitutive not only of a singular moment of history, but of various individual histories. In this sense, the protesters did not protect the wall as such, but the affective relation to the past it enables,[85] thereby expressing their ownership of a personal but (shared) history of walled life.

In this sense, the protest (once again) traumatically collapsed time and expressed the crystallization of the histories attached to the wall as various personal encounters and stories across different spaces and generations. Simultaneously, there seemed to be an insistent demand to repress the wall and to return it to an absence. People demonstrating with slogans such as "the wall must stay" uncannily reversed the 1989 image of people demanding "the wall must fall."[86] In a similar way, one German newspaper's headline stated "No one has the intention to destroy a wall,"[87] echoing Walter Ulbricht's announcement in July 1961 that "no one has the intention to build a wall."[88] Despite the protests temporarily stopping construction, the company responsible ultimately managed to take down further sections of the wall by the end of March 2013. A first demolition took place, hidden in darkness, at 5 o'clock in the morning and was "protected" by a 250-strong police force.[89] The scene not only mimicked the mechanism of repression in which the psychical forces work to maintain the exclusion of a forbidden thought from consciousness, but also ironically re-invoked the scene of the wall's creation in 1961, hence projecting history in more than one way and transferring it to the present.

Ultimately, the struggle over the Eastside Gallery suggests that despite the demise of the wall and the political system that created it, walled life has left visible and invisible marks across the physical and psychological landscapes of the post-communist world.[90] It thereby affirms the wall at the center of a struggle between competing attachments to the past and present. Interestingly, "wall-art" increased *after* the fall of the wall and around the 20th anniversary of its demise in 2009. On the one hand, this revitalized engagement with the wall as a canvas may be explained by a more general renewed interest in the wall in the context of its first major anniversary and the countless attempts to "unearth" various materials, stories, and "testimonies" in order to signify and mediate the date's historical importance. On the other hand, the notion of (re)surfacing also suggests a need to continuously reimagine a lost structure and thereby echoes the compulsive repetition associated with trauma.

The reactivated engagement with the wall may then further be read as an attempt to provide a retrospective view on the now seemingly absurd experience of a walled city. As Kristensen explains, the absent wall conjures up a loss of a definite shape of history, as "there is nothing onto which the present can reflect."[91] Echoing Fukuyama's famous exclamation about the "end of history," the loss of the wall in the post-communist world denotes "the point where time and space collide,"[92] suggesting that the spatial organization of the absent wall is in need of frameworks of understanding—frameworks that are spatial, temporal, and sometimes sentimental in the way they provide meaning. Mediating a walled experience in the form of artistic reiterations in the present then also evokes Freud's concept of *Nachträglichkeit*, in which an absence in the present is undergirded by a particular dynamic of the past, folding back on itself and making "possible a different understanding of what was remembered."[93] Such notions of reconstructing history via memories, feelings, and Freud's uncanny temporalities thereby utilize the wall as a mode of understanding or a need to make sense of the past in the context of the present and vice versa.

One More Time with Feeling: Commemorating the Fall

One way of anchoring affective investments in the past within official narratives is the public commemoration of national events. In the case of the Berlin Wall, this has also meant that the politics of sentimentality have been utilized to repeatedly reproduce a particular delight in the wall's fall in order to support Western ideas of freedom and democracy. Acts of public memory favor perspectives and meanings that imbue time and space with significance, retelling the affective stories that are meant to assist in the overcoming of a growing distance to the people and spaces that are being remembered. In a sense, efforts to restage the sentiments of the fall thereby also mark an attempt at institutionalizing and memorializing specific forms of forgetting, reinterpreting, and instrumentalizing historical pasts in the service of power dynamics in the present. Of course, commemorations of Berlin's infamous wall are still largely based in living memory and therefore often fashion moments of remediation of a particular event in time—the iconic fall of the wall and the feelings and excitements associated with it.

The notion of *remediation*, however, is not simply linked to efforts of re-experiencing the euphoria and hopes that saturated the early 1990s. The act of remediation is central to understanding the wall as a medium or as a means of the affective formations that undergird the political space. Following Bolter's and Grusin's definition of remediation as "the representation of one medium in another," the dynamic suggests that the wall repeats a psychological mediation preceding the wall's physical appearance and thereby makes visible the narratives, ideologies, and sentiments that inform political settings. However, where the wall is remediated as part of the communal memory of the nation, it also serves to expose how the present is imagined before all else. In this context (re)mediation can also be understood as the repeated negotiation of conflictual divides (inherent to the wall and its mental remainders), potentially implying acts of reconciliation and the possibility of remedy in the context of working through the individual and collective affects associated with the wall.

For example, when the wall's demise neared its first major anniversary in 2009, the twenty-year commemoration readily drew on an image which had already been circulated and reaffirmed within the national (and global) imaginary. Turning back time became the logic of the televised spectacle, symbolically re-staging the fall of the wall in a manner carefully designed to reaffirm the course of history since 1989, and thereby the course of democracy. The various reconstructions of memories such as Chancellor Angela Merkel re-enacting her crossing of the bridge at Bornholmer Strasse in 1989,[94] or the masses of people gathered around the Brandenburg Gate, plus various exhibitions, panel discussions, newspaper articles, and film festivals all worked toward the climactic falling of a 2-kilometer *Domino Wall* in the center of Berlin. In this way, the established meaning of the 1989 images was playfully reasserted and retrospectively affirmed. In order to create a celebratory space, the "Freedom Fest"[95] mixed entertainment and politics, elsewhere carefully avoided by German politicians. The "show" was hosted by the popular German entertainer Thomas Gottschalk, who welcomed high-ranking political guests, such as Hillary Clinton, Nicholas Sarkozy, Dimitri Medvedev, Gordon Brown and Angela Merkel, as well as Mikhail Gorbachev and Lech Walesa,[96] while leading mass chants spelling the word F R E E D O M.[97]

The image of the fall was carefully scripted in order to "remember" the "domino-effect" of the "falling" communist countries opening their borders to the West. Following a 100,000-voice countdown, Lech Walesa initiated the falling dominoes, just as he had symbolically done twenty years earlier when he helped to open Poland's borders. During the thirty-minute spectacle, 1,000 dominoes, individually painted by more than 15,000 children and adolescents, were toppled in a row accompanied by a screaming audience along the route. Screens along the way enhanced the televisual experience of the falling dominoes, and of course the event ended in a huge firework show above the Brandenburg gate, referencing the New Year's Eve celebration of 1989/1990, now often confused with images of the night of the fall of the wall. As Lech Walesa summarized it in an interview a few days prior to the event, "The fall of the Berlin Wall makes for nice pictures."[98] In other words, the falling wall of the commemoration was first and foremost meant to create a (pleasant) image of (and for) Western democracies, suggesting that the image of the falling wall works for Berlin both in terms of aesthetics and also as a point of a self-projection to the public, affirming the course of history rather than questioning it.

In other words, the event suggested a certain way of remembering and attempted to prescribe the experience of the participants, creating a celebratory space for the status quo. The wall served as a backdrop for political staging (as it always had), mediating a carefully orchestrated and conclusive history lesson about the "single world of freedom and democracy"[99] celebrated in 1989. In this sense, "world leaders became history teachers,"[100] as Ben Gook puts it, spreading the values of democratic societies and toasting to (German) national unity. Although the falling domino wall referred to a historic event, it also worked to affirm the present and the current coordinates as the valid future orientation. Drawing on his own experience of the event, Gook characterizes the commemoration as a form of "intensified remembering with others (...) anchored in place."[101] Crucially this "anchor" worked to signify German unity as the epitome of free people and free markets.

Tellingly, Gook also found the commemoration to be "unfulfilling"[102] and characterized by "an affective gap"[103] between the emotions created by the set-up of the celebration and the actual experience which it sought to articulate. Whereas for Gook this led to a disappearance of the subject "behind the appearance of involvement"[104] (and thereby, it seems, ironically mimicked the countless marches and demonstrations prescribed by the GDR and more or less routinely endured by its flag-waving citizens), it also adhered to the logic of spectacular (televisual) production, reviving the wall as an ideological screen upon which the desires of and about the West can be projected. In this regard, the commemoration is the perfect example of Guy Debord's claim that "the fall of the Berlin Wall, repeated over and over again, immediately attained the incontestability of all the other signs of democracy,"[105] leaving little room for personal investment or political contestation.

This is particularly evident in the spectacular falling of the dominoes and the accompanying exultory speeches, verifying that the falling Berlin Wall is not simply the hallmark of freedom but also a stand-in for the "nation" itself. The symbolism of the event was meant to represent Germany as such and to "restore a sense of unity and purpose"[106] by staging a "closed harmonious totality,"[107] which marks, as Renata Salecl reminds us, "a fundamental impossibility"[108] otherwise. This is problematic, precisely because it reinstates the fall of the wall as a clean slide of history and encloses the wall's meaning without exploring the "historic echoes" reverberated in the fall. The uncanny coincidence of November 9, marking both the fall of the Berlin Wall in 1989 and the atrocities of the "crystal night" pogrom in 1938, was mentioned by Merkel but not incorporated into the event. Similarly, when the band U2 blocked their free concert from the view of those who had failed to get "tickets," the situation produced an abundance of historical ironies, referencing the "Concert for Berlin" in 1987[109] and of course the very wall whose demise was celebrated. Read in this way the image of "walling" at the 20th anniversary commemoration and the accompanying events involuntarily evoked an affective presence of the wall, precisely because the event necessarily referenced other times and spaces that problematize "the end of history" instead of reinstating it. These referential scenes meant to mark an ending, instead revealed uncomfortable continuities or what Gook identifies as the "continuing of endings."[110]

To the extent that the 2009 commemoration was both a repetition and a continuation, it echoed Freud's work on repression. According to Freud, "repetition replaces remembering"[111] and "gives way to acting out"[112] absences, which may well illuminate the condition of continuous re-enactment of the wall (and its dramatic fall). In this way, the past inhabits the present and vice versa. This is reflected in the way in which the commemoration self-reflexively pointed out "other walls" in the world. Although this was primarily an effort to internationalize the event,[113] it also created a web of political experiences across time and space, pointing toward the invisible (global) structures mentioned by Kristensen. About one-fifth of the dominoes were shipped off to parts of the world in which visible and invisible walls persist. These dominoes predominantly went to Cyprus, Turkey, Palestine, Israel, and Korea, to be painted by children who continue to live a "walled" life. The two most famous dominoes were those returned from South Africa, where they had been painted by Nelson Mandela, his children, and grandchildren, in an effort to draw attention to the invisible divisions still haunting South Africa. The point was to highlight the way in which political walls, as means of exclusion, always work primarily invisibly before exercising their visible presence or visible effects of alienation, hence evoking a mental separation as much as a corporeal one. Read in this way, the iconic Berlin Wall both represents and covers over an invisible wall that somewhat persists.

While the memory of the Berlin Wall mediates perspectives on contemporary politics, it also functions as a gateway to return to specific political fantasies, firmly anchored in the experiences of 1989 (and their mediations thereafter). In some respect, the image of the Berlin Wall's fall now works like a Proustian madeleine, able to take the onlooker back to a political moment marked by openness, and perhaps hope, and yet vulnerable to absorbing the dominant narratives of the present. Unsurprisingly, then, the celebrations for the falling wall's 25th anniversary made use of a similar concept as the spectacle five years earlier, using balloons instead of dominoes and Beethoven rather than U2. Gook points out that these grand attempts to reproduce 1989 hinge on a thinly veiled nostalgia for the televisual quality of the Berlin Wall's demise, "only this time it would be properly captured: shot, filmed and managed by experts; illuminated by just-so lightening; a schedule dictated by advertising breaks, celebrity interviews and projected historical footage of 'key moments'."[114] Gook maintains that these structures work (if unsuccessfully) to return the audience to "a moment of unconsciously celebrating the brief visibility of an open situation," as well as invoking the fantasized democratic ideal of the West produced in those days.[115]

Atmospheric Poetics and New Walls

The re-enactment of the wall's fall has remained a staple of commemorating German (and European) unity, although the 25th and 30th anniversary celebrations have seen a shift from clunky dominoes to a focus on what might be considered an atmospheric poetics concerned with approximating a feel of the wall. The balloons that were released in the air in 2014 and the colorful streamers floating weightless between the Brandenburg Gate and Straße des 17. Juni in 2019 appeared to animate the wall's affective presence, rather than simply attempting to re-create the televisual spectacle of the wall's fall. This representation of the wall as de-substantialized and suspended in ethereal weightlessness marked the event in feelings instead of strictly re-materializing the wall. As Derek McCormack explains, balloons are "atmospheric media" capable of eviscerating "the extrusive presence of affective materials."[116] Similarly the streamers of the *Vision in Motion* installation at the 30th anniversary of the Berlin Wall's fall achieved a particular distribution and a sense of affective release, creating an "atmosphere of occasion,"[117] residing in a tension between giving shape (to the lost wall) and letting go (of the past).

Both installations thereby unfolded an ambivalent archive of affective encounters with the wall, ranging from melancholy to grief and mourning, to hopeful joy and elation. In other words, despite the fact that commemorations of the Berlin Wall's fall (of course) continue to be steeped in national narratives that affirm Western democracy, the balloons and streamers enhanced the atmospheric complexity of the Berlin Wall's fall, making palpable a kind of imparting withdrawal, or weighty absence, without quite substantiating this presence of the fallen wall. By animating the wall as diffuse, ambivalent, and invisible, these installations were less interested in the televisual technicalities of the spectacle but worked to draw out its affective compositions and thereby offered new ways of reflecting on the historic event and by extension broaden opportunities to make sense of the present.

However, the image production of the wall's commemoration not only celebrates a particular narrative about German national identity and more broadly democracy in the West, it also produces institutionalized forms of forgetting. For example, Jeffrey Jurgens points out that the wall's effects on migrants have been largely excluded from the grand narrative of German reunification, despite the fact that the wall's construction was closely linked to the influx of Gastarbeiter into postwar Germany and that many of these migrants literally lived in the shadow of the wall in the Western part of the city.[118] Jurgens links this commemorative omission of migrants to "a moment of selective forgetting that renders migrants largely invisible within memorials and narratives that cast the wall as a central figure of national trauma and redemption."[119] The omission is, of course, largely consistent with the walling up of European countries in recent years and the treatment of refugees arriving at Europe's shores. While Angela Merkel welcomed thousands of refugees to Germany in the early stages of 2015, her open-door policies were met with strong resistance within Germany and the European Union. Subsequently, it was in the year after the 25th anniversary of German reunification that the European Union engaged in a notable resurrection of walls, fences, and barriers. From Hungary to Slovenia and Croatia, to Austria, Italy, and France, more than 1,000 kilometers of walls and fences have symptomatically reappeared at Europe's outer limits since the fall of the Berlin Wall.[120]

These new dynamics of walling play out spatially; however, like their historical predecessor, they articulate "mental" barriers as well. Unsurprisingly then, simultaneous to the appearance of physical fences all over the continent, popular right-wing movements within Europe and Germany gained traction—most notably the PEGIDA movement in Germany, protesting the "islamization" of Germany and the AFD (Alternative for Germany) party, whose then head, East German politician Frauke Petry, publicly called for a shoot-to-kill policy at the border (thereby creating a direct link to the lethal legacy of the Berlin Wall). The AFD has since managed to enter the German parliament as a result of the 2017 federal election, where they continue to further their fear mongering right-wing agenda, spearheading the anti-lockdown movement during the Covid-19 pandemic and consistently lobbying against migration. It is worth noting that apart from the many disquieting historical echoes these examples create, these developments also reproduce the wall as a shield and mirror in the European imaginary. While Western democracy was (not too long ago) staged with recourse to the image of a falling wall, the notion of the West now appears to utilize walls in order to reinvent itself in opposition to an exterior other. Materializing xenophobic ideas about the other and restaging the colonial boundaries of the past, this new Europe endeavors an idealized affective space, which is predominantly fantasized as exclusively white and Christian. The new walls, in other words, create a variety of affective investments in belonging as a problem of (sufficient) whiteness, and thereby reveal Europe as a postcolonial, post-holocaust, and post-socialist palimpsest, in which different histories of racial violence and political domination both disguise and reanimate each other.

In light of these developments the commemorations of the fall of the Berlin Wall in 2014 and 2019 seemed to suggest a slightly different relation to the present than the previous celebrations had staged. Rather than affirming the status quo with recourse to the past, the affective animation of the wall's suspension unsettled the notion of a stable (political) present, while grappling with the emergence of new walls. In particular the commemoration in 2019 displayed a tangible nostalgia for the civil courage presented by the agents of the peaceful revolution in the late 1980s and early 1990s in order to confront (if arguably insufficiently) the troubling forces upheaving Western democracies today. Utilizing the Eastside Gallery and other monuments in the city as literal screens, to showcase video installations that produced a kind of affective collage of the protest, the celebrations aimed to project the sense of optimism and solidarity that pertained the days of the fall. The 2019 commemoration thereby sentimentalized the struggle for democracy and its affective potentials, instead of simply monumentalizing a specific historic outcome. Frequently referencing the rise of right-wing populism in Germany, Europe, and the United States, the wall's artistic suspension with the help of projection screens thereby intimated an opposition to the creation of ever new (mental and physical) walls, urging a note of caution—a shift in tone which was markedly different from the victorious euphoria displayed ten years earlier.

In other words, the commemoration suggested an appeal to civil courage in order to resists the emergence of anti-democratic structures—of course, aiming to cement established political structures, but also somewhat posing democracy as a question (rather than something that is to be taken for granted). Exemplary of this attitude were the comments of Berlin mayor Michael Müller, who stated, "then and today it is important to stand up for freedom. We are fighting against any form of alienation and exclusion."[121] Of course, what these comments overlook is the fact that many people in the East still feel alienated and the ways in which this dynamic correlates with ongoing xenophobia in response to migration. The comments also evade the exclusion of migrants, not simply from the commemorations of the fall but also principally from the safety of Western democracy by way of a deadly (global) border regime. In this sense, the remediation of the atmospheric wall was also a missed opportunity to reimagine the stakes of Western democracy and Europeanness in light of shifting global mobilities and with recourse to a more inclusive past.

Ultimately, the transition from affirmative celebrations of history to a more introspective reflection on the uncertain positions of democratic structures produced a move away from fixed ideological references but stopped short of critiquing the culpability of existing political structures in the creation of contemporary exclusions. Commemorations of the now absent Berlin Wall thereby also signal the fallibility of creating atmospheres of historical belonging, most notably reflected in the omission of migrant experiences and the avoidance of the colonial undertones sustaining the contemporary securitization of (Fortress) Europe. Overall, then, repeated enactments of the Berlin Wall's fall can be read as attempts at approximating the catharsis of walled life; however, they also mark an ongoing struggle over the affective arrangements that undergird national identity and political action today, reproducing the wall as a means of far-reaching forms of politically relevant absence(s).

Continuous Endings

Read as a temporal image, the falling Berlin Wall generates a sense of affective endurance or repetitive forms of reconstruction and falling, marking the end of history as an event that, just like Sontag's photograph, "will forever happen."[122] The fall of the Berlin Wall hence exceeds a specific moment in time, which is reflected in the numerous medial reproductions of the episode since 1989, and also in the way in which the event was anticipated. Even on the night of November 9, 1989, the actual fall was metaphorically preceded by its media image, in the sense that Western media proclaimed the opening of the wall before it was actually opened and thereby enabled the literal opening to a great extent.[123] Hence, before the Berlin Wall actually fell, "the fall" was already an image (and imaginary), perhaps an affect, staged before and beyond the actual chronology of the event. Such stagings had both anticipated the demise and have been re-enacted after the fact. In this sense, the falling Berlin Wall provides "a scene" that reappears in different times creating a sense of timeless meaning, or an act never quite fulfilled that has found its reversal in the re-construction of new walls all over the world.

In this way, the Berlin Wall poses a challenge or task to deal with the affective repercussions of its twenty-eight-year-long existence. As a political setting, this barrier has always relied on the ferocity of absence and invisibility, evoking complex attachments, ambivalent intimacies, and creative resistances in its shadow. Today, it still poses a task "of coming to terms with absence,"[124] as part of a broader engagement with national imaginaries and the remnants of walled life. The staging of the fall of the wall hence affords a paradoxical reading. On the one hand, the image of the wall is firmly integrated into a network of "incontestable" significations of the spectacle, as Debord points out. On the other hand, this image also opens the possibility of connecting to experiences across time and space, potentially reconfiguring meaning through resonances with political and historical contexts that are not necessarily foregrounded in the immediate history of the Berlin Wall itself, but nevertheless firmly attach themselves to its image. There is an affective resonance that unfolds from wall to wall, and from one context to another; the wall as a concept thereby collapses temporalities while re-projecting the scenes of an "absence" that continue to stir walled life.

3

Looking to the Other Side: The Walls between Us

Exploring the intricate layers of walled life means to read the Berlin Wall as more than a political barrier and to look beyond the material and symbolic meanings it offers. Turning the view to the affective resonances the wall (still) echoes and shapes, I mean to foreground the personal experiences informed by political architectures and to explore the ways in which political walls solidify the various silent walls we erect between and within ourselves. In other words, by investigating the wall as an affective formation, I want to point to the ways in which political settings generate emotional space and collective atmospheres that link individual lives to larger formations of power, and, which, sometimes, persist as a scene of feeling or sustained sense of crisis long after these formations have changed or disappeared. In this regard, it is vital to approach the Berlin Wall through the personal encounters it has shaped and to acknowledge that the wall is as much an expression of a state of political affairs as it organizes psychological, affective, and fantasmatic responses on a collective and individual level. Beyond its political efficacy, the Berlin Wall, in other words, engenders a mental occupation or a felt experience that has outlived the fall in 1989. Flickering between absence and presence, the wall continuously destabilizes self-knowledge and historical attachments, animating, again and again, the various retrospective imaginaries and narratives projecting walled life.

Crucially, the wall implicates an affective residue that cannot be fully erased on a national and intimate level, stirring not simply a country and its politics, but also the many people who, in one way or another, have lived with the wall's presence/absence. In other words, the wall is not simply an object in the sense that it acts as a spatial impediment or a political monument, but it is also an experience, an anxiety, a memory, an investment, in short: a feeling. In this sense, the wall poses a problematic encounter with the past, long after its fall, perpetuating walled life as an ongoing enigma or task. What this infers is that the wall is compelling not simply through its physical and visual obstruction, but also because it is affectively internalized, often by neglecting the past while compulsively repeating its repercussions. Put simply, when walls are torn down, their psychological efficacy and emotional impacts do not humbly disappear; rather the sentiments of the walled existence are brought to the surface and, sometimes they get energized, precisely because a fallen wall can remain effective and affective in the way it shapes a country, a family, a person, and a life.

While exceeding the meaning of trauma as a pointed rupture, these attachments, confusions, and memories beckon to be narrativized, mediated, and in some sense, perhaps, to be worked through. Otherwise, collective histories of violence accumulate to "haunting legacies" as Gabriele Schwab explains, evoking protective, yet equally distressing, forms of forgetting. At the same time, such legacies also shape the individual stories that evolve in these contexts, frequently sealing them off from direct engagement and understanding. Often, the experience is "walled in, silenced, and removed from consciousness and the public sphere,"[1] while exerting pressure on the present of collectives and individuals. This interplay between a physical and psychological sense of "walling in" perpetuates a kind of "memory prison" or "walled past" and hence replicates the mechanisms of repression. In this context, the past remains inaccessible; however, like trauma it has a way of resurfacing, ensuring its compulsive repetition. Schwab points out that trauma is made accessible by finding "a form... that translates into language or symbolic expression an experience that is only unconsciously registered and left as a mere trace on the affective and corporeal levels."[2] Similarly, the wall as a sustained crisis or traumatic routine can be located at the point of meeting between "unthought knowledge"[3] and shared signification, enabling a projection of history's unassimilated affects.

The Cinematic Nation: Memories of the Wall

Whereas Freud psychologically locates the possibility of *Wahrnehmung*, or availability to consciousness, on the screen of the preconscious, a similar mechanism also plays out via collective engagement with the screen in the cinema. The projection is possible because, on the one hand, "film and photography have inserted themselves like protective barriers between us and the real"[4] and hence afford a sense of (psychological) security. On the other hand, these media are prone to re-envision and screen our "unconscious optics,"[5] conflicting affects, and knotty investments and thereby enable scrutiny of the hidden depths of the psyche. Because of this capacity, the cinema is often said to facilitate Freud's *dreamwork*—or the condensation, displacement, and finally representation of (collective) unconscious material. Film, in other words, makes our "unthought knowledge"[6] available to public engagement, by translating it into the shared images and stories we see on screen.

As a collective medium, the cinema mirrors the nation and envisions its formative fantasies; however, it also simultaneously reiterates them. Films are utilized to retell the story of the nation, as they reimagine its past and narrativize its aspirations. Thereby, films simultaneously draw on and recreate the fantasmatic investments and collective fictions that enable the imaginary formation of the nation (and its captivating illusions) in the first place; or, as Anthony Smith points out, they "disseminate and perpetuate the idea of the nation itself, its history, its development and destiny."[7] Hence, the cinema screen offers a powerful point of identification for a national imaginary and rearticulates the nation's core fantasies. However, similar to the workings of such fantasy, film is capable of visualizing affective knowledge and thereby also provides "a powerful ground for transference,"[8] in Schwab's sense, assisting in the act of continuously imagining and reworking a national memory and walled-off past. In this way, the film screen, more than anything, enables the negotiation of repressed (national) histories. It provides a form of engaging with the walled-in memories that stir us collectively, by mediating their intimate frictions and impacts and by creating stories that help us explore the experiences of the past in the present context.

Film self-reflexively interrogates memory and the affects it generates, addressing the way in which media documentation may uncover and maintain private and public recollections of the past, on the one hand, and manipulate and even eradicate them, on the other. In particular, the cinema adheres to "the often noted visuality of memory"[9] but also allows for the articulation of affective disintegration, precisely because the film screen produces a link between spectator and collective imaginaries via the circulation of feeling. Exploring memory and its ideological designs visually, film provides the opportunity to investigate and foreground the wall's (invisible) psychological architecture as encoded in its spatial arrangement. At the same time, the screen also brings to the surface the contours of what Katharina Gerstenberger and Jana Evans call "an invisible wall [that] stands for more complex reflections about our ability (or inability) to imagine something that once was but no longer exists."[10] In short, the cinema envisions the emotional complexity and affective remnants of walled life.

Both Cynthia Beatts's *The Invisible Frame* (2009) and Bartek Konopka's *Rabbit à la Berlin* (2009) explore the physical and psychological space left behind by the Berlin Wall as a means of investigating a specific perspective on and about the East, tangible in the visible and invisible remainders of this monument. These films debate historical perception and invite reflection on identity and the mediation of repressed histories in a (post)walled world. *The Invisible Frame* poses questions about the ambiguous relationship between past and present, following Tilda Swinton on a philosophical bike ride along the absent wall in an impossible attempt to access the "other side" of history. The haunting invisibility of the monument comments on the obstacles of understanding the past from the point of view of the present and evokes a sense of retrospective separation and introspective alienation. Similarly, Konopka's allegorical reimagining of the past through his documentary about the rabbits that inhabited the former death strip defamiliarizes the wall's meaning and simultaneously projects its totalitarian effectiveness, reminding the viewer of the ambivalence of historical mediation. Hence, both films complicate the accessibility of the past, particularly the East's past, and thereby re-envision processes of historical othering, and perhaps willful forgetting through reflections on the Berlin Wall.

The crisis of accessing a collective past is countered by remediating experience creatively. Thereby the past is continuously (re)imagined, foregrounding its affective links to the present. In other words, although history remains "both absent and unrepresentable,"[11] as Kaja Silverman reminds us, the memories negotiated in and through film bring to the surface the fantasmatic and affective investments that have shaped and continue to shape a walled life. However, "there is no way of thinking about memory outside its histories and politics";[12] and therefore, investigating the "felt" dimensions of the past (often through the lens of private memory) unveils the intermingling of national fantasies and individual experience. In this sense, film can provide the link between the political and the personal, the publicly displayed and the intimately guarded. This is important because the wall functions as a mediation of rigid identity politics and inconsistent collective imaginaries, while molding the subjective trajectories of individual lives.

Films such as *The Lives of Others* (Donnersmarck, 2006) and *Kawasaki's Rose* (Hřebejk, 2009) explore the intimate effects of silent walls cutting through the lives of people in a walled existence, while exposing the larger political narratives and national fantasies that constitute these walls. Florian Henckel von Donnersmarck's *The Lives of Others* unearths the psychological walls sustaining an oppressive system of intimate surveillance. Following an adherent Stasi officer who becomes increasingly absorbed in the lives of the artistic couple he monitors, the film interrogates a national fantasy of the good man and thereby reveals further fantasies of reconciliation with (or perhaps despite) an atrocious past. Jan Hřebejk's *Kawasaki's Rose* explores similar parameters (albeit to different ends) and suggests that the notion of walled life is sustained in the present, exploring how we may deal with its enduring repercussions in public and private. In this way, both films destabilize a simplistic distinction between victim and perpetrator and simultaneously provoke discussion about the politicization of memory. Memory-making plays out in the logic of the present and engages with history as a form of experience, by which established binaries of understanding are subverted, providing insight into the intimate complexities evoked by political settings.

The Spaces between Us: *Rabbit à la Berlin*

Bartek Konopka's "natural documentary" *Rabbit à la Berlin* (2009)[13] explores the space in between the no-man's land of the two Berlin Walls (erected to the East and the West). The film draws on the expanding rabbit population that actually lived in the walled-off pasture and retells the history of the GDR from the rabbits' point of view. In this version of history, the wall was erected to protect the rabbits, providing plenty of food and equal access to underground caves. Exploring the different phases of the regime's increasing fortification of the social experiment, Konopka creates an allegory for the troubled comfort of totalitarian imprisonment and civil apathy, investigating the rabbit's microcosm as an analogy to East German life. Approaching history like an exercise in zoology, Konopka's "fairy-tale allegory docu-genre"[14] posits the wall as a physical and psychological space. The film reimagines the past through defamiliarizing the wall's meaning, while simultaneously projecting its totalitarian effectiveness, thereby reminding the viewer of the ambivalence of historical mediation. In this way, the film complicates the accessibility of the past and reconsiders processes of historical othering and forgetting in relation to the Berlin Wall. More to the point, the satirical tone that accompanies the film's allegorical form and ironic distance addresses history through defamiliarization and reveals a crisis of accessing the irretrievable past. The experience of the East is estranged through the rabbit perspective, putting pressure on historical truths and challenging dominant forms of storytelling. Human truths are reframed as bizarre, mirroring the way in which the East has been made strange (to) itself. The wall can hence be read as a memory landscape. However, it also alludes to W. J. T. Mitchell's idea of landscape "as a cultural practice, evoking a visual field which does not merely signify the structures of political power but also functions as an agent of its ideology."[15] This in turn suggests that the wall's politics are encoded in its spatial design.

The landscape of the death strip exemplifies the inherent spatiality of politics and rearticulates the politics of the walled state from the forgotten no-man's land at its margin. The wall as both limit and condition of Eastern life condenses the meaning of politics in the GDR and provides insight into the mechanisms of oppression. Carl Schmitt points out that political and social orders become visible through "the initial measure and division of pastureland"[16] in an act of order and orientation that produces an "enclosure" or "spatially concrete unity"[17] through which the law of its politics, or *nomos*, is established. This is precisely what happens to the rabbits in the beginning of the film when soldiers set up the cozy nature reserve that frees the rabbits from the pains of natural struggle. However, the "settlement" also coincides with the act of establishing the walled state as totalitarian entity, reiterating that the mechanisms of utopia and dystopia play out concurrently. Nomos, in its etymological resonance with a literal wall,[18] spatially evokes "a kind of no man's land,"[19] according to Hannah Arendt, that enables a political community in which the wall secures political life on one side and shelters the biological life of the family on the other. Following this logic, it becomes possible to read the political through the enclosure. By situating the biological life of the rabbits on the pasture inbetween the GDR's wall(s), Konopka allegorizes the political order of the GDR as a totalitarian entity, precisely because the space in which the rabbit life takes place collapses the notion of home and homeland. This dynamic becomes visible in the spatial negotiation of the death strip as a nature reserve but also alludes to an Eastern life in which the sanctuary of the home was permanently subject to arbitrary state surveillance and intrusion. As Arendt explains further, "to have no private place of one's own... meant to be no longer human,"[20] and one may add, in the logic of Konopka, perhaps to be a rabbit.

The wall creates a political order alongside psychological imperatives, and thereby creates a particular identity reflecting both on East and West. The "rabbit identity" is documented as a "species," cynically alluding to Zinovyev's *Homo Sovieticus*,[21] provoking critical commentary and historical othering alike, and evoking community as a psychological consequence of living a walled or ignorant life. As Konopka puts it, the film is about "the rabbit's people of the world (...) those people who want to have a simple life and want to have at least some area of fresh grass."[22] The rabbit-identity is hence associated with the notion of fear and ignorance, evoking a timeless middle-class mentality that privileges private comfort over civil courage. The German terms *Angsthase* (literally "scared rabbit" in reference to a coward) and *Versuchskaninchen* (literally a "test rabbit" and the equivalent to the English "guinea pig") both comment on the psychology of the GDR's "niche society"[23] as evasive and passive. The suggestion of *Angsthase* is evoked in the first minutes of the film, introducing the species as "naturally fearful" and "hiding in caves" when feeling threatened. The notion of *Versuchskaninchen* further alludes to the idea of the GDR as a social experiment which treated its citizens as dispensable. Whereas such ideas comment on East German civil debility, they may also satirize the common view of East Germans as a simple species that tends to portray "the East as a quainter more natural Germany,"[24] as Hodgin explains, a portrayal through which the FRG could in turn affirm its superior credentials, as suggested by Paul Cooke.[25] The Eastern identity, in other words, remains ambivalent, as expressed through the ironic distance provided by the figure of the rabbit. Konopka, who was born in Poland in the early 1970s, explains, "I feel myself as a rabbit and I know that many people around me psychologically feel themselves as rabbits [sic]."[26] His film then explores a gap in the post-communist experience, an inbetween space shifting between East and West, past and future, nostalgia and shame. With the loss of the wall as a referent for identity, the past is projected as a means to make sense of the present, locking identity into discussions that characterize the East as either a callous dictatorship or a caring homeland.

The Eastern experience is characterized by a complex position of being simultaneously a victim and a pillar of the regime. Engaging this dichotomy from the perspective of the death strip hence utilizes spatial and psychological inbetweenness. This is reflected in the archival footage of people happily waving their flags during a parade juxtaposed with images of increased fortification and surveillance, leading to an even more peaceful existence for the rabbits. *Rabbit à la Berlin* alludes to media depictions of the GDR as "a noble experiment gone wrong,"[27] but turns this notion on its head by depicting a sudden shift from paradise to terror state that allegorizes the unwarranted aggression of the regime against its own citizens through images of lethal crop-spraying in an attempt to control the expanding rabbit population. The traumatic implication of such routinized cruelty is addressed through the defamiliarizing tactic of using animal imagery as a stand-in for humans, as has been done in works such as Art Spiegelman's *Maus* or John Marsden's *The Rabbits*. A powerful disruption of this logic is then most hauntingly demonstrated in a former guard's assurance that no one shot the rabbits, a statement which is ironically placed alongside contrasting gun shots and images of dead or injured humans being carried from the death strip. The juxtaposition satirizes the infamous commentary of a Western journalist about escapees from the East being shot like rabbits, while it lays the ground for the numerous scenes in which the rabbits are massacred as a way to visually articulate the traumatic enforcement of the shoot-to-kill policy on the death strip. The walled-off pasture becomes a microcosm onto which the ambiguities of the Eastern experience are projected to enable a nightmarish awakening, evoking an East German paralysis that outlives the wall's physical demise. After the wall has fallen, we see an elderly couple awkwardly standing in a gap of the wall looking disoriented, as if they did not dare to cross the line. The pair signifies the fact that the Eastern self remains confined by the death strip of a walled past.

The rabbit perspective on history renders the past absurd and bizarre through the eyes of the rabbit on the one hand and through our own looking at the rabbits as the center of historical events on the other. The two perspectives oscillate in the film, reimagining the facticity of the archival footage and diverting it from established meanings. Such a "naïve" history allows for an examination of history outside itself, in the form of "the strange behavior of humans"[28] easily reframed from the rabbit's point of view as being all about them. By focusing on the banality of historical detail in order to access larger truths, Konopka opens up questions of representation and the ambivalence of historical mediation. Similar to the numerous (filmic) rewritings of GDR history, the past in *Rabbit à la Berlin* is easily twisted with the help of media images and archival footage. This comments on the representation of the twentieth century through the media and functions as a reminder that all history is essentially mediated and that meaning is negotiable, depending on one's perspective. *Rabbit à la Berlin* further highlights this dynamic in the depiction of the numerous high-ranking visitors on both sides of the wall who use the obstruction as a projection screen for their own politics, reframed as a supposed attempt to impress the rabbits. While such a reframing never seems to stray far from its underlying histories, it establishes the allegorized image on screen, "both as a site of vanguard political analysis and as a space of aesthetic alterity,"[29] as Katie Trumpener might put it. In this sense, Konopka's depiction of the GDR is not simply a study of political immobility and intransigence; it simultaneously encapsulates the notion of resistance through a slight twist of the focal lens.

Ultimately, it is precisely the image of the rabbit that signifies a history of resistance. Whereas the film positions the rabbits as naively engaging with a wall that falls as inexplicably and suddenly as it had appeared, the interviews with Thierry Noir, Peter Unsicker, and Manfred Butzmann reinstate the rabbit as a symbol of political struggle. All three artists have focused their work on a criticism of the wall, using it as a screen for political commentary and utilizing the rabbit as a symbol of freedom, precisely because it was the only creature capable of occupying the pastureland. Thierry Noir created a rabbit homage through graffiti on the surface of the western side of the wall, as did Butzmann from the East when the border was opened, while Unsicker designed an Easter postcard depicting a giant rabbit breaking through the obstruction. In the context of art, the rabbit of course also evokes provocateur

Joseph Beuys, who famously also felt himself to be a rabbit,[30] but to whom the rabbit represented an element of movement and action (rather than passivity and fear) and hence could be used as a sign of transformation.

Most notably, however, the very notion of a "rabbit film" evokes a reference to East German filmic resistance. Similar to Konopka's work, Kurt Mätzig's 1965 reformative drama *Das Kaninchen bin ich* (The Rabbit is me) addressed the problem of political disengagement as a way of supporting the structures of totalitarianism. The film (constructively) criticized the law-making of the GDR system as having fatal social implications and was subsequently singled out by the state and withheld from release, paving the way for a wave of film bans in the same year. These films persisted as underground legends and are still collectively known as the *Kaninchenfilme* or *Rabbit Films*,[31] now touring the Goethe Institutes of the world.[32] Barton Byg explains that, because of their belated circulation after the fall of the wall, these films now ironically attest to the regime's failing, instead of contributing to reform as had been anticipated by their creators.[33] The meaning of the rabbit is hence layered and carries multiple truths beneath the surface, similarly to the workings of political allegory itself, reminding us that historical truths are transcribed and projected, evoking different readings in different contexts. *Rabbit à la Berlin* attempts to negotiate and perhaps transgress the historical encryption of space, whereby the concretization of history and its spatial organization, as exemplified in the Berlin Wall, gives way to contemporary perspectives on enduring political alienation.

Searching the Wall: *The Invisible Frame*

Investigating the interplay between outward and inward perspective within historical space, Cynthia Beatts's *The Invisible Frame* (2009)[34] resonates with her earlier attempt to mediate the wall through a bike ride in *Cycling the Frame* (1988). Both films show Tilda Swinton cycling along the wall's 160 km route through Berlin and Brandenburg as she contemplates her experience of the space through inner monologues. Although the two films are meant to stand independently, according to the director, both journeys communicate different "underlying layers of consciousness"[35] across the historical space and thereby articulate the wall as a physical, metaphorical, and also psychological demarcation across time. In this sense, both films provide "psychogeographic, philosophical mediations,"[36] as Anke Westphal points out, and invite an exploration of expressed and repressed history. Utilizing the "outsider" as the catalyst of inward and outward perspective, the two films negotiate identity in a landscape that is maintained by the ambivalent appearance and disappearance of Cold War history, yet enable an engagement with the wall beyond its physical imposition.

The first film, *Cycling the Frame* (1988),[37] was produced by non-Germans for a TV series called *Looking from the Outside* and presents the physical imposition of the wall as a sense of frustrating finality. However, this perspective also positions the outsider in relation to the wall as an artificial margin, and therefore perhaps in relation to a philosophical endpoint as a limit to thinking. Kristensen explains that this immovable viewpoint allows Swinton's character to achieve increasing assurance in response to the concrete obstruction.[38] In this way, Swinton is directed by the wall and her perspective toward the physical and psychological imposition is unequivocal: she hates the wall, and she wants to shoot a hole in it. Twenty-one years later, the wall, if not completely gone, is absent and, in this way, disrupts the indisputability of the experience. The introspection enabled by the wall in 1988 is now replaced by the search for new frames.[39] Swinton's 2009 journey reveals an impossible desire to understand the other side of this space by returning to the excluded perspective in search of what has emerged from it—only to reveal that the East's perspective is still walled off.

With the object of the wall gone, the engagement with the past in *The Invisible Frame* is experienced as increasingly contentious, leading to a nostalgic search for definite frames of encounter. As Swinton sets out on her journey, she passes the various memorials across Berlin that seek to preserve a sense of what the now-absent wall was like. It seems that Swinton does not gain any insight from these cues, as her inner monologue is silenced. Rather than accessing the past, the monuments echo Mila Ganeva's criticism of the city's continuous effort to "bring the past back to surface, of course in a neat, clean, attractive form,"[40] since this sense of "clean" history denies the significance of absence as a form of horror vacui accompanying the fallen wall. Swinton expresses a wish to complete her experience of the historical space in a way that is no longer limited by the physical obstruction of the wall. "I want to know what the wall was like from the other side," she states as she leaves the tourist attractions behind to follow the invisible frame.

However, her impossible journey to the other side of history is disrupted by a sense of permanent disorientation. She gets lost repeatedly, encountering haphazard pathways and graffiti-covered roadmaps. The encounter with the wall is complicated by the loss of its physicality, leading Swinton to seek it through other objects such as fences and hedges, always searching for direction and a way back. Kristensen remarks that with the "wall as something that gave shape to history"[41] gone, her perspective is no longer anchored, as "there is no 'outerland' where the self can be reflected and space internalized."[42]

However, the confusing loss also reinstates the wall as a potential mirror and projection screen for the historical identities reflected in spatial arrangements. If, as Étienne Balibar outlines, the notions of partition and walling are a means to "maintain oneself as unified,"[43] then the disappearance of the barrier creates the demise of unity in the physical and psychological sense, ironically leading to a nostalgic projection of all kinds of borders, fences, and partitions, such as can be seen in the numerous *Kleingärten* or garden allotments that can be found all over Berlin and Brandenburg. In this way *The Invisible Frame* also articulates nostalgia for a lost object of history, for a sense of direction, and the possibility of "definite" knowledge. Although such definite knowledge is of course illusionary, this notion of a "self-evident and definite"[44] framework is not simply sentimental, but also functions as a reminder of the wall's own pervasiveness or affective presence, which led people to believe it was simply an inevitable part of their lives.

By way of her own ideological dislocation, Swinton is able to investigate the mechanisms of the wall's psychological functioning as a mental barrier. This is sustained precisely by systematically evoking the erasure still tangible in the historical space that was once governed by a dynamic of visible and invisible limitation. In this regard, it is important to recall that a wall does not simply work to erase the other side, but ultimately invites the viewer to forget the sight of the wall itself. This is reflected in the blank screens that famously marked the Eastern side of the partition, but it is also observed by Swinton in 1988 when she explains that "West Berliners seem to be so studiously ignoring the wall." Whereas Swinton initially contrasted this phenomenon with the "enormous attention given to the wall by the men in the towers from the East," twenty-one years later the whole space seems to be submerged in a sense of willful amnesia and historical forgetting. In her study of *Postwall German Cinema and National History*, Mary Elisabeth O'Brien remarks that such willful amnesia is symptomatic of the filmic engagement with events of German reunification, or *die Wende*, and that this phenomenon attests to an effort "towards unanimity by erasing all evidence of conflict."[45] However, in "digging under the surface of reunification,"[46] Beatts articulates this persistent erasure by focusing Swinton's attention on the wall's absence, thereby questioning and challenging the prerequisite to ignore it and opening up the possibility of deconstructing the wall's logic. As Swinton puts it, "when this wall, this ex-wall, this manifestation of a ghost-wall was here it felt so much more invisible than it is now. It has my attention in a way it never did before." In other words, it is only through the wall's absence that she comes to understand the wall's brutal pervasiveness—a brutality she identifies as "translated into some kind of stoic acceptance" and now decidedly forgotten in the landscape of the present. This notion of amnesia aligns the wall's pervasiveness with the loss of memory evoked by traumatic crisis. It communicates a need to forget "what has become useless, or too difficult to accommodate,"[47] and further suggests that a traumatic walled past still exerts pressure on the present.

Since the wall's invisible structure is internalized by those who live with it and/ or outlive it, the wall becomes a means of an ongoing traumatic routine that evokes post-communism's radical inbetweenness, manifesting itself within the shifting trajectories between us and them, here and there, now and then. Such twofoldness echoes the notion of a traumatic crisis precisely because trauma occurs "on the threshold between remembering and forgetting, seeing and not seeing, transparency and occlusion, experience and its absence,"[48] as Huyssen puts it. Similarly, the wall draws on these dialectics to exercise its psychological and affective efficacy. However, the fact of absence recalls the wall as that which can never be adequately represented but persists as an internal conflict. For Swinton the wish to bring the two sides together through some kind of knowledge of "what the wall was like from the East" remains hence unfulfilled and, yet, her impossible desire acknowledges this throbbing wound and its uncanny resonance within the present. We see her zigzagging the line of cobblestones that mark the wall's former route, "as if sewing the two sides together."[49] Her futile attempt to conjure up the wall in this way expresses the desire to heal the troubled past and the haunted present through "instinctive ghostwork,"[50] as Beatts describes the journey in an interview. However, it is the melancholic articulation of this impossibility that summons the meaning of Swinton's excursion. Quoting Russian poet Anna Akhmatova, Swinton frames her last kilometers as an acknowledgment of ongoing loss when she addresses the historical other, stating,

> I bear equally with you the black permanent separation.
> Why are you crying?
> Rather give me your hand, promise to come again in a dream.
> You and I are a mountain of grief.

It is this impossibility of closure and yet continuous entanglement of past and present that suggests the historical space can never be adequately read; rather, it must be permanently rewritten.

Of course, the rewriting of historical space is always twofold in the sense that it is as revelatory as it is evasive. In the case of German reunification, it was made clear instantly that there was no intention to preserve GDR history. As the then Minister of the interior, CDU politician Wolfgang Schäuble, put it in 1990, my dear citizens, what is taking place here is the accession of the GDR to the Federal Republic, and not the other way around (...) We are not seeing here the unification of two equal states. We are not starting again from the beginning, from the position of equal rights.[51]

The historical space of the East was literally rewritten in light of the West, most evidently reflected in the obsessive renaming of streets after unification. Swinton encounters examples of this cultural absorption as the signposts of a rewritten history. She passes streets called *Einheit, Freiheit,* or *Kuckucksruf* (Unity, Freedom or the Cuckoo call[52]). The houses are restored and polished, making room for new generations that have no active memory of the wall. The long shots of graceful house facades are underlined with sounds of children that remain absent from the image, as if the future was haunting a present that cannot deal with its own past. "Acres of shame and rewritten history," as the actress puts it, prevent Swinton from gaining a perspective of the East, often leading her to lose her orientation or to question whether she is in the East or the West. On the other hand, the past erupts unexpectedly in ruins that attest to the East's decaying presence. Swinton utilizes these moments to put herself into the shoes of the other, taking the perspective of a border guard from a watch tower and reciting a to-do-list while cycling around the remainder of a monument in the shape of a soviet star. Yet, none of these enactments provide retrospective meaning; despite and because of everything being open, the historical space is instead layered with new experiences across time.

Although Swinton never accesses the past, her journey attests to the nonlinearity of historical time. In this regard, Richard Terdiman points out that "human temporality, (...) is always underlain and rewritten by other times"[53] and therefore we cannot assume the past's persistence (and thereby liberate ourselves from it). Instead, we have to engage it through a continuous "confirmation, as the form the past takes now."[54] Swinton expresses this notion when she muses "now you see it, now you don't. It's like a trick of the light and then you come around a corner and something is completely unchanged." As the wall flickers between past and present, it becomes impossible to write it into a map (or find it solely according to its former route), precisely because it is also a temporal phenomenon attesting to the circularity of historical occurrences. Swinton often fails to locate the wall on the map she is using, finally leading her to the conclusion that "maps are very fake things. They tell you that time has stopped but it hasn't. It's going on, remaking itself all the time." This realization is reflected in Swinton's literal circling, singing a repetition of "round and round and round and round," and in her constant encounter with and musing about "new walls." In this way, the historical space of the wall is shown to circulate and to itself be associated with cycles of history and nature.

The image of nature is repeatedly utilized in order to evoke the circularity of history, but it also provides a sense of metaphoric estrangement, allowing for commentary on the politics of space. Beatts continuously evokes nature in order to ironize the politics associated with the wall. The poppy fields that have taken over the space of the wall, for example, evoke former chancellor Helmut Kohl's often-quoted (and much criticized) promise of blossoming landscapes in the East,[55] while also attesting to a naturalization of the wall's absence. This is interesting because the earlier *Cycling the Frame* utilizes the image of nature in order to contrast with the wall and to reinstate the monument's monstrous and artificial disruption of ordinary life. When Swinton states that she "want[s] to shoot a hole into the wall," the aggressiveness of the statement is contrasted with the fact that the hole is meant to save a little bee. This opposition reinstates the wall's impediment to the ways of nature and defies it by privileging the bee over the concrete obstruction. In *The Invisible Frame* then, the space has been taken back by nature and hence the wall itself, in its "absent" presence, has been rendered natural. Despite Swinton's best efforts to become part of this naturalized landscape by disappearing in a bush or lying in a field waving her hands with the rhythm of the wind blowing through the grass, she therefore does not ultimately emerge in the historical landscape. Despite nature's best efforts, the wall still cuts through space, as signified in the image of a dead snake lying on the concrete. This reiterates a historical space in which the past is still active yet overtly ignored and thereby imprisons the present. Swinton hence concludes that real freedom is not achieved through getting over the past but through a fearless engagement with it—fearless precisely because such engagement does not accept the silent and persistent walls of the heart and the mind.

Intimate Terror: The Lives of Others

Walled life is signified by intimate barriers that cut through the personal lives of ordinary people. These silent walls demand to be assessed as part of political and historical negotiations. In fact, regarding history as part of the intimate sphere is a crucial premise for approaching the past via the means of fantasy and feeling—a way of reimagining history that has been predominantly achieved by the fictional accounts of cinematic drama. Exemplifying this maneuver, *The Lives of Others* (2006),[56] directed by Florian Henckel von Donnersmarck, tells the story of the adherent Stasi agent Gerd Wiesler who takes the lead in a surveillance operation, targeting the playwright Georg Dreyman and his girlfriend, actress Christa-Maria Sieland. While monitoring the couple's every move in their East Berlin apartment, Wiesler is increasingly moved by the intimate negotiations of their private desires and political confines. Sieland and Dreyman unwittingly introduce Wiesler to the pleasures of art and music, but they also testify to the oppression, humiliation, and destruction perpetuated by the state, despite their political standing and cultural capital. When blacklisted director Jerska commits suicide, Dreyman begins working on a regime-critical text. Wiesler conceals the playwright's subversive endeavors, and thereby protects him from violent persecution by the state. Accordingly, the film was widely received as advocating a "classical model of redemption and humanization through art,"[57] which, culminating in Dreyman's piano rendition of "The Sonata for a Good Man" as the footing for his own and Wiesler's transformation, also led to the film's controversial critical reception.

On the one hand, the film's tragic treatment of Eastern surveillance has been hailed as an authentic view of life in the GDR and a much-needed corrective to the late 1990s phenomenon of Ostalgie.[58] On the other hand, the film has been accused of aestheticizing historical inaccuracies and endorsing a humanization of the perpetrator, and by extension a humanization of the dictatorial state apparatus of the GDR.[59] Anna Funder in particular took issue with the film's "odd relation to historical truth"[60] and argued that it was merely "a fantasy narrative."[61] However, taking such claims seriously, it is important to realize that *The Lives of Others* neither denies the cruelty of the East German regime nor does it aim to document "historical truths"; rather, the film draws attention to the fantasmatic investments and affective intricacies sustaining (national) history and, thereby, suggests, as Timothy Garton Ash points out, that "these objections are in an important sense beside the point."[62] In other words, it is precisely the "fantasy narrative" that accounts for "the shifting registers of unspoken ambivalence"[63] as vitalizing the workings of the regime's intimate violence.

Inherently linked to the act of remembering, the fantasmatic lining the film articulates provides insight into the affective truths and intimate negotiations that shade historical experience but also shape the politics in which they are embedded. In fact, *The Lives of Others* suggests that intimacy itself works to perpetuate the terror of the state, securing the psychological walls that help to sustain it. By this I mean the way in which the state participates in the private life of its citizens, often by exploiting personal attachments and dilemmas, or by instrumentalizing emotions, investments, and relationships. Yet, intimacy also offers a mode of subversion, precisely because it is linked to the transgressive capacity of fantasy and therefore is capable of circumventing these inner walls. Ultimately, then, intimacy works as a mode of identification on the level of the private as well as on the level of the political and thereby lays the foundation for a transformation that is primarily grounded in the personal relations all politics entail.

Set in the Orwellian year of 1984, the film illustrates a politics of intimacy through which the totalitarian state systematically collapses individual desire in order to bureaucratize (and hence control) the intimate as such. The administrative state produces the faceless perpetrator dedicated to a system of oppression, much in the way Hannah Arendt has famously outlined "the banality of evil." It facilitates a psychological culture in which the state attains the role of the intimate Other. Rouvillois points out that the state's "drive to monitor intimacy"[64] reiterates "that the citizen's body belongs to the collective."[65] In other words, the state disciplines the corporeal, precisely because totalitarianism clashes with "the rebellious and perturbing potentialities of desire itself."[66] Wiesler's internalization of this subjection is reflected in his strict self-control and the reduction of his physical needs to a bare minimum, defining his existence through an absolute "renunciation of desire in service of the state."[67] His apartment is sparsely furnished and his meals are functional at best. His contact with humans is reduced to his students and superiors, with the exception of occasional mechanical sex with a prostitute working on schedule for the "MfS guys." Wiesler never ceases to be the Stasi agent; rather, his identity is completely subsumed to this role.

Wiesler' most intimate relationship is with the state and it is for this reason that he instantly finds Dreyman to be suspiciously "arrogant" (and perhaps unwittingly attractive) in his ability to combine private intimacy and public standing. These conflicting feelings lead Wiesler to suggest monitoring Dreyman, volunteering himself for the task. Wiesler's internal surveillance of his own desire is thereby projected onto Dreyman as the other of a desired self. His need to investigate the playwright's political commitment is driven by the wish to subject the artist as well to the bureaucratized intimacy of the state and, hence, to prove that the structure of self-renunciation is necessary to maintain the state's righteous superiority. In this way, Wiesler personifies the terrifying structure of the state designed to distrust and control its citizens at all times, supporters and opponents alike. He also attests to what Foucault has famously termed governmentality, epitomized in the totalitarian state's attempt to regulate its citizens from the inside by establishing an omniscient self-control, which is then projected outward.[68]

The intimacy associated with governmentality is best reflected in the notion of an all-encompassing surveillance mechanism that turns the state into a giant panopticon. Resonating with this notion, the film sets up a hierarchy of looking, similar to the spatial arrangement of the theatre, in which each of the main characters takes part. Tellingly, Wiesler first encounters Dreyman during one of his plays, to which the Stasi agent is taken by his senior commander Grubitz, an unapologetic careerist, who is seeking an opportunity to introduce himself to Minister Hempf. Establishing the scene for the choreography of power that will determine the intimate surveillance of the couple, the two Stasi men are positioned in the upper box, allowing them to monitor the theatre as a whole. Christa Maria performs on stage while Minister Hempf is seated in the center of the frame, in close proximity to the stage in the stalls. Dreyman, closely watched by Wiesler through a pair of binoculars, sits in the VIP loge. The setup literally sets the stage for "Operation Lazlo," based on Wiesler's suspicion and Hempf's desire for Christa Maria, reflected in the particular dynamic of looks exchanged between the participants in the scene.

Indeed, throughout the film everyone engages in a curious routine of surveillance. The majority of characters spy on one another; at the same time, they carefully hide secrets and habitually tell lies to protect themselves or loved ones. People doubt, discern, and manipulate each other constantly, reflecting that the GDR's bond with its citizens did not necessarily rest on the notion of political affect as "feeling politically together," in the way that Berlant describes the desire of the political,[69] but was experienced on the grounds of permanently imagining oneself to be enclosed and observed (a fear which was of course always realized through the means of the wall and the scrutiny of the State Security system). In fact, Preuss argues that because the movement of GDR citizens was restricted at all times, life in the East played out as if on a stage, and turned the "immobilized citizens into an audience."[70] In this sense, the broad distrust and cruel habit of mutual monitoring the film introduces, suggest, as Ewa Mazierska points out, that "Wiesler is by no means an exception among the citizens of the GDR."[71] In fact, Sieland and Dreyman observe each other, Grubitz watches Hempf, Hempf orders his driver to follow Sieland, and even Wiesler is watched by Dreyman's neighbor. Intimacy plays out via the means of the look, whether it is the intrusive look of the Stasi or the tender looks exchanged between lovers. However, it is the look that bypasses the state that serves to undermine it.

Surveillance functions as a form of intimate terror, as exemplified in Wiesler's secret intrusion into the private sphere of Dreyman's home, but it also renders the Stasi agent an unvoluntary participant in the couple's intimacy, which implicitly destabilizes the state's predominance. Indeed, Dreyman and Sieland's home appears as an island of interpersonal warmth and creative possibility in the otherwise grey and meagre landscape of the East. Unlike Wiesler's own apartment, their home is warmly lit and furnished with a wealth of books, art, and even a grand piano. The couple's apartment exemplifies how "the private sphere functioned for many citizens as an outpost of individuality, potential dissent, and alternative identity formation,"[72] as Betts asserts, in which the intrusion of the state was anticipated but also tacitly ignored. The privacy of the home thereby also epitomizes the German word *heimlich*, referring to both homely and secretive, in the double sense of private secrecy and a secret presence, imagined or real. The private sphere is then cynically "connected to a profound sense of shared intimacy,"[73] a dynamic in which Dreyman, Sieland, and Wiesler engage alongside each other. Indeed, Wiesler is positioned at the heart of this intimate exchange. He knows about the little lies and profound secrets the couple hide from one another as well as about their shared intimate moments.

However, Wiesler also functions as the other to this discourse of intimacy in the psychoanalytical sense. Miller asserts that "the most intimate is at the same time the most hidden"[74] because it marks "a point of opacity"[75] or otherness which Lacan calls *extimacy*. As Miller further explains, "extimacy says that the intimate is Other—like a foreign body, a parasite"[76]—or a Stasi agent in the attic. Wiesler is hence the extimate to Dreyman and Sieland's intimacy, positioned as "the Other who, more intimate than (...) intimacy, stirs [them]."[77] In this way, Wiesler is never simply an observer but always a participant in the intimacy of the couple and their affective circuits, casting his own position increasingly into doubt. When Jerska commits suicide, Wiesler cries secretly (*heimlich*) in the attic, attesting to his emotional investment in the shared agony that plays out downstairs. Hence, the implied mutuality of intimacy stirs Wiesler, too, and he is confronted with himself as part of the encounter, instinctively locating the other in the self and the self in the other. The small and profound dramas experienced by Dreyman and Sieland affect Wiesler, moving him as a person of flesh and blood, rather than addressing him as an agent of the state. Ultimately, this leads him to realize that the other, in the negative sense, is the state, and not Dreyman.

In fact, Wiesler increasingly identifies with Dreyman, which paves the way for his transformation from cold adversary to empathetic ally. However, notably, from the outset, Wiesler and Dreyman are not as antagonistic as they may seem. Both share a deep commitment to the GDR, which is based on an obdurate sense of idealism, albeit they negotiate this investment to different ends. Dreyman is a personal friend of the General Secretary and Head of State's wife Margot Honecker and is described by Grubitz as "pretty much the only non-subversive author we have." Indeed, Grubitz further points out that to Dreyman, "the GDR is the most beautiful country in the world." Dreyman often tries to balance a peculiar middle ground between the "perturbing potentials"[78] inherent in art and his political idealism and commitment to the GDR. His rebellious friend Hauser points this out when he tells him, "you're such an idealist that you are almost a bigwig," urging him to understand that "if you don't take a stand, you are not human." Similarly, Wiesler's devotion to the state also relies on the utopian ideals inherent to communism but rarely accomplished in its lived experience. He sits with the lower ranks in the ministry's cafeteria, asserting to Grubitz that "socialism has to start somewhere." He also reminds his commander of the oath they swore when Grubitz explains the benefits of Dreyman's persecution for both their careers.

Wiesler identifies with Dreyman on the grounds of this shared idealism and simultaneously disidentifies with the careerist exploitation of power by those representing the state. Laplanche and Pontalis explain that identification works via modes of recognition,[79] which in the case of Wiesler is channeled via the intimacy that develops as part of his surveillance of Dreyman and Sieland. Crucially, such identification in the psychoanalytical sense marks "the operation itself by which the subject is constituted."[80] In this way, Wiesler is intimately confronted with the question of the self and realizes that his political idealism is incompatible with the state's abuse of power. Rather, his desire for a utopian ideal is mirrored in Dreyman's reformist hopes, leading Wiesler to be "transformed, wholly or partially after the model the other [Dreyman] provides."[81] As Laplanche and Pontalis further explain, identification "expresses a resemblance and is derived from a common element which remains in the unconscious"[82] and which they identify as "a phantasy."[83] Hence, the common element that links Wiesler to Dreyman (and us, the spectators, to both of them) is precisely the intimate fantasy of the good man persisting in a terrible world.

The fantasy of the "good man" resonates throughout the film, binding the characters in their actions, but also determining the historical and societal approach of the film. Whereas Wiesler understands himself to be the good man fighting the enemies of the state, Dreyman's own fantasmatic investment in the image of the good man is reflected in his non-conflictual manners and self-confirming narcissism. By intimately linking the characters through modes of identification, the film here most overtly participates in this shared fantasy. However, rather than dismissing this as a somewhat idealized "fantasy narrative that could not have taken place,"[84] as Funder would have it, such investment may also provide insight into the larger cultural fantasies that support a national memory of the wall. National reconciliation (and perhaps redemption) is then achieved by imagining the good in man and by evaluating the present in light of the intimate resistances of the past, instead of focusing on the glaring atrocities—a tactic Germany is well accustomed to from the engagement with its Second World War past.

Indeed, Dreyman is modeled on a cultural icon—Bertolt Brecht—who like Dreyman was capable of writing anti-fascist, communist texts that were "still interesting enough to be read in the West"[85] and whose work insistently considered the question of how to be good in a bad world, as most poignantly explored in Brecht's drama *The Good Person of Szechwan*. This link between Dreyman and Brecht finds its most explicit expression when Wiesler reads the Brecht book he stole from Dreyman while imagining the playwright reading the words. In this way, Dreyman is presented as the good man Wiesler aspires to be, which the latter realizes (in a Brechtian Lehrstück (or learning play)) in the (educational) drama that plays out in the couple's apartment. This literally stages Laplanche and Pontalis's explanation that fantasy is linked to a "private theatre,"[86] in which "our most intimate possessions"[87] play out as scenes. Fantasy provides "the stage setting of desire,"[88] eventually allowing for both Dreyman and Wiesler's desire to literally transgress the law. Crucially, both men overcome their inner prohibition the moment they find this fantasy confirmed by Sieland. She adores Dreyman and finally chooses him over the powerful Hempf, who threatens to destroy her (and eventually initiates her persecution). She also tells Wiesler that he is "a good man" the moment he introduces himself as her "audience."

Ironically, the fantasy of the good man ultimately provides the link between Dreyman and Wiesler, engaging them in their shared complicity in Sieland's death. However, their righteousness is never questioned by the film, precisely because the women in the film are depicted as weak rather than good and, hence, they support but do not sustain the film's fantasy. As GDR poet Wolf Biermann elaborates, "we are all addicted to evidence of people's ability to change for the good,"[89] alluding to cinema's ability to initiate the examinations of "social issues through the lens of fantasy"[90] in the process of imagining the collective self. The fantasy of the good man hence resonates with aspirations of reconciliation, which haunt a nation still in the process of reuniting on the ruins of an atrocious past. In this sense, Dreyman and Wiesler serve as collective fantasies of the good man, despite their implication in Sieland's destruction, distilling "the question of individual morality, a value easily integrated into Western capitalism and ultimately antithetical to Lenin and Brecht's intentions."[91] Donnersmarck hence creates "a metaphorical hyperrealism"[92] rather than a historical document, or as the director himself argues, the reality of the film is "verdichtet."[93]

Verdichtung, which implies both condensation (*dicht* = thick) and dramatization (*Dichtung* = poetry) in Freud's discussion in *The Interpretation of Dreams*, enables Wiesler's transformation but also characterizes the intimate treatment of history itself. In the Freudian dream, *Verdichtung* appears in the sense of both a distortion of poetry, or mis-fictionalization, and an enlargement, or over-fictionalization, and is thereby linked to the notion of fantasy. This evokes the playwright in the private theater of desire, which, like Wiesler's identification with Dreyman, expresses itself through Wiesler's transformation into "the good dramatist." Wiesler interferes in Dreyman's and Sieland's relationship, causing Dreyman to find out about Hempf and convincing Sieland to liberate herself from Hempf's exploitation. Hence, Wiesler orchestrates the couple intimately, while fabricating the scripts for their everyday lives. Crucially, these scripts contrast with his intimate experience of the lives of others, despite their factual correctness. This makes apparent that the Stasi language "obfuscates and confines experience, rather than defining and communicating it,"[94] as Paul Cooke asserts, attesting to Wiesler's inability to experience a life of his own.

Affected by the language of Brecht (through the voice of Dreyman), Wiesler becomes the playwright. He transforms life into fiction by concealing the "revolution" that develops within the walls of the apartment. While he overhears the creation of Dreyman's text, he experiences the state's terror expressed through literary language, or *Dichtung*, which he translates by inserting the affective truths of the situation into the fabricated files, without exposing what is really taking place. When Dreyman reads his file after the fall of the wall, it is revealed that Wiesler actually created an imaginary play for the 40th anniversary of the GDR on Dreyman's behalf. Incredulously, Dreyman reads (now through the voice of Wiesler) the first act, in which "Lenin is in permanent danger," but "despite increasing pressure from the outside he holds on to his revolutionary plans." This opening betrays the actual events but also, in a way, rightly communicates Dreyman's (and Wiesler's) increasingly precarious situation. In other words, despite *Verdichtung*'s thickening and distorting of reality, "the affects have remained"[95] appropriate in the Freudian sense. Hence, Wiesler rewrites history but intimately retains its affective truths, much in the way Donnersmarck insists on the film's emotional (rather than historical) accuracy. Perhaps the film's historical infringement is then not simply linked to Wiesler's fantastical transformation into Dreyman, but suggests the possibility that this could also work in reverse; or, to borrow Jacqueline Rose words, "fiction's greatest offense becomes its ability to turn us all into perpetrators, each and everyone of us."[96] Acknowledging the fictional quality of all history then intimates that the way we access history describes, but also destabilizes, our (political) positions in the present.

Silent Walls: *Kawasaki's Rose*

The Czech film *Kawasaki's Rose* (2009)[97] destabilizes simplistic distinctions between perpetrator and victim by exploring the ways in which political affect is transmitted and preserved via the personal memories shrouded in family secrets. The walls of the political past remain present as the silent barriers between family members, dividing not only public narratives but also private stories. This suggests that political contexts are multi-layered, hinging on a range of affects that often supersede the frames of national narratives and commemoration. Utilizing this ambiguity of memory as a vehicle, *Kawasaki's Rose* investigates the East's totalitarian past as the basis of a walled life in the present. Enduring patterns of guilt, shame, and silence are examined as the cornerstones of intergenerational memory and ultimately work as building blocks for a psychological prison that resists simplistic understandings of what the communist past has meant or means. Specifically, director Jan Hřebejk examines the guilt of the collaborator and the sacrifice of the dissident as "two sides of the same coin,"[98] suggesting that the layers of personal and political history elude one-dimensional narratives of heroes vs. villains. Instead, *Kawasaki's Rose* asserts that the act of remembering reworks individual and national identities across different times and spaces, projecting walled life under constant revision of mediated affect.

Set twenty years after the Velvet Revolution and the fall of the Berlin Wall, *Kawasaki's Rose* interrogates the past through the family drama that erupts when former dissident and highly acclaimed psychiatrist Pavel Josek is revealed to have collaborated with the secret police in the early 1970s. Pavel assisted in the expatriation of his rival Borek in order to win back his then ex-girlfriend and now wife Jana. Set to receive the Memory of the Nation Award for "his moral credit in spite of unfavorable political circumstances," Pavel is confronted with a compromising file unearthed by a documentary film team that unravels the family secret and situates the personal conflicts emerging as part of a walled life as firmly anchored within national history. Underpinning the notion of forgiveness, the film reconstructs this intimate history through the eyes of both its immediate participants and succeeding generations.

The characters' personal lives are indefinitely shaped by a walled-off past that demands to be confronted. Resonating with Freud's notion of *Nachträglichkeit*, or "deferred action," the process "in which early memories and experiences are revised and rearranged at a later date to fit in with fresh experiences,"[99] *Kawasaki's Rose* negotiates the meaning of national and personal acts of remembering as a process or task. According to Roger Kennedy, it is precisely this "rearrangement of memories"[100] that constructs (and sometimes imprisons) history. However, acts of remembering are less helpful for discovering truths about the past, "than to understand the impact of the past in the present."[101] Thinking (and feeling) historically in this way is then not simply about forgetting certain narratives and foregrounding others; rather, approaching the past in this way marks an attempt to access walled-off memories that affect the constitution of the self in the present.

Kawasaki's Rose depicts the emotional prisons of a walled life as built on unbearable memories and unspoken experience that exercise their continuous control on the present. Such secrets are necessarily a direct outcome of the political (walled) context; however, these intimate legacies play out as highly personal feelings of guilt, shame, and fear. Indeed, Freud associates the very notion of repression with a "dark trace,"[102] referring to Oedipus' "ancient guilt"[103] and thereby, from the outside, connects emotional confinement to a sense of felt culpability in the past. Yet, Freud also explains that such a remnant of felt turmoil "acts like a foreign body,"[104] fully capable of asserting its impact on the present "long after its entry."[105] Driving the narrative of the film, this powerful interplay between past and present is reflected in Pavel's own guilt, which persistently hovers (walled off) behind an appearance of what his deceitful son-in-law Ludek repugnantly calls "a paragon of virtue." Pavel seems to carry his façade as a burden, pushing him to the verge of (forbidden) emotional collapse.

However, as Pavel never allows himself to articulate his own guilt, "the foreign body" disseminates its affective bearings, curtailing not simply Pavel's well-being but also impacting negatively on the lives of his descendants. The toxic dynamic is literally evoked through his daughter Lucie's tumor, the removal of which opens the film. It is also reflected in his granddaughter Bara's unsettled position in the family. Without knowing it, Bara seems to enact Borek's displacement and sense of alienation, after he has been exiled due to her Grandfather in 1972. Bara does not have any direct access to these guarded histories, but she compensates for her lack of understanding the silent legacies that affectively work through her family with eating compulsively—preferably shop-lifted chocolate bars. This habit of stealing sends her to a literal prison, uncannily evoking her Grandfather's guilt.

Schwab explains that internalized guilt leads the children (and grandchildren) of perpetrators to be "always on the run."[106] Illustrating this dynamic, Bara runs from the shop owners who catch her stealing, poignantly leading her to her grandfather's study—after a detour to the police station. The repressed material comes to the surface when Bara suggests keeping the incident a secret and Pavel unwittingly articulates his own imprisonment. He explains that "everyone who cheats or who steals isolates himself," maintaining that guilty secrets are destructive, precisely because the "inner prison is much worse"[107] than confessing one's misdeeds. Although this leads Bara to own up to Ludek, Pavel actually reinforces the structure of self-imprisonment by not addressing his own implication in this moral truth, despite Bara asking about the tension between him and Ludek. Dan Bar-On explains such a dynamic via the notion of a "double wall,"[108] which describes the erection of walls between the past and the present by victims and perpetrators alike, leading their descendants to build their own walls, etc.[109] Together these walls work to maintain a "conspiracy of silence,"[110] as any attempt to break through is instantly met by "the wall of the other."[111] In this way, prisons of memory are inflicted, again and again, on succeeding generations, on account of the silence of the previous one.

The silent legacies of past atrocities resurface in the present most commonly enveloped in the family secret and delivered, from one generation to the next, with the help of the affective circuits that maintain these enigmas. As Schwab explains, "children read their parents' unconscious more generally in the embodied language of affects."[112] They intimately negotiate their parent's emotional conflicts and intimate secrets, routinely attaining an expertise at "listening to the unspoken,"[113] or all that is reflected in the shifting moods and affective tensions surrounding them. In this way, children develop what Marianne Hirsch has coined a "postmemory" to describe "the experience of those... whose own belated stories are evacuated by the stories of the previous generation."[114] The idea is most poignantly articulated through Pavel's betrayal and Lucie's subsequent loss of (her biological father) Borek prior to her own birth, her own marital problems (also marked by betrayal), and the harmful disease she is fighting. Lucie's postmemorial struggle is channeled and anticipated by the parents' guilt, unwittingly echoed in Jana's explanation that the hardest thing was "to decide on behalf of the child" when confronted with the secret police.

In other words, *Kawasaki's Rose* demonstrates how the destructive force of the state erupts within the family frame. Illustrating the fatal entwinement between state terror and family biographies, former secret policeman Kafka recounts the family secret in a chilling voice over accompanying shots of private photographs that depict the fragile idyll of Pavel, Jana, and Lucie. These images exemplify the hidden location of postmemory as identified by Hirsch, and attest to a family chronicle demanding belated reinterpretation—by Lucie foremost. The scene intimates that it is up to the children of those who orchestrated the past to develop the stories and meanings that connect one historical moment with the other, providing an opportunity to integrate the unassimilated affects that shape these children, their families, and nations. As Hirsch further explains, "perhaps it is only in subsequent generations that trauma can be witnessed and worked through, by those who... receive its effects, belatedly, through the narratives, actions, and symptoms of the previous generation."[115]

In this sense, Lucie painfully builds her own narrative by untangling the threads of the past. As she confronts her father and mother, and travels to Sweden to meet Borek, Lucie enables the transitory movement of affective histories across time and space and thereby achieves (at least temporarily) some kind of affective catharsis, most poignantly echoed by the communal reciting of Czech swear words at Borek's Swedish dinner party. This release of tension is later repeated in Prague, when Borek humorously bombards Pavel with a seemingly endless list of swear words, taken from a book he has been given by Lucie. In this way, Lucie becomes the knot of a complex past, assembling the various strings of affective histories located in different moments in time and dispersed across space.

The spatial distribution of traumatic histories resonates with the psychological arrangement of memory as organized through modes of attachment and exclusion. Exploring memory in the context of social and spatial specificities enables a sense of cultural transference and relational remembering. Pavel's guilt is an exemplary dilemma of the Eastern experience and its particularity functions as a means of investigating Czech history. However, this specificity is complicated by Borek's expatriation, demonstrating the way in which history (and its walls) may stretch across different cultural contexts. Hence, although memory "unfolds within a spatial framework,"[116] as Maurice Halbwachs points out, it is essentially also about traversing these spaces. Borek's expatriation to Sweden has literally made him the foreign body Freud associates with repressed memory, unfolding Pavel's dark trace of a purposefully forgotten story all the way to Sweden. Hence, when Borek travels to the Czech Republic and attends Pavel's medal ceremony in Prague, he personifies the return of the repressed. However, as the complex image of the rose Borek's painter friend Kawasaki dedicates to Lucie signifies, transference, in the sense of displacing unassimilated affects from one idea to another,[117] is ultimately not linear. The film instead suggests a composite relationship of various histories made apparent through layers of violent pasts across different cultural contexts.

There is a sense of intimate belonging animated by overlapping legacies of violence and loss, an idea which is most apparent in Borek's friendship with the equally displaced Kawasaki. The Japanese artist, who lost his family in the Tokyo Sarin gas attack in 1995 and subsequently stopped painting, is "adopted" by Borek, who lost everything in 1972. The two men seem inseparable, connected by a mutual understanding of each other's pain and intimately linked by a sense of interpersonal transference. When Lucie unlocks the past for Borek, Kawasaki hence also feels a sense of the knot unravelling. This transferential affective release finds expression in his painting of the rose for Lucie and resonates with the voice of Pavel reading a poem on remorse and suffering that overlays the scene. Such spatial and generational compositions of memory sites exemplify Schwab's argument that "histories of violence can be put in a dialogical relationship with one another, thus creating a transferential dynamic for those who participate in, witness, or inherit those histories transgenerationally."[118] Suggesting that we are all implicated in each other's experiences, affective transference, in other words, enables collective forms of remembering that do not foreclose cultural, historical, and national particularities, but, rather, draw on them to underpin self-formation in the context of shared histories of violence.

Of course, national identity heavily relies on this kind of shared feeling, utilizing the affective self-knowledge of individuals as a metric for communal realizations. Moments of collective identification such as the commemoration of historical turning points, occasioned here by Pavel's Memory of the Nation Award, on the one hand cement certain political positions in opposition to others, but, on the other hand, they also destabilize such stances, thereby also unwittingly foregrounding the way in which the nation engages with the affective details of its past. Pavel's ceremony illustrates history's continuous narrativization and, like all commemorations, it marks an attempt to cleanse inconsistent fantasies about the past. However, the official narrative proposed by these formalities is complicated by the protagonist's intimate ambiguities, and thereby the film ultimately privileges human dilemmas over historical valor.

In this regard, the fantasy of "the good man" plays out differently in *Kawasaki's Rose* than it does in *The Lives of Others*. Whereas Wiesler and Dreyman perpetuate a strong sense of righteous integrity in an otherwise cruel world, Pavel asserts a moral vulnerability to historical and political force, suggesting a different kind of reconciliation. As Pavel points out in his acceptance speech, "some things cannot be atoned for," and hence he does not attempt to undo the past but rather advocates remembering it as formative. "If memory is lost we cease to exist," he explains, accepting the award as a "punishment" instead of some kind of "perfection" as Borek cynically describes it earlier. Hence, the film suggests a movement from collective guilt to collective responsibility, as advocated by Schwab,[119] which is reinforced by Pavel's apology—a commitment to moral complexity that *The Lives of Others* lacks. Crucially Pavel's plead for forgiveness is directed at Lucie (and not Borek), and thereby it addresses the generation that carries the silent repercussions of these legacies, rather than those participating in their creation, precisely because the past cannot be reconstructed in a more favorable way.

The fallen hero on the pedestal thereby voices the nation's most affective dilemma, suggesting that heroes and villains go hand in hand, without attempting to resolve this contradiction. This undermines the historical dichotomies upon which national identities rest and suggests that the official collecting, archiving, and publicizing of past atrocities have to account for human complexities. Pavel's inauspicious weakness is ultimately not forgiven; however, because of this, open guilt, rather than a private prison, becomes the premise of integrity and a process of healing personal and national wounds. Instead of highlighting resistance in private, the film thereby foregrounds human weakness as an incipient, but also vastly exploited, driver of state terror. The entanglement nevertheless does not operate as an excuse; rather in personalizing the ethical vulnerability of states and nations, the film counters the moral abstraction of history.

The approach resonates with the stinging case of Czech writer Milan Kundera, who was accused in 2008 of denouncing military deserter Miroslav Dvoráček. Allegedly, Kundera's collaboration with the regime in 1948 resulted in Dvoráček deportation to a labor camp, where he served for fourteen years before emigrating to Sweden. Kundera has rejected these claims and was widely supported by other prominent writers; however, the incident underpins the affective charge of the nation's memory as ambiguous, contradictory, and ultimately lost. Kundera writes that "the struggle of man against power is the struggle of memory against forgetting."[120] Similarly, Pavel's story provides a counter-narrative to the neat resolutions projected by the state. Demonstrating the personal ambivalences of those who make up the nation, *Kawasaki's Rose* thereby challenges the official discourse that seeks to reduce walled life to binaries of exemplary vs. fallen citizens.

The Past Is Irretrievable

Kawasaki's Rose investigates the location of memory as firmly situated within the domestic realm of the family, in a similar way that *The Lives of Others* negotiates history as belonging to the intimate sphere. Both films thereby function as a reminder that complex politics are ultimately small in the sense that they tangibly play out through the everyday trajectories of ordinary people. This idea is particularly relevant for a memory of the walled past in Eastern Europe, precisely because communism has always maintained a complex interplay between the personal and political. With the state venturing deep into the private sphere of individuals, people were forced to negotiate a public identity in accordance with official political scripts. On the other hand, this also led to the importance of creating a private idyll, promising a kind of intimate self-preservation. Ironically, Pavel and Jana continue this performance long after the end of the Iron Curtain, this time maintaining their image as distinguished dissidents. Hence, the walled era and its aftermath exemplify Hirsch's point about the family structurally being "a last vestige of protection"[121] against the threats of the political but also becoming "particularly vulnerable to these violent ruptures, and so a measure of their devastation."[122] Both *Kawasaki's Rose* and *The Lives of Others* examine the historical implications of the past through the lens of personal repercussions or, to borrow from Mazierska once more, "politics enter [the] characters' lives through their bedrooms and kitchens,"[123] creating enduring liabilities. Private settings hence provide access to the production of meaning which politics and history enforce.

Drawing on the individual memories and affective knowledges embedded in political structures, the cinema continuously remembers and projects the intimate imaginaries that sustain historical events. In this way, cinema is capable of somewhat engaging with an otherwise irretrievable past, offering perspectives, decentered from the fixed positions of grand narratives and relegating history to productive affective revision. The films discussed demonstrate how spatial politics produce meaning; however, crucially they also address the repercussions of affectively internalizing these meanings. The process is reflected in the reconstruction of the family secret by the documentary team following Pavel, who set out to celebrate the polished image of the virtuous dissident but when his betrayal is discovered, move from supporting a public image to investigating the private memories that challenge such one-dimensional accounts. The interviews with Borek, Kafka, Jana, and Bara confront different points of view, yet juxtaposed on the screen, they create a multifaceted, ambiguous, and thereby truly intimate narrative of the past. Similarly, Wiesler rewrites the lives of others in the private theater of the home, allowing the viewer to intimately reconsider the public staging of historical fantasies through the Brechtian *Lehrstück* Donnersmarck creates. The affective complexities resulting from this kind of *verdichten* are as fabricated as the official accounts they aim to trouble; however, similar to the genre of cinematic history accounts, the confrontation is less concerned with adequate reconstructions of the past than with the creation of narratives that help to make sense of the past's complex impacts on the present.

Of course, reiterating memory as something active and creative, cinema also suggests that one personalized story can come at the cost of obliterating another; yet, those intimate recollections on the national screen also serve to diversify shared narratives. Konopka's rabbit perspective satirizes this idea, suggesting that media truths are subjective, constructed, and instrumental, and therefore comment on the politicization of memory via its public mediation. However, when Tilda Swinton leaves the public display of history behind in order to explore the wall's meaning through an internal dialogue, she reminds us that the past is only ever assessed through an experience of the present—an experience cinema helps to provide. We may remain "cut off from the pasts that have created us,"[124] but at the same time the cinema screen channels "the temporal imaginings of past, present and future,"[125] crucial to making sense of the affective shapes of intimate publics today. All four films represent an examination of the past through the lens of the present and, hence, ultimately attest to the ways in which "cinema memories travel through time and from one historical moment to the next."[126] They interrogate the wall as that which has been and now remains absent—in the most affectively present way. These films thereby project collective feelings and experiences about walled life that insist on the past as an emotional (if messy) compass—a creative endeavor, which, at the end of *The Invisible Frame*, is tellingly "dedicated to the people of Palestine."

4

Palestine: Dreams of Walls and Undead Lives

Following Yitzhak Rabin's announcement in 1994 that "we have to decide on separation as a philosophy,"[1] Israel began to construct the iconic wall of the present: the West Bank separation barrier. Similar to the Berlin Wall, this partition works to exclude "the other side" physically and mentally, projecting a visual symptom of divisive politics and affectively reinforcing the parameters of the enclosed nation. However, Israel's barrier, more than anything, substantiates a need for security from an "other," who is experienced as an overwhelming, intolerable threat and in its most immediate manifestation evokes the Palestinians (or more precisely the ideological image of the Palestinian terrorist), but arguably gestures further to the violent history of Jewish persecution. The wall in Israel is complicated by the legacy of the Holocaust and existing anti-Semitism, enacting, both racialized colonial aggression and a response to a historically warranted fear of (racialized) violence. Far from offering permanent security, however, Israel's walls thereby mediate perceptions of precariousness, instability, and marginalization that animate myriad forms of technological, political, and crucially psychological defenses. As a result, Israel's infamous barrier and the Berlin Wall share (different sides of) the same historical legacy, but they are also linked in the present, not simply by means of a visual similarity, but due to their aesthetic connotations. Like the Berlin Wall, Israel's wall can be read as an "overriding presence of absence,"[2] or more precisely as constructing an "aesthetic absence"[3] out of the cultural and political presence of Palestine.

Most notably, the Israeli wall epitomizes the emotionally charged national screen, both in the sense of a shield erasing the other(ed) side and as a projection surface on which the collective imaginary of Israel comes into being. It thereby highlights, perhaps like no other wall, the potency of dreamwork in the wall-screen-affect cathexis. As Ella Shohat puts it, "while, as we know, all nations are invented... some nations are invented more than others, especially since in the case of Israel, the state can be said to have invented the nation."[4] Put simply, the collective identity of Israel is dependent on the notion of screening out, which has ensured a continuous expansion of Israel's mental and physical barriers in an effort to secure the Israeli collective by excluding the Palestinians. Exploring these projections, I want to approach Israel's wall as a medium that organizes political alongside affective space, occupying a landscape which works as the central enigma in the cultural imaginaries of both collectives. Israel and Palestine are locked in a highly charged relation, negotiating opposing claims to the land and competing meanings of and fantasies about it. As a result, the West Bank separation barrier stands as a "security fence," but functions as a projective screen, making palpable the conflicting intimacies, deeply held attachments, and innumerable ambiguities of Israel-Palestine.

Israel's wall establishes a dynamic structure of feeling, resourcing a national identity that seeks to protect itself from, and simultaneously blind itself to, the existence of Palestine. Conceptualized as an affective presence or atmosphere by Raymond Williams, a structure of feeling "mostly goes without saying,"[5] as Berlant would add. However, it might also be capable of apprehending the collective affective scenes or emotional commons of Israeli-Palestinian existence, interrogating the visceral charges of the occupation while imagining how political and ideological spaces are mapped onto each other. Of course, this kind of projection is always a work in progress, which, in turn, is reflected in the way the West Bank separation barrier does not strictly operate as a geopolitical border, but is more overtly an instalment of power, or an architectural symptom of divisive politics, that simultaneously prevents and reveals the intimate encounter between the two conflicting sides, while joining them in the visible manifestation of a violent structure. As Judith Butler puts it, "violence renews itself in the apparent inexhaustibility of its object,"[6] and Israel's wall works accordingly, continuously and progressively reinventing its route, despite the International Court of Justice declaring in July 2004 that the "wall is a political measure, unjustified on grounds of security, and a defacto land grab."[7]

Israel has since then repeatedly expanded its attempts, and the anticipated route of the barrier under construction will be 712 kilometers long, with 85 percent of it appearing within the West Bank, thereby increasingly annexing Palestinian land and livelihood.[8] By 2018, approximately 64 percent of the projected wall had been completed, which amounts to a length of nearly 460 kilometers.[9] Most of the barrier takes the form of barbed-wire fences and trenches, but in some places the barrier evolves into a 6 to 8 meter-high concrete wall that, according to the IDF, will make up about 30 kilometers in total once construction is finished.[10] When completed, the "security fence" will imprison at least 210,000 Palestinians between the barrier and the green line,[11] cutting them off from their lands, families, olive groves, workplaces, hospitals, etc. In 2012, Israel also began to construct a high-tech fence along its Sinai Peninsula in an effort to curtail immigration from Africa. In 2018, the first concrete sections appeared along the border with Lebanon and in early 2019 Israel started construction of a 6-meter-high fence along the Gaza Strip, which by June 2019 began taking the form of a solid wall. Israel's walls thereby highlight the way in which a rhetoric of othering is directly translated into the field of vision by inscribing political landscapes onto human space.

However, what I want to point out is that the collapse of political and personal space also works as a meaningful point of contact, precisely because the physical entity of the wall gives shape to an everyday politics of walled life and thereby concretizes the relationship between the two sides in the form of a telling symbol. The ambivalence of the wall is reflected in the way it reveals the encounter between the two sides and simultaneously prevents it. The wall as a shield strengthens the grand narratives of division and threat by verifying a need for self-protection and by defining the parameters of security for one's own identity—an identity that seemingly needs to be walled off in order to be experienced as coherent. On the other hand, the wall does not simply fortify the narratives of its creation, but also lays them bare by bringing the relationship between Israel and Palestine into view.

Read as a medium, the West Bank wall stands in for the relationship between the two sides and can provide insight into the cultural sensibilities that circuit the conflict, potentially uncovering the identities it conceals. In other words, the West Bank wall is not simply a means of division but marks a point of intimacy, in the sense of both meeting and confronting the other(ed) side, because it crucially appears as the physical and psychological manifestation of a (political) relationship between Israel and Palestine. This is important to acknowledge because the problem posed by the wall is in the first instance the collapse of a shared history and hence of a shared narrative. However, the underlying relationship between the two sides is encoded in the political, psychological, and physical elements of the landscapes, and thereby reinforces, but also potentially challenges, the politics of walls and the way they open intimate conflicts onto modes of political discourses.

Dreaming Political Landscapes

The interplay between landscape and politics relies on the role of the land as a central component of the national imaginary. The imagined homeland at the core of national narratives and political identities is primarily an image of a landscape which has the capacity "to naturalize and render transparent"[12] the ideological ideas from which such imaginaries take their effectiveness. The very foundation of Israel relies on such a claim to the land and is echoed in the motivation of "making the desert bloom." In the *Question of Zion* Jacqueline Rose explains that Israel's national imaginary works through a "language of redemption of the land via settlement."[13] This mode of redemptive occupation reinstates a wish to enter "history though territory"[14] and to reclaim the "promised land." Thinking through the Zionist project, in other words, has to begin with the notion of a powerful and charged attachment to the land—a land which is assumed to be empty and hence available as a protective haven for the homeless Jews. This is the idea exemplified in the Zionist slogan, "A land without people for a people without land,"[15] reinforced by the horror of anti-Semitism that spread across Europe and peaking in the atrocities of the Holocaust committed by Nazi Germany during the Second World War.

Haunted by this painful past, the drive for protection at the heart of Israeli ideology must then, as Edward Said points out, rely on "the refusal to admit, and the consequent denial of, the existence of Palestinian Arabs,"[16] in order to avoid the conflict of securing one people at the expense of another, thereby confronting the violence Israel sought to escape. The tragic dynamic is reflected in a spatial politics of avoidance (or repression) and introduces an emotionally charged vision as a claim to the land in the sense that the parameters of the visible define the (political) reality of the inhabitants. Landscape establishes a scopic regime that extends to a collective sensibility, both of which provide modes of belonging and exclusion. In this way, the spatial organization of Israel works to undermine the Palestinians' very existence by making them invisible and negating the Palestinians' own "indissoluble bond with the land,"[17] as Edward Said further maintains. The conflict between Israel and Palestine is hence significantly realized through the construction of landscape and narrative, shaping the perspectives and realities of walled life. To no small part the conflict plays out as a battle over what and who is seen as part of the legitimate field of the visible, and who is negated through effacement.

Israel's spatial politics perpetuate a fantasy of separation and carefully orchestrate the architecture of the homeland accordingly. Such an organization of space exploits the landscape in order to secure a coherent identity. Since, in the logic of Zionism the landscape needs to be "redeemed" as part of a divine plan,[18] as Rose elaborates, Israel practically accomplishes an affective grounding in the place through the accoutrements of settlements, walls, and towers. However, the spatial arrangement is only a first step: Ideologically, the land also "needs to be filled by the dreams (…) of its beholders."[19] The Zionist dream, in its perpetual deferral as a promise, a wish to be fulfilled, continuously occupies the site of Palestine and manifests itself in concrete spatial designs. This exemplifies Salecl's claim that a country is always "a kind of fiction" but also reminds us that such fictions gloss over the "absence of the nation" through the concealment of fantasy.[20] Both Palestine and Israel share this notion of absence, but it is Israel's power to create and manifest its dream in the spatial organization of the land and the fantasmatic realm of identity politics that seems to afford its unresponsiveness to Palestinian suffering. The visual distribution of power largely denies Palestinians their own national dream, while the fantasy scenario evoked by Israel imagines landscape as an ideological screen that protects Israel and hides Palestine. The landscape hence stages both "a defensible and homogeneous Israeli political space"[21] and an affective screen projecting (and protecting) national identity. In this sense, to create the homeland is to dream the nation, and, according to Said, "Israel has [largely] succeeded in shutting its own and the world's eyes"[22] to the social, cultural, and political relations embedded in this dreamscape.

The invisibility of Palestinians is evoked on an imaginary level *and* carefully enforced in the physical construction of space. Importantly, however, the dream serves as the scheme for constructing this reality. This is not to say that Israel rests upon delusions; rather, it "foregrounds its own fantasmatic dimension"[23] while engaging architecture as a form of constructed reality, instead of confronting the fact of Palestinian existence as indissoluble from Israeli identity. As Rose points out, "Zionism (...) is a violation of reality that knows its own delusion and runs with it."[24] Despite the rhetoric of an empty land, Israel is of course aware of the conflict of occupation, but it settles the land on the basis of the dream (and the wish to which the dream pertains) rather than encountering the actualities of (shared) suffering. Israel's first president Chaim Weizman explained as early as 1909 that "we have to create our title out of our wish to go to Palestine."[25] Analogously, Freud explains that the "motive force of the dream"[26] is the wish which is "represented as a scene."[27] Such a scene can be read as the Palestinian landscape, but in this case it also marks a concrete instalment of power.

Israel's politics is manifested in an intricate system of ideological and spatial forms of separation and effacement that work to divide Israelis from Palestinians.[28] In fact, Eyal Weizman has compellingly demonstrated that Israel's architecture is a strategic tool to exercise power over the Palestinians, locking them into engineered prisons, shaped by roads, water pipes, and barriers that isolate and divide them from Israel and each other.[29] Simultaneously, the constructed realities of Israel's landscape design maintain that these atrocities remain invisible, hence affording a "psychological blindness" that secures the notion of redemption as well as the "continuation of the dream."[30] Weizman explains that the process of "building the land of Israel"[31] essentially entails a complex system of "comfortable, traffic free roads, completely devoid of Arabs,"[32] vertically reinforced through a three-dimensional matrix of roads, tunnels, and bridges,[33] which create the "land without people" so as then to claim it. Put simply, the invisibility of the Palestinians is built into the spatial organization of an Israel without Palestine and at the same time this design is disguised as it naturalizes the architectural erasure of Palestine. In turn, the wall cutting through the land, as a monumental, political imposition is hence paradoxically capable of rendering visible the fantasy of separation concretized in the architectural making of the landscape (while also reinforcing it).

Creating the Cinematic Dream

Alongside producing the nation politically and architecturally, Israel has self-reflexively utilized the cinema and other narrative forms to imagine the nation as a site for identity formation. Acknowledging the pivotal role of cinema in the founding of Israel, Shohat explains that the movement of Zionism, as a process of shaping collective national imaginaries and memories, emerged concurrently with the invention of film and therefore has always been well aware of cinema's ability to produce the Zionist dream on the national screen.[34] In fact, she argues, "Zionism invented, as it were, the Israeli nation partly through its literary and cinematic narrative."[35] As early as in the works of the Lumière brothers (*Palestine* was released in 1896 and *Leaving Jerusalem by Train* was produced a year later),[36] cinema has envisioned the empty land at the heart of the Zionist endeavor and thereby fantasmatically inscribed the place on the mental map of the collective imaginary.

Following Anat Zanger, this idea is enhanced rather than necessarily limited by the inability of cinema to "write the Israeli place as anything other than a fantasy,"[37] precisely because fantasy, as has been shown by Renata Salecl, provides the motive force for the establishment of the affective nation.[38] In this context, cinema becomes a means of reading the Israeli space and the borders it establishes as "reflect[ing] mental maps of belonging, setting boundaries between 'us' and 'them'."[39] Mediating the walled space in this way, cinema not only enforces, but also reveals the intimate attachments, and sometimes violent investments, that forge and prevent relationships in Israel-Palestine. In her discussion of Israeli cinema, Shohat therefore concludes that film does not simply "register[-] perceptions and perspectives on reality,"[40] revealing the ideological dynamics and intimate ambivalences of conflict, but that it is also a "means to actively shape that reality."[41] This in turn suggests cinema's central role in creating and sustaining, but also in challenging Israel's wall(s).

More to the point, contesting the confined space of Palestinian erasure is a matter of (literally) giving a face to Palestinians in an effort to reinscribe them into the political landscape and cultural imaginary. Palestinian cinema is hence not reducible to a national aspiration (although this often happens, particularly from within the Palestinian community, as director Elia Suleiman explains[42]), but it is primarily a medium for renegotiating Palestine's deeply problematic relation to the visual, as Edward Said has explained. Said asserts that "Arabs were always being represented, never able to speak for themselves."[43] In his keynote speech for the 2003 Palestinian film festival *Dreams of a Nation* in New York, Said considered the subversive potential of Palestinian cinema to be twofold. He explained that "on the one hand, Palestinians stand against invisibility... and on the other hand they stand against... a visual identity associated with violence and terrorism."[44] Both of these problems constitute a form of effacement, described by Judith Butler as either "producing a symbolic identification with the face as inhuman,"[45] or "foreclosing our apprehension... so that there never was a human, there never was a life and no murder has, therefore, ever taken place."[46] The face of Palestinian cinema as a challenge to the walls of Israeli domination, in other words, re-establishes the grievability of Palestine in Butler's sense—by rehumanizing Palestinians and simultaneously unmasking the stereotypes projected by the wall. The effort aims to rework the emotional organization of geographical and ideological space. However, it remains difficult to accomplish these changes where the production of the cinematic landscape is intimately bound to the political one.

The cinema of Israel-Palestine has to consider the indissoluble bond with the other(ed) side, even where it does not address this intimate link explicitly. Palestinians and Israelis are locked into a shared landscape—affectively, imaginatively, and geographically. Nationhood, for both, hence "constitute[s] an intellectual space of conflictual and independent utopias and dystopias."[47] Exemplifying this dynamic, Hamid Dabashi argues that the structural (traumatic) core of both cinematic traditions is Israel's establishment in 1948, called al-Nabka (the catastrophe) by Palestinians and the War of Independence by Israelis.[48] The events of 1948 are traumatic for Palestinians, in the sense of an exodus, but arguably this act of violent repression (per definition) also manifests itself traumatically within Israel's collective imaginary. Dabashi suggests that this central wound is precisely "the defining moment of Palestinian cinema"[49] and structures the stories around remembrance of a lost homeland, just as Zionism envisions the homeland epically unfolding on the collective screen. Although these competing narratives are radically different, they are also intimately linked, creating a cinematic landscape (alongside the political one) that reveals rather than conceals the foundational relationship at work.

Walling the Land: *Lemon Tree*

Set near the Green line in the West Bank, Israeli director Eran Riklis's and Palestinian writer Suha Arraf's *Lemon Tree* (2008) tells the story of the Palestinian widow Selma Zidane, whose lemon grove is declared a "security threat" when the fictitious Israeli defense minister Israel Navon (who literally stands in for the country Israel by virtue of his political standing and name) and his wife Mira move in next door. Selma hires lawyer Ziad to prevent the lemon grove from being uprooted, while Israel and Mira increasingly struggle to negotiate their demand for security both politically and privately. When the lemon trees are fenced off, the relationship between the neighbors rapidly deteriorates, eventually leading Selma to take the case to the Israeli Supreme Court. Whereas the conflict reveals ever new walls (legally, politically, and emotionally), Mira, nevertheless, comes to identify with Selma, and thereby is confronted with her own and her husband's hypocrisy. Despite publicly maintaining the importance of building relationships among Israelis and Palestinians, Israel and Mira are incapable of doing so with their own neighbor. The couple becomes estranged over the dispute, as their own relationship is increasingly disaffected, alienated, and finally walled-off.

The film's central concern is the wall's destructive impact on an emotionally rich bond between the people and the land, which plays an essential role in both the Israeli and the Palestinian imaginary. Negotiating the physical and emotional space shared between neighbors, walled life, in this instance, is imagined in the form of a profound anti-relationality enforced by the wall, stretching from the spatial to the intimate. Demonstrating the ways in which political acts (and walls) impact on the lives and bonds that are possible within a particular arrangement of power, the partitioning of the land, as the constitutive act of forging these relationships, works to organize the context, both politically and intimately. In this sense, the creation of the political realm, or *nomos*, is both a function of the law *and* a means of intimacy, precisely because the nomos not only initiates a particular order of power,[50] but it is driven by the wish to establish relationships and a sense of belonging in order to create the home or homeland affectively. In the context of Israel-Palestine, the claims to this "homeland" are of course two-sided and mutually contested. The wall hence aggressively signals Israel's visual claim to territory. However, mirroring these dynamics on the micro-level of neighborly encounters, the film utilizes Selma's lemon grove as the affective sight of Palestine's own investment in the land.

The landscape of the lemon grove mediates a larger politics of division, critiquing Israel's ignorant policies and walls. The film opens with a slow tracking shot into the lemon grove, establishing Selma's relationship to the land by focusing on the labor and care she invests in the plants that in turn provide for her. Selma's grove is contrasted with a long shot of the West Bank wall, along which Mira and Israel's possessions are being transported, foreshadowing the gradual erection of the physical and mental barrier, which will separate the neighbors but also cause the death of the land. The scene reverses the myth of redemption, as it shows the Israeli couple detached from the lemons, which otherwise "serve as a charged metaphor for the Jewish people's relationship with their land,"[51] as Zanger explains, implying that walled life ultimately estranges both sides. Exposing the inconsistency of the Israeli imaginary, the wall (cutting through the garden and the nation) makes visible the political intimacies prefiguring the divided space; it also suggests that these conflicts are immediately erased.

Reworking the trajectory between the political imaginary of Israel and its reliance on the psychological repression of Palestine, the film introduces the physical and emotional barriers that emerge between Selma and her new neighbors by way of partitioning and fencing, rather than dialogue and engagement. As soon as the couple arrives at their new home, the secret service enters the grove and sets up a fence and a watch tower, ignoring Selma's presence and never discussing the problem with her. Israel and Mira establish their new home through acts of partitioning and "primeval division"[52] as opposed to creating connections, thereby treating the land as empty and denying the present inhabitants a voice in the political reality constructed by the "new" home/nomos. Of course, this colonial logic echoes the country Israel's politics at large, which, as David Theo Goldberg puts it, rests on a "tension between denial and repression that fuels Israel's sense of Palestine, and so of itself also."[53] According to Edward Said, this attitude is characteristic of Israel's dealing with the Palestinians as "an inconvenient nuisance"[54] rather than "a population with an indissoluble bond with the land."[55] In fact, Selma and her worker Abu, like Palestine at large, are "refused a decent place in actuality—even when they sit on the land."[56] Selma's own claim to the land, reflected in emotional memories and a deep attachment to her trees, is literally cut off by the fence, negating the relationships already "in place."

The film suggests that the violent structure perpetuated by the wall entails the nonrecognition and erasure of the individual which is further substantiated by an arbitrary and discriminatory law. Selma epitomizes the "absent Arab" who is caught up in a surreal confinement based on obscure regulations, in which "those in control (the authorities) and those being controlled... are trapped in the same topographical field following orders from above."[57] This supports Sundberg's claim that borders wall-up not only people but also (necessarily) the law.[58] Starting with the letter Selma receives about the military's decision to uproot the grove being written in Hebrew rather than Arabic, and, hence, preventing her from fully understanding her situation, Selma finds herself caught up in the horrors of a one-sided bureaucratic system which does not recognize her and in which she is left without support. Israel's legal state of exception (in response to the threat of terrorism) completely absorbs checks and balances, obliterating the individual in favor of what the Israeli military lawyer calls "imperative military necessity."

In fact, Selma and her grove are barred from the law's protection altogether and merely addressed by the "inclusive exclusion"[59] that characterize Agamben's bare life. Folding her into the violence of Israeli sovereignty, Selma's legal nightmare stands in stark contrast to the enormous efforts that go into Mira and Israel's security. This nonrecognition of and by the law mirrors Selma's journey to the Israeli Civil Administration in the West Bank, where she is told after hours of waiting that her problem is not important—a strategy seemingly aimed at the political surrender of Palestinians, but also situating the Palestinian outside of the protection of the law. Correspondingly, the Palestinian village men show little compassion or will to help Selma. As if accepting their position outside the realm of the (Israeli) legal system, the men refrain to active retraction from Israel, which includes an insistence to "not take their money," leaving Selma with no options or defense. When she decides to challenge the order, Selma relies on self-motivation and is only assisted by the outsider Ziad. Hence, it is not simply the relationship between Israel and Palestine that breaks down, but, as the film suggests, human relationships as such, like the soil of the plants, deteriorate through the lack of care that develops in the shadow of walls.

In this sense, the wall not simply compromises the relationship between Palestinians and the land, it also refutes a meaningful connection for Israel. For example, the defense minister continuously reiterates the importance of good relations with the Palestinians while defending the construction of the wall. However, the conflict in his backyard exposes the contradiction running through these public commentaries and demonstrates (both the country and the man) Israel's inability to confront the mental barriers. Instead of "redeeming" the land, Israel's relationship with country and people is constructed self-consciously and functions as an artificial component of his public image. Israel's failure to connect with his Palestinian neighbor is doubled by his inability to bond with the land and in turn to respect Selma's (and Palestine's) own foothold in the place. He mindlessly "borrows" lemons from the grove for his party and does not understand Selma's outrage over the intrusion. Later, he launches a public campaign for the protection of Palestinian olive trees while insisting on the destruction of the lemon grove. These contradictions originate in Israel's inability to acknowledge the link between his mental barriers and the physical wall he is building, which in

PALESTINE: DREAMS OF WALLS AND UNDEAD LIVES

turn exposes the country's paradoxical policies. The "homeland" is destroyed rather than protected, because Israel excludes human relationships from his concept of security.

Negotiating these political failings on the level of the intimate, the film reflects on the ways in which relationships are limited in the context of a walled life. The more fences Israel puts up (in both the physical and the psychological sense), the more the relationship to his more open-minded wife is deteriorating, eventually leading her to leave him. Just like the country, the defense minister avoids acknowledging the connection between escalating conflicts, affective alienation, and the politics of walls. When Israel finds out that Selma is challenging the court's decision to fence off her grove and prevent her from entering it, he shows little empathy, initiating the confrontation with his wife that will eventually leave him alone, crushed, and desolated. As Israel denies the relationships between land, people, and wall, he cuts himself off emotionally and fails to create a home for himself and his family. Israel's emotional ineptitude, by extension, serves to highlight the nation's increasingly estranged relation to the land.

While the film carefully traces the deadlocks of Israel's walls, it also offers openings for rethinking these politics through modes of shared sensibility and recognition, made possible by the women on both sides. The connection that unfolds between Mira and Selma arguably fails to establish a dialogue between the Israeli woman and her Palestinian neighbor, but it nevertheless produces acknowledgment and empathy across fences. Mira increasingly identifies with Selma's struggle, as she participates in her neighbor's vulnerability through the violent scenes Mira observes playing out across the fence. These moments of "witnessing" Selma's harassment by the Israeli secret service challenge the invisibility afforded by the wall and disrupt Mira's ignorance, enabling the recognition of commonalities.

Both women are isolated and feel neglected. Selma's husband is dead, and Mira's is absent. They are both estranged from their children and attempt to carve out their home (Selma lives off the land and Mira is an interior designer) within the confines of aggressive male jingoism. Of course, Mira finds herself in a privileged position (the secret service protects her; the grove needs to be uprooted for her safety); however, her identification with Selma can be read as an inability to maintain Israel's "psychological blindness." Mira is unable to turn her eyes away from the grove and Selma's confrontation with the military. She feels increasingly urged to *meet* her neighbor. However, Talmon and Peleg argue that Mira, who represents the Israeli Left, ultimately does not communicate with the Palestinian side but only reflects on herself.[60] Exemplifying this limitation, the authors quote a scene in which Mira approaches Selma's house, but instead of talking to her neighbor, Mira encounters her own reflection in the window, which causes her hesitation and leads to the secret service's intervention.[61] Talmon and Peleg explain that Mira's failure to establish a dialogue stems from the barriers she "erects around herself."[62] However, this moment of self-reflexivity also leads Mira to contemplate her own and by extension her country's impediment on Palestinian livelihood and thereby suggests that the wall also offers a chance for encounter and perhaps reviewing the current politics.

In fact, Mira develops a sense of responsibility for Selma's situation and realizes that the walls meant to protect her also work as a prison, from which she can only free herself by acknowledging her neighbor. When Mira is prevented from knocking on Selma's door by the secret service and she protests, it is made clear to her that the agents do not take orders from her, but her husband. The incident causes Mira's depression, leading her to consider the larger parameters of her country's and family's history and future. Talking to Gera about children, she confesses mourning a child she never had and thereby indirectly reflects on the state's inability to build a future. As Mira puts it in regard to her family, "my mother always used to say, Israel needs to sort out the problems with his father before he can become one himself." This of course insinuates (the country) Israel's ongoing struggles with the trauma of the Holocaust, raising the difficult question of response and responsibility. Here, the film implicitly encourages a negotiation of the past, perhaps asking whether the memory of persecution and genocide can be met with militant protectionism and dispossession of another people, or whether it beckons compassion for the other and a recognition of (mutual) vulnerability. These questions remain crucial to Israel's and Palestine's future, whose tentative status is reflected in the absence of both Mira's and Selma's children. Hence, when Mira finally appears in court, it is primarily to acknowledge Selma's existence.

Lemon Tree foregrounds the claim that competing memories and attachments to the homeland can only be reconciled through human interaction. Mira's act of acknowledging Selma's struggle by appearing in court recognizes that the "other side's" relationship with the land is the precondition for human and also political rapport. In other words, the land provides a chance to connect the people to the place but also to each other. As Abu puts it to the court, "Trees are like people. They have feelings, they need to be talked to, need tender loving care." The uprooting of the trees is hence synonymous with the dispossession of people and the neglect of human relationships.

Of course, the dynamic also foregrounds the fact that the wall does not simply divide the land but also substantiates division between, and perhaps within, people. Unable to adhere to this logic as the basis for protection of her country, Mira appears in the Supreme Court, where Selma explains, "My trees are real. My life is real. You are already building a wall around us isn't that enough?" Selma unwittingly perhaps also speaks for Mira, who subsequently leaves the husband who has been walling her in. With the separation wall now running through his garden, signifying the breakdown of human relationships, Israel has fortressed and defeated himself. In the last scene of the film, he stares at the wall while the camera pans to the other side, showing Selma equally defeated among her pruned trees. She is also looking at the wall and thereby (unknowingly) directly at Israel. The final image intimates that Israel's fear of terror is ultimately destructive for both sides, as the face-to-face encounter is made impossible in the dying walled land.

Facing the Terrorist: *Paradise Now*

Contemporary anxieties about terrorism are a driving force in legitimizing the wall, which officially functions as a protective shield against such attacks. On the word of the IDF, the wall marks a direct response to the violence Palestinians committed during the second Intifada (2000– 2005), at the height of which, according to Israel's Ministry of Defense, over 200 Israelis were killed during suicide bombings.[63] The wall, in other words, neatly aligns with Western anxieties about terrorism—a perception that was only heightened in the aftermath of 9/11. However, the traumatic intersection between Israeli security needs and US vulnerability has alleviated Western investments into retribution and militant protectionism, particularly against Arabs. The (global) narrative of anti-terror security, in this sense, is a significant building block in the foundation of the West Bank separation barrier and its various expansions since 2004. Discursively reducing an entire people to a threat and excluding them under the auspices of security, the IDF views the wall primarily as a defensive bulwark, able to guard Israel from terrorism.

As part of this discourse, Palestinians are largely relegated to the role of the callous suicide bomber, an image which works to aggressively dehumanize them, equating Palestine with terror and thereby projecting all kinds of fears and hostilities onto the Palestinian. In *Paradise Now* (2005),[64] director Hany Abu-Assad challenges the stereotype of the terrorist by controversially giving "a human face to the suicide bombers,"[65] and exploring the social conditions that lead to the making of "martyrs." The film thereby invites the viewer to rethink the difficult issue of suicide bombing beyond the parameters of an irrationally evil and fundamentally inexplicable action, instead contemplating the context of walled life as imposing an already experienced (political and social) death-in-life as the precondition for such atrocities. The film aims to challenge the narratives and emotions that assist in the creation of terrorists, exploring the repercussions within the communities from which they emerge. *Paradise Now* thereby critically examines the notion of terror as intimately linked to enduring modes of victimization, but the film also experiments with the possibility of alternative resistance.

Paradise Now envisions the last hours before the two childhood friends Said and Khaled are due to carry out a suicide attack in Tel Aviv, including their last moments with family and friends, the shooting of the martyr video and their reflections on their motivations and doubts. When the two eventually cross into Israel, they are discovered by soldiers and separated in the subsequent chaos. Although Said crosses back into Israel, he finds himself incapable of carrying out the bombing. Meanwhile, Khaled is trying to find Said in Nablus, as his absence becomes increasingly suspicious. A cat and mouse chase begins in which the two friends try to find each other (and perhaps also themselves), in the midst of which Suha the daughter of a martyr, with whom Said shares a growing affection, tries to prevent the attack. However, when Said and Khaled finally find each other and their group, Khaled surprisingly decides to refrain from going through with the plan, whereas Said, at last, makes a strong claim to the leader Jamal, explaining why he wants to carry out the bombing regardless. The film ends with Said pulling the trigger in a public bus in Tel Aviv.

Paradise Now reclaims the image of the terrorist but simultaneously attempts to open up a "meaningful discussion about the real issues at hand."[66] The film harshly disrupts Israeli perceptions of moral integrity and consequently has been criticized for being a one-sided, "vile, terrorist glorifying movie"[67] that attempts "to trivialize mass murder."[68] Yet, the film does not condone the murder of people or legitimize the perpetration of violence; rather, it unmistakably denounces these atrocities as being harmful to both sides. Examining the point of view of the occupied nevertheless, Abu-Assad seeks to explore the cycle of violence leading to such radical acts. In doing so, the film unsettles ideas about irrational terror as the mechanism that secures the victimization of the oppressor; yet, it insists that aiming to make sense of a position does not equate to legitimizing it. Rather, the analysis is meant to open the possibility of highlighting the ways in which violence is discursively and affectively framed. Discussing the links between narrative and power, Edward Said explains that the discursive and affective realization of the Israeli-Palestinian conflict has meant that Palestinians have nearly always been spoken for, subduing them to a narrative that characterizes Palestine as inherently violent and backward.[69]

By contrast, *Paradise Now* challenges common political, often emotionally charged, understandings of "what terror looks like." Interrogating the face of the bearded Muslim as the pivotal "symbol of evil" in the post-9/11 world, the film lays bare how the terrorist image "efface[s] what is most human about the [Arab] 'face'," to reinstate Butler's point.[70] Instead, the film reiterates that terror acts are committed by human beings, whose motivations are based in complex political and personal trajectories. As Butler puts it, "certain faces must be admitted into public view."[71] In admitting the face of the suicide bomber, *Paradise Now* shifts a narrative about unfounded terror toward a more complex investigation of violent intimacy that implicates both "sides." However, as Butler further points out, the very act of showing the human face (and hence what is particular about it) is also the point that representation must fail.[72] In this way, *Paradise Now* explores the possible conditions that tragically lead to suicide attacks, while simultaneously refusing to provide universal solutions.

The mediation of the terrorist image is part and parcel of an ambivalent process of meaning production, invoking a fragile field of power. Joseph A. Massad points out that "terror" is an act that collapses into an identity or image controlled by the enemy; hence, both Israeli and Palestinian acts of violence have been labeled as terror (by the other side).[73] Who is seen as a terrorist (and conversely who counts as a human being) is determined relative to the power structure within which such a discourse takes place, precisely because controlling the image of the terrorist assists in approving one form of violence as legitimate and denouncing the other as simply evil. This has been well understood by the Israeli forces (and the West in general), forming the basis for the exclusive alignment of terrorism with the Arab face post 9/11. However, acknowledging a complexity of violence that links both sides does not diminish the suffering of terror victims. Rather, such an acknowledgment works to unravel a hierarchy of suffering, which in turn is often used to authorize more violence.

Paradise Now complicates the image of the terrorist, focusing on Said's face as the site of negotiation. Playing on the preconceived ideas of the film's decidedly Western audience, an unkempt but likable Said gets his picture taken at a run-down photo studio, just before he is recruited by the terror group's ringleader Jamal. The photograph bears witness to Said's devastation, displacement, and apathy, yet also renders him somewhat feeble. Staring into the camera, his look is empty; his eyes are encircled by dark shadows and framed by an untidy face and haircut. In some sense, the photo mirrors the stereotypical terrorist image (albeit with great sympathy); however, it also secures the ambivalence of Said's face in relation to this idea. Later we learn that the photographer specializes in both martyrs and collaborators, heroes and traitors, tragedy and elegy, thereby foreshadowing Said's own wavering between these positions. The ambivalence is enhanced when the stereotypical face of the terrorist, which Said neatly conveys while working as a mechanic, is juxtaposed with the clean shaven handsome appearance Said takes on to carry out the attack, which seems to transform him into a completely different person. When Said encounters his "new" face in a mirror reflection, assuring himself that "you cannot alter fate, there is no other way," he ultimately disrupts the image of the bearded terrorist. The moment is juxtaposed with Suha contemplating the photograph of the broken young man, taken only hours before. Complicating the function of the face as a proof of identity, the various mediations position the face as subject to shifting processes of meaning production.

Paradise Now explores the productions of the face by interrogating ways in which the terrorist image is projected, discursively and technically, by way of political narrative, and through the creation of specific media representations. The film engages with intricate processes of media making, producing the terrorist image excessively through photography, posters, the martyr video, an enthusiastic use of mirrors and of course through the film itself. The "terrorists" in the film both humorously indulge in these images while also ridiculing their artifice. Drawing on a variety of these media, the group recruiting Khaled and Said makes a strong effort to communicate their politics by navigating established codes of terror and martyr portraits; however, the distance between the terrorists these images help stage and the human beings who are introduced by the film unsettles the process and, hence, subverts these portrayals throughout. Ridiculing the terror genre in order to remind the viewer that such mediations have little to say about the complex personal and political motivations behind the attacks, the film, in a self-conscious nod, positions these images as failed illustrations.

This kind of representational collapse is particularly obvious in the use of the martyr video, of which there are two instances in the film. The first is made by the group and pokes fun at the motif of the khuffyr-covered, machine gun holding terrorist, giving a dramatic speech. When Khaled records his message, the camera repeatedly fails to function, which leads him to deliver his speech less and less energetically. When the team starts to eat during the recording, Khaled is reminded of his mother, which prompts him to address her, advising her where to buy the cheapest water filters while holding back his tears. The scene locates the "terrorist" in the sentimental everyday of family activity, making the image of the fanatic seem somewhat absurd. By contrast, but to similar effect, Said's video message is performed with his trademark apathy and mute affect, leaving little room to understand his personal investments and reasons to carry out the attack. Both attempts, in other words, reveal an affective gap, preventing the viewer from assessing the men's motives. Later, the director seeks to explore precisely such objectives when Said gives his (second) speech to the group leader. Self-possessed, certain, and candidly addressing the camera, Said emanates affective authenticity when he explains why he wants to carry out the attack, and thereby presents the viewer with the "actual" martyr video of the film. This time, Said details what the occupation has intimately meant to him, having grown up in Nablus and having experienced his father's execution for being a collaborator. The personal account reclaims the face of the terrorist, providing a set of motivations, albeit not necessarily legitimizations.

Said's speech interrupts the discourse of terror rather than terror itself by disavowing its underlying dynamics of power and providing a discomforting counter-narrative. Disrupting the myth of the fanatic, Said reveals, to borrow Massad's words, that "what the discourse on terror seeks is the erasure of power relations as the central problematic of violence."[74] In other words, as long as the suicide bomber remains an irrational extremist, the other side does not need to engage with the way in which the violence on both sides is linked. In the case of Israel/Palestine, this dynamic is central to the maintenance of existing power relations and one-sided global support for Israel. As Edward Said puts it, "Zionism's sense of the world as a supporter and audience has played a considerable role"[75] in the shaping of the conflict, but also in the distortion of the reciprocity of violence.

The idea that the victim also constitutes the perpetrator is sustained by the image of the "faceless" terrorist; however, by addressing the audience Said articulates this structure of violence, explaining to the spectator that

> if you are all alone faced with this oppression, you have to find a way to stop the injustice. They must understand that if there is no security for us, there will be none for them either. It's not about power—their power doesn't help them... even worse, they've convinced the world and themselves that they are the victims. How can that be? How can the occupier be the victim? If they take on the role of oppressor and victim, then I have no other choice than to also be a victim and a murderer as well.

This reversal of power relations and problematic zero sum logic also exposes the imaginary of the suicide bomber who, through using the body as the last resort of absolute violence, seeks a utopian equality in death. Khaled explains this earlier to Suha who heavily contests the idea, insisting that equality cannot be achieved by means of killing, because violence sustains the conflict and its injustice. While Suha and Khaled's exchange questions the modes of violent redemption, it also intimates that the more walls Israel builds, the less it can engage with the issues that cause a need for security, leaving it vulnerable to future attacks. Conversely, Palestine cannot escape the sequence of violence either, as each form of violent measure is met by more violent counterforce. The two "sides" are locked in a cycle of deadly antagonism, where the avoidance of vulnerability is precisely what ensures its persistence. Hence, it is essential to look at the unconscious dynamics that intimately entwine occupier and occupied in the violent structure of walled life.

Crucially, *Paradise Now* links Palestine's physical and political territorialization to a corresponding psychological and emotional occupation. The film utilizes icons of spatial subjection to make visible the psychological deadlock that generates affective formations of enclosure. As Shohat puts it, "the checkpoint forms a metaphor and metonymy for structural violence even if no spectacular bloodshed unfolds on screen."[76] Tellingly, the film opens at the checkpoint, establishing Suha's return to her home, but also documenting the ways in which Israel's military mediates hostility through the organization of space and feeling. The architecture of violence testifies to a complete lack of Palestinian sovereignty; it also produces a kind of visceral, affective grip, played out via the tensions, anxieties, and sorrows confining the place. The apprehensive looks exchanged between Suha and the border guard create a chilling atmosphere, exemplifying the way in which (spatial) power aims at psychological defeat by way of intruding the personal (belongings) and affective realities of those who wish to cross the checkpoint. Assigning particular identities of power and subjection respectively, checkpoints, borders, and walls all reflect affective maps of (dis)belonging that design boundaries between "us" and "them," but also reinstate the power imbalance between occupier and occupied performatively. Accordingly, Said cannot go to Tel Aviv without a permit, but is restricted to the West Bank, where the psychological prison effected by his physical confinement finds expression in excessive boredom, a claustrophobic state of inertia, and a feeling of not being able to change the face of (his) reality.

The aggressive impassiveness experienced by Said and Khaled prior to their recruitment constitutes what Hage designates as the affect of colonial humiliation.[77] In this context, the psychological occupation produces a particular emotional charge, which is linked to feelings of political impotence and resignation or "the inability to dream a meaningful life."[78] Such affects invoke an atmosphere of constant submission and shame—an emotional grid lock that drives much of the action by the young men in the film. Reflecting on the meaning of the occupation (and providing a thinly veiled allegory for political castration), Khaled recalls memories of his limping father whose leg was broken by Israeli soldiers during a home invasion, after they made him choose between the left and the right one. Similarly, Said is marked by the indignity he experienced due to his father's desperate cooperation with Israel, which to Said epitomizes the military's ability "to exploit the people's weaknesses and turn them into collaborators" and which he identifies as "the worst crime" of the occupation. Fueling feelings of dishonor, resentment, and anger, both Khaled's and Said's memories attest to an all-encompassing "colonial affect,"[79] felt as a sense of political emasculation, which Hage identifies as the affective motor driving the social conditions of suicide bombing.

Giving shape to the political organization of such affects, Achille Mbembe maintains that the occupation of Palestine epitomizes a state of living death.[80] Mbembe refers to the "creation of death-worlds, new and unique forms of social existence in which vast populations are subjected to conditions of life conferring on them the status of living dead."[81] Drawing on Orlando Patterson's concept of social death and Baruch Kimmerling's notion of the politicide of Palestine, Mbembe explains that what is at stake in the occupation of Palestine is no longer a biopolitical distinction between the living and the dead, as Foucault would have it, but more precisely a disciplinary, biopolitical, and necropolitical concentration of power by which Palestinians are subdued to a number of political, social, psychological, and physical death(s) or what Mbembe call the "the most accomplished form of necropower."[82] In order to counter Said's doubts about the operation, Khaled expresses this sentiment literally, stating, "you said there was no other way under the occupation we are already dead." Later Said's final decision to carry out the bombing is wordlessly communicated when we see him resting on his father's grave, bombs strapped to his body, lying silently and motionless (as if) dead already.

The film, in other words, insinuates that terror attacks, at least in part, are connected to a fantasy of breaking free from the psycho-political structures of walled life. In this regard, Said's chilling decision to carry out the attack in the end is also an attempt to violently challenge the psychological walls of the affective occupation. Defying his own living death, Said seeks to contest Israel's necropower through an act of self-annihilation that, in the logic of martyrdom, is re-read as a means of transgression and liberation, or paradoxically, "a sign of life,"[83] as Hage would put it. This fantasmatic "logic," according to Hage, works as an "*illusio*"[84] constructed around a "highly masculine"[85] competition for symbolic capital, forging the "swapping of physical existence for symbolic existence,"[86] so as to reclaim a sense of control and even aliveness (in death). Hage understands this act as a social practice meant to channel colonial affect and to boost personal status. In other words, Said and Khaled participate in a fantasy of political (masculine) revitalization through death.

However, through the perspective offered (once again) by the women in the film, *Paradise Now* also challenges this masculine discourse of lethal agency and thereby questions the promises and principles of terrorism. Suha, in particular, defies the fantasy of masculine retribution, critiquing the rationale outspokenly. Her point further highlights the suffering the martyr *also* inflicts within the Palestinian community, mainly onto those who lose family members and loved ones to the cycle of violence—those who are left behind with no cathartic outlet for their pain: the mothers, daughters, and wives. Though she is a privileged outsider, who studied abroad, Suha is angry at the losses imposed by masculine vengeance, which is most explicitly articulated via her own difficult relationship to her late father, himself a martyr, who has caused her unspeakable grief by his absence. Said painfully repeats this vicious cycle, causing Suha to lose, again, a loved one to the same violent, and to her decidedly senseless, cause. Hence, Suha's position as both a victim of violence and an emotional advocate for change (either way) challenges the idea that terror can bring justice or redemption.

Ultimately, the film wrestles with the ambivalent intimacies of violent conflict without providing definite answers. A critique of suicide bombing is also reflected in the wavering positions of Said and Khaled, whose stands on the issue are anything but clear. In fact, it is through their questioning and reasoning that the film engages terror as a point of discourse and debate. Finally, the somewhat surprising change of heart for both, the determined Khaled (who backs out of the plan, after talking to Suha and considering his mother) and the hesitant Said (who ends up carrying out the attack after visiting his father's grave) complicates expectations about violent extremists. It also reinforces the gendered positions laid out by the film. In this way, *Paradise Now* attends to a visceral quality of the occupation, a colonial affect that erupts in shame, anger, boredom, or violence. The film thereby questions a readily available pool of suicide bombers; instead, it suggests that such acts are driven by the social conditions, personal experiences, and finally the emotional regimes that emerge within the context of walled life. To counter terrorism is then to dismantle the exclusionary politics that maintain structures of violence, including their accompanying images, deadly affects, and unconscious walls.

Feeling Occupied: The Cinema of Elia Suleiman

Focusing on the affective orchestration of the occupation, the cinema of Elia Suleiman humorously (and often tragically) destabilizes the violent structures of the status quo and, despite the director's claim that he has "absolutely no imagination [about what to] do with the wall,"[87] his films, like few others, draw out, the visceral qualities of a walled life. Regarding cinema as a possible form of resistance, Elia Suleiman engages with the mundane and absurd in order to visualize the claustrophobic space of Israel-Palestine, articulating the intersection of the private and the political as a form of comical choreography. Suleiman's work speaks of displacement, sketching an affectively flattened world and laying bare the ways in which politics encroach on the intimate spaces of the private, and even on the unconscious, of what he calls "estimated Palestine."[88] In this way, Suleiman's cinema expresses the affective occupation that troubles walled life, but he also disavows it by exploring nonlinear means of representation, which convey the absurdity of oppression as a form of exaggerated reality. Privileging the visual over the verbal, Suleiman recontextualizes Palestinian trauma with recourse to what Lauren Berlant has aptly described as "flat affect,"[89] a politically charged, deliberate underperformance and gestural deflation that in the case of Suleiman's films speaks to the dispossession and imprisonment of everyday Palestine. Suleiman's trademark deconstruction of narrative further works to disrupt ideas of finality and truth, particularly in their alignment with forms of nationalism, in favor of multiple trajectories of fantasmatic identification. The image in his cinema is hence decentered and destabilized, communicating the "absence of Palestine."

Negotiating the affective and psychological implications of walled life through everyday fragments of absurdity, Suleiman's Israel-Palestine trilogy, which consists of *Chronicle of a Disappearance* (1996), *Divine Intervention: A Chronicle of Love and Pain* (2002),[90] and *The Time That Remains: Chronicle of a Present Absentee* (2009),[91] reflects on the particular political climate of Palestine in its intersection with the private spaces of the director's family and immediate environment. *Chronicle of a Disappearance* combines a personal with a political diary in order to express the structural interventions that lead to stagnation and helplessness, transcribing an unbearable sense of passivity and waiting as characteristic of Israeli-Palestinian existence. Because it received Israeli funding and lacks nationalistic overtones, the film was boycotted by the Arab world, leading critics to accuse Suleiman of "treason, Zionism and cooperation with the enemy."[92] The next film in the trilogy, *Divine Intervention*, allows the tension built up in *Chronicle of a Disappearance* to erupt in more explicit depictions of violence, with "all hell breaking loose,"[93] as Suleiman, somewhat ironically, describes it himself. The film most notably engages fantasies of (female) empowerment and liberation, providing a sense of catharsis. *Divine Intervention* was received enthusiastically around the world, but its submission to the Academy Awards was rejected on the grounds that "Palestine is not a country,"[94] only to later receive the Judges' Choice Award in the 2002 Cannes Festival. Finally, *The Time That Remains* unveils the traumatic core of Palestine's confined (non)existence. Using his father's diaries, Suleiman gives an account of the conflict's development, or as the director suggests, its regression, starting with the crucial envisioning of the 1948 foundation of the state of Israel—the unrepresentable traumatic moment of al Nabka. The film thereby visualizes the return of the repressed, depicting the loss of the homeland through the lens of family history. Articulating Palestine's ambivalent status as "absent presence," in the political, historical, and affective sense, Suleiman uncovers the violent structures of un/feeling projecting walled life.

Characterized by a distinct under-performance of emotion or recessive expressivity, a Buster Keaton-esque comedy to some, Suleiman's films communicate a kind of "subtracted response to the urgency"[95] of Palestine's confinement, uncovering, politically and aesthetically, what Berlant might call a "structure of unfeeling."[96] Animated by a mode of flat or flattened affect, in Berlant's sense, Suleiman's cinema downplays the expected melodrama of a situation in favor of articulating a form of apprehensive muteness, which, at first glance, mimics the dissociative genre of trauma, but, on second view, more overtly "foregrounds affective diffusion" or "what is overwhelming"[97] about a walled existence. Pointing just as easily to comedy as "to tragic and traumatic situations,"[98] unfeeling in Suleiman's films remains subdued, repetitive, and even numb, as if to say that sense and emotion in Palestine can only ever occupy "an empty time, time that never passes"[99] or an affective space that is utterly besieged and "dominated by the other's emotion"[100] and trauma (hence denying Palestine an emotional ontology of its own). In other words, Suleiman's films respond to a world that, in one way or another, has been emptied out of "Palestine," as a place that is spatially and imaginatively inhabited, inflating its political, communal, and emotional substance. Articulating a voiceless existence, most powerfully, with recourse to the non-expressive charm of the director's face, Suleiman's films affectively scream of mute resistance, refusing "to have emotions for the other"[101] or to reproduce trauma within the familiar codes of Western aesthetics. Instead, Suleiman creates an affective remediation of Palestine's occupation in all its uniquely suffocating violence.

Suleiman's films utilize silence as a form of defiant witnessing. In all of his movies, Suleiman appears as the mute and expressionless character E.S. who connects the sequences through his vigilant presence. E.S. is an observer, through whom the viewpoint of the film unfolds, although he often cannot see properly or is ignored by other characters. E.S is the "absent" witness, as Getz and Khleifi point out,[102] whose powers are subsumed to the politics he interrogates with his look, but whose silent and relentless testimony nevertheless works to destabilize these structures.[103] As Suleiman put it in an interview, "silence is very political… [it] can destabilize a certain microcosm of power."[104] Silence expresses a reluctance to communicate within the structure of the status quo and thereby circumvents existing power relations, even if this means that E.S. is reduced to a ghost-like existence.

PALESTINE: DREAMS OF WALLS AND UNDEAD LIVES

Furthermore, silence challenges the arbitrariness of power by reinserting the Palestinian witness into an environment which subjugates Palestine's presence. This idea is enhanced insofar as E.S. does not invite the viewer's identification, due to remaining quiet and expressionless; rather, he puts the spectator in a position of witnessing E.S. witnessing and thereby enables a contemplation of the viewer's own (distanced/flat) positioning in relation to the political frame. In some sense, E.S. reiterates his own absence and brings it to the forefront of perception, as famously staged in *Chronicle of a Disappearance* when we witness E.S. witnessing a police raid in his own home, during the course of which the policemen seemingly remain oblivious to his presence.[105] Reporting on the incident, the police list all the items in the house carefully, before ending the call with the statement, "at last a guy in a pajama, over," thereby cynically testifying to their ignorance of a Palestinian presence, objectifying E.S.'s existence and rendering him utterly irrelevant. However, through his look E.S. "dialectically answer Zionist blindness,"[106] to use Edward Said's expression, unfolding the Israeli imaginary imposed on Palestinians as absurd, performative, and thereby somewhat ridiculous.

Drawing on the obscenity of performance, the controversial intervention made by Suleiman's cinema is then the application of humor to the harsh reality of occupation and conflict. The director disrupts genre expectations but is also capable of re-articulating the unspoken dynamics of power. The joke is embedded in and draws on a political choreography, uncovering the underlying structure of violence, making it visible in a scene, and hence accessible as a critical moment. On the one hand, this works by utilizing enjoyment as a form of resistance and catharsis, whereby laughing at the things one is not supposed to laugh at disrupts the rigidity of the existing power structure. Rancière reminds us that "shifting the generic frame can constitute a political act,"[107] precisely because "the world is divided between those who can and those who cannot afford the luxury of playing with words and images."[108] By interrogating the situation with humor, Suleiman, in other words, contests the existing division between those who have reason for laughter and those who are excluded from it by virtue of their dehumanization. Humor and laughter thereby constitute a humanizing, yet defiant act in the face of injustice while never striving far from the underlying tragedies. Always maintaining the anguish of the situation, humor carries the unspoken registers of suffering and exclusion with it, precisely because its function is to overcome these categories while simultaneously exposing them. As Suleiman puts it, "there is something not subversive per se but resistant about humor"[109]; or, as Dabashi explains, Suleiman creates "the precise critical moment when the depth of tragedy mutates into the height of comedy"[110] and then "remembers the dark dread at the heart."[111] Exposing the political layers of everyday interactions, the joke, as Freud reminds us, thereby always borders on the socially unspeakable.[112]

Suleiman's films mingle anti-authoritarian gestures with a sense of being overwhelmed in order to illustrate a dominant structure of feeling. For example, in *Divine Intervention*, after spending the night observing a sadistic soldier at the checkpoint, E.S. begins a staring contest with the settler in the car next to him. His attempt is assisted by sunglasses and a song working to build tension, as E.S captures the settler by means of his look. Contrasted with this demonstration of antiquated male competitiveness, the music turns into a female voice singing the lyrics "I put a spell on you," Natacha Atlas' rendition of Nina Simone's famous song, at the moment the settler returns the look and accepts the challenge; E.S.'s attempt to display overt masculinity is swiftly undercut, and the confrontation is re-read as simultaneously aggressive and flirtatious. As the lights turn green, the two keep staring (instead of racing), attesting to the impotence of the challenge and the inability to move forward, ridiculing the inert dynamics of chauvinistic nationalism. The situation is drawn out to absurd length without providing any cathartic result. The scene hence reveals a sense of entrapment, but further documents E.S.'s (and by extension Palestine's) incapacity to challenge the Israeli face-to-face, as E.S. fails to either match or change the connection between male heterosexuality and aggressive nationalism epitomized in the unmovable settler. The joke thereby punctuates the obscenity inherent to the existing structure of power and its associated walls by addressing atrocity through an absurd scene.

Exploring violence as a form of absurdity shaping ordinary crisis, Suleiman often utilizes the intimacy of the personal as the locus for political negotiation. The private space marks the focus of Suleiman's cinema and is explored as a means of apprehending the political, rather than simply escaping it. Starting from the cynical "premise" that "Palestine does not exist,"[113] as famously exclaimed by Edward Said and reiterated by Suleiman in various contexts,[114] the director turns to the intimate realm in order to renegotiate Palestinian absence. In other words, because Palestine is politically absent, it can only be explored by means of the domestic and the personal. Suleiman's private spaces (which are often the director's own) are "divided, disjointed, apprehended only bit by bit,"[115] offering contradictory scenes of (a)politicized existence. For example, E.S.'s parents, Fuad and Nazira, are often shown in their routinized activities, such as checking the mail or eating breakfast. On various occasions, they are seen resting and sleeping or staring out of the window, disengaged and (e)motionless, "waiting like the rest of Palestine,"[116] as Haim Bresheeth puts it. The whole of Nazareth (Suleiman's hometown) seems to be trapped in violent boredom and aggressive passivity. The camera frame remains completely static in these scenes and often provides the spectator with a disadvantaged point of view.[117] The image works like a prison that hinders movement and agency, underperforming or walling the daily routines of the protagonists. While, in the logic of Berlant, this recessive anti-drama might well "represent a big emotion under the discipline of comportment and crisis,"[118] it also (once again) intimates how the political emerges into the private in the form of a routinized pervasiveness, invisible yet prevalent.

The political infiltrates the private, provoking an internalization of the power structures because the psychological occupation "has seeped into the mind and body"[119] as Refqua Abu-Remaileh explains. Indeed, the political can blend in so well that politics appear irrelevant or even remain unrecognized. For example, when E.S.'s father feeds his bird in *Chronicle of a Disappearance*, the radio brings the political back into the private space; however, the commentators discuss the war in Bosnia rather than the events in Israel-Palestine. Hence, political violence subtly leaks into the private but, just like trauma, it is articulated only in relation to another time or space. This kind of transference renders the political inescapable, but also suggests that a retreat into the private is nevertheless politically insightful, precisely because it explores the affectivity of confinement. In *The Time That Remains* such a withdrawal recounts the immediate reaction of Nazareth's inhabitants to Israel's declaration of independence in 1948. As one of Fuad's friends puts it, "My family needs me; the country is lost." Engaging a delusional separation between the private and the political, this attitude bespeaks a domestic repression of the social oppression. However, this denial inevitably comes up against the intimate ruptures created by the political occupation and hence viscerally clutters the space with palpable tension.

Political deterioration and misdirected social violence erupt as the symptoms of social and domestic repression. For example, *The Time That Remains* chronicles a continuous "regression of the status quo"[120] in correspondence with the movement from active to inert resistance. Since the political frame cannot be changed and the dominant powers remain unmovable, the inhabitants of Palestine eventually "unleash their frustration against each other."[121] Violence seems to erupt as an absurd and irrelevant act of self-defeat or a non-sequitur, whose meaning is transferred onto another context. In *Chronicle of a Disappearance,* we repeatedly see cars stopping in front of a café. Each of the drivers subsequently attempts to beat his passenger but is prevented from doing so by the men in the café. Similarly, in *Divine Intervention* we see a group of neighbors involved in an extended beating, shooting, and finally burning of what turns out to be a snake. Such scenes pay witness to a collectively built-up, inert tension that is epitomized in the image of the pressure cooker of *Divine Intervention's* final shot. In *The Time That Remains* Suleiman eventually shifts his lens and lays bare the structures of political confinement Palestinians are subjected to. We see a Palestinian man taking out the garbage while talking on the phone. The man remains seemingly oblivious to the long gun barrel of a tank directly next to him, which follows his every move. In each case, the invisible violence of the occupation is brought to the forefront and at the same time it is obliterated or envisioned as belonging/restrained to the unconscious.

Political confinement emerges in the settings of private routines, recovering the invisible oppression from the depth of walled life. Suleiman's cinematic unconscious articulates itself by evoking a political choreography that creates the scenes enacting the visceral excess of repression. For instance, Suleiman negotiates the notion that the two sides are inseparably interlocked in the conflict, to the point where the Palestinian psyche lives under occupation of a trauma or "a foreign body" as Freud would say. In *Chronicle of a Disappearance* Suleiman exemplarily creates a scene, which he entitles "The hidden conscious of estimated Palestine," designed spatially as a basement at the center of which there is a chair in the colors of the Palestinian flag. We see the female lead Adan taking a seat. While watching a group of Arab men performing a traditional *dapke* dance on an old TV screen, she sings a traditional Jewish song about gazing toward Zion, which works perfectly in sync with the Arab dance. The scene has been read as "a powerful statement on shared culture between Arabs and Israelis"[122]; however, it also lends itself to Freud's idea that we are indeed most other at the point of our greatest intimacy, or as Rose puts it, "we are peopled by others"[123] in a way that Butler describes as "not only persecuted but besieged, occupied."[124] Hence, where the political is inescapable in the private sphere, it leads to psychological confinement. This is further acknowledged in *The Time That Remains* when E.S. pole-vaults the separation barrier in an attempt to escape the political absurdity of Ramallah, only to land in the obscene reality of his life in Israel. Neither the private, nor the political, or even the imaginary, realm provides an exit from the walled reality. Affective relief, however, is possible on the level of fantasy.

While the fantasy scenes in Suleiman's cinema highlight the absurdity of the occupation and its repressed realities, they also provide a sense of affective catharsis. Echoing Freud's notion of the dream, Suleiman utilizes fantasy scenes in which a strong sense of wish fulfilment drives the dream-thought or cinematic image. In this sense, the jump over the wall expresses not only the impossibility of a utopian escape, but also the wish to overcome this deadlock. The fantasy scenario, in other words, enables a move from passivity to action, perhaps even empowerment—a release that obviously betrays the "reality" of the situation, but is nevertheless experienced with affective authenticity. As Suleiman explains, "there is an activity, even if it's in the fantasy,"[125] and thereby the fantasy scenario pushes the viewer beyond the inert experience of the occupation, utilizing cinematic adrenaline as the cathartic moment of communal liberation. This kind of fantasmatic release occurs in *Divine Intervention,* in which we see E.S. causing a tank to explode by simply throwing an apricot pit at it, or we witness his girlfriend appearing as a Palestinian ninja single-handedly eliminating a special unit of the Israeli military. In another surreal sequence, we see the woman crossing a checkpoint at gunpoint, staging an empowering catwalk in which she seems to literally make the watchtower fall apart by virtue of her confidence. To Suleiman these forms of fantastical empowerment provide a critical reversal of the absurdity of reality, but they also work as a means of hope. Fantasy, used as the tool of visceral oppression, can also become the tool of affective liberation, challenging the effectiveness of Zionist fantasy.

Un/feeling the Wall

Ultimately, the cinema of Israel Palestine, in one way or another, makes palpable a structure of un/feeling pertaining to walled life. Envisioning the affective intensities and emotional residues of the occupation, the films under discussion foreground the ways in which political discourses are tethered to personal experiences that say something about belonging (or disbelonging) to a particular way of seeing or being seen in the world. Emotional activity translates into political form (and vice versa), producing a collective sensibility that simultaneously unites and separates the "two sides" and their respective cultural imaginaries. The act of dreaming the nation and affectively populating it through the relationships it enables and forecloses thereby marks a dynamic that provides insights into the fears and hostilities sustaining walled life—in this case presenting a lesson on how collective affects interrogate and shape the intimate lives of both Israelis and Palestinians. However, in confronting these structures of un/feeling the cinema of Israel-Palestine also points to ways in which the affective occupation negotiates power differentials about whose feelings count, whose face is seen, etc. In turn, such an engagement with the visceral repercussions of ideological and physical obstructions suggests opportunities to access walled life through the emotional ruptures that challenge the status quo.

In this sense, the films I've explored are primarily concerned with laying bare how a politics of avoidance evokes the breakdown of human relationships, the effacement of the other, and the occupation of the intimate. Shedding light on the unconscious dynamics of Israel's walling (*Lemon Tree*), Palestine's suicide bombing (*Paradise Now*) and the viscerality of a walled life (*Chronicle of a Disappearance, Divine Intervention,* and *The Time That Remains*), the cinema of Israel-Palestine draws attention to the importance of affective screens (in the protective and projective sense) within political conflict; however, it also grounds the violence inscribed into these settings in the (undead) trajectories of crisis and trauma. Of course, Freud identifies "affect as the operative cause of trauma"[126] and conceptualizes the affect of trauma as changing the tension of repression into compulsive repetition (of violence). In other words, the affects (both undead and newly produced) circulating on and through the surfaces of the various walls Israel builds chart a traumatic encounter for both sides that finds expression in the image and imaginary of walled life—one which is remediated by the stories told at the cinema, and, which, perhaps, animates processes of un/feeling the wall.

5

Mirror, Mirror, on the Wall: Ambiguous Projections

The West Bank separation barrier has gained global notoriety as a canvas for art in the contemporary political landscape. Photographers, painters, and performance artist from Palestine, Israel, and around the world regularly flock to the "security fence" in order to confront the political structure creatively, often by engaging in a shared artistic dialogue about ongoing political exclusion. The wall in Bethlehem, in particular, is famous for its elaborate graffiti exhibition, attracting busloads of curious (mostly Western) visitors eager to see the colorful bricks every day. While seemingly bringing the wall into full view, the wall's infamy thereby upholds a number of ambiguities that are worth to take a closer look at. For one, the reputed wall, uncannily, reverberates with an early argument by Israeli architects that the wall should be turned into an "attractive structure,"[1] capable of drawing international tourists rather than international critique. In other words, the separation barrier's popularity as a travel destination speaks to the unsettling aestheticization of violent structures and the ambiguous emergence of conflict tourism with all its affective pitfalls. Still, this questionable fame propels the wall's visibility as a message board for the world—one that has gathered increasing global attention for its ability to communicate the oppression it materializes. Projecting the barrier's politics into a space that otherwise largely renders its underlying ideologies invisible, art may hence channel another reflection of walled life's unconscious parameters.

In this sense, the art projections on the separation barrier's surface can be read as a means of recognition and civil disobedience, opposing the disciplinary invisibility facilitated by walls. At the same time, and perhaps more interestingly, they also draw attention to the wall's inherently ambiguous mediality. Of course, the act of creatively engaging on and with the wall is about reclaiming an occupied political space as lived in; it may even offer a personal (though often politicized) response to the inert experience of walled life. Projections of image and text create a "voice" that aims to challenge the grand narratives of the political situation, turning the wall into a medium of its own critique. Yet, such mediations always have a potential to be absorbed by powerful narratives. In this sense, visual protests operate in the hazy borderland between affirming, naturalizing, and even beautifying an architecture of imprisonment while aiming to disrupt, rework, or reclaim the structures they oppose. Wall art sits somewhat uneasy, yet, productively within this complexity, reflecting on the murky intimacy between artistic inscription and political walls. Two sides of the same coin, art and wall compulsively evoke and provoke each other, reeling ambiguous projections.

Crucially, the wall is at once a symbolic image of separation and a medium of its mechanisms and politics. It acts like a mirror by which the (political) identities are thrown back to the viewer, but it is also used as a surface of expression, a media screen, that allows communities to rethink and reclaim the meaning of the wall's efficacy—often with reference to other walls around the world. Indeed, Eyal Weizman explains that the separation wall works effectively "as a powerful image within a media economy of the conflict"[2] which has brought to Palestine "an international audience."[3] He asserts that this image resonates "within a Western historical imagination still engaged with unresolved memories of its colonial and Cold War legacies."[4] Similarly, the Israeli wall became an important touchstone for the Trump administration to prove a point about Western security politics, ostensibly legitimizing the US president's ambition to build a wall between the United States and Mexico. Recontextualizing the US border plans as part of a (successful) narrative of international walling, the Israeli wall worked as a frame for reaffirming the need to protect "a Western-style modernity"[5] as Ghassan Hage might put it. From each of these perspectives, the Israeli wall is capable of utilizing global narratives that situate the conflict, and its mediation, within a broader context of political division and (neo)colonial acts of segregation.

In fact, the wall in Palestine intimates (global) processes of cultural separation at the same time as it projects the specific political narratives cementing such processes. The wall hence manifests political oppression, but simultaneously it provides a material medium for resistance through art. Since politics has a spatial and aesthetic dimension, art utilized in this space can gain a political dimension. Politics create common landscapes that work to construct the affective, cultural, and spatial realities of those who inhabit them. In this context, Jacques Rancière asks, "what landscape can one describe as the meeting place between artistic practices and political practices?"[6] It appears that the encounter between the wall as a symptom of politics and as a screen for art presents itself as a literal manifestation of this "meeting place." Such an encounter must also be understood as a confrontation and emerges where a political practice is used to create an artistic one—or, more precisely, where a political wall becomes a screen for the art that seeks to resist it.

The artworks I want to discuss in this chapter project the ambivalent legacies of walled life in Israel-Palestine, introducing the face as a significant medium. Operating between affirming and disrupting the structure of un/feeling imposed by the wall, the graffiti, murals, installations, and photographs I introduce access the memory work of walled life, engaging its traumatic affects, and emotional investments, often by exposing, in one way or another, the intimate reconstitution of belonging. Engaging a dialectic between face and effacement, art makes readable, and sometimes forecloses, channels of mutuality that entwine political with human settings. In many ways, I am concerned with the ways in which art, wall, and face come together in the walled space of Palestine, often challenging one another and sometimes producing affective commons (for better or worse) that expose the ambiguity of intimacy as part of the conflict. Each presenting a screen in its own right, art, wall, and face articulate the properties of the visual as a vital measure of political orchestration: making people seen or unseen is a central mechanism of organizing affective space; it is also the central tenet that unites these three conduits and the complementary sensibilities (and surfaces!) they each provide. While each artwork engages these parameters to different ends, collectively these works renegotiate an otherwise repressed relationship between the two sides, unpacking and reworking, pulling apart and reconstituting the politics of vision.

The Graffiti Mirror

Graffiti is unsurprisingly the prevalent medium of choice in oppressed spaces. Allowing for a disruptive response to heavily constrained environments through the visual negotiation of different voices, narratives, and imagery, graffiti displayed on public surfaces inscribes the subjugated back into the space that has made them invisible. Put simply, graffiti constitutes a form of community and attunes the environment to debates about who or what is excluded from it. Hence, graffiti marks an inscription in which aesthetic and political practices coincide and rearticulate the public field of vision. In this regard, graffiti shares its mode of appearance with that of political walls, although it works to disrupt an order as opposed to sustaining it. However, this also makes political walls irresistible to graffiti. The medial capacity of the wall, its function as a mirror and a screen, appeals to the possibilities of expression provided by graffiti. Put simply, the spatial logic of the wall as the epitome of order and visual rigidity presents the natural antidote to the subversive and disruptive nature of graffiti—and vice versa.

The visual vocabulary of graffiti is traditionally associated with the invasion of spaces and the formation of subcultural exchanges. In this way, graffiti has always been linked to modes of politicized disruption in the sense that it functions as a response to the social needs of those who seek to affirm their presence in a visual field that tends to ignore them by subverting the visual order. This order, if examined in terms of the politics of visibility, has always functioned as a form of exclusion by denying certain representations as opposed to others. In this sense, graffiti can be read as "a mode of protest"[7] or a form of empowerment because it achieves an "unlawful disruption"[8] of exclusive environments, as Anna Waclawek explains, writing identities back into the visual landscape through the accumulation of signatures and images that are linked to particular groups or individuals.

Because of the potential to interfere with public order and to disrupt the visual occupation of the political, graffiti has often been juridically treated as a form of vandalism and even social crime,[9] while also attracting attention as an expression of alternative urbanity or counterculture. At the same time, graffiti artists have always laid an emphasis on their engagement with a subculture by creating a form of "internal dialogue with each other"[10] that is more concerned with its own styles and ethics than it is interested in communicating with the general public.[11] However, these boundaries between subculture and public have become increasingly merged since the 1970s and 1980s, highlighting graffiti's subversive potential on the border between illegality and high art.[12] The development reinforces the idea that the politicization of graffiti is not solely reducible to content and form, but more importantly emerges out of its context of exhibition.

In Palestine, graffiti as a surface expression demonstrates the wall's functioning as a screen by inscribing a narrative of resistance directly onto the wall's concrete. More to the point, the politics, which the wall seeks to naturalize are revealed, and in a sense debated, where those who are excluded from the public realm utilize graffiti to assert their existence and resistance. In the Palestinian context, such acts of writing gain particular significance as they mark an act of "voicing" and civil disobedience. Reinstating a Palestinian presence and re-inscribing it onto the material landscape, graffiti is capable of disrupting the existing power relations which otherwise deny Palestinians such agency. As Julie Peteet points out, graffiti invites response,[13] emotionally and cognitively, sometimes viscerally, and also reflexively. Such reactions, in one way or another, gain a subversive significance in a political landscape that largely ignores the Palestinians and remains impassive to their suffering.

In fact, graffiti challenges the public denial of Palestine's struggle. Highlighting Edward Said's point that due to always being spoken for "a Palestinian cannot be heard from (or represent himself) directly on the world stage,"[14] the use of graffiti on the West Bank separation barrier can be re-read as a form of voicing. In other words, the wall provides a significant medium for Palestinian resistance: It marks the visual articulation of a Palestinian voice. Of course, such writings are ephemeral, fragmentary, and often erased soon after they emerge. However, the very appearance of such graffiti undermines Israeli surveillance and problematizes what Said calls a Palestinian "civil extinction"[15] through forms of aesthetic expression, projecting the public image of a silenced people onto the wall as *the* screen of Israeli occupation. Since this screen is embedded in a global media economy of conflict, graffiti as the visualization of an otherwise unheard Palestine is capable of communicating a different perspective on the conflict to a global audience. Most often, the graffiti on the West Bank wall envisions Palestine as a "symptom" of walled politics, producing an image that (through other forms of media) readily resonates with global notions of imprisonment and resistance and thereby draws attention to a people that is otherwise largely invisible.

Additionally, the separation barrier plays a vital role in the visibility of Palestinians to each other, by mirroring a Palestinian presence to itself. One of the main consequences of the wall is the fragmentation of the Palestinian population and the separation of villages and communities. The division within Palestine makes it difficult for Palestinians to collectively organize in the face of occupation and further displaces them from the land. By extension, this undermines Palestinian national aspirations and the creation of collective and shared narratives, crucial for the attempt to "mobilize people around a common goal."[16] As Said explains, "perhaps the greatest battle Palestinians have waged as a people has been over the right (...) to possess and reclaim a collective historical reality."[17] Such collective affirmations are essential in the formation of cultural imaginaries that sustain Palestine as valid, authentic, and alive.

Graffiti is capable of creating identity-based community by initiating a form of "everyday" dialogue as a communicative accumulation of everyday exchanges about and among Palestinians. Hence, a re-inscription into the field of the visual does not necessarily have to be highly politicized in order to be effective. In fact, the most "banal" of graffiti (if examined in terms of resistance)—the writing of one's name—becomes an effective statement of identity, as it demands the recognition of the individual as part of the collective, inserting the human being back into the social configuration. In other words, the wall can function as a (Lacanian) mirror that makes a people visible to itself, reflecting their image back into the public space from which they are excluded and thereby assisting in the formation of (collective) identities. Israel's separation barrier is effectively turned into a political palimpsest for the world's exclusionary practices, capable of critically responding to Israel's politics while creating an archive of resistance. Many of these messages may hence be "devoid of any seemingly direct connection to the occupation or barrier";[18] however, it is the act of writing on the wall which deeply resonates with a project of Palestinian resistance.

Robert Sauders points out that during the first popular uprising of the Palestinians, the Intifada from 1987 to 1993, Palestinians made use of graffiti in order to circumvent media censorship by the Israeli authorities.[19] Graffiti became a means of political speech and enabled the dissemination of information, thereby assisting the organization of resistance and the mobilization of communities.[20] During this time, graffiti was regarded as "a low-level politically motivated offense akin to throwing stones or Molotov cocktails,"[21] as Sauders points out, and "a running political commentary on the progression of the uprising,"[22] as Peteet explains. It is in light of these (rare) moments of Palestinian voicing that the opposition to Israel's divisive politics in the form of graffiti can be read as globalized and not necessarily trivialized. On the other hand, embedding these messages in a global iconography of resistance raises the risk that the Palestinian voice might (once again) be overpowered by a range of international voices that seek to reappropriate the wall as their own medium without necessarily providing concrete help or input for the situation.

Indeed, the separation wall is endured by Palestinians, but largely painted and beheld by an international audience, complicating simple notions of ownership. The extent to which various artists effectively respond to the Palestinian situation before the eyes of a global audience cannot be decided unambivalently. On the one hand, it can be pointed out that the paintings and graffiti on the surface of the separation wall turn this political imposition into a tourist attraction that makes it "too easy for tourists to feel as though they're politically engaged."[23] In this sense, the separation wall appears as what Badiou calls the "world's wall,"[24] functioning as a depot for all kinds of statements from a global audience that range from the ordinary and banal, to broader commentaries on the state of the world. Such discourses transgress the particularity of the situation by drawing attention to more general contexts of human interaction that serve as prisms for collective ponderings of the everyday.

On the other hand, to dismiss the inscriptions on the wall as mere tourist memorabilia is to ignore the global response and affective engagements invited by the wall and thereby to invalidate the way in which these graffiti may work as political commentary. A global response is important in so far as it counters the wall's invisible pervasiveness. As the example of Berlin has shown, a political wall is otherwise easily normalized, internalized, and forgotten, overwhelming the space with a structure of un/feeling. Hence, the Palestinians may well not "need its presence underscored for them"[25]; however, in the struggle for visibility it is important that the presence of the wall is taken to a global stage in order to debate its impacts and ongoing expansion.

The Mystic Writing Pad

The wall can be utilized as a medium to pitch the Palestinian cause as part of broader political debates, precisely because the visual commentary also works to "reterritorialize the space as a global forum."[26] Bethlehem's wall works like an international graffiti stage, often showcasing political commentaries that also exceed the wall's immediate context. Displaying imagery that ranges from highly politicized to comedic or everyday statements, the various murals on the concrete segments accumulate an image and imaginary of the West Bank wall that can be readily broadcast to the rest of the world. In many instances, these images rearticulate and recontextualize the West Bank wall in relation to a larger phenomenon of (global) walling. Addressing a local and global audience simultaneously, artists have to operate within the tensions of Palestinian specificity and at the same time reclaim the issue as an international responsibility. In many cases, these works hence exemplify the shifting, rebuilding, falling, and resurfacing of the conceptual wall as a historical signifier of divisive politics. This referential wall is affectively saturated and operates as a memory trace that connects the political barriers from Berlin to Palestine and Mexico, revealing and concealing the histories these settings repeat.

The idea of retaining a history that lurks beyond the immediate surface of the wall, a structure of un/feeling in William's and Berlant's sense, also recalls Freud's famous analogy of the "mystic writing pad" to illustrate the (mystic) interplay between forgetting and remembering.[27] Explaining the functioning of the psyche's mnemic apparatus, Freud utilizes the writing device in order to showcase the relation between the conscious and the unconscious. According to Freud, the writing pad shares similarities with our psychic "topology" because the "receptive surface that can be used over and over again, like a slate"[28] works as a "protective shield,"[29] behind which "the permanent trace of what was written is retained."[30] Analogously, Freud suggests, our mind erases conscious memories in order to manage stimuli and perception, but nevertheless stores these impressions on the "wax slab" of the unconscious. As Freud puts it:

> If we imagine one hand writing upon the surface of the Mystic Writing-Pad while another periodically raises its covering sheet from the wax slab, we shall have a concrete representation of the way in which I tried to picture the functioning of the perceptual apparatus of our mind.[31]

Freud's explanation intimates a topography of the unconscious, which in turn may provide a way into thinking the unconscious of (political) spatiality.

I want to push Freud's analogy a step further and consider the wall as a kind of "mystic writing pad" in its own right. From this perspective, the graffiti on the surface may be ephemeral, temporary, and easily erased; however, it resonates with the affective structures and political unconscious inscribed "underneath" the wall's surface. The writing on the wall, in other words, establishes a complicated dialogue with what lies "hidden" behind the physical manifestation, precisely because the wall appears at the intersection between a political unconscious and its materialization. However, whereas Freud maintains that the mystic writing pad's invisible traces are only "legible in suitable lights"[32] and "cannot 'reproduce' [the writing] from within,"[33] the wall is arguably capable of inverting the function of the shield by means of the screen, thereby making readable the affectively charged, unconscious political space it delimits. In a way, the graffiti on the wall can hence bring to the surface the ways in which each political wall is underwritten by the histories and traumatic traces of another, revealing a hidden (or mystic) trajectory of walls around the world.

In its most obvious form, the memory trace emerges in the form of references and allusions, but it may also link broader narratives of walling as a way to recontextualize ideologies. For example, a famous (and much photographed) section of the wall in Bethlehem displays the slogan "Ich bin ein Berliner," a nod to Kennedy's infamous 1963 speech in response to the then newly built Berlin wall, but also suggesting that the Israeli wall is (no different from) the Berlin precedent. While attaching the Berlin Wall's histories of imprisonment and authoritarian control firmly to the Palestinian example, the statement also invokes emotional connections between the two settings and provokes an almost hereditary relationship between walls around the world in the sense that one resurfaces as another. The West Bank wall is hence utilized to create chains of affective associations with the familiar imaginaries of its Western counterparts, suggesting a reappearance of "old" problems in new contexts, in the hope of remembering these histories productively.

While the approach of reading one wall through the lens of another may (rightly) evoke concerns about universalizing ostensibly local problems into global narratives, the connections can also remember such interplays optimistically. In this regard, it could be argued that juxtaposing the heavily restricted space of the West Bank wall with a global memory of the Berlin Wall does not simply invoke the political crisis of ongoing division and control, but also produces cathartic associations, such as anticipating "the fall of the wall" and the freedom of movement in the Palestinian context. These images hence regenerate art's (and by extension graffiti's) ability to create an archive of resistance that is central to transformative political narratives. The ephemeral nature of graffiti, of course, poses a problem to the establishment of such a record, but it also mimics memory's instability and characteristic rewriting as a counterweight to history and official narrative, while simultaneously drawing on these trajectories.

Expanding the trace of the wall's collective imprint, the barrier in Palestine has not only been linked to the histories of walling in Germany; it is also increasingly used as a point of reference to make sense of more contemporary US border politics. Read in this way, the wall as a concept accumulates the xenophobic fears and neoconservative populism brought to the surface by the 2016 election campaign of Donald Trump, remediating these ideologies from Palestine to Mexico (and vice versa). Largely propelling him to become the president of the United States in 2017, the walled imaginary has been crucial to Trump's political rhetoric, mirroring his divisive politics in the evocative proposal to build a wall between the United States and Mexico. The West Bank separation barrier has subsequently served as a potent screen onto which the fantasy of a walled United States could be projected and enlarged. For example, in early 2017 Trump used the Israeli example to reinforce the effectiveness of walls around the world, explaining that: "A wall protects. All you have to do is ask Israel. They were having a total disaster coming across and they had a wall. It's 99.9 percent stoppage."[34] Despite the factual falsity of the statement, Trump's confident turn to the Israeli wall as a shield and model-wall demonstrates the ways in which it serves as a reflection for political ego ideals, actively disremembering the implications of political walls in the past and present. Accelerated by the neo-colonial power of walls to keep out (and zone in) an unwanted other, the US president used the interconnections of political barriers to project an international expertise of walling, invoking one wall in the context of another.

However, the separation wall has been utilized to both support and challenge Trump's proposal, highlighting the ambivalence of political walls as shields and screens once more. While Trump may be able to project an ego-ideal of "his wall" onto the Israeli example, the same mechanisms can be used to subvert his politics. Drawing attention to this dynamic Australian graffiti artist Lushux dedicated two murals on the West Bank separation barrier specifically to Donald Trump. Satirizing Trump's intense investment in the politics of walls, the first image shows the American president wearing the kippah while kissing a watch tower. The comical innuendo intimates Trump's libidinal attachment to the wall, and simultaneously jokes about the US president's overt reliance on narcissistic masculinity or need to turn everything into a phallus in support of his ego. Put simply, the watch tower plays out as a phallic object of affection (much in the sense that Trump Tower works to assure Trump's masculine credentials). Lushux's mural hence provides comic relief in relation to the terrifying persistence of the idea that "walls work"[35] and Trump's egotized commitment to the megalomaniac project.

Operating in a similar vein, however commenting on how Trump's politics in turn feed into the Palestinian-Israeli context, Lushux's second image more explicitly articulates the political relationship between the United States and Israel. The mural shows Trump placing his hand against the wall, again affectionately, promising to build "a little brother." The image makes a reference to a photo taken during Trump's visit to Jerusalem's Western Wall in May 2017, while drawing attention to the familiarity between Israel's and America's walls. It also firmly positioned the planned wall as the "love child" of the Trump administration, while critically highlighting a vitalized bonding over divisive politics between the United States and Israel. Lushux's art works as a reminder that while Trump had vowed to broker "the ultimate deal" between Israel and Palestine, his position had been anything but neutral. Trump's determination to debunk former US President Barack Obama's Iran deal led to an increasingly close relationship between the United States and Israel (and more so between Donald Trump and Benjamin Netanyahu), putting the Palestinians at a disadvantage in the negotiations let by the United States.[36]

Highlighting this point, Trump tended to his new ally by moving the US embassy from Tel Aviv to Jerusalem in 2018, de facto recognizing Jerusalem as the capital of Israel and effectively sabotaging the Palestinian's own long-standing claim to the city. The move provoked severe violence in Gaza and the West Bank territories, costing more than sixty Palestinians their lives. Poking (bitter) fun at Trump's alignment with the politics of walls, Lushux's mural reflects on these developments, while also suggesting a trajectory between the walls of the past (the Western Wall in Jerusalem onto which Trump originally placed his hand), the walls of the present (most pertinent exemplified by the section in Bethlehem onto which the mural was painted) and the walls of the future (which Trump planned to build). While remaining invisible on this mystic screen, such a trail of walling of course also echoes the resurrection of walls all over the world (e.g., Europe's new walls, Israel's Sinai fence, the partition between India and Pakistan) and those that came before them—again the Berlin Wall, but also the Irish peace walls, the colonial walls of European settlements, etc.

Furthering this visual trajectory of Trump's lasting love affair with past, present, and future walls, Lushux added another image in October 2017, cementing the intimate politics between Israel and the Unites States. Depicting Netanyahu and Trump kissing, the mural subverts the politics of male jingoism embodied by both leaders through a questioning of heteronormative aggressivity, and by mirroring the political "courting" between the United States and Israel. The image also, once again, remembers the Berlin Wall's authoritarian overtones on the screen of the West Bank separation barrier, referencing the Berlin Wall's famous *Brotherkiss* between Erich Honecker and Leonid Brezhnev, and thereby suggesting a love affair with Cold War dependencies. The image recontextualizes both Trump's and Netanyahu's approach to walls as the repetition of failed politics, while renegotiating the security discourse linking the United States and Israel with regard to the traumatic imprisonment symbolized by the Berlin Wall.

In this regard, Lushux's work operates like a mystic writing pad revealing the unconscious imprints that connect the graffiti mirror in Israel-Palestine to a trajectory of walling around the world. The memory traces revealed in these images not simply lend meaning to the wall by creating associative chains to the walls of past and future, they also intimate the ways in which these contexts draw on each other politically. Such works provide contextualization, but they also engage with the unspoken histories that inform the politics of walls then and now. Seen in this light the murals resituate the conflict, but they also work to showcase and highlight the wall itself. As Lushux puts it, "the wall is a message in itself" and hence the image may be comical and expressive, traumatic or referential, but ultimately it also foregrounds its exhibition context by making the wall visible as an enduring global issue of local politics.

The Banksy View

Of course, Lushux's work must be read through the lens of British artist Banksy's iconic work on the West Bank separation barrier, which laid the groundwork for opening the wall to an increasingly international audience, approximately twelve years earlier. Operating within a context of the wall as a global image and local confinement, Banksy's murals self-reflexively engaged the ambivalences that persistently work through the aesthetics of political walls. Because of the artist's popularity, Banksy's infamous murals on the wall in Bethlehem in 2005 increased the visibility of the West Bank separation barrier and its function as what the artist labeled "the world's largest open air prison."[37] However, Banksy's art has also generated large-scale "Banksy Tourism," drawing increasing numbers of Western spectators (and graffiti artists) to Bethlehem. His artwork thereby perfectly exemplifies the ambiguous intersections between affirming and interrupting a political structure through aesthetics.

Banksy's images evoke and transcend the setting of the wall in an effort to highlight ambiguous sentiments about utopian escapes from the heavily constrained space. We see a girl flying over the wall holding on to a handful of balloons, while a little boy paints himself a ladder; on various occasions, the wall opens up a window onto a beautiful beach or an impressive mountain scape.[38] These images comment on the wall as physical impediment by providing a contrast or a backdrop against which to examine the imposition. The exaggeration of this contrast plays with the wall's flickering status between visibility and invisibility. On the one hand, it can be argued that Banksy's work marks a "reclaiming [of] public space as a space of public imagination"[39] and thereby invites the spectator to circumvent the "barriers to thought and awareness"[40] that define this setting. On the other hand, his work turns the wall into a beautiful and photogenic travel destination and hence runs the risk of inviting a forgetting of the impediments endured by the inhabitants of the space.

Rather than resolving this ambivalence, Banksy incorporates it ironically into the images, literally depicting beautiful holiday spots as the unattainable point of escape. This cynical commentary is echoed in the artist's framing of the work, which not only points a finger at the "open air prison"[41] but further explains that the wall marks "the ultimate activity holiday destination for graffiti artists."[42] In other words, Banksy utilizes the wall's ambiguity as part of the commentary he is making, complicating the notion of visibility and invisibility. The concrete monstrosity is turned into a tourist attraction and thereby remains forgotten in its very visibility. Paradoxically this is precisely the way the wall's presence as a political prison can also be understood: as long as the wall is ignored by the world, the Palestinians will remain invisible. Tourists may hence not encounter the wall with an obvious political agenda; however, this does not mean that their attention cannot be channeled toward political activism.

Of course, the Banksy effect accelerated "wall tourism" and has drawn an increasing number of largely Western spectators to Bethlehem, who often encounter the political situation as a kind of byproduct of the trip. Taking photos with Banksy's art and buying prints of his work, many tourists do not seem to be overtly politically engaged in the local situation; yet, tour guides and locals make great efforts to communicate the politics that have led to the cementing of the separation barrier and other walls in the area, creating a didactic tourism, complete with explanations and colored illustrations on the West Bank wall. The dynamic remains ambivalent: While Palestinians have utilized the tourist phenomenon in order to "educate" Westerners about the situation, and hence use the attention in order to claim a long denied forum to tell the Palestinian side, the wall as a tourist attraction also uncomfortably spectacularizes a Western gaze projected onto the local situation, without necessarily procuring support.

Exploring and satirizing this ambivalence further, Banksy opened the *Walled Off Hotel* in Bethlehem in early 2017, capitalizing on "the worst view in the world,"[43] in order to comment on the political situation in Palestine. While the hotel actually hosts tourists and art connoisseurs, as a piece of architecture, it operates somewhere at the intersection between art exhibition, political activism, museum, and theater stage, provoking a range of controversies and ironies (as is to be expected from the artist). From a practical stance, *The Walled Off Hotel* has meant a boost to the local economy, creating employment, drawing (more) tourists, providing a stage for local artists and returning the profits to the community.[44] However, beyond these benefits the hotel also works as a political museum and piece of performance art in and of itself. Indeed, Banksy's hotel offers information about the wall while firmly situating the barrier in a historical context. Additionally, each of the hotel's nine rooms is a visual statement (like the wall itself), communicating politics through interior design. For example, by contrasting the lavish decor with the bleakness of the environment or by utilizing objects that are associated with the conflict (think: army bunk beds and bullet-strafed water tanks[45]), the hotel space is making a (deliberately unsettling) point about the political conflicts and divisions undergirding walled life/wall-tourism.

Capitalizing on the notion that the political efficacy of walls depends on their invisibility or effective "blending" into the landscape, Banksy's work does not simply question the wall, but also draws attention to the landscape it works in and through as well as the political legacies that have informed it. Crucially, these histories rely on the colonial practice of dividing up space as a way into marking boundaries and hierarchies.[46] Understanding this practice as a key feature of the walled life in Palestine, Banksy's walled-off hotel exuberates a distinctly "dystopian colonial theme" in its design. The interior draws attention to the role of the British mandate between 1920 and 1948 (the year Israel was established) as well as to the neo-colonial overtones inscribed in the tourist gaze administered by the hotel, the construction of the separation barrier itself, and ultimately in the view of the British artist reinscribing the landscape through his artistic interpretation. In other words, the hotel self-consciously foregrounds and commercializes the colonial grounding and atmosphere of walled life.

For example, the tea-room with self-playing piano and safari imagery references a persistent coloniality, which frames the situation in Palestine as the outcome of a Western history that posits the colonial exercise of violence as a defense.[47] The resulting construction of an exoticized other is at the heart of Edward Said's critique of orientalism, positioning the colonizer as the "superior"[48] agent of Western civility who conquers and tames a foreign land. Countless props in the hotel bitterly satirize this process, displaying a range of African wildlife and colonial furniture and firmly placing them in the context of Palestine's occupation. One of the walls is plastered with animal trophies, whose heads have been replaced by old surveillance cameras; a monkey in uniform serves as the concierge.[49] Banksy's hotel hence recontextualizes the walled life of the area within the historical and political forces of colonial conquest, treating the wall not simply as a canvas for images, but a projection screen for (self-reflexive) political narratives that stretch from past colonial exploits in the occupied territories of the other to the future of walling around the world.

In this sense, the art on the wall is caught up in inevitable ambiguities that open debates about public modes of seeing on the one hand and complicate art's function in the aestheticization of politics on the other. This is most poignantly reflected in the numerous graffiti responses both in favor and critical of Banksy's work that overwrite or copy his pieces, adding to them or dismissing them altogether.[50] Similarly Banksy's hotel and artworks have sparked ongoing debates about "encouraging the normalization of occupation" and Western decadence.[51] In his reflections on the murals, Banksy quotes a conversation with a Palestinian man which exemplifies this dilemma: The old man commented, "You paint the wall, you make it look beautiful," to which Banksy replied, "thanks," prompting the old man to respond, "We don't want it to be beautiful. Go home."[52] In this sense, graffiti art serves as a resistant, yet contradictory mediation of walled life, which is always caught between the two sides of concealment and exposure, security and vulnerability. The intervention of art into such a space/experience, hence, demands self-reflexivity on the part of artist and viewer. Inviting both blindness and seeing, the image always flickers between affirmation and challenge, disguise and exposure, protecting and projecting.

Gilo's Invisible Wall

Wall art does not simply run a risk of beautifying a monstrosity or erasing the Palestinians from a narrative of resistance. It may also actively assist the wall's effectiveness by supporting the invisible structure of political appropriation.

Indeed, art may assist the narrative of alienation, and thereby the narrative of the wall, by blanking out the wall and making it less criminal, less hideous, and less absurd. In this way, the former wall in Gilo,[53] an Israeli settlement in the south-western part of East Jerusalem, has gained much attention as an example of painting the wall into invisibility. Cementing the status quo and concealing the ostracism of the wall's imposition, the wall in Gilo projects a fantasy landscape that works to exclude and hide the other side, but also to hide the wall itself. The concrete slabs exhibit large murals that replace the landscape lost to the physical imposition of the wall with the psychical "reality" of an empty and peaceful land. The wall envisions an empty land, which awaits to be settled, literally painting Palestine out of the landscape and imagining an Israeli space devoid of Arab people. The pastoral view suggests a picturesque homeland marked by impressive pine trees (at times validated by actual tree crowns seen over the wall), romantic ruins of forgotten times, and distant idyllic villages of unspecified Europeanness.

In this way, the Gilo Wall exemplifies an architectural unresponsiveness to the landscape's actualities and achieves a kind of murky whitewashing of the conflict between Palestinians and Israelis. The wall stages Zionism as the negation of Palestine and thereby (again literally) inscribes a psychological barrier in the form of an invisible physical wall. However, this invisible wall is not simply a blockade, but also a medium, even if it is not explicitly utilized as such. The wall "speaks" to the side it is viewed from and also implicitly says something about the "other(ed)" side, which it seeks to displace. Unlike the graffiti found on the Palestinian side, the Gilo wall largely articulates an Israel based in the denial of Palestinian existence, which is physically enacted through the murals on the wall and their inscription of Palestinian absence. The Palestinian village of Beit Jala (situated behind Gilo's wall) is effectively blanked out and replaced with an idealized imaginary of the fantasized homeland.

The Gilo wall is plainly turned into an ideological screen, which does not simply efface the other side, but stages Zionism and its "immensely traumatic (...) effectiveness."[54] Such a dramatization of the national imaginary needs to blank out the wall in a way that evokes a vast and empty landscape, precisely because Israel is careful not to suggest that the separation wall marks a border. As Rose remarks, since "Israel seeks to be the state of all Jewish people... it supersedes the means of territory."[55] By rendering the wall invisible, this illusion of territorial infinity is maintained. Rose further suggests that this perspective marks "a historically embedded failure of vision,"[56] a notion which is literally reflected in the Gilo paintings. However, it has been pointed out that Zionism is perfectly adaptable to the staging of the fantasy and the creation of a dreamscape (see Chapter 4). "It knows itself as a child of the psyche, a dream, a figment of the brain,"[57] Rose explains, leading her to the conclusion that "like the unconscious, Zionism had to be staged."[58] In this sense, the fantasy landscape on the Gilo wall literally enacts and cements a notion of the national self in relation to a utopian idea of complete mastery over the "peaceful" land.

In other words, the Gilo wall exemplifies the vicious cycle by which Israel's architecture reappropriates the narrative that finds its physical manifestation in the very sight of the wall: Gilo cements the status quo by repressing Palestine and replacing it with a narrative that can only be perceived as coherent if Palestine is repressed. This narrative is a self-absorbed and narcissistic mediation of the national ego-ideal as self-contained, similar to the self-absorbed discourse mediated by the bare wall in the first place. Simultaneously, this mechanism stimulates the psychological blindness that allows the state of Israel to maintain an idealized version of the land, as the literal and metaphorical means of national self-protection. The dynamic is echoed in the wall's initiation as a reaction to the second Intifada after conflicts between Palestinians and Israelis escalated in the area. In the course of these conflicts, Gilo was attacked by Palestinian sniper bullets and large parts of Beit Jala were destroyed.[59] The wall, although controversial for its admission of defenselessness, was subsequently erected to protect the inhabitants of Gilo.[60]

Crucially, the construction of the Gilo wall (like the rest of the West Bank separation barrier) was conducted without the involvement of any architects and thereby resonates with a more general criticism about the "exclusion" of architects from the "security fence" project. The complaint relies on an aesthetic argument rather than an ethical one and goes something like this: In 2004 architect Gideon Harlap lamented in his campaigning speech at Israel's Architect's Association that the West Bank separation wall could have been beautiful or impressive (rather than disturbing and offensive) had the Israeli authorities involved architects in its design.[61] Harlap expressed a wish to turn the wall into an international attraction (apropos of Banksy) comparable to the Great Wall of China rather than a locus for international criticism.[62] Similarly, Weizman quotes Israeli architect Ayala Ronel envisioning "transparent plastic partitions"[63] where Israel had to part with particular beautiful landscapes and to further propose "camouflaging the partitions as landscape elements."[64] In Gilo, such a mindset eventually materialized when the then head of the culture department of Jerusalem's municipality, Shlomo Brosh, decided to hire Israeli and Russian artists to "paint the wall with the missing view, in an effort to alleviate some of the ugliness of the concrete slabs."[65] He justified this with the following reason: "We did not want to part with the view, but they forced us to. So we copied the view."[66] The result of this is a fantasy landscape beyond the wall, which simultaneously conceals and reveals an idealized national identity.

Gilo creates a blind spot in the landscape, but at the same time it mediates and renders visible a national dream about Israel. The wall mediates a (neo-colonial) fantasy element that expresses a national wish to erase Palestine ("a land without people") and start a new sketch ("for a people without land"). The Palestinian side is obscured and avoided, and the void this leaves in perception is filled in with a fantasy about the other. Renata Salecl's argument that the void of political discourse is in fact "the nation" and that fantasy functions as a scenario that conceals the impossibility of representing this nation, points to the traumatic structure of this dynamic. The fictionalized character of a country (such as Israel) exposes the nation as not a place, but rather "a narration about this land."[67] The fantasy of the "homeland" provides a structure for the national fantasy; it is "the scenario"[68] that allows society to perceive itself as consistent, a *Schauplatz*, as Freud would say, that needs to be filled with dreams about the nation. The nation is then always a fantasy projection, though this is rarely so clearly manifest as in the murals on the Gilo wall. Securing the structures by which the nation is imagined and narrativized, the fantasized landscape hence does not simply conceal the wall as such, but inevitably also reveals the larger fantasy upon which it rests as a symptom of politics.

Moreover, the wall as a medium functions as a mirror by throwing the gaze back at itself, reflecting a fantasy of Israel without Palestine and exposing the mechanism of denial at the heart of Israel's identity. The wall uncovers this dynamic, but at the same time renders it traumatic, since the nation arrives with a need to repress the persecution of the other. In the first instance, this parallels Israel's discourse of the Jewish state and its core narrative of victimhood (resulting from a traumatic history of Jewish persecution and genocide), on the basis of which it secures its effectiveness and coherence through blanking out another persecution, the violence it exercises against Palestine. Rose points out that "although it is one of the most powerful military nations in the world today, Israel still chooses to present itself as eternally on the defensive, as though weakness were a weapon, and vulnerability its greatest strength."[69] Complicated by traumatic affect, such an idea nevertheless remains unresponsive to the vulnerability of the Palestinians to ongoing occupation and violence.

However, if we take seriously that Zionism acts upon a shared fiction and does so effectively by establishing "a narration about this land" as the means of national aspirations, then the notion of vulnerability also intimates that we are dealing with the configuration of trauma with all its overwhelming impacts on the felt experience of the present. To be sure, Rose addresses her reader in *The Last Resistance* with the disclaimer, "You are analyzing a trauma."[70] In this context, the dream of the nation, and the dream of Israel in particular, does not simply work effectively but it also works affectively. As Rose further asserts, it is this "affective dimension, as it exerts its pressure historically, that has been blocked from view."[71] In this sense, the wall in Gilo, more precisely, serves to block the *affect* of Israel's trauma at the same time as it represses the Palestinian trauma from recognition. Hence, while the inscription on the wall evokes and symbolizes Palestinian trauma, it simultaneously mediates Israel's traumatic encounter with its own history. The wall acts as the very mechanism of trauma, of having to repress something intolerable from perception, namely the persecution of the (Palestinian) other.

While drenching the setting in affective complexity, the role played by vulnerability and trauma in Israeli identity formation may also provide an opportunity to invite the return of the other into the conflict. The politics of division, and hence the denial of an underlying relationship between Israel and Palestine, is as artificial as the Gilo murals on the wall. Israel and Palestine are most obviously intertwined in their shared attachment to the land, their dream of national selfhood and their sense of vulnerability. Both people share the intimacy of conflict, which binds them as "each other's other"; or, as Said puts it, "the actuality is that Palestinians and Israeli Jews are now fully implicated in each other's lives and political destinies."[72] A shared perspective, and perhaps a shared narrative, is then played out in the various layers of what Zionism means to the Israelis and what it has meant to the Palestinians in return.

The image perpetuated by the Gilo wall obscures this mutual perspective; rather, it turns it into a blind spot, signifying the "historically embedded failure of vision"[73] mentioned by Rose. The images on the Gilo wall, in other words, reconfirm the very narrative upon which the wall rests, cementing the status quo of Palestine's repression/oppression. This then marks a self-contained and ultimately self-absorbed mediation of national selfhood but manifests it as a normative mode of public seeing. Said explains that progress in the conflict can be achieved only "if both peoples make the attempt to see each other within a common historical perspective"[74] and he grounds this assumption in the inevitable relation between "the people of Palestine—Arabs and Jews—whose past and future ties them inexorably together."[75] As Said further explains, "their encounter has yet to occur on any important scale. But it will occur… and will be to their mutual benefit."[76] This reciprocal recognition demands forms of mediation that acknowledge and enable the relation between the self and the other. In this sense, the narrative of division must be opened to the "other side" in order to expose the self as vulnerable and to encourage a mutual facing.

Artists without Walls

Artists without Walls is a collaborative project between Israelis and Palestinians who utilize the wall as a medium capable of evoking transparency. In 2004 the group initiated a project in response to the Gilo wall, aiming to disrupt its philosophy of avoidance. Somewhat echoing the approach of the Gilo wall murals (but with a twist), *Artists without Walls*, too, played on the organization of the visual by disguising the barrier, effectively rendering the wall invisible with the help of projection technology. However, as a result the wall was literally made transparent and thereby expunged. Unlike the Gilo murals, the *Artists without Walls* project then framed this transparency in the form of an opening in the wall that did not attempt to erase the other; rather, it enabled a view to the other side by projecting a live transmission from each sector onto the opposite side of the wall, making each side visible to the other. Remarkably, the event thereby not only circumvented the other side's absence, but also created a kind of affective release, prompting "two hours of cheering and waving,"[77] and thereby (at least temporarily) unsettled the structure of feeling imposed by walled life. If Gilo blocked the traumatic affect of Israel-Palestine's emotive entanglement via the wall, *Artists without Walls* managed to discharge the encounter.

The installation acknowledged the wall's presence and used it as an affective screen: producing acts of mutual seeing, and thereby laying the grounds for the affective commons between the two sides. Reflecting on the traumatic erasure mediated by the Gilo wall, the artists rested their endeavor on the presumption that "the wall is merely an expression, in a concrete form, of what is already there, a high degree of segregation and wish for separation, a mentality, a feeling which is widely present in the public [...]."[78] By denouncing such a "mentality" as resting upon a wish, the artists implied that in actuality a narrative may also be shared and that a different structure of feeling can be made possible. The premise echoes the notion that Palestine and Israel are already implicated in an indivisible relationship that exposes the wall's psychological barrier as a fantasmatic division from the other. For the artists to work against the wall, then, meant to be "working against this, changing the mentality,"[79] and enabling joint forms of community or a shared "intimate public,"[80] as Berlant might put it. Reclaiming public space as a medium of public bonding and mutual recognition in order to affectively reorganize the walled space, the installation aimed at a momentary overcoming of the wall as an affective gridlock, thereby disrupting normative modes of public vision and traumatic blindness.

In other words, *Artists without Walls* reintroduced the dynamics of engagement into an otherwise restricted and rigid political space, reworking the emotional setting of the conflict by enabling human interaction. The event thereby created an image of bonding and empowerment, achieved by acts of looking and gesturing as the condition of mutuality. Involving artists and communities from both sides of the conflict, there was a sense of activity and agency, an affective charge, pervading and animating the project, thereby unmistakably challenging the rigid immobility cemented by walled space. Of course, such forms of stasis are encoded in the "lifeless" imagery of the Gilo murals that depict landscapes devoid of humans and thereby foreclose the possibility of human encounter. The *Artist without Walls* project, on the other hand, set in motion what can be described as community effort, accompanying the event with meetings, discussions, and mutual exchanges. *Artists without Walls* hence resonated beyond the moment of transparency projected onto the wall, because the project ultimately reintroduced (perhaps somewhat released) the human space concealed beneath the projected ideological landscape.

As a result, artists and community disseminated a variety of activities, debates, and meetings, each challenging the stasis of walled life. Terry Boulatta, a Palestinian teacher and member of the group, recounts her impressions of the event as follows:

> Our Israeli artist friends brought two projectors. The Palestinian community around the wall brought us electric cables and chairs. People gathered to watch what was happening. When it was totally dark, the projectors screened people standing on one side of the wall to the people standing on the other side of the wall. My neighbors came down to salute their family members who came to the other side. After two hours of cheering and waving the projectors were turned off. The Israeli and Palestinian artists came around to our neighborhood for tea and dancing. We felt very victorious.[81]

In this way, the artistic event was capable of creating community through participation and further enabled personal experience of a political space that otherwise denies such possibilities (of facing, waving, dancing, etc.). Hence, the *Artists without Walls* project not only projected an affective overcoming of the wall, but more precisely expressed a new political setting—turning the wall into a medium communicating the other's presence.

The affective responses evoked by the *Artist without Walls* project: the spontaneous expressions of excitement erupting on the two sides upon seeing each other rearticulate the repressed relationship animating the conflict. Contrary to the division invoked by the wall, affect here becomes the catalyst of encounter and potentially provides what Berlant calls an "affective register of belonging."[82] In this case, community is defined by both Israelis and Palestinians who have a common interest in challenging the wall and the setting of occupation.[83] Although this ambition is restricted by the powerful political reality of an unequal conflict, such an endeavor is nevertheless politically relevant, precisely because public spheres are always, as Berlant asserts, "affect worlds" to which people are bound by feeling and in which they negotiate a "common interestedness."[84] In other words, the "affective projection"[85] alludes to the artist's statement about the need to also change a (public) *feeling*. It allowed them to develop a shared interest in abolishing the separation evoked and symbolized by the wall and the traumatic mindsets it manifests. Berlant insists on the importance of such felt encounters in the political realm. "A public's binding to the political is best achieved," she writes, "neither by policy nor ideology but the affect of feeling political together."[86] The affective channel provided by the *Artists without Walls* projection hence enabled a new binding of communities.

In this scenario, affect gains a double function, evoking a structure of feeling that can either support the walled space or somewhat "unfeel" it. On the one hand, traumatic affect alludes to the fantasmatic dimension of the politics that create the wall, as it underpins (and blocks) the underlying relation to the other (side). This is important, as Rose points out, precisely because when it comes to challenging the intricacies of the Israeli imaginary "reason will not settle it. You cannot argue with a dream."[87] A shared affect, as released by *Artists without Walls*, however, may (at least) redirect the meaning of this projection and unlock the affective prison of walled life, admitting the other into full view. In this context, Freud reminds us that ultimately affect is true to the repressed, rather than serving the disguise of fantasy.[88] At the same time, affect individuates vulnerability marking the "body's belonging to a world of encounters"[89] as reflected in the mutual response to facial expressions and visceral reactions of dancing and waving. Bodies and faces sharing affect thereby also stage the human as the site of conflict. In short, those affected by the politics of erasure reinstate their presence and relationality by virtue of their body and mutual facing, hence providing the means for a shared human experience.

Face2Face

A mutual facing is intimate, but by far not always peaceful. The assumption that the face-to-face encounter lies at the heart of a politics of recognition is grounded in the sense that the other's face works like a mirror of the self, enabling the exchange of affective channels through empathy. Emmanuel

Lévinas imagines this encounter as transformative insofar as the other's vulnerability (as reflected in the face) posits an ethical demand or an insistence to respond.[90] Conversely, such forms of recognition harbor a potential to erase the other behind one's own reflection—or more precisely, in the mirror of the other's face. Effacing the power relations that structure the encounter, such recognition relies on the omission of the other's difference (rather than preserving a radical alterity as Lévinas would have it). In order to evoke the face-to-face as a politics of recognition, it is therefore essential to challenge the universalizing appeal of mutuality; instead, the face-to-face encounter must be read as a form of confrontational intimacy, mediating the circuits of conflict, affect, and even violence that structure the encounter between one's self and one's other.

Facing the other intimates that the other's face mirrors my own face, relying on channels of mediation. It is then not surprising that Roland Barthes identifies the creation of the body in the feeling of posing in front of a camera—in the act of being photographed. Barthes suggests that the camera creates the body,[91] which is according to Judith Butler "political[-] in part by virtue of social vulnerability."[92] To quote Susan Sontag once more in this regard, "to take a photograph is to participate in another person's (...) mortality, vulnerability, mutability."[93] Portrait photography, especially when framed by political conflict, hence mediates an attempt to create a socially relevant, face-to-face encounter aware of its own violent intimacy, potentially resurrecting the body in the landscape of effacement, posing one affective surface (the face) against another (the wall). Sharing vulnerability in this way can be unequal; however, it points to the capacity of mediation to reconfigure the realm of the possible by mutually exposing the other and the self through channels of vision and feeling. Recognizing such an intervention then becomes a political act, demanding a negotiation of the intimacy between the self and the other—an intimacy in which the onlooker is always also mirrored and implied.

The 2007 French project *Face2Face* by artists JR and Marco draws on this capacity of the photograph by screening the face of the other as the site of shared intimacy. The project thereby seeks to question grand narratives of division; instead, it reinstates a relation with the enemy. *Face2Face* returns to the notion of facing as a straightforward challenge to effacement and offers engagement with the intimacy of walled life. The project collects portrait photography of everyday people, shot with a 28-millimeter camera (and thereby allowing for maximal closeness of the subject), who make "funny faces." The close-ups are then enlarged and presented in pairs of shots, each projecting an Israeli and a Palestinian who share the same occupation side by side.[94] The images were shown in what the artists themselves called the "biggest illegal expo ever"[95] on(to) both sides of the wall and in several Israeli and Palestinian cities. JR and Marco explain the idea of the project as follows: "With our project, we wanted to show the face of 'the other'... to reveal the complexity of the situation to show a resemblance in those expressions."[96] The notion of a face-to-face, in other words, reinstates the presence of the other, demanding engagement with the other's reality. Encountering the other through facing, through mirroring, and by screening the self in the other, the artists negotiate intimacy and empathy. As Barthes writes in *Camera Lucida*, "The photograph is the advent of myself as other,"[97] which works to him through channels of looking, but which also indicates a recognition of the other as indivisible from the self.

Citing the political encounters that run through individual life paths, faces tell stories of walled life: each line, each smile, each expression is affected by what has come before, archiving the intimate dynamics of grand narratives. The photograph makes available an encounter with these stories, allowing the viewer to linger and to examine the face, without concrete knowledge of the picture's reality. In this instance, the face intimates forms of sincere doubling and silly caricature at once. To be sure, Lévinas reminds us that the notion of resemblance implied by the image does not sustain a direct encounter with reality; rather, it creates a "shadow," which, in a sense, is "more real than reality"[98] resonating with the perhaps utopian sense of commonality suggested by the photographs. JR and Marco's faces do not specify a situation of violence and they do not attempt to directly communicate a sense of suffering, conflict, or power. Instead, they manifest silliness and humor as the ultimate means of human connectivity. In this instance art "does not belong to the order of revelation"[99] in the sense that it discloses the conflict. Yet, the "caricature" of resemblance subtly invites us to rethink the face as a site of narrative. *Face2Face* makes use of the comical face to probe the narratives about the other and in particular to question the separation between other and self.

The images show the face as a site capable of reinstating specificity, but the (human) difference implied by this process is simultaneously questioned in the way the faces resemble each other. In this instance, caricature exposes common social roles and affirms, as Sontag explains, that "the camera cannot help but reveal faces as social masks."[100] Exaggerating this idea, the images play with modes of expressivity as forms of caricature and exemplify the face as the site where being and being a picture coincide.[101] In other words, we are reminded that the "person bears on his [or her] face (...) always [his or her] own caricature"[102] or a social and political mask. The photograph in this sense does not reveal the face as such, but represents the mask it bears as an image, a notion which in the case of the *Face2Face* project is simultaneously meant to unsettle the image. The dynamic echoes Barthes claim that "the photograph cannot signify except by assuming a mask."[103] To Barthes then it is only through the lens of these masks that a face is made "into the product of a society and history."[104] Consequently, "the mask is the meaning,"[105] a meaning which in the *Face2Face* installation expresses a relationship through the shared narrative of everyday occupations and activities. At the same time, the images attach these resemblances to social roles and occupations but not to nationality, effectively producing commonality on the level of the broadly social.

The relationship between self and other, the face-to-face of two sides, is primarily an instance of intimacy negotiated along the lines of a particular encounter. Such intimate encounters are potentially both violent and peaceful, too alienated and too close, but they negotiate an ambivalent relationality, despite the imposition of borders or walls. In fact, intimacy itself foregrounds all kinds of conflicts, divides, and ambiguities. It is grounded in the exchange of affects and feelings that have to be negotiated as they shift perspectives and relationships. Berlant asserts that "in its expression through language, intimacy relies heavily on the shifting register of unspoken ambivalence."[106] Such exchanges are conflict-laden, even violent, and sometimes traumatic; at the same time, they insist that intimacy is a dynamic, which we constantly "negotiate" in relation to others. The photograph can provide the means of such a relationship, but it works as both a tool of power, implying a potential aggression, as Sontag points out, and a means of reaching out, by making things closer, "like a pair of binoculars with no right or wrong end."[107]

Face2Face establishes intimacy by way of the photograph, its particular artistic method, precisely in the instance of Barthes's "posing" to create a body. The 28 millimeters lens only allows for a few centimeters of space between the subjects and the artist, who is involuntarily "listening to their breath."[108] This implies a point of closeness and intimacy that demands trust and produces a negation of separation (reflected in the images) in order to make room for a new way of looking (at each other). As the artists assert, "this intimacy does not distort the faces but offers an original perspective."[109] *Face2Face* brings the other closer—so much so that it becomes hard to distinguish the other from the self. In most instances, people were actually unable to tell the Palestinian and the Israeli apart.[110] In this sense, the faces are indeed "more real than reality," reinstating a relationship that is otherwise repressed in the sphere of walled life. The face in its pure expressivity rehumanizes the political setting by exposing the other and the self as intimately related—for better or worse.

Projecting this perspective into the political landscape (literally posting the images onto the wall), *Face2Face* accomplishes the dissemination of intimacy, face-to-face within the public eye, and thereby the project renegotiates the politics of vision. Berlant explains that "the inwardness of the intimate is met by a corresponding publicness."[111] The ideal of the democratic public sphere hence rests on "the advent of intimacy as a public mode of identification and self-development."[112] The intimacy of and in the *Face2Face* portraits projected on the wall exemplifies this closeness between politics and the intimate of the everyday. The project reinstates the faces that sustain and endure the politics of division, but it also turns the wall into a public screen of self-reflexivity and self-development. Portrait photography is itself strongly associated with privacy, but the intimacy it generates here is, in resonance with Berlant's understanding of intimacy, indivisibly connected to a "narratives about something shared."[113]

The perspective provided by JR and Marco encourages the viewer to consider a common narrative between Israelis and Palestinians, at the same time as the project reminds us that this relationship is already at work. The images project "commonalities" back into the political setting of walled life, which otherwise signifies division. Berlant suggests that "spaces are produced relationally,"[114] as borne out by the juxtaposition of multiple realities that recreates the walled space through the intimacy generated by the images and the similarities they reveal through mirrored facial expressions. The political space in which the wall erupts as a symptom is then reconsidered through shared channels of feeling and thereby creates a space of and for engagement with walled life. Communicating personal narratives through the faces that address the cameras within their given political context, JR and Marco provide a vehicle to retell the narrative of the wall from the point of view of the human beings it works to hide on each side.

Finally, the face reintroduces affectivity as necessarily constitutive of (and constituted by) the realm of the political and the narratives that strengthen it. What is of interest about the faces in the photograph makes itself felt if we allow for an understanding of intimacy as a part of politics (rather than its opposite). The image of the face can express, and affectively so, an experience of humanity in a political space rather than simply an image of it. Barthes writes that "whatever it grants to vision and whatever its manner, a photograph is always invisible: it is not what we see";[115] rather, "the photograph touches me if I withdraw from its usual bla bla to say nothing, to shut my eyes, to allow the detail to rise of its own accord into affective consciousness."[116] In other words, we are asked to make an affective investment in response to the image.

Such a notion of responsiveness as responsibility, or the ability to respond, must be created in resonance with a relevant political consciousness, but it is ultimately accomplished only when the photograph thinks beyond itself to "feel, intuit—what is beyond it, what the reality must be like if it looks this way."[117] In this sense, the *Face2Face* project is most subversive at the moment we do not consider the faces as representations of Palestinians and Israelis—or even of an Israeli-Palestinian commonality, but when we understand them to communicate the incommunicability of human experience to our own specific position as viewers. In this regard, it is important to point out that the images ultimately do not face each other (they are projected side by side); they face the public eye and therefore the viewer. The intimacy of the face-to-face is hence taking place between the photographer and the subject, though it is mediated by the onlooker, who is situated in a broader public field of vision. To look at these photographs is then to be asked to respond from one's own position, because the onlooker is addressed and individuated by these faces. Again, such a response may be understood as a form of responsibility. Being responsible is then to be open, even vulnerable, to the face and its affective circuits that link the self and the other and project them side by side. When the face becomes a pure expression, rather than a signification, it may in fact encourage an affective encounter to interpret and (re)experience the particularity of collective conflict.

All the Way to Mexico

The artworks displayed on political walls (re)negotiate the politics of walled space and the way it makes those living in its shadow see each other and themselves. In this regard, art is capable of reorganizing the field of representation produced by the wall, including its structure of feeling and the way it directs political vision. Art, may it be in the form of graffiti, installation art, murals, or photography, thereby negotiates the relations between different registers of the visible and the feelable. This poses an interesting dilemma, whereby one affective screen (the wall) is confronted with another form of emotive projection (art), suggesting that art and wall imply each other ambiguously, potentially reinforcing, or else, severely challenging one another. Renegotiating the politics of vision, the artworks under discussion, in one way or another, engage with this entanglement and, in the course of this, reveal the significance of memory, fantasy, and intimacy in sustaining and undoing the conflicts of walled life.

However, turning the structure against itself and providing new forms of aesthetics, these artworks also enable a reorganization of political spaces and ultimately walled life. In many cases, wall-art in Palestine achieves *other* forms of identification while commenting on the constitution (and shifting meanings) of the political situation. This may assist in challenging the politics of walls and working through the traumatic experience sustaining a walled life in the area. It also lends itself to rethinking the appearance of walls in other parts of the world. Ultimately, it is through means of the imaginary, the fictitious, and the artistic that the boundaries of the political can be renegotiated as political landscapes are reconstructed and sometimes momentarily overcome. Correspondingly, the work of art must operate within the structures it seeks to challenge and thereby always runs a risk of being absorbed and re-appropriated. It is precisely this ambivalence that allows art not only to challenge the logic of the political via means of the fantastic, but to lay bare the structural entanglements between politics and fantasy.

Crucially, the wall in Palestine consolidates the political fantasies, neo-colonial narratives, and affective legacies of Israel; yet, these same structures are also reimagined in other context, sometimes, as in the case of the United States, using the West Bank separation barrier as a kind of template. In mediating the political landscapes of walled life, condensing local and global histories, the West Bank separation barrier, as both a mirror and a screen, provides a frame (in the literal and the epistemological sense) through which to apprehend the politics of contemporary walling, fencing, and barricading. Both critically recalling a means of imprisonment familiar from European history and projecting a neo-colonial ego-ideal central to US border-fantasies about the future, the West Bank wall can be read as medium of the traumatic past, the "colonial present,"[118] and divisive future. Wallart persistently renegotiates these meanings intimately, provoking a mutual facing and affectively reorganizing the structures of feeling pertained by the wall. It is important to remember that these affective circuits travel far and wide: from the walls of the past, such as the one in Berlin, to the walls of the future: from Palestine all the way to Mexico where the specters of walled life persist.

6

Mexico: Colonial Ghosts, Walled Minds

Long before Donald Trump cemented the idea of a wall in the US American imagination, the US-Mexican border preluded a structure of otherness while physically separating, perhaps like no other barrier, the Global North from the Global South. Often referred to as the "Great Wall of Capital,"[1] the US-Mexican border is one of the largest and most controversial border regions in the world, provoking reflections on contemporary forms of militarization, cultural othering, and spectacular enactments of national imaginaries. Similar to the West Bank separation barrier, the US-Mexican border exposes the wall as a tool of colonial occupation, structuring, zoning, and enclaving the other as a means to highlight and to fortify sovereign power, while revealing "a tremulousness, vulnerability, dubiousness, or instability at the core of what [it] aim[s] to express."[2] However, the US-Mexican border also shares its ghosts with the Berlin Wall, insofar as it blocks and blinds a closed-off national identity and manifests a kind of haunted landscape in the service of producing and projecting fantasies about the other (side). In this regard, the border mediates forms of imprisonment that uncomfortably reverberate with the authoritarian control of the GDR, but also reproduce the legacies of colonial violence. Collapsing these pasts in the present (and increasingly anticipating a variety of walled futures) the US-Mexican border attests to the mending (and even suspending) of laws in order to stage ever more bellicose forms of sovereignty, "walling up democracy"[3] and minds (and not just a nation), as Sundberg asserts.

While enacting division politically and culturally much in the way that the Berlin Wall and the West Bank separation wall have showcased, the US-Mexican border also differs from these walls in the sense that it appears to be trapped in a perpetual state of materialization. Since it is not quite a wall of brick and concrete (yet), the US wall mainly exists as an affective and effective imaginary, a fantasy or specter, haunting American politics—be it in the form of Trump's proposal to build "a big fat beautiful wall,"[4] as a symbol of US American bigotry, or as a lived obstacle to those seeking to cross into a new life. Of course, the US-Mexican border also manifests itself as partial fencing and even concrete blocks, while also entailing a lethal desert and the dangerous currents of the Rio Grande—all of which substantiate political ideologies with physical obstruction. Concrete or not, as Roger Bartra puts it, this border is experienced as "a wall we can only cross if we have the necessary documents."[5] It prominently functions as a restrictive death zone, by which the im/permeability of the American way of life is solidified. From the US side the imaginary of the wall hence serves to assuage a psychical wish for protection and containment,[6] ghosting Mexico, while from the *other* side it works as a means of social, political, and cultural exclusion that anxiously blends place with grief and fantasy. In this regard, it is helpful to consider the US American wall as a formation of Western imperialism, projecting colonial (anti)relations as well as organizing a logic of human hierarchization that recalls the ghosts of the past.

Linking contemporary border politics to the history of the American frontier, the US-Mexican border makes itself felt through a politics of spectrality. As Eve Tuck asserts "the United States is permanently haunted by the slavery, genocide, and violence entwined in its first, present and future days."[7] This sense of haunting procures a kind of productive *after-life* of these histories, animating "repressed or unresolved social violence"[8] as Avery Gordon might put it and thereby it invokes a particular form of political affect, or "creative anxiety"[9] apt at describing the difficult memories, experiences, and prospects of walled life in the United States/Mexico. In other words, the specter of the border as wall impresses upon an architecture of haunting, attaching the divisive feelings of unresolved trauma (or ghosts) to processes of barricading, and simultaneously somewhat punctuating the past in the present, the self in the other, etc. Building on this notion of spectral wounding and utilizing Maria del Pilar Blanco's sense that haunting insists on "that transnational, transcultural anxiety of the tensions that are occluded, but nevertheless palpable within a specific American nation,"[10] I want to explore the US-Mexican border as a ghostly remnant or impending arrival that registers particular kinds of social violence in past and present—sometimes blatantly and other times more discreetly—while always anticipating (and partly achieving) to materialize the wall in the physical and psychological sense.

In other words, the US-Mexican border must be viewed in its specific historicity, but it also takes us beyond its own context, referencing its precedents in Berlin (the wall of the past) and Palestine (the wall of the present) while representing the wall of the future. The US-Mexican border, hence, has the potential to conjoin temporalities as well as the political and psychological undercurrents of all three walls and simultaneously provides insights into the distinctive conditions of walled life in America. Crucially, the US-Mexican border is a structure and a mentality that gives way to all sorts of racialized violence, ranging from physical assault and extermination to cultural erasure, social exclusion, and psychological aggression. As Edward Casey and Mary Watkins put it, "understanding the border wall requires seeing the border as part of a historical lineage of displacements that were perpetuated to create the United States."[11] Ultimately, in providing a projection screen for the relationship with the other, the US wall envisions local histories of colonial violence and global processes of persecution and fortification at the same time. As such the wall, ironically, enables forms of crossing, collapsing life and death, here and there, then and now. It thereby produces a kind of haunting "simultaneity,"[12] as Blanco would put it, that emplaces the wall in a specific landscape but also "forces an imagination of others in other locations,"[13] adjoining the traumatic legacies of walled life.

To be sure, in her pivotal discussion of *La Frontera* Gloria Anzaldúa conceptualizes the US-Mexican border as an "open wound"[14] and thereby evokes the language of trauma. While broadly applicable to a global wounding through walls, in the American context this wounding imposition makes itself primarily felt on the Mexican side, maintaining a colonial relation that has been injuring land and people for centuries and which continues to assert its ghostly presence in the form of an ever-emerging militarization of the borderlands today. However, the border as wound also exudes a "psychic colonization" on the part of those who have crossed into the United States, recreating the intimate barricades of walled life that lock the Americas into a reality of segregation, which is often reinforced by concrete policies and everyday obstructions. Forcing migrants into invisibility, the wall's shadow casts far into the United States, where it is reprojected in the form of commonplace exclusions (such as restricted access to housing, education, medical care) and routinized internments (e.g., detention centers, prisons).

Yet, when Anzaldúa evokes this wound, she also conjures up the uncanny double of walled life and thereby suggests that haunting, as a social phenomenon, relentlessly impacts on all "sides" involved. Addressing those who find themselves in positions of power, she explains that "where there is persecution of minorities, there is shadow projection. Where there is violence and war there is repression of shadow."[15] Her comments suggest that the relationship between Mexico and the United States cannot be disavowed by a wall—that it cannot be erased by contempt or stereotypes, nor split off by repression. Instead, the border screens an intimate encounter to both sides, invoking "the doppelgänger in [the] psyche,"[16] or the uncanny other side. In one way or another, the examples discussed in this chapter resonate with these forms of doubling and repetition, imagining a crossing of boundaries in various forms: the boundaries of political sides, the boundaries between life and death, past and present or self and other, or those between conscious and unconscious histories, they all are permeated, in some way, in order to discover a haunting simultaneity or presence of the other in the nation and, by extension, in the self.

Focusing on the performance art of Guillermo Gómez-Peña and the cinematic work of Chantal Akerman, my discussion of the US-Mexican wall begins with the liminal artist and the liminal filmmaker in order to explore their subversion of a haunting division through resistance to conventional representations and fictions that exclude the other. Providing a strong sense of how various forms of othering collide in the US-Mexican borderscape, Gómez-Peña and Ackerman exercise the kind of "creative anxiety" evoked by ghosts, reflecting on the ongoing formation of identity in relation to unfinished histories. Gómez-Peña utilizes performance to negotiate his own otherness in a colonial space, while Akerman is interested in unconscious trajectories of othering and the traumatic interfaces they reveal among different political and historical settings. Both Akerman and Gómez-Peña facilitate a collapse of walled binaries in order to question the global processes of othering invested in the migrant. The US-Mexican border hence provides a useful platform for investigating forms of "otherness" that may emerge in all kinds of walled contexts and spaces, revealing a trajectory of racialized violence that stretches from the founding moments of settler colonialism to the walled life experienced in the twentieth and twenty-first centuries.

Colonial Walls

Although the United States is often referred to as an "immigrant nation," it is useful to recall that the country's formation rests on the violence of settler colonialism. Like other expansive European powers, the United States is founded on the aggressive acquisition of political and economic control through the principle of subordination. This includes the dispossession and extermination of the native population, through genocide, erasure, and assimilation[17] and the institutionalization of racial, cultural, and economic segregation as a national raison d'etre. From the outset the nation's realization is hence based on the "mapping and marking of boundaries"[18] (both in the literal and in the imaginary sense) in order to lay claim to the land as property, enabling ownership and capital on the one hand, and creating an order of (white) privilege based in citizenship on the other.

Reflecting this "dual violence of race and capital,"[19] to borrow Achille Mbembe's words, the Southern border of the United States is closely linked to a colonial (and economic) expansion into Mexico. In particular the Mexican-American War (1846–8) saw Mexico lose approximately 55 percent of its land,[20] largely subjecting indigenous peoples to the newly ordained territorial regulations. Yet, the border, as Reece Jones explains "was marked on maps but not necessarily on the ground" invoking a kind of arbitrary porosity that was a far cry from the heavily militarized territory the border denotes more recently,[21] and thereby implying a process of violent and continuous materialization over time. Today, the border stretches across a length of 1,969 miles (3,169 kilometers) and 62 miles (100 km) to either side, hosting a border population of approximately 15 million people.[22] Its most crucial legal documentations are the Treaty of Guadalupe Hidalgo (1848) and the Gadsden Purchase (1853), with the former not only legally confirming American settlement of Mexican land, but also promising those conquered full citizenship and property rights in the United States.[23] Notably, US citizenship was tied to whiteness, and Mexicans were "categorized as racially inferior,"[24] hence, the document also established an ongoing colonial relation "based on domination and exploitation,"[25] fortifying the racialized imperial subjugations still relevant today.

In fact, Ramon Resendiz, Roslava Resendiz, and Irene J. Klaver suggest that we consider the US-Mexican border as an "imperial structure,"[26] reinforcing racial inequality as the organizing principle of the social and political fabric of the United States—then and today. The dynamic echoes Patrick Wolfe's argument that settler colonialism is better understood as a structure, rather than simply an event,[27] thereby producing a continued and intricate experience of domination and violence. Weaving together a traumatic condition of vulnerability, exploitation, and disposability on the part of the colonized, such a structure is mirrored in the political and cultural formation of division and manifests itself in the appearance of colonial boundaries in the physical, cultural, and ideological sense. Tellingly, many Mexicans express this sentiment, explaining that "we did not cross the border, the border crossed us."[28] While referring to the territorial annexation in the aftermath of the Treaty of Guadalupe Hidalgo and the Gadsden Purchase, the phrase also describes an imposed state of precarity, or even, a walling of the mind, conditioned by the literal and imaginary walls of settler colonialism.[29]

The violence of partitioning, zoning, and walling assembles the colonized as objectified in the service of settler profit. For Mexicans this has always meant that "while their labor was exploited, their full personhood was denied."[30] Despite relying on cheap and illegal labor from the South economically, the United States has always sought to exclude Mexican immigrants politically. Solidifying this structure of exploitation, formal guest worker systems confirmed "the role of Mexicans as dispensable workforce"[31] while the porosity of the border has ensured a large crossover between the two nations. Yet, these programs were then sporadically punctured by surges in mass deportation in order to control surplus labor (most notably during the Great Depression in the early 1930s, during Operation Wetback in 1954, and in the context of Operation Gatekeeper during the Clinton era in the 1990s). In other words, objectification and profitability (rather than "the logic of elimination"[32] alone) are the driving forces of the US settler colonial structure. However, these functions rest on the erasure of local histories that challenge such an understanding of people and land.

The "imperial structure"[33] constituting the US-Mexican border as an imaginative limit, or wall, is crucially the result of a double colonization, revealing, and connecting layers of historical violence and racism(s). In particular the indigenous people of the border region (such as the Lipan Apache/Nde') "who have lived, and continue to live, on their traditional land despite colonial, imperial, and postcolonial efforts to dispossess them of it"[34] have long been subject to a twofold erasure. Initially colonized by Spain, indigenous communities were forced into hiding (they were symbolically ghosted) later surviving US aggressions by passing as assimilated Mexicans.[35] Their erasure remapped local relationships insofar as the Western lens reinterpreted land and people as property and resource. The invisibility and erasure of indigenous people was subsequently relentlessly enforced through "various forms of genocide, ranging from military violence to biological and cultural assimilation,"[36] and served as the founding encounter of the capitalist US settler whiteness still prevalent today, as Evelyn Nakano Glenn explains.[37] Projecting the identity of the colonizer while (doubly) erasing those of the colonized; this moment of walling in US history also conditions the subsequent hypervisibility of the racially marked bodies of African Americans and Mexicans in the US national imaginary.[38] Interlocking these different racisms, the wall as an imperial structure, oscillates between racial invisibility and racial projection, exposing the "racializing assemblages"[39] that underwrite US nationhood historically and fantasmatically.

While the US national imaginary has always heavily relied on the means of dividing, zoning, and barricading land, people, and identities, the materialization of the US-Mexican border into yet another wall has been accelerated in the last few decades, and particularly post 9/11.[40] Most notably in 2005, the US government began the construction of a physical fence in the border region through the Secure Border Initiative, repeating the double-aggression of settler colonialism once more by fortifying a racial line to Mexico and by violating tribal lands in the borderzone. Authorizing about 850 miles of the border wall, the Secure Fence Act brought in by the Bush administration in 2006 legalized vast interference with the border ecology, including indigenous-land relations, by blocking access to ancestral remains and by creating a vast symbol of exclusion toward the Mexican side.[41] The Fence Act, furthermore, allowed the Department of Homeland Security to waive more than thirty-six federal laws interfering with the building of the wall, effectively creating a lawless area,[42] in which US military power can be tested, staged, and escalated with little to no restrictions.

Under the Obama administration this development of the border was reinforced by an increasingly virtual wall, including 24/7 drones, sensor cameras, and elaborate surveillance technology, turning the Southern border region into a playground for the military-industrial complex.[43] However, this "state of exception," which Agamben describes as "the legal form of what cannot have legal form,"[44] also materialized in the guise of paramilitary border squats, such as "border patrol" (who are not actually part of the border patrol) or the Minutemen project. These self-appointed vigilantes roam the "lawless" borderlands in search of migrants trying to cross the border illegally, often projecting the nationalist aggression of fascist militias. The escalation of border violence and border discipline hence attests to Aime Césaire's claim that "no one colonizes with impunity."[45] While aiming to dehumanize the other through violence and erasure, settler violence firstly decivilizes the colonizer.[46] This "law of progressive dehumanization,"[47] as Césaire calls it, marks the border as an ongoing project of violence, projecting the history of colonialism and simultaneously reattaching it to the present.

At the same time, the US-Mexican border also works as a shield that obscures these legacies. The border as wall functions as a kind of fantasmatically produced shelter[48] that rests on a "national imago of goodness, one that wholly externalizes the nation's ills and disavows its unlovely effects on others, its aggressions, needs, and dependencies,"[49] while strengthening the cultural hatred it projects visually. If, as Michel Foucault maintains, "invisibility is a guarantee of order,"[50] then the bringing to surface or making visible of power structures by acknowledging the border as wall is, however, precisely the first step to subverting and disaggregating the existing political order. Wherever the dynamics of walling are projected, forms of intellectual, artistic, and literal crossings may hence be enabled to renegotiate the meaning of the border. Returning to the politics of spectrality, the border as wall, in other words, may not be fully materialized; however, it emerges as a colonial ghost or residue of unresolved histories, by which the legacies of an enduring exclusion make themselves (increasingly) known in the present and future. The screen hence does not simply operate a shield, concealing the atrocities of then and now; the wall as screen is also always projective, in the sense that it reveals, insistently, this point of erasure.

The Birth of a Nation

The founding demarcation of the US national imaginary rests on the grand narratives that harden divisions today and constitutes the psychological, social, and political "reality" the wall secures. In a focal interview with Cahiers du Cinéma in 1976 Jacques Rancière suggested that we understand this "reality" as the "dominant fiction,"[51] a privileged mode of representation consisting of images and stories through which the members of a society are invited to "identify themselves."[52] To Rancière the dominant fiction of the United States is epitomized in "the birth of a nation"[53] and more specifically in the cementation of boundaries between "whites/ American Indians, North/ South, the lawman/ the outlaw, etc.,"[54] that underwrite this narrative. The dominant fiction, like the wall, functions as a screen (and on screen) projecting the categories of US hegemony in an effort to mirror the nation back to itself. Drawing on the ghostly appearance of cinema and image technology, this spectral encounter with the national imaginary allows the ghosts of the past to return: the screen, in other words, invokes a politics of haunting. Once again congealing the conceptual mortar between wall, screen, and nationhood, cinema thereby captures the afterlife of empires that refuse to be put away, repeating, again and again, a unique sense of violent exclusion at the heart of the collective US imaginary.

The fantasy of the "birth of a nation," itself eternalized in G.W. Griffith's 1915 controversial (read: profoundly racist and sexist) film of the same name, firmly raises the phantoms of gendered and racialized siege narratives sustaining white privilege. Vilifying people of color and reinstating the need for walls, boundaries, and separation as the fundament of social reality in the United States, the film reworks the ideological glue of whiteness in America. Connoting a powerful imaginary, "this is fiction presenting itself as fact,"[55] as Deborah Shaw asserts, and it has been endlessly reproduced on the screen of the nation and the cinema alike. For example, films such as *Traffic* (2000), *Man on Fire* (2004), or *Savages* (2012) reinstate the threat of the borderless world (played out foremost on the white female body as a proxy for US nationhood) and the corruption of the American family through drug trafficking, advocating a binary of good and evil in the American imagination, which plays out as equivalent to the coordinates of North and South. The screen/wall hence projects the racialized subject positions available within the US dominant fiction, cementing the violent divisions and binaries at its foundation, but also suggesting that the ghosts of the past are present in the future.

On the other hand, such ghostly projections of the wall have also been used as artistic challenges to these national fantasies. For example, in 2003 artist activists in Tijuana evoked the wall as an arrangement of colorful coffins (apropos haunting), each displaying a particular year and the numbers of deaths recorded in the borderlands.[56] Placing the coffins on the Mexican side, the installation effectively dramatized the (ghosted) Mexican side of the border's deadly and restrictive landscape. The display of loss invoked the specter of violence that permeates the landscape at all times, and thereby, the installation candidly characterized the border as a wall that poses a threat to the lives and security of those that try to escape its shadow, rather than condemning the people it keeps out. In this way, the "dominant fiction" of a Mexican threat was decentralized by exposing the true victims of this power structure and registering the wounding inflicted by a walled life. The coffins articulate that the racial hierarchization sustaining US American nationhood is concretized in the border wall and therefore can be made visible. However, this manifestation is ambivalent, in the sense of being both subversive and immersive, espousing a continuous negotiation of the wall's meanings and consequences.

Crossing Walls

Indeed, the subversion of the US-Mexican border has always taken place in the form of literal, artistic, intellectual, and most crucially illegal crossings. In this sense, the US-Mexican border epitomizes the notion of crossing in the physical and psychological sense. Practically, the US-Mexican border registers approximately 250 million legal crossings per year, supplemented by an (estimated) one million illegal crossers risking their lives in the midst of the lethal desert, many of them dying on the way.[57] However, the ambivalence between possibility and restriction, the change of one's current life at the risk of death, is not limited to physical exclusion but also plays out through the crosser's subjectivity. The border is a transitional space, in which one (cultural, social, or fantasmatic) identity is exchanged for another through the process of crossing, rendering this wall "the magic curtain"[58] in the Mexican and American imaginary.

This idea of "crossing" and ultimately confronting "the other side" opens up the possibility of examining the wall beyond the rigid binary of the politics of "us" and "them." Instead, the borderscape that underwrites the desire for a materialization of a US wall threatens the demarcations of the rigid Western imaginary, precisely because it lays the ground for a state of ambivalence and "inbetweenness." Rather than separating one political, social, and imaginary entity from another (as the wall's architecture wants to ferociously suggest), the borderscape between the United States and Mexico conditions a state of "neither here nor there" or the point where one "side" melts into another. The idea of crossing once again invokes the spectrality of the wall imago; however, it is also closely related to the notion of liminality, and its implication in ambivalence, potential, and subversion.

Lauro Zavala suggests that we understand liminality as "the paradoxical and potentially productive condition of being situated in between two locations,"[59] be they physical, intellectual, or cultural. Paul Stenner further considers this state as a means for intervention, explaining that "liminal experiences are experiences that happen during occasions of significant transition, passage or disruption."[60] In other words, the notion of liminality subverts the binaries and divisions enacted and enforced by political walls, instead asking us to consider the potentialities of crossing they also necessarily entail. In this sense, the US-Mexican wall in particular allows for a discussion of the wall's conceptual "other side." It encounters the other as a multiplicity located in the reflexive space of the actual and conceptual "in-between." More precisely, exploring the US-Mexican border in the context of crossing denotes this border as a liminal space from which we can explore the wall's "otherness" or perhaps its de/colonial ghostliness. I suggest that this perspective articulates the correspondences between different "walls" without reducing them to "sameness." Instead, we may think of the wall as a borderland of possibility and transformation, where identities are fluid and perspectives multiply continuously, provoking "creative anxieties."[61]

Performing the Border: Guillermo Gómez-Peña

Challenging the enclosed perspectives offered and projected by the wall, Mexican-born Chicano artist Guillermo Gómez-Peña utilizes the medium of performance in order to explore the notion of crossing and multiplicity as markers of a "border subjectivity." Investigating difference and diversity in relation to the border, both as a physical site and as a psychological setting, the artist builds up a "counter fiction" to exclusionary patterns of settler colonialism and the binary politics it evokes by situating identity within the "border space." Engaging in a process of social communication and "cultural translation,"[62] Gómez-Peña suggests, in resonance with Homi K. Bhabha, "that all forms of culture are in some way related to each other, because culture is a signifying or symbolic activity."[63] Hence Gómez-Peña's performances create a possibility of political negotiation, or a shift of perspective in a landscape of binaries, by insisting on an inherent cultural hybridity.

The artist celebrates identity as a form of multiplicity and understands his performance "as a strategy to become visible"[64] made available to those who embody unwanted diversity and cultural otherness. His performances, to borrow the words of Patricia Zavella, "become a reflexive space which fosters agency by allowing for critiques of politics from outside and from within Mexican communities."[65] Border art thereby becomes "a conceptual territory,"[66] in which the border's restrictive meanings and associated identity politics are renegotiated and the border space itself is reclaimed "as a worthwhile place of creation."[67] Hence, the wall as a means of separation is subverted by the notion of the border as a screen or a stage, working "as the site of specular performance"[68] that seeks to make visible the unconscious assumptions about culture and identity it otherwise so strictly maintains. Exploring the concept of otherness along these parameters, Gómez-Peña's investigation of the US-Mexican border opens up questions about the encounter of cultures as opposed to the erection of walls. Through his performance he seeks to challenge the dominant fictions and histories associated with national identities by reinventing the relationship with a cultural other and constructing alternative fictions of the everyday.

In his performative engagement with the wall, Gómez-Peña explores the crossing of borders, in terms of both the collective and the individual and the physical and the psychological, and thereby draws attention to multiperspectval encounters. This reveals the border's interplay between a site-specific politics that mostly re-enacts (post)colonial racialized violence and its more universalized psychological form of alienation. Drawing on Jeff Kelly, Claire Fox explains that an artistic practice which is concerned with site-specificity investigates how "a place is not merely a medium of art but also its contents."[69] Conversely, the exploration of the psychological undercurrents of such a place is more concerned with the way in which the space itself is internalized.

This interplay is reflected in Gómez-Peña's two most border-focused works: the establishments of the *Border Art Workshop/ Taller de Arte Fronterizo (BAW/TAW)* in 1984 and his performance character *Border Brujo*, which he performed between 1988 and 1989, and which enjoyed a significant "afterlife" in the form of a video installation and performance scripts.[70] The BAW/TAW primarily investigated the border area as a site that revealed heavily coded cultural, historical, and political layers of structuring subjectivity, whereas *Border Brujo* was interested in the investigation of a "border personality" or "border ghost" as a widely applicable experience in the (post)colonial context. With these artworks Gómez-Peña hence traced a movement from the specificity of the border's site to the internalized conditions of the border as a psychological restriction. In so doing, as Claire Fox observes, he insisted that "the border was something people carried within themselves, in addition to being an external factor structuring perception."[71] Both projects, *BAW/TAW* and *Border Brujo*, in other words, invite an exploration of the borderlands as a liminal or ghostly space, in which the specific and collective traces of dominant fictions, identities, and walls can be found and experienced, at the same time as they are subject to a hybrid renegotiation of multiple cultural and political—but also psychological—encounters.

The *BAW/TAW* was a bilingual artist collective, which predominantly challenged the politics of the US-Mexican border between 1984 and 1990 by claiming it as "a laboratory for social and aesthetic experimentation."[72] The group proposed "the artist as a social thinker and binational diplomat,"[73] staging cross-cultural performance encounters in the US-Mexican border region. For example, in 1986 the group performed a "roundtable" on the border between Chicanos, Mexicans, and North Americans, literally placing participants around a table that was bisected by the US-Mexican border. Turning the tables in the practical and metaphorical sense, the group then staged illegal crossings of the border as well as illegal exchanges of food and affection.[74] The performance resulted in what the artists have described as "siesta,"[75] proposing a sense of border culture marked by the inherent crossing of its participants and suggested a "community of difference... fragmented, ever changing, and temporary"[76] as opposed to the enduring binary division enforced by the border as wall. This sort of insistent site specificity then became "a guiding principle of the group,"[77] showing the US-Mexican border "not merely as a delimiting factor or dividing line but a social and cultural world unto itself."[78] Playing with the structure of colonialism, the setting allowed the artists to stage a kind of reverse cultural invasion, according to which the relationships between Anglo-American, Mexican, and Chicano cultural identities could be renegotiated.

Projecting such collective negotiations back onto the psychological screen of the individual, Gómez-Peña's performance character *Border Brujo* furthermore foregrounded idiosyncratic experiences and perceptions of the border, while articulating political and cultural criticism through the multiple voices of the character. *Border Brujo*, whom the artist has described as "a psychological border crosser,"[79] "a guide for border crossers,"[80] and "a ghost from the future"[81] combined multiple identities that reenacted and also traversed the broader cultural assemblages. The character of *Border Brujo* consists of fifteen different personae, each speaking a different "border language"[82] or dialect, who reflects on the various relationships between North and South.[83] The character thereby implies the kind of haunting simultaneity, or politically relevant "now moment"[84] that registers how identity is reflected through lived spaces that are themselves marked by a kind of relentless endemic violence recurrently reproducing its impacts on the everyday.

Border Brujo continuously reenacts colonial attitudes and stereotypes of the exotic and somewhat backward other, before offsetting these images with articulate cultural criticism. "I'm ready to fight, I'm ready to rape, don't like me too much, 'cause I'm a drug smuggling welfare recipient to be,"[85] one of *Border Brujo*'s personae proclaims, before he blatantly rejects this stereotype, lamenting that "if it wasn't for the fact that I read too much Foucault and Baudrillard… I could fulfill your expectations much better."[86] The various personae speak with different voices—ranging from "authorative" to "drunk," "vulnerable," "agitated," and "epiphanic"[87]—and enact different accents as well as varying levels of intelligibility, affirmation, and antagonism. Producing a kind of affective stylization of haunting, *Border Brujo* thereby enacts Ambrose Bierce famous designation of the ghost as "the outward and visible sign of an inward fear,"[88] in this case processing the anxieties of the Anglo-American side. Speaking from a candle-lit postmodern altar consisting of a mix of cultural icons; such as the Lady of Guadalupe, the Star Wars robot R2D2, a football and a plastic figure of an American Indian, *Border Brujo*, himself covered in "ironicized" pop culture buttons, a giant banana necklace and a Corona hat, works the image of the Mexican through different apparitions of culture, art, film, and literature. The character thereby questions the notion of a fixed identity, continuously reenacting multiple perspectives, anxieties, and sensibilities across continuums of cultural identification.

The performance of border subjectivities draws attention to the border's vulnerability or imaginary inconsistency and thereby challenges the border's own performance of stability, unveiling its underlying structures. The connection between crossing and the concept of the transcultural is thereby prominently expressed in the various hybrid genres Gómez-Peña applies. In a combination of Mexican popular culture and fluxus,[89] Gómez-Peña's performance art draws attention to cultural contrasts and shifting identities that make up the borderscape, challenging the rigid territorialization evoked by walls meant to segregate "a new mankind, the fourth world, the migrant kind."[90] *Border Brujo* is not willing to maintain such distinctions, or as he puts it to his audience, "I am not your tourist guide across the undetermined otherness."[91] Instead, Gómez-Peña pleads for "a pluralistic sense of self"[92] and for the application of "multiple repertoires of identity"[93] as reflected in his multilingual performances, which mix cultural costumes and hybridize Mexican and Anglo American cultural icons, ranging from a Tequila bottle to a Batman sticker. To Gómez-Peña these images and acts of multiplicity subvert what he identifies as "the borderization of the world,"[94] staging a cultural clash or "border experience"[95] and thereby exercising, as he says, "the freedom that my two countries have denied me."[96]

Similar to the fantasy scenario evoked by Freud and the wound evoked by Anzaldúa, such an experience works through the negotiation and expression of different identificatory roles and positions, and suggests that, like *Border Brujo*, these multiple roles are performed in multiple contexts and communities. By investigating multiplicity as a means to map identities, Gómez-Peña challenges the ideological fictions that support division by walls. He deconstructs the grand narratives that stigmatize and exclude the cultural other by renegotiating the meaning of the border, and by challenging the parameters that define identity. This is possible precisely because "borders frame national and cultural identities"[97] in specific ways that are reiterated through dominant fictions, and Gómez-Peña disrupts these patterns of power via "creative appropriation, expropriation, and subversion of dominant cultural forms."[98] His aim is to position the other and the self in a continuous project of crossing, precisely because the "arrival" on either side suggested by the wall "is just an illusion."[99] Gómez-Peña's artistic intervention is the positioning of the other (including himself) "in a fictional center, pushing the dominant (or colonizing) culture to the margin."[100] In this way, the parameters of walled life are rearranged, "turning and forcing the dominant culture to become the other."[101]

Illustrating this dynamic, the *BAW/TAW* released a press statement on el Día de la Raza/ Columbus day, claiming that "the continent had been turned upside down,"[102] leading Columbus to arrive in Tijuana. The fictional event was then itself replayed by the "roundtable" situated across the border. Exploring a similar approach of decentering the facts fictitiously, Gómez-Peña called for a Gringostroika movement, advocating "the complete economic and cultural reform of US capitalism."[103] Such a strategy of fictionally rearranging meanings not only aims to make "a parodic, dramatic, and humorous theatre out of the dominant fantasy,"[104] but also exposes the global and local power structures that purport to be centers of dominance. In this way, political contingencies are fictitiously recontextualized to explore the underlying structures of meaning. In each case, the wall is challenged through a multiperspectival engagement of the spectator, through which the dominant narrative itself becomes strange or just one possibility among many alternatives.

The construction of alternative fictions does not only aim to destabilize the grand narratives on which walls are built, remapping the boundaries of the political through strategies of (counter) fictionalization. It also serves as a form of resistance, by which the other negotiates his or her position as an outsider from within the field of meaning constructed by the dominant collective. The migrant thereby epitomizes the other on the inside, much in the way Gómez-Peña evokes *Border Brujo* as "he becomes self and other within himself."[105] The character demonstrates the interrelation of self and other; however, this relation can play out along different fictitious trajectories. For example, the nation may not strictly seek to eradicate the other; rather, the (fictive) other is needed "to reproduce an illegality that in turn justifies the repressive measures"[106] of the state. Gómez-Peña persistently reenacts this illegality of the Mexican migrant and recontextualizes it in order to open such processes to critical reflection. The illicit exchange of food and affection across the border table similarly highlights this strategy of illegalization and renders it absurd, while also staging such boundaries as the means for successful crossings.

Negotiating different cultural, political, and psychological subject positions, Gómez-Peña acknowledges the production of alternative fictions as a "significant way for immigrant cultures to deal with the new reality"[107] that allows for a remapping of the new setting, often through "reterritorialization, rejection of the new reality and the construction of a fictitious past."[108] To Gómez-Peña these parameters are essential to the Chicano movement; however, the elaboration of alternative fictions is useful to migrants and "others" in varying contexts of segregation, colonization, and walling who find themselves in unfamiliar and often hostile surroundings. The reconstruction of reality via alternative fictions is a powerful means for addressing the element of otherness within a particular collective self and rearranging the coordinates of this collective's self-understanding. In this way the figure of the conceptual other is reinstated as crucial to the imagination and re-imagination of an unbounded collective.

Gómez-Peña aims to challenge national identity, reimagining its psychological undercurrents and thereby broadening the forms of community it enables. *Border Brujo* in particular exemplifies Gómez-Peña's claim that crossing the border evokes a "multiplicity of selves."[109] However, the many facets of *Border Brujo* also make a point of the psychological process of bringing out these selves, "many of which are unconscious."[110] *Border Brujo* "articulates fear, desire, trauma, anger, and misplacement,"[111] switching among the fifteen personae that make up his character. Continuously oscillating between the extreme emotions of a "borderline personality," the performance explores the spontaneous eruptions of these seemingly repressed characters, which functions as a cathartic release. These moments of outburst are often enacted as "drunk talk," through which *Border Brujo* uncovers uncomfortable truths from the postcolonial unconscious. "You think we have nothing in common?"[112] he asks before revealing, "well, well you are a victim of your government and so am I... of yours."[113] Confronting his Anglo-American audience, a drunk *Border Brujo* explains, "I am here 'cause your government went down there, to my country without a formal invitation and took all our resources, so I came to look for them, just to look for them, nothing else. If you see a refugee tonight, treat him well; he's just seeking his stolen resources."[114] Such efforts of refiguration ultimately challenge the collective imaginary of the nation with the aim of critically addressing its power centers in order to reimagine community as multiple, diverse, and both self and other.

The starting point of this encounter is the recognition of "otherness within,"[115] which relies on the idea that "one has to understand otherness to understand oneself."[116] However, as Gómez-Peña asserts, "the problem is that the North continues to project stereotypes onto the South, as the center does onto its perceived margins."[117] This is reflected in the various Mexican stereotypes that continue to circulate through a border discourse, and which Gómez-Peña enacts and radicalizes, most overtly in the appearance of the romantic mariachi or the drunk antagonistic migrant. He thereby seeks to debunk the stereotype, enlarging the image to point out its fractures for the audience. As Gómez-Peña puts it, when you confront the audience with the stereotype, "you shatter the mirror in front of their faces and you make them aware of the political implications of the construction of this stereotype."[118] In this way, the screening of otherness marks a political practice aimed at destabilizing the rigid divisions of political power and settler colonial subjugation.

In this way, political wall art engages in a complex process of working through (and with) political division in order to reinstate the otherness within, ultimately reimagining practical forms of political community. As Gómez-Peña explains, in some sense, border art can evoke "a process of healing, articulating, subverting, reinventing, this relationship with the cultural other";[119] however, in its spectral presence it also insists that "for the ghost the haunting is the resolving, it is not what needs to be solved."[120] Gómez-Peña seeks to reintroduce diversity, noise, and affective resonance into an otherwise culturally impoverished and politically inert space at the margins of power. Haunting the patterns of political alienation established by the wall, art thereby makes palpable the unfinished pages of collective hi/stories. This proves helpful in culturally nourishing political margins through affective scenes that reinstate diversity and acknowledge that "no one belongs to only one community."[121] In this sense, artists evoke the wall's other side, by providing a stage, on which the multiple roles of the social can rearrange the given "reality" and dominant fictions of social division.

Screening the Border: Chantal Akerman's *From the Other Side*

Similarly, to the art of Guillermo Gómez-Peña, Chantal Akerman's films display a profound interest in the liminal encounters between self and other, continuously exploring their underlying relationships and the evocation of

MEXICO: COLONIAL GHOSTS, WALLED MINDS

racialized violence. However, Akerman's films utilize this relationship primarily in order to investigate the layers of trauma underlying everyday politics. Her documentaries in particular investigate political and historical settings but are ultimately interested in bringing the repressed to the surface as part of the social criticism they evoke. In particular, Akerman's documentary *From the Other Side* (De L'Autre Côté, 2002)[122] is attentive to the abstract meanings of space and the psychological demarcations to which space is linked, exploring the unconscious of the border-wall setting.

From the Other Side investigates the Mexican border as a wall that carries fatal symbolic and practical implications for the Mexican people, imposing a political and psychological segregation from the United States. Unveiling the multiple aspects of this problem on both sides of the border through interviews, while showcasing the wall itself in its full physical (and imaginary) weight, Akerman encounters the political implications of space via adamant interrogations of the personal. Screening the walled life of the Mexican borderscape, the film is interested in revealing traumatic and ghostly intersections between the walls of past and present, projecting their cementation of "otherness" and ultimately joining these different historical contexts. This is achieved by investigating the psychical dynamics revealed by the border as both medium and barrier, insistently exploring the wall on—and as—screen.

In fact, the screen allows Akerman to explore the trajectories of trauma through her complex documentation of the return of the repressed and her incessant collapse of conceptual binaries. She hence perpetuates a cinema of blurred boundaries—between the self and other, the personal and the political, the factual and the fictitious, the director and her subjects, and thereby the film adheres to the sensibilities of haunting. This bringing together of registers that are otherwise routinely kept separate allows Akerman to think (and feel) the operations of the wall across different cultural and historical spaces, to reveal a common trace of ghostly collision and simultaneity or a map of traumatic encounters and racialized violence that link the various contexts.

In other words, for Akerman, walls erupt in and through a variety of settings, but they always implicitly lead her back to the haunting recurrence of the Holocaust as the ultimate traumatic experience and the post-memorial burden, she inherited from her parents.[123] Walled life, as unresolved repetition, in other words, is manifested and revealed via its link to "a post-Holocaust imaginary"[124] and Akerman patiently reproduces this "post-memory" or "after-life" through the investigation of alternative fictions, settings, and realities. The engagement offers insight into the haunting evoked by political walls and intimates how they might unconsciously be linked. Indeed, Akerman conjures up a cinema of the past in the present, of endurance and passage; ultimately, she evokes a cinema of the unconscious, "obsessed with borders and liminal spaces,"[125] across different contexts and times. Similar to the work of the psychoanalyst, her films are characterized by patience and waiting in order to allow the ghosts of the past to (re)surface and to explore the invisible dynamics between the concrete and the abstract, the manifest and its others.

From the Other Side begins on the Mexican side, where Akerman interviews the inhabitants of the Mexican borderlands about stories of crossing. The interviews are interspersed by long shots of the wall to reveal that family tragedies are embedded in poor economic conditions and fatal attempts to find a better life. While turning the wall into the protagonist and setting of the relationship between North and South, the first half of the film thereby makes clear that the wall is primarily a Mexican reality, restricting life to an inert and unproductive space. The first scenes reflect the inertia of walled life, which is heightened in the extended filming of the actual wall. As we see shots of the wall cutting through a picturesque landscape, the camera's movement is reduced to a minimum, foregrounding "the rigor of the frame"[126] and the durability of the wall. Few people enter the static frame, which approximates a sense of uncanny arrest, or suspension in time and space. We see people only from afar, passively waiting or trying to work the dead land without tools. These people (many of them children) are caught up in an unproductive and futureless space, limited by an enormous fence and the inequalities it has materialized. Akerman captures this agony in the accounts of a fourteen-year-old who wishes to cross over in search of a better life. She reiterates the bleakness of his future in Mexico with a long-tracking shot along the wall, whose felt endlessness and ghostly presence is finally offset by a 180° turn that leads the viewer back into Mexico, where the tracking shot of the wall is now mirrored by an outward-looking scene of its reflection: an empty, lifeless, and silent Mexican neighborhood.

Indeed, as the traumatic consequences of the political situation in Mexico slowly emerge, Akerman's interviewees become more and more silent; simultaneously the static shots of the wall increase. Literally drowning out the voices and faces of those it oppresses, the wall, in this sense, takes center stage as the camera (re)approaches it in another tracking shot, as if to take it on once more. These scenes foreground the wall as the defining object of the Mexican space, absorbing all attempts to create meaning and reproducing a Mexican invisibility as the (post)colonial condition of the relationship between the two sides. Mexico, in effect, is ghosted, relegated to what Rob Nixon has famously called an "unimagined community."[127] Placed under conditions of "administered invisibility" and "spatial amnesia" such an unimagined community remains "uncoupled from the idea of both a national future and a national memory":[128] Forgotten and suspended, it haunts

MEXICO: COLONIAL GHOSTS, WALLED MINDS

"the visible nation"[129] on the other side. Tellingly, Terri Ginsberg observes, the wall can only be shown on the Mexican side (of the film),[130] where it is constantly present, intraversable, and cutting through the everyday lives of the people Akerman encounters. It is "positioned as looming... in any case mortally impenetrable"[131] and always framing Mexican life. However, when Akerman's camera finally crosses over to the US side, the wall disappears from the screen. From there on the wall "is veritably absent—from the mis-en-scène, as well as, the film insinuates, from US consciousness,"[132] as Akerman explores the political and mental barriers that characterize the US side as a profound sense of xenophobic anxiety and inability to deal with the postcolonial narrative that connects the two countries. In this way, North and South replay the division between conscious and unconscious settings of the psyche, much in the way Freud had imagined the topology of the mind.

However, the eventual filmic crossing into the United States creates a profound sense of disorientation, and thereby mirrors the unstable (national) imaginary on which the wall rests, dislodging it from its particular location. The shot leads the viewer to the other side of the unconscious, away from the repressed scene of postcolonial exploitation to the encompassing reality of a stable US economy and culture. Here the wall works primarily as a psychological barrier, which is reflected in the xenophobic accounts of interviewees and poses an implicit limit on those who criticize the lethal handling of the situation or try to improve it. In other words, the wall is invoked as a force of traumatic recurrence and ghostly presence within the nation, precisely because the film is concerned with the other that the barrier introduces in fantasy and the fictitious nationalism this production entails. We hear a border patrol agent, reciting a eulogy, refer to "the front lines of this daily war," and a couple of farmers explaining their right to use gun power against potential threats to their property. The same couple also expresses a profound fear of the "diseases" Mexicans could bring, underpinned by an anxiety that "there won't be enough vaccine for everybody." Such fantasies of invasion not only produce an abundance of ironies in a postcolonial context, but also reveal that the wall serves to delimit the siege fantasy of the settler,[133] securing a false sense of moral integrity despite the inequality, exploitation, and dehumanization perpetuated in the shadow of colonial walls.

Once again, the conceptual and physical wall is exposed as a medium of shielding the aggressor from his own descent into violence while enforcing human hierarchies that resonate with traumatic forces of exclusion and racialization across histories. In this way "the wall transcends the specific context of the film and becomes an allegory of all barriers that have divided and continue to divide humanity,"[134] as Schmid puts it; here, the xenophobic and aggressively defensive fantasies about the (Mexican) other resonate with the aggressively self-protective rhetoric that also characterizes the spaces of Berlin and Israel. Hence, the film exemplifies the fact that walls "inadvertently produce a collective ethos and subjectivity that is defensive, parochial, nationalistic and militarized,"[135] to borrow Brown's words once more. In this sense, the wall screens the social injustices it perpetuates, both in the sense of concealing these processes and in the manner it inadvertently makes them visible.

From the Other Side focuses on the wall as a means of exclusion, sustaining the fictive identity of the United States while denying the two sides' mutual interdependence. Because the film acknowledges that the separation is one-sided for Mexico, it hence also carefully deconstructs the ideological position of the United States as self-contained. In the first few minutes of the film (while on the Mexican side) we are confronted with the story of Delfina's son, who, after years of trying to help his Mexican community to progress and sustain itself, realizes that the means to achieve the aim of relative economic and social stability are only located on the other side, north of the border. Invoking her child's ghost in a painful account, Delfina recalls her son's idealist enthusiasm, which eventually sent him on a journey he did not survive. The scene projects the ghostly hopes of the dead who were lured by the wall/screen. After all, walls invite those they exclude to project a wish for a better life beyond the limits of the barrier, and to risk their own lives in the process of overcoming them.

The film deconstructs the myth of the magic curtain, which suggests that the US-Mexican border "is transformation itself, the embodiment of change,"[136] promising "the beginning of one sort of life"[137] and "the ending of another."[138] Instead, the border is literally evoked as the wall Bartra describes and, thereby, works as "a filter that is supposed to purify the passing flux."[139] The Mexican, as the cultural other, is then manifested as the "impure," which recalls the language of Jewish persecution yet seeks to implicitly legitimize the ignorance toward suffering and cruelty displayed by the other side. As a sheriff in Arizona explains, the border policies are ineffective, provoking a "large increase in deaths of migrants," but he accepts these deaths as a "calculated consequence." Hence, the image of the physical wall we encounter on the Mexican side is meant to signify the mental barrier maintained by the United States.

Akerman utilizes personal trajectories in order to destabilize these political patterns, reinstating the intimacy of the personal in order to challenge bounded space and to circumvent separation. In particular, Akerman makes use of the interview to reveal the personal aspects and facets that lend meaning to the wall through the experiences it creates. Many of her subjects are filmed with the same enduring, patient camera as the images of the wall. The camera waits for meaning to emerge and provides the space for the details of a protagonist's story to come to life. This circumvents the border as a barrier that makes invisible the suffering it induces. Rather, the film stages multiple ways of transgressing boundaries in both content and form, all in the service of experiencing the face of the other, or the faces of the other side.

The patience on the part of the filmmaker also reveals the affective nuances that exceed verbal communication, as mirrored by the face. The camera stays fixed on Delfina's agonized face long after she has finished her story. Her expression of despair is then mirrored by a long shot of her husband's face, who eventually continues the story, to which there is no closure, before the camera returns once again to Delfina. The same sense of silent agony and grief is then epitomized in the image of the barber who faces the camera in complete silence, never uttering a single word. It seems that the losses experienced by the protagonists cannot be expressed by language and narrative alone but are revealed in the screening of the affective circuits of their wordless, despairing faces. Because of this the film can, as Klaus Ottman remarks, be "almost unbearable for the show of human suffering expressed by the parents or grandparents of migrants who have perished in the desert."[140] These images pitch the visceral force of intimate ghosts against the static politics of the border in order to reveal the traumatic legacies of walled space.

From the Other Side suggests that walled life is confined by the histories it sustains, in the conceptual and physical sense, and thereby raises the specter of imprisonment and control. Akerman articulates this dynamic through issues of surveillance and incarceration as being directly related to the camera (and hence the screen/wall), whether it is in the service of a documentary or to track down illegal crossings. This self-reflexive ability of Akerman's camera to recreate imprisonment is mirrored toward the film's ending. Following the shadows of illegal crossers through the eyes of an infrared surveillance camera, the film asserts a cinematic connection to a feeling of being watched, not only because film and surveillance "inhabit the same technological field,"[141] but also because they give expression to the inner boundaries of psychological imprisonment. The images depict the crossers as mere shadows and thereby invoke them as phantoms or ghosts. At the same time, the presence of the invisible camera insinuates a haunting apparition of the military other, always ready to strike with violence. The film hence draws attention to the unspoken, the bounded and the impenetrable as reflected and maintained by the ghost-wall, reinstating the silent visuality of trauma.

In fact, treating the wall as a screen (and vice versa), the film projects the haunting legacies of walled life on several levels. The history of persecution, imprisonment, and dehumanization underwrites the colonial structure the border upholds; however, to Akerman such forms of racialized violence also explicitly link this structure to the history of Jewish persecution. From the claustrophobic gaze of the surveillance camera lining up unspecified migrants, whose extended walking through the lethal borderlands restages a memory of the "deathmarch" in Europe, to the images of open highways accompanied by Akerman's narration about loss and memory, the closing images of *From the Other Side* resound with Jewish trauma. Indeed, Akerman explains in an interview that her interest in the US-Mexican border had been sparked by an article in which an American was quoted comparing migrants to "dirt."[142] As she read the words "we don't want that dirt,"[143] Akerman was instantly reminded "of other times in history when the word 'dirt' was used,"[144] most evidently in the hateful expression of "dirty Jews."[145] Hence, Akerman's exploration of the US-Mexican wall is a study of human repression of "the other who is impure"[146] as linked to the crimes of the Holocaust, but also marks an attempt to respond, or take responsibility, on account of this history.

Akerman concludes her documentation of the border with the fictitious story that overlays the final scenes of the film. Reciting the story of David, who is in search of his mother, the last words are themselves recollections and constructions of the other. The story is told from the point of view of a landlord who speaks of an anonymous "her," whose identity we never learn. Akerman's words (now in French) insist on a disturbing non-specificity of otherness and subtly incorporate familiar prejudices, commenting on the woman's tidiness, her supposed mystical powers, and her determined distance from neighbors. The account intimates a divestment of responsibility on part of the fictitious speaker and simultaneously blames the victim. What happened to the woman remains unknown and is subject to unreasonable speculations as well as uncomfortable repression of her possible death (which is at the same time strongly implied). Echoing the persecution of the Jews and the insistent denial of bystanders, the story (once more) reinvokes a recurrence of ghosts, the trauma of the Holocaust, but also proclaims walled life's inability to deal with its legacy.

Reimagining this fragmented traumatic experience at the core of an artistic border transference, *From the Other Side* first screened as a video installation exhibited at the Documenta 11 in Kassel in 2002. Besides employing twenty-four video screens that projected and fragmented the walled life captured in Akerman's film, the installation also featured a large screen importing images from the Mexican border desert into the gallery space in Germany. At the same time, another screen envisioned the final moments of the documentary,[147] invoking the traumatic trace of the border as closely associated to the psychological and physical internment of the camp, the epitomal space of the other's persecution. As daylight began to light up this scene, the image slowly dissolved to expose the surface of yet another screen, which, as became apparent, was located in the Mexican desert. Obscuring the distinctions between here and there, collapsing distance, and traversing spatial and historical contexts, this screen functioned as a medium of ghostly simultaneity, capable of invoking the haunted landscapes of (different) walled lives while reinstating the screen as a (common) psychic device.

In the darkness of the Mexican desert the screen worked as the preconscious of a border mentality. However, in light of the day it reinvoked the barrier, dissolving the transparent image. Marion Schmid reads this move as staging "the dissolution of the American Dream,"[148] and as such it may well also comment on the wall as the national screen. Freed from its spatial particularity, the screen of traumatic history reinvokes the walls of the past, the present, and the future (whether they are set in Berlin, Palestine, or Mexico). Linked in projective repetition and subdued to the flickering presence of the haunting other, they collectively echo the film's final words: "it must have been a mirage." Materializing the historical unconscious, the ghost-wall is revealed as a traumatic trace. Wherever it appears, the wall marks a local projection of a global repetition of xenophobia and violence, separating the self from the other and simultaneously denying this. Akerman's film invites us to reconsider this trajectory in light of past, present, and future walls, and, of course, from the other side.

Pasts, Presents, Futures

Long before the promise of definitively materializing the wall in the form of a physical, built obstruction became a concrete tool for mobilizing fear, anxiety, and hatred in order to accumulate votes, the works of Guillermo Gómez-Peña and Chantal Akerman attested to the ways in which the wall as a concept, a fantasy, and even a ghost already operated within the political imaginary of the United States and Mexico. Shielding and resurfacing repressed histories of violence, subjugation, and erasure, the US-Mexican wall thereby projects the relationship between the two countries. "It is," in the words of Maria Del Pilar Blanco, "the site that waits to be made answerable, where the limits of American imagined communities are jealously guarded and violently enforced."[149] In a way, the histories that make up the structure of this wall (concrete or not) hence exercise pressure on the ways in which landscape promulgates a spectral wounding and national trauma from the past to the present, from the other to the self. Understanding this dynamic, Gómez-Peña and Akerman both treated the US-Mexican border as a screen for the racialized hierarchies that mediate histories of personal otherness and communal persecutions to link the legacies of walls across time and space. By utilizing the US-Mexican wall as a transnational liminal medium, both artists aimed to re-tell implications of the border, recounting and subverting the various walls through their resonance with other places, contexts, and stories.

Gómez-Peña has explored this trajectory with a focus on the internalized walls that condition the creation of a postcolonial border subjectivity, holding the potential to disrupt the dominant fictions of the global North. He thereby exposed the dependence of the colonial structure on the maintenance of imaginary and concrete partitions, barriers, and walls, while utilizing them as a fantasmatic playground for the staging of "alternative fictions" (perhaps already as opposed to "alternative facts"). This kind of creative haunting considers the entwinement of geography and un/conscious, present and past, in order to read the fluctuations of subjects across different political communities and cultural imaginaries. From the other side, Chantal Akerman reminded viewers that the wall works primarily as a traumatic barrier in the Western psyche. Returning the repressed racialized violence at the core of European histories, and thereby recalling the West's inability to deal with its "others" while simultaneously depending on them, Akerman's work chronicles a map of traumatic encounters across walled lives, reminding us that those who build walls risk to lose their humanity in the process. Working with the site-specificity of the US-Mexican border, both artists projected a global lineage of walling that entwines the histories of colonial violence and authoritarian control long before Donald Trump appeared on this stage. In one way or another these artworks hence foreshadowed the aggressive appeal of the wall's materialization along with its violent historical and political foundations in the US American context and elsewhere.

Tellingly, the trauma of racialized violence underwriting this trajectory links the different contexts in Berlin, Palestine, and Mexico at the deepest, most intimate level. The Berlin Wall works as a symptom of denial, and of the German inability, and perhaps refusal, to deal with the guilt and shame of the atrocities committed during the Second World War. Serving to repress the legacies of the past on both sides, the wall literally builds a barrier against the past in an attempt to remodel the (collective) self without having to address earlier atrocities. Inevitably linked to this denial, the wall in Palestine also works as an expression of the trauma associated with the Holocaust. It projects the fantasy of the enclosed Israeli nation in order to secure its people, coping with the past by eliminating vulnerability. The wall in Mexico (though having made its presence felt affectively and effectively for decades) has become a symbol of cultural anxieties and capitalist hounding, reviving a racialized and gendered structure of privilege that hails back to the imperial foundations of US nationhood. Like its precedents in Berlin and Israel, the US-Mexican wall hence resonates with the traumatic legacies of the past; however, in its insistent evocation of temporal, contextual, and cultural simultaneity, the US wall most acutely summons a politics of haunting.

In her discussion of "Imperial Ghosting," Anne McClintock explains that the remnants of the nation's violent foundation, its fictional investments, and "administered forgettings"[150] reveal themselves in the reappearance of national phantasms and the compulsive repetitions of imperial violence.[151] Haunting the political present, the ghosts of the past return in "the form of a doubleness (...) material and spectral traces, shadowy after effects, and temporal disturbances,... scarring the landscape"[152] and its inhabitants alike. We may well read the US-Mexican wall in line with these "ghosts," as the recurring remnant of a violent past, reminding us of the perils of modernity. Of course, in the United States this process of re-walling and dividing has been primarily linked to the election of Donald Trump as the US president in 2016. Affectively reviving a well-worn national (and as has been shown global) imaginary of a rusty (perhaps even ghostly) hierarchy of privilege, Trump's politics are firmly situated in the context of racialized violence inscribing walled space. In other words, with the appearance of Trump, the colonial ghosts of past and present have gone rampant in returning to the surface, materializing the defensive whiteness, gendered power, and parochial nationalism encoded in the project of a "big, fat, beautiful wall."

7

To Trump Them All: The Most Beautiful Wall

In 2015 real estate mogul, turned Reality TV celebrity, turned presidential candidate, and finally the nation's most controversial "anti-establishment" twitter troll, Donald J. Trump announced that if he was elected president of the United States, he was going to build an "impenetrable, physical, tall, powerful, beautiful, southern border wall" and "make Mexico pay"[1] for it. Attaching (perhaps unsurprisingly) yet another enormous building structure to his name (consider the phallic resonance of Trump Tower or the former Trump Taj Mahal), the great wall of Trump became an important symbolic building block in the construction of Trump's highly gendered, cultural, and political persona as president of the United States.

Crucially, Trump was not the first to suggest the building of a wall at the US-Mexican border in an effort to ascend to the presidency. Michelle Bachman promised to build a fence along the southern border in 2001, and Herman Cain aspired to a "twenty-foot wall, barbed wired, electrified on top," which he compared to the "Great Wall of China" in the same year.[2] Neither was Trump the first to attach the wall-imago to a return of America's greatness. During the 1980s Ronald Reagan already rejoiced to "Let's Make America Great Again" while promising strong measures to prevent migrants coming into the country from the South. The recipe of containment, self-indulgence, and nostalgia has long provided powerful resonance within US political discourse. Yet, no other politician has managed to project his or her name onto the imaginary concrete of the national phantasm of a "great wall" as ferociously and "bigly" as Donald J. Trump.

While the wall proposal earned the then soon-to-be-elected president a great amount of mockery and criticism due to its obvious impracticality, outrageous symbolism, and untenable cost, the "build the wall" slogan has also accounted for astonishing waves of enthusiasm, support, and applause during the 2016 Trump campaign and beyond. Arguably, the proposition to build the wall was instrumental to Trump's successful move to the White House, provoking intense affective resonance with his supporters and opponents alike. Despite (or perhaps because of) the sheer absurdity of its obsessive literality, Trump's wall seemingly enabled a (Freudian) condensation of a range of affects and fantasies associated with the politics of walls. More precisely, Trump's wall reverberates with powerful fantasies of a gendered nationalism that are reflected in the evocation of nostalgia for a lost greatness and secured in the reassurance of national anxieties through the comfort of containment. Enveloping some of the more aggressive affects of the United States' political unconscious, this nationalist fantasy of walling is rooted in a simultaneous yearning for omnipotence and a perceived disavowal or besiegement, mediating an anxious (if imagined) sovereignty that is highly dependent on the archaic artifice and prop-masculinity of nationalist fantasy projections.

Seen in this light, it is important to remember that the wall Trump invoked did not introduce the racism, sexism, and bigotry it has come to symbolize in the US political discourse. Rather the wall, as a national phantom, remediates an existing mythology that utilizes these parameters in order to produce what Salecl calls "the fantasy structure of the homeland, the nation (in the sense of national identification)."[3] In the context of the United States, this structure is necessarily bound up with a European past and a colonial modernity, which constantly reproduce and renew each other through the means of territorial circumscription and racial hierarchization. Within this frame a pan-European "whiteness" is historically treated as "synonymous with the nation"[4] as Evelyn Glenn Nakano explains and thereby "encircled whiteness" (literally evoked in the form of wagon forts during the frontier expansion) operates as the structural fantasy of the nation. Resting (not so far) underneath the surface of US politics, this fantasy structure conjures up the uncanny specter of European fascism and American empire through rhetoric that links racial supremacy and the evocation of camp spaces to a myth of "manifest greatness." Projecting this fantasy to a national audience, the wall in Trump's politics is hence primarily a medium that helps to create the fantasy-nation in terms of a bordered (and hence secure), great, white America (of the past and future).

While many people are fascinated with the powerful, visual, and palpable physicality of walls, it is precisely the border-wall's timeless, invisible intensity, and affective sponginess that generates political force in this case. Trump may hence have struggled to build his wall, while critics continue to point out its overall inefficiency; however, what we can take from the ongoing enthusiasm of his followers is that the power of Trump's wall has little to do with such practicalities. Rather, it is the wall's "affective economy," its ability "to align individual and collective bodies to the very intensities of [the] attachments"[5] it generates—that is, the promise of a better future rooted somewhere in an imaginary past—which is capable of mobilizing people into responding to the collective fantasies that amplify the wall's political ferocity. In fact, the wall-imago provides a point of fantasmatic identification, and thereby organizes, in the words of Salecl, the "economy of enjoyment"[6] surmised by Trump's outrageous politics.

Trump's appeal may hence be linked to "the discursive power"[7] of his offensive rhetoric, his ability to "tell it like it is"[8]; in actuality, however, the affective resonance of his words has just as much to do with what remains unspoken and instead is being projected onto the imaginary wall. Following Salecl, "the level of unsaid fantasies"[9] in Trump's politics propels the enthusiasm of his followers (and the horror of his opponents), providing a space that can be filled with racists and sexist scenarios by which America is returned to "greatness." Such fantasies find a projective screen in the medium of Trump's wall, even where (or perhaps because) it only exists as an imaginary. Hence, rather than providing a feasible immigration policy, Trump's wall is capable of mediating various fantasy scenarios of dispelling "the proverbial other" (in the form of foreigners, criminals, and, crucially, non-whites) and returning the nation to the hetero-patriarchal masculinity that anchors a history of white privilege in the United States.

Most obviously the wall enables fantasies of exclusion that are both racialized and gendered. The wall is hence crucial to projecting what Kevin Bruyneel calls "Trump's counter subversive memory politics,"[10] envisioning "a past in which American individualism embodied in the white settler hetero-masculine figure reigned supreme with neither constraint nor critique, but rather esteem."[11] The wall provides the frame and context, the *Schauplatz* as Freud would say, in which various forms of this performance can take place, countering anxieties about the porous whiteness central to both fascist and colonial fantasies of mono-cultural sovereignty. As Mark Burnett, producer of Trump's larger than life TV persona on *The Apprentice* once put it, "He's like the guys who built the West,"[12] and who has now (re)appeared on the political stage as the business mogul who can rebuild it.

Practically, such a "renewal of white supremacy's relevance to capitalism"[13] takes the shape of ethno-nationalism, which operates by enforcing imaginary, legal, and concrete walls. Under Trump such barriers were primarily pitched to exclude Muslims "as the post-soviet 'enemy' of the American Empire"[14] on the one hand and reject Mexicans as the postcolonial rival on the other. In other words, these boundaries renew (and forcefully guard) imperial investments into American whiteness. While many news outlets and commentators have warned about Trump's uncomfortable flirtation with fascist politics, it is hence the underlying project of "the colonial present"[15] that provides him with a mythological footing for a contemporary version of modernity's authoritarian tendencies. As Cornel West puts it, "[Trump] is a product of American empire. He's a product of American civilization, the vicious legacy of white supremacy still operating,"[16]—and we may add, so is his wall.

The mirage of Trump's border wall must therefore be read as a medium in its own right, projecting the political unconscious of his time—or the time of Trump's presidency. Just like its physical counterparts in Berlin and Palestine, Trump's imaginary wall functions as a screen in the sense of both shielding and revealing the political context from which it emerges—not least because all walls are primarily a function of the imaginary. In order to read such a screen and the political fantasies it simultaneously disguises and projects, it is important to consider the wall's contextual specificities by which it has attained its politically affective resonance. For example, Trump's wall amplifies a disturbing "affective fascism"[17] that is often linked to, but simultaneously exceeds, European history, signaling the authoritarian surmise at the heart of the American fortress. Yet, Trump's wall also emerges from (and simultaneously reproduces) a distinctly postcolonial context in which its totalitarian overtones are grounded.

Ultimately, Trump's wall tells us something about the historical legacies that operate within, but are often forgotten by, American political discourse, and which are linked to a European modernity that has repeatedly appeared cloaked as interventionism, fascism, totalitarianism, or dictatorships. Reminding us that these histories have always joined forces with imperial partitions, the wall, in other words, exemplifies the constant replenishing of white supremacy in the United States. In this context it is often overlooked that Trump's imaginary wall appears as a colonial remnant, an "imperial ghost" as Anne McClintock would say,[18] and thereby it returns us to the forgotten imperial structures, which have always underwritten the fascist ideologies of megalomaniac men. Crucially, such a return of the repressed highlights a difficult history that exercises pressure on the politics of the present, but also offers points of engagement and remembering.

The Wall as It Stands (-ish)

From his initial week in office (until his very last day[19]) Donald Trump framed his presidential term with the image of the wall, proclaiming the emergence of an administration openly banking on authoritarian control and imperial disciplining in order to violently guard and forcefully reestablish what was perceived as the country's vanishing sovereignty. In the first instance this meant that Trump energized the fantasy of the wall to reinforce multiple parameters of exclusion, as a way to assert his own power (and perhaps to test the malleability of the US constitution). On January 25, 2017, only five days after his inauguration, Trump issued executive order 13767 on Border Security and Immigration Enforcement Improvements, demanding to "immediately plan, design, and construct a physical wall along the Southern border."[20] and effectively putting 11 million people at risk of deportation.[21] Only two days later this initiative to redraw the line between what Trump and his followers perceived as true and deserving America and the other(ed) side of this fantasy was followed up by executive order 13769 (otherwise known as the Muslim ban), which temporarily prohibited refugees and citizens of seven (predominantly Muslim) countries from crossing US borders. One week into the presidency Donald Trump had therefore well-established a kind of exclusionary public feeling in the service of rebuilding the American fortress, or what we might call an "affect of walling," as the centerpiece of his politics, utilizing the wall to identify and target the non-white others crucial to sustaining his political imaginary.

The Southern border and the president's hostility toward Muslims and Mexicans in particular intersected at the conjunction of fantasy and materiality where an imaginary exclusion manifests through concrete restraints. Hence, while the "affect of walling" resonates beyond the material construction of the border wall, Donald Trump was intent on giving shape to rhetorical and legal division through architectural exclusion. Trump insisted that the wall "be physically imposing,"[22] stand at a height of 30 feet (although 18 feet may be acceptable) and sink into the ground by at least 6 feet in order to prevent illegal migrants from entering the United States through tunnels.[23] Furthermore, Trump had specified that the wall was meant to "be aesthetically pleasing"[24] (bearing in mind that one day it might carry his name), although he had also made clear that this was only a requirement from "the north side."[25] This focus on physicality and visuality highlights the wall's function as a "hyperbolic token"[26] in the performance of the Trump presidency. While the wall may be impractical for an effective immigration policy, its theatricality was central to Trump's understanding of his own "spectacularized power."[27] Consequently, Trump's wall has emerged from a rhetorical device to somewhat of an ego-project, which the president had to pursue against all odds.

The flickering presence of the wall-mirage between invisibility and visibility, projection and physicality, flimsy rhetoric, and actual bricks quickly became a central battleground of the Trump presidency despite facing a range of obstacles. Most people in the United States opposed the building of a physical wall (62 percent were against the construction in February 2017).[28] Congress was reluctant to finance the wall at an estimated cost of $10–12 billion dollars[29] and had "only" approved $1.6 billion dollars for the construction by 2018.[30]

It was also unclear where the $750 million dollars of costs in maintenance per year[31] were meant to come from, not least because Mexico had (and still has) no intention to pay for the wall.[32] Furthermore, the federal government does not own most of the land that the wall was meant to stand on. Rather, the land largely belongs to native tribes and private owners, suggesting that the path to construction (then and now) is plastered with an endless array of legal battles.[33]

Such practicalities aside, Trump was fully immersed in the mirage of his wall, going as far as tweeting misleading photos in March 2018 that suggested the construction of the barrier had finally begun.[34] At the end of the same year the president provoked a government shut down over funding for his wall and in January 2019 the dispute resulted in Trump's first nationwide presidential address, during which he insisted a wall was "absolutely critical" to meet "a growing humanitarian and security crisis"[35] at the southern border—despite the factual inadequacy of these claims. Trump eventually declared a state of national emergency (which was only suspended by his successor Joe Biden in 2021) to be able to draw money for his wall from the defense budget. In the end Trump managed to build a fraction of his promised wall—452 miles to be exact,[36] most of which were replacing existing fencing, and left an array of unfinished structures (some of them ironically undermining the surveillance technologies such as radars operating along the border) while claiming he had "ended the immigration chaos and re-established American sovereignty"[37] in 2021. Trump's anxious obsession with the construction of the wall throughout his term intimates that as a powerful fantasy structure, the wall was the Lacanian mirror to Donald Trump's presidential ego ideal, but it also worked as a central part of the fantasy the president had about himself. The wall was a decisive prop in performing "presidential" Trump, Commander in Chief, patriarch of the nation, and gatekeeper of "Americanness."

More precisely, by bringing to the surface the racist and sexist fantasies that organized "enjoyment" of the Trump presidency (Trump's own and that of his supporters), the wall mediated the gendered nature of racialized division as a point of ideological identification. For example, Curtis Marez suggests that the wall reproduced "racialized and gendered dynamics of subordination and humiliation,"[38] and thereby became an attribute of Trump's hetero-patriarchal power (and by extension that of his male supporters). In this regard, it is no coincidence that the development of eight wall-prototypes to "test and evaluate the anti-destruct characteristics"[39] of the mock-up walls early on in the project had been largely framed as Trump's wall "beauty pageant"[40] by the media. Reflecting not only on the importance of appearances and celebrity for Trump, but also "feminizing" the wall itself, such a frame exposed how the wall sustained the hetero-patriarchal imaginary from which it emerged.

The wall became the impenetrable membrane in the fantasy of protecting the (feminine) nation from intrusion—a protection only Trump, the presidential construction tycoon, could provide.

The Concrete Beauty Pageant

Of course, such a mediation also has the potential to fold back on itself, offering points of critique. Suggesting an imaginary reversal of nationalist paranoia, the mock version of the Border Wall Prototype Beauty Pageant, organized by the San Diego art group Magpie, featured students showcasing "prototype outfits made from cardboard, tinfoil, and recycled materials"[41] on a red carpet. By drawing attention to the political cosmetics underlying Trump's wall project, the students articulated the media celebrity of the wall's chief creator, simultaneously rendering it absurd. Hence, the prototypes exhibited in the Tijuana desert invoked a critical remediation of the politics from which they emerged, suggesting that if the wall is regarded not simply as an obstructive barrier but as a setting for theater, performance or as a piece of art in its own right, then it communicates its hidden premises.

Following the same logic, Swiss-Icelandic artist Christoph Büchel issued a petition in which he argued that the prototypes should be considered "sculptures" that "have significant cultural value and are historical landart."[42] The proposal was largely read as a sarcastic commentary on the wall, invoking Joseph Beuys's humorous request to raise the Berlin Wall by 5 cm in 1964; however, it also reflected Roxana Velásquez's point that "these eight examples of an overall architectural form are a profound reflection of the cultural barometer, as they leave an indelible mark on the moment we are living."[43] In other words, the wall segments were critical media in their own right, both in the sense of reflecting the symptomatic incoherence of Trump's project and by providing a projective screen that allowed "other" critical commentary to emerge.

Of course, the wall-screen also works as a literal projection surface and hence it did not take long for this capacity of the wall segments to be put into action. Soon after the prototypes appeared, a group consisting of members of the Overpass Light Brigade San Diego, People over Profits San Diego, and graduate students from UC San Diego used the wall segments to project light graffiti onto their surfaces.[44] With the help of a spotlight and stencils the group cast images that recontextualized the meaning of the wall. For example, a ladder mocking the structure's impenetrability was projected onto one of the segment's surfaces, suggesting the possibility of overcoming walls by simple means. Further reframing the narrative of division imposed by the wall, a projection of the Statue of Liberty reminded viewers of the importance of immigration for the US national imaginary. Finally, a human shadow highlighted by the word "¡LLEGALE!" (evoking "illegal" in English; yet, meaning "come in" or "go on" in Spanish) poked fun at the signifying possibilities of signs and symbols (such as the wall), highlighting the functions of walls as both a means of separation and a necessary point of contact. In this regard, the wall may be crucial to the image that Trump seeks to project of himself; however, the various meanings of this image exceed his control, presenting competing ideas about "the nation."

American Greatness

Trump's wall encapsulates the ambiguity of the border-wall-as-medium, shielding an encounter with the past while also remediating it in the present. The wall, hence, works as a Freudian screen, inadvertently returning repressed histories to the political scene by making them visible, palpable, and relatable, while simultaneously distorting these memories. Under the guise of national security and sovereignty, the wall draws on the legacies of the imperial past; yet, at the same time, it effectively provides a medium for "forgetting" the ways in which these violent histories have energized "Americanness" from its founding moments to the way they still animate power formations today. In this regard, it is important to realize that the wall can never be read outside the context of imperial modernity from which it emerges and which it simultaneously seeks to rework.

For example, while the wall reinstates the colonial partition as a way to reinforce territorial sovereignty and political discipline over Mexicans and Native Americans in particular, it also dis-remembers the histories of their violent expulsion and deep entanglement with the land. At the same time, such repressed histories push to the surface precisely at the point where the "colonial present"[45] attempts to renew itself. Forgotten pasts become visible in the protest the wall evokes, the political programs it sustains, as well as the affects their ideologies generate, and, finally, in the visual symbolism of the wall itself. In other words, the wall exposes a double-function of the political discourse: Just like the screen of the wall, political power works both as a means of articulation and as a medium of erasing the historical conditions on which the present social structure is built. The wall hence always reproduces the political fantasies that hide behind its discursive structure.

More to the point, Donald Trump's wall can't help but project the hidden crux of his power performance: that is, a historically anchored gendered and racialized mythology of Americanness. This is important because, as

Matthew Flisfeder argues, "Trumpism has its own distinct historical logic. It is a protofascist movement but one that is particular to its own historical conditions."[46] In particular, the wall links the Trump phenomenon to the affective force of European totalitarianism, exposing the fact that populist movements have always relied on the racialized, gendered hierarchizations that have sustained Western expansionism and colonial exploitation. As Wolfe puts it, "settler colonialism was foundational to modernity"[47] which in turn found its most atrocious expression in the European dictatorships of the twentieth century. Trump's wall screens these conditions in the US context— in both senses of projecting and shielding—providing further insight into the national imaginaries that underwrite Trump's appeal by demonstrating how modernity's most violent impulses renew themselves through fascist rhetoric and empire nostalgia.

More precisely, Trump's wall can be read as a medium of imperial modernity, highlighting a particular white masculinity rooted in the mythology of the nation's foundation (and extending it to Trump). While such mythologies work as "screen memories" (in Freud's sense[48]) in and of themselves, often disguising the violent encounters that have formed them in the first place, the wall also provides a "projection surface" on which they can be examined with closer scrutiny. Remediating the fantasmatic structure of national mythology through the act of territorial circumscription, the wall suggests that political discourse in the United States is underwritten by a distinct and enduring coloniality. Of course, this imperial foundation has always determined the way in which the nation is fantasized; however, it crucially also has been deliberately "forgotten" in the US context, thereby obscuring the conditions of the nation's production. In this sense, Trump and his wall return the nation to a mythology of destined masculine whiteness as brought about through the control of women, racialized "others," and territory. This myth enables Trump to project a narrative of American greatness, without directly addressing the racial and gendered violence that lies at its heart.

McClintock explains that the national narrative (or the nation's "fiction" as Salecl would put it) has not only disguised the settler colonial structure at the foundation of the United States, but it has also enabled the re-reading of US history as tragic destiny[49] or what I would call "manifest greatness" in the context of Trump. McClintock asserts that, "in much United States history, the slow genocide of American Indians is naturalized as the unavoidable tragic outcome of the manifest destiny of the exceptional (white) nation."[50] This re-fictionalization of the founding encounter between Europeans and Native Americans ironically prefigures the exclusionary treatment of migrants today, reframing the violent territorialization of the land "not as imperial policy but as the sloughing off vanishing peoples unfitted by nature for modernity."[51]

Similarly, the wall works to reject anyone who is supposedly in the way of American greatness, economically, politically, affectively, and crucially by virtue of their non-white ethnicity. In this way the wall itself becomes a token of manifest greatness as whiteness, while fictionalizing, disguising, and camouflaging the persistent efficacy (and affect) of colonial histories.

The interplay between the visible and the invisible, the repressed and the renewed is central to the operation of the wall and American coloniality. In fact, McClintock explains that "the founding tenet of American Empire is that it is no empire at all." It is "an empire in camouflage and denial,"[52] or as Bruyneel puts it "the settler part of white settlerness [...] is generally ignored in US political discourse."[53] Nevertheless, US coloniality is always in the process of reemerging or pressing toward consciousness, precisely because, as Kim explains, "settler colonialism and military empire [constitute] an ensemble of relations that continually need to re-create and renovate themselves, for they are incomplete and unexhausted projects."[54] In this regard, Trump's wall moves beyond the haunting of previous materializations of the border as a signpost for the persistence of colonial ghosts. Rather, Trump's wall helps to project a return of repressed coloniality, repeating the nation's foundational violence and constituting what McClintock calls "an imperial déjà vu"[55] in contemporary US politics.

While the wall seals off colonial histories, replacing them with a narrative of (self)protection, it also reveals Trump's entanglement with American empire through the lens of "greatness." This is important precisely because when Trump promises to "make America great *again*" he does not refer to a specific point in time. Rather he invokes an imaginary of lost privilege linked to the myth of Western self-determination and sovereign control. The wall reinstates this imaginary symbolically while soothing anxieties about the loss of racialized and gendered privilege. As Lloyd and Pulido put it, "the fixity of the US settler colonial mentality is the petrified remnant, besieged by demographic trends and delegitimated by decades of social and cultural struggle, of the philosophy of manifest destiny."[56] The wall on the other hand reinstates this project, partitioning, fencing, and zoning the land, which can subsequently be subjugated, owned, and exploited (thereby affirming a historical domination). Creating clear parameters between the "inside" and the "outside," the wall restores the racialized fabric of the great American nation, working as a frame within which the "procedures of differentiation, classification, and hierarchization"[57] central to colonialism can be reinvigorated (or so it may seem).

The politics of space are crucial to understanding the racialized politics of Trump's claims and their affective ferocity. Indeed, Trump invokes the myth of American greatness with reference to the spatial hierarchies afforded by the wall: a monument to the national fantasy of delimiting, disciplining, and reclaiming the country through territory. Utilizing the biopolitics of citizenship as a way to assign identities of (non)belonging, the wall thereby also reinstates an imagined American exceptionalism through means of territory. Cohen and Gorden assert that such a biospatiality "denotes the deployment of... biotechniques to demarcate, control, manage, shape, and ascribe significance to space"[58] in an effort to initiate the political mechanism "by which space is constituted as racialized or in racialized terms."[59] It is through the conquering of the land that a (settler-colonial) political identity can emerge—or in the case of Trump, reconfigure itself. The wall is hence a biospatial medium, determining boundaries as a means to reassert self-definitions; or the formation of greatness is simultaneously spatialized and racialized.

Of course, the spatial boundary provided by the wall is crucial to the development of national identity as whiteness. The wall delimits the scope and margins of citizenship that is historically and fantasmatically underwritten by a trope of whiteness that defines the "hidden surmise" of greatness. As Aileen Moreton-Robinson puts it, "the USA as a white nation-state cannot exist without land and clearly defined borders; it is the legally defined and asserted territorial sovereignty that provides the context for the national identification of Whiteness."[60] Trump utilizes this imaginary of national whiteness and provides it with a spatial frame (and projective screen) in the form of the wall. Attaching xenophobic rhetoric and racialized stigma to the building of the wall, he consequently does not need to spell out the racist fantasies that underwrite America's greatness (although he does not pass off the opportunity). Rather the fantasy of restored national whiteness is mediated on and through the wall, appealing to the empire nostalgia for conquest, progress, and power.

This mythological footing of the wall reproduces John L. O'Sullivan's idea of a manifest destiny, according to which the United States was historically positioned as an "innocent" sovereignty "possessing a messianic destiny" to spread democracy politically and territorially across the continent from the Eastern ports to the shores of the Pacific Ocean in the West. In the logic of this cultural imaginary, politics became a function of a religious investment in the belief that "God had revealed that it was his will for the United States to spread across all of North America"[61] or as O'Sullivan put it, America has a claim, "by the right of our manifest destiny to overspread and to possess the whole of the continent."[62] The wall as a tool of colonial expansion reworks this colonial mythology, staging a contemporary version of American greatness through territorial conquest, by which "the expansion of the United States westward is identical to the expansion of the democratic principle."[63] Resonating with this idea, Trump claims to cure a system that is "rigged,"[64] "fixing" the government and establishing true democracy, not least by means of a wall delimiting the southern border of the US West. Rhetorically excluding African Americans, Native Americans, and South Americans from such claims of "rightening" the system (in both senses of the word), while also appealing to segments of these groups, Trump's affective resonance thereby also highlights the centrality of imperial whiteness as a fantasy position (rather than simply pigmentation of the skin) to the mythological grounding of US sovereignty in the spatial, cultural, and political sense.

Reproduced in the project of Trump's wall, such histories situate greatness as maintained through conquest and settlement. This kind of subjugation of landscape is excruciatingly exemplified in the waiving of a variety of laws that concern the border's environmental protection, including "the Endangered Species Act, Clean Water Act, Clean Air Act, Safe Drinking Water Act, Native American Graves Protection and Repatriation Act, Migratory Bird Treaty Act, and the National Environmental Policy Act," as Sundberg points out.[65] Similarly issues of land ownership, recolonization, environmental concerns, and disruption of ceremonial rites are at the heart of Native American resistance to the project.[66] The wall as an "imperial structure"[67] works as the antidote to natural environments. Instead, it appears as a powerful disruption of open landscapes and ultimately stands as a monument of Western modernity or, more simply, of Western ownership of "nature."

This sense of dominating nature is also echoed in Trump's promise to "drain the swamp" and reclaim the country, once again exposing the "manifest destiny" fantasy at the core of Trump's politics (and his wall). Crucially, in the US context, "draining the swamp" originally referred to the termination of disease-carrying mosquitos and plays on the notion that Washington was built on swampland. However, as a campaign motto the idea has long encompassed the political velocity to rally Americans behind a monumental change: to reinvent the nation. For example, the slogan was used by the far left (to drain out capitalism), by the far right (to get rid of big government), and (surprise!) by Ronald Reagan (to make America great again).[68] Trump reutilized the catchphrase to energize his campaign, positioning himself as simultaneously anti-elitist (he was going to drain the swamp from lobbyists, corrupt politicians and the likes of Hillary Clinton, whom he successfully placated as the embodiment of the "establishment") *and* an authority in returning order to the swamp of Washington (conquering and renewing political territory). While bearing the rhetoric of "cleaning up," restoring, and rebuilding a broken political system, the idea strongly resonates with the "cultivating" of political, economic, and physical landscapes as the outcome of colonial refurbishing. The premise is of course central to the mythology of making America great (in the first place). In this sense, Trump revisits the phantasm of America's origins, re-mythologizing the narrative as a way to fantasize regressive change as "manifest greatness."

Conservative artist John McNaughton recently picked up on the sentiment by recreating Emmanuel Leutze's iconic painting *Washington Crossing the Delaware*. In his version, however, McNaughton replaces the first president of the United States with Trump, reimagining the nation's political foundation in the present. The painting shows Trump, his wife Melania, and notably armed members of the Trump administration dressed in camouflage jackets and denim uniforms, as they make their way to the White House by crossing a swamp. Trump himself is dressed in the famous aviator Jacket that signifies him as the Commander in Chief, holding a light to lead the way. Melania, submissively kneeling by his side, is holding on to Trump's arm (we can only assume she might fall out of the boat otherwise). She is flanked by Vice President Mike Pence who (instead of Melania) stands by the president's side, carrying the American flag. The picture recalls the toxic romanticism of fascist nostalgia, but it also reproduces a distinctly colonial fantasy of conquering swampland somewhere in "the heart of darkness" in the United States. This imaginary provides the fantasmatic context within which the wall must be understood; that is, the wall is situated within the colonial imperative of mapping the grounds for securing the political order of Trump's political empire. Based in a fantasy of protecting and invigorating the frail nation through a hardened (or masculine) performance of domination, the (collective) Trump-fantasy reestablishes affective (and actual) boundaries between the nation and its others, reinserting a gendered whiteness as the defining shield of American greatness.

The Gendered Nation

Nira Yuval Davis, Anne McClintock, Ghassan Hage, and Sara Ahmed have all discussed ways in which the national body is imagined as gendered to map the conflicts and aspirations of the nation.[69] In this scenario women have served as symbols that lend affective meaning to the nation, assisting in defining the boundaries of the homeland in relation to a threatening inside/outside.[70] If the nation is always already fantasized in the sense that it has to be filled with meaning and imagined as a community, then the women-as-nation and the nation-as-woman emblem secures the intimate investments that charge these fictions with consequence. The feminized nation must be protected, controlled, and idealized in order to secure an exclusive relationship between national subject and homeland. Drawing on this affective setting, Trump's wall relies on a gendered discourse, which to many of his supporters appears to provide a path (back) to physical and economic protection, recovering political virility, while his opponents are wary about a democratic nation under threat. In each case, the gendered walled state serves as a screen that enables intense attachments to the political identities an "intimate public"[71] subscribe to as a way of organizing political desire.

Recalling imperial fantasies of fortitude and domination as well as fascist discourses of strength and force, Trump, the Man, who can "fix *it*"—the system, the future, America, white manhood, and more—utilizes the wall as a projective screen for his performance of the gendered politics of the past and thereby demonstrates the grip of these ideas on the present. Trump's wall reflects a defensive imaginary of the fortress-nation within which a white hetero-patriarchal settler masculinity once controlled, disciplined, and dominated the land by ruling over territory and its bounds. Trump's political performance draws on these mythologies of the past and simultaneously reproduces the imperial fantasy in the present. In this regard, Trump's wall provides a magnified stage for the gendered politics of fences and barriers as the grounds for masculine sovereignty.

The American masculinity Trump seeks to exude (although not always successfully) depends on the means of props and walls, precisely because it is primarily a dramatic performance or theater. The wall here works as a podium, a setting, or a screen, projecting the Lacanian mirror to Trump's masculine ego-ideal and that of his supporters—both men and women, who reclaim a seemingly lost privilege by resuming and rejuvenating the traditional gender divisions that have always informed racial, economic, and political hierarchization. Producing a counterpoint to what many commentators have labeled a kind of "wound of whiteness"[72] motivating his voters' support, this performance promises to restore a hetero-patriarchal system that advances whiteness economically and politically. Trump thereby reminds us that ultimately all political discourse, including the racialized, xenophobic ideas, and exchanges that underwrite his wall, are always already gendered within a given system of power. Most obviously, Trump is largely framed and perceived through an obsessive (and anxious) engagement with his own masculinity, and therefore willingly or not, his politics foreground the function of gender to divide and hierarchize.

Protecting the contours of an ethno-nationalist imaginary, the wall is part of the gendered fetishization of the "nation." In his book *Against Paranoid Nationalism* Ghassan Hage asserts that "nationalisms, by their very nature, invite a defensive posture."[73] Similar to the way in which Salecl explains the fictionalization of the nation, Hage suggests that nationalism's defensiveness (which sometimes escalates into paranoia) relies on the production of reactionary narratives that draw on "two modes of imagining the nation."[74] Firstly, the nation is imagined as territorial entity, a "social/geographical space"[75] with clear delimitations and boundaries. Secondly, the nation is imagined as "national will" or as "a unified national body [...] hovering above the territory and defending"[76] its national collective "we." While producing the "imagined community"[77] needed to sustain all national collectives, as Benedict Anderson would put it, this fantasy "conceals the ultimate inconsistency of society"[78] within the nationalist imaginary, as Salecl further explains. More precisely, the nation is projected as homely, nurturing, and caring in order to disguise the nation's mythological artifice, alleviating anxieties about belonging but also promoting fears of loss.

What is of interest here is the way in which this imaginary invites a conceptualization of the nation as *body*, specifically a female body, or the personification of the homeland as woman, often depicted as equally maternal and sexualized, mighty, and vulnerable. One only needs to recall the image of Lady Columbia who embodied America in John Gast's famous painting *American Progress* from 1872 (the "manifest destiny" image per se) in order to understand the importance of the female body for the national imaginary from the early stages of US settlement. Hovering over the landscape, Columbia dominates the image in size, carrying a book and a telegraph wire to symbolize colonial westward expansion as inevitable, enlightening "progress." While rendering her powerful, even unstoppable, the image also attributes an ephemeral (white) femininity to America. Accentuating her *body* with a sparse and floaty white dress, embellishing her with graceful gestures and framing her with angelic golden hair, the painting utilizes Columbia's femininity ultimately as a way to imbue this imaginary of the nation with a sense of delicate beauty and erotic splendor—a combination of fantasies that necessarily cumulates in the nation's unmistaken whiteness. This portrait of the nation, hence, conjures up a serene pride and simultaneously achieves a form of defenselessness and exposure in the national psyche that appeals to patriotic (male) protectionism, devotion, and support.

Under Trump this imaginary has been somewhat reinvigorated, as the wall provides a screen for the gendered investments into the nation from both sides of the isle. More obviously the President himself invokes the gendered imperial mythologies which are often backed by the brand of white femininity enacted by his female staff and family members. The uniform spray tans and blonde highlights of Kellyanne Conway, Kaleigh McEnany, and Ivanka Trump are indicative of this performance, but they are also hyperbolically punctuated—such as when the First Lady sported a colonial Safari outfit on one of her tours.

Invoking Amy Kaplan's point that (white) women have always played their part in reproducing what she calls "manifest domesticity," whereby women help define "the contours of the nation and its shifting borders with the foreign"[79] or other, the women Trump tends to surround himself with stage (and enable) a gendered attachment to whiteness. However, the notion of the gendered nation is deeply recognizable within the American imaginary, animating a variety of investments and, hence, it cannot be disavowed by political affiliation alone. Rather, the gendered nation also appeals to progressive critiques of Trump, suggesting that the wall as screen enables a variety of attachments to national protection.

The Statue of Liberty, for example, often serves as a stand-in for the progressive nation embodying the United States symbolically; she thereby visually provides the female body on which Trump's assault on democracy and nation is imagined by his opponents. Like Columbia, Liberty towers over the nation and exudes maternal reassurance for the American psyche. Overlooking New York, the Statue defiantly holds the torch of freedom and safeguards the Declaration of Independence. However, in countless contemporary political cartoons she is framed as a feminine counterforce to the parochial masculinity embodied by Donald Trump, often showing her violated, upset, or abused by the president. In countless variations she is deported by Trump or told to go home. While these instances articulate the nation's vulnerability in the explicit shape of an assaulted women in order to criticize Trump's objectification of women, his disrespect for democratic processes, and attempts to wall-off the country (thereby effectively linking these processes), this picturing of the nation also exposes a gendered nationalist trope at the heart of US political fantasies. Ultimately, both examples, Columbia and Liberty, demonstrate a predilection to imagine the nation as a woman to provide the means for affective investment while positioning politics as masculinized (portraying executive power either in the form of protector or assaulter or both).

If the nation is thought to be a female body, the wall must be read as a patriarchal gesture of protection as control—and, depending on where you stand, as assault. In each case, the nation, or the motherland, is linked to fantasies of (male) possession and anxieties over foreign and domestic "penetration." As Hage suggests, nationalism's most potent fantasy is the threat of various "other" bodies corrupting the body of the nation, thereby positioning the idealized nation as a "forever deferred finale"[80] that can only be achieved once the nation is "purified." Within the psychosexual imaginary of the gendered national body this means that the nation is never quite (yet) the nation of our dreams (or the great nation of the past) because it is constantly under threat from "others" and must be defended from "intrusion."[81] As Lefort asserts, "what is at stake is always the integrity of the body"[82] and hence it is the fantasmatic other who intrudes that ruins enjoyment of "the nation." The wall, on the other hand, promises to secure a privileged access to, or, conversely, threatens to disavow, national belonging. Trump's wall is hence throwing the paternal shadow, so to speak, "looming over the motherland"[83] by subjugating the motherland to the father's law/nomos/wall.

Similarly, the effort to project and to re-hegemonize white masculinity is bound to the gendering of others in order to reinstate increasingly unstable racial hierarchies. This is reflected in the gendered rhetoric Trump uses to dismantle his opponents (remember "Little Marco" and "Low-Energy Jeb") or the way in which he expresses xenophobia through gendered language. For example, Trump often frames Mexicans as either too feminized (not man enough to contribute to the American economy) or by way of escalating masculinity, that is, calling them "rapists" (apropos intrusion). The same (gendered) logic applies to the exclusion of Muslims, who Trump described as "young, strong men,"[84] "bad dudes,"[85] "trying to take over our children."[86] Simultaneously producing a fear of terrorism as deadly intimacy and of otherness as "excess masculinity," such rhetoric repeats the gendered project of racial hierarchization. Within the bounds of the United States this gendered discourse of racial exclusion solidifies the notion of a feminized nation under siege to be contained by the masculine commander who comes to her protection.

Sealing off the nation from intruders, the wall soothes collective (paranoid in Hage's sense) anxieties that position the national body as vulnerable, infringed, and even violated. In the nationalist imaginary the threat of "other" bodies is persistently compromising the nation's integrity from without and within.[87] For Trump and his supporters, the threat from within takes the form of anyone who does not fit the white hetero-patriarchal ego-ideal of the Commander and Chief and his alt-right followers, including African Americans, Muslims, members of the LGBTQ community, nasty women, democratic "snowflakes" and of course the equally corrupt and "stupid" political "elite." Looking to the "outside," Trump projects the national threat in the form of migrants, terrorists, and drug cartels. The affectivity of these fears of penetration strongly resonates with the emotional outbreaks that characterize Trump's rhetoric and the spectacle of anger he channels for his supporters. What Trump has made palpable in this scenario is that when the threat of national intrusion collapses into what Misha Kavka calls a pleasure in "negative affect,"[88] policies don't convince the anxiously inflamed and intoxicated nation. Instead, what is required, according to this fantasy structure, is the strong (if tiny) hand of hetero-patriarchal imperial masculinity and of course one big "*impenetrable*" tall, solid, beautiful, powerful wall.

The White Imperial Anxiety Complex

Where defensiveness escalates into populist anxiety, the wall exceeds its function as a protective structure; instead, it turns into a projective screen. The screen ensures that the fantasy about the nation can be collectively reproduced, visualized, and maintained. Sara Ahmed explains that the gendered imaginary of the nation can lead to anxieties about a kind of (political, economic, territorial, and also emotional) softness of the national body, that needs to be countered at all costs.[89] In particular the "soft nation" provokes fears about a vulnerable white nation, which by extension, is then equated with "the vulnerability of the white body."[90] Conversely, by enabling the masculine protector (in this case Trump) to assume his role as providing and regulating access to the motherland, the wall assures an affective screening of the collective investment in his potency. In this context nationalism under Trump has propelled new levels of affect, energizing white panic about proximity to vulnerability and besiegement (whether rooted in reality or not) and subsequently (irrationally) charging the president, as well as his wall, with the exceptional proficiency to toughen up boundaries between us and them, so as then to "make America great again."

Yet, it is important to consider that to many of Trump's supporters the motherland has become disappointing and corrupt, leading to a conflict in the nationalist psyche about how to sustain the patriotic investment.[91] In an "anti-oedipal"[92] twist Trump voters appear to be endowed with the idea that the macho-president alone can return them to a lost relationship with the motherland by sealing and dividing the nation as a means of (patriarchal) objectification and control. This suggests that what is ultimately at stake under Trumpism is not simply the integrity of the nation (which may be better protected by other means than a wall), but the identification with the *fantasy* of the nation as threatened by the prospect of neoliberal inequality reinterpreted as loss of racial privilege.[93] In other words, Trump's angry supporters express a discord in the imperial fantasy structure that otherwise ensures the obstruse dispensations of white supremacy.

In this scenario, the unraveling of the imperial order by forces of globalization, advancements in civil rights, and gender equality against the backdrop of neoliberal capitalism are *perceived* to go hand in hand with economic losses and political alienation of those who once thought themselves at the center of the system's care. Leading to an "unhomely motherland" in the eyes of Trump's supporters, these dynamics are the grounds on which the president's hateful rhetoric can subsequently thrive. Indeed, those invested in the narrative of manifest destiny and the (white) American Dream see Trump as someone who can heal the wound of what they perceive to be a loss (or impending loss) of predestined rights and privileges. In this respect, the wall is also a symbol of white woundedness, a bandage for the bruised national ego it protects and projects. Maureen Sioh points out that Trump's supporters are less motivated by economic inequality than they are terrified of economic convergence with minorities,[94] since they experience the loss of white privilege as "traumatic."[95] The wall works as a psychic barrier, containing the wound and deflecting the anger back onto those whose economic and political advancements are feared.

By positioning himself (and by extension his followers) as rightful owner and protector of the nation as bounded and delimited by the wall, Trump performs an imperial nostalgia that is highly affective and monumental in the American psyche. However, the affectivity of Trump's imperial masculinity in particular relies on the fact that, like his wall, Trump's masculinity is artificial, decorative, performative, and ultimately a prop. The macho-cult he likes to cultivate, hence, suggests that like all performances of hypermasculinity, Trump's too is clandestine, fragile, and always already an imitation of something that can never be reached. Conversely, this infringement is matched by a need to contain transgressive femininity by all means necessary. This obsession with containment is epitomized in the proposal of an almost 2,000 mile long wall. It also echoes across Trump's America with the pivotal demand to "lock *her* up"—Hillary Clinton or "the nation," either way, *she* must be contained.

Nasty Women

It is precisely the anxiety at the core of imperial masculinity that drives this gendered discourse of Trumpism and the wall. At the same time masculine anxiety also offers a hole in this structure: a point of critique. Women in particular have been quick to pick up on the fragility of the masculine artifice sustaining Trump's politics. Drawing primarily on the president's self-image and size obsession, Trump's performance of masculinity has invited caricature and ridicule. More precisely, women have challenged Trump's phallus claim, exposing the possibility that status and power are linked to masculine artifice, performance, and props. As congressional leader Nancy Pelosi sharply observed after a heated and much publicized stand-off with the president about the funding of his wall, "it's like a manhood thing for him."[96] Resonating with this anxious staging of hyperbolic masculinity, Trump has gained notoriety for his demeaning attitudes toward (certain) women, creating a climate in which chauvinistic antics are (once more) exhibited as the order of the day.

Of course, many women on the right have also supported Trump despite his alarming sexism. White women in particular were instrumental in electing Donald Trump to be the president in 2016,[97] upholding a vast legacy in promoting conservative aspirations as Emma Blackett has shown.[98] From Phyllis Schlafly's ERA in the 1970s to Sarah Palin's Mama Grizzlies in 2010 and Women for Trump in 2016, conservative women have long proclaimed a kind of feisty depoliticized feminism, which is often deeply rooted in archaic frontier fantasies and present anxieties about the impending loss of class and racial privilege. As Roxane Gay explained shortly after the election in 2016, it seems that women who support Trump "are more invested in their whiteness than they are in their womanhood."[99] By sustaining the gendered nationalism invoked by Trump, they hence see their privileges secured (rather than threatened), adopting an attitude, as Jane June remarks, whereby conservative women are "second in sex to men, but first in race to minorities"[100] and hence embrace the gendered logic of US imperial capitalism while sustaining its boundaries.

On the flipside, many women—and women of color in particular—have also posed a major challenge to Trump's racist and sexist agenda, most notably by what the newspaper the *Guardian* has called "a female-led resistance movement forged in opposition to the election of Donald Trump."[101] Resonating with this claim, the US Congressional mid-term elections in 2018 saw a record number of ninety-two women elected to the House, including two Native American women, Sharice Davids and Deb Haaland, the youngest woman elected to the House, then 29-year-old Alexandria Ocasio-Cortez, and two Muslim women, Rashida Tlaib of Palestinian decent and Ilhan Omar, who came to the United States as a refugee from Somalia. Aside from this surge in political representation, women in all spheres of society recovered their own empowerment through offering distinctly feminine perspectives on the portrait Trump likes to draw of himself. Female artists, in particular, aptly disavowed the construction of hyper-masculinity as a way to critique a system of racialized and gendered power and division by invoking the president's most obvious anxieties (and using them against him).

For example, in early 2016 Los Angeles-based artist Illma Gore painted an 11 inch by 14 inch portrait of Donald Trump, showing the president naked and with a notably small penis. The painting, humorously titled *Make America Great Again*, is exhibited at Maddox Gallery in London and is now priced at around 1 million pounds. The painting's success is of course in part due to its famous subject; however, much of the image's viral infamy relies on the controversy and affective charge it was able to generate (particularly from the white men who felt diminished by proxy). While the image has been largely read as an (unforgivable) attack on Trump's masculine credentials, Gore has stated that the painting was meant to raise questions about the way in which we mythologize the relationship between masculinity and power by challenging the equation of phallus and penis-size. As the artist put it, "if I painted Trump with a massive penis, why would we then take it as a signal that he is powerful? Why would a small penis be viewed as effeminate? And what is wrong with effeminacy to begin with?"[102] In other words, pointing out the difference, "indeed the gulf between phallus and penis"[103] according to Jacqueline Rose, requires a rethinking of authority and status within a masculinized discourse of politics. It also plays with the gendered assumptions underlying division and walls.

A president who understands himself (and is popularly understood) through performative phallic power creates a fantasy template "willing to resort to just about anything to fulfill itself."[104] In this respect the wall itself does not work as a phallic symbol (the Trump Tower is a much more obvious example of this); rather, the wall is the tool that allows for an enactment of phallic power over a feminized territory and therefore itself becomes a symbol of containing transgressive femininity. Gore's image, on the other hand, raises questions about the core assumptions that sustain this discourse, not simply emasculating the president, but reconsidering the fantasmatic foundations of masculine power formations. However, in a political climate in which Trump's hypermasculine artifice has become central to the staging of supreme white manhood, the gendered imaginary of parochial nationalism serves as a limitation to any one of these questions. The divorce between phallus and penis is too challenging for the fantasy structure of the hetero-patriarchal imaginary, overwhelming the hypermasculine ego.

Feminine transgression of this kind is hence (unsurprisingly and, yet, disturbingly regularly) met with hostile sanctions, exposing the fragility of these hegemonic structures. Gore's painting provoked a disproportionate amount of (mostly white male) rage, highlighting this point. The insult of the small penis, itself reinforced by Trump's own obsession with the size of his hand, the size of his audience, and the size of his wall, quickly became a means to concentrate masculine anxiety. In this sense the outrage provoked by the image demonstrates how the affective intensity underwriting male anxiety is reproduced as anger and violence. Whereas such an affective concentration evokes a sense of thrill and bonding among Trump's support groups and rallies, it turns into menace and abuse toward anyone who threatens this core energy and the fantasies it sustains.

Highlighting the fragility of Trump's transgressive prop-masculinity, the abuse Gore faced in the aftermath of making the image public emphasizes the way in which the anxiety produced by male fallibility is compensated for by a spectacle of aggression and hostility. In this context outbreaks of violence are accompanied by a pleasure of "misbehaving with impunity," of doing whatever one wants to do and saying it "like it is," thereby retrieving the phallus from all those who are perceived to have no rightful claim to it (women, migrants, Muslims, Democrats, etc.). Women who challenge this affective crux are perceived as "nasty," "crooked," and "shrill," as the president himself has exclaimed on countless occasions (most often by referring to his opponent Hillary Clinton—another "phallic woman"). Women who are perceived to cross the line, in this sense, must be locked up, punished, and contained.

After publicizing the image on social media in February 2016, Gore reported that she received "death threats, rape threats and anonymous phone calls demanding [she] remove the image from [her] social media accounts or risk going to court."[105] In April the same year, Gore was attacked on the street by a group of Trump supporters, one of whom punched her in the face while yelling "Trump 2016."[106] The affect of reproducing white male anxiety as group exhilaration and violence is an exercise in reclaiming the phallic order Gore's painting unraveled, putting this "nasty woman" into "her place" but also demonstrating a public acceptance of violence against women in the era of Trump. In this sense, Gore's image challenged the mythology of masculine power to which the wall is attached. It thereby disrupted the boundaries which the project of hetero-patriarchal aggression constructs and enacts.

Similarly, in 2016, just days after Trump won the election, artists Roxanne Jackson and Jessamyn Fiore began curating the exhibition *Nasty Women* in order to challenge the misogyny of the incoming administration. More than 700 self-identified "nasty women" contributed to the exhibition, raising more than $50,000 dollars, $42,325 of which went to Planned Parenthood.[107] Accompanied by the "Stay Nasty" program, consisting of "performances, lectures, screenings, and workshops,"[108] initiatives such as these, along with the Women's March on Washington and the explosion of the #metoo movement, respond to the gendered divisions Trump's politics reinforce, as exemplified by the administration's hostile stance on abortion or consideration to delimit "gender as a biological, immutable condition"[109]—another notable containment. While Trump may return an archaic masculinity to the presidential office, insisting on traditional gender divisions and definitions, his efforts are hence also met with a revival of feminist action and artistic resistance.

In the vein of these movements and similar to Gore's disruption of the psychosocial structure of hetero-patriarchal rhetoric by questioning the phallic master signifier, artist Sarah Levy troubled Trump's hyperbolic masculinity by way of feminine materiality. Invoking an abject counterpoint to the hypermasculine fragility that underwrites Trump's aggressive misogyny, the artist painted a portrait of the president using her own menstrual blood as paint. Patiently collecting her material with the help of a tampon and a Diva cup over time, Levy's image was a focused response to Trump's attack on Fox

News host Megyn Kelly during the Republican primaries in 2016, challenging the male anxiety that undergirded this exchange.

Confusing hyper-defensiveness with masculine power, Trump infamously berated Kelly, not simply as a journalist but distinctly as a woman. When asked by her about his verbal attacks on and sexist comments about women, Trump aggressively rebuffed Kelly, later exclaiming "there was blood coming out of her eyes, blood coming out of her wherever."[110] Trump's remarks, which played on archaic fantasies of feminine monstrosity and female abjection, can be read as part of a sexist discourse by which hypermasculinity must be barricaded, stabilized, and secured through delimiting itself in opposition to all things feminine, but especially menstruation, which simultaneously implies castration (a wound) and its disavowal (women bleed without injury). Establishing (and aggressively insisting on) such boundaries (in resonance with the fantasy structure of the wall) thereby works as a means of exercising control over women, disciplining their behavior, and questioning their integrity, even sanity, on account of biological "difference." However, by using menstrual blood to make a portrait of Trump, Levy crossed these boundaries of the hypermasculine identity and self-definition, taunting the integrity of Trump's fragile ego with the feminine abject.

Indeed, Julia Kristeva conceptualizes the abject as the antidote to borders and walls. The abject is that which crosses boundaries, "shatters the wall of repression and its judgments,"[111] and in fact "signifies the other side of the border."[112] Abjection "does not respect borders, positions, rules,"[113] it "disturbs identity, system and order"[114] and ultimately "it kills—in the name of life—a progressive despot,"[115] as Kristeva further elaborates. Menstrual blood, in other words, can be read as a threat to hypermasculine imaginaries—their orders, borders, and walls. As Kristeva further writes, the abject challenges "an ego, wounded to the point of annulment, barricaded and untouchable [that] cowers somewhere, nowhere."[116] This insight takes on an uncanny resonance with the fortressed male ego Trump projects, while positioning the materiality of menstrual blood as a counterforce of signified femininity which is hence capable of unraveling the masculine ego-ideal, and, by extension, its boundaries.

Ultimately, then, Illma Gore, *Nasty Women*, and Sara Levy provide examples of women destabilizing the masculine fantasy, which Trump discernibly likes to cultivate about himself, thereby disrupting the gendered national imaginary at the core of his cultural project through means of political art. Their artworks thereby resonate with Trump's discourse about walls and divisions, exposing the gendered logic of control, containment, and expulsion. More to the point, Trump's obsession with rhetorical, imaginary, and physical walls, whether to exclude the other that is threatening from the outside or to discipline those within, all work in the service of a nationalist fantasy of gendered whiteness.

Often associated with cleanliness in the racist imagination, whiteness proper (that is gendered) disavows the abject and reassures the anxious psyche of its own "clean [white] self."[117] While this is an unstable claim (as the examples have shown), it is the logic that underwrites a need to redraw boundaries, sometimes by means of rhetoric or symbolism, sometimes by means of violence and walls. However, by challenging these masculine fantasies through artistic expressions, (nasty) women pose an important opposition to the racist hetero-patriarchal discourse sustaining the wall.

Tiny Wall

The gendered efficacy of the wall must finally be read in the context of the fame it promotes and projects. After all, while the president is undeniably obsessed with sizable props, Trump also links his phallic power and embodiment to the force and intensity of his celebrity status. Many commentators have rightfully argued that Donald Trump's celebrity as a Reality TV star in particular has paved the way for his political ascendency.[118] This legacy is reflected in the way he runs the White House like an *Apprentice* season (lots of drama, competition, and frequent firing), but it also channels his appeal to mass audiences, which is then further amplified by Trump's emotional use of hostile, xenophobic, and sexist rhetoric (all crowd pleasers on the stage of history). Trump's ability to "entertain" the nation and occupy the media to a large degree determines the dissemination and effectiveness of his outrageous (and often plainly ridiculous) political stands. Understanding this perfectly well, Trump appears less invested in running a country than in producing a great show. He is less interested in polls than he is in ratings, frequently worrying about perceptions more than "realities."

Suggesting that the projective power of Trump and his wall depend on the fame we grant him, British artist Plastic Jesus criticized Trump's wall through a literal challenge to his stardom and gendered performance. The artist poked fun at Trump's hypermasculine insecurities by using his own props against him, building a "tiny wall" around Trump's star on the Hollywood walk of fame in 2016. Encircling the president's claim to fame by literally walling in (and thereby containing) the symbol of his stardom, *tiny wall* was made of 6 inches of concrete, complete with razor wire, and keep out signs.[119] Linking the president's wall to the gendered discourse about his tiny hands and his status as a celebrity, the miniature wall worked as a reminder that both of these discourses are constructed through artifice.

Crucially, *Tiny wall* goes beyond the idea of the wall as a masculine gesture to protect the nation; instead, the installation suggests that the wall helps to protect and project Trump as spectacle in the nationalist imaginary. Highlighting the much-criticized celebritization of politics as a requirement of contemporary political communication, the installation thereby draws attention to the "affective function"[120] of Trump's star image to mobilize public opinion, particularly among his base. Of course, the importance of celebrity as "political weaponry"[121] cannot be overstated in the case of Trump; the wall as the screen magnifies a "cult of personality," the key feature of fascism no less, while securing support from Trump voters. Because of this Trump repeatedly utilizes the wall to stage solidarity with his supporters and to reinforce his own masculine resoluteness, anxiously refusing to compromise on the barrier's materialization, as the government shut down in early 2019 has made clear. In this regard Trump's insistence on the wall itself becomes a pseudo-event in the media narrative of the celebrity president.

This implies that the success of Trumpism, which is largely dependent on the creation of the "celebrity politician,"[122] relies on the complicity of a media culture fascinated with the Trump phenomenon. Indeed, Trump followers and opponents alike engage in a kind of political fandom, based in adoration and repulsion respectively. As Emily Nussbaum suggests, we "continue to see him [Trump] through the filter of Burnett's TV hit,"[123] *The Apprentice*, and hence the president of the United States becomes a "real-life fictional character"[124] onto which the anxieties and fantasies of a whole nation can be projected. Containing this celebrity in turn, or so Plastic Jesus maintains, works to resist the negative affect of Trump's emotive populism and imperial thrill. In other words, plastic Jesus criticized the celebrity status Trump capitalizes on, using the tagline "stop making stupid people famous,"[125] as a reminder that celebrity is sustained by a complex system of media attention and audience support. Ultimately, *tiny wall* highlights (once more) the self-defensiveness of Trump's gendered politics as well as the self-isolation and pretentiousness encapsulated by his wall. Both Trump and the wall are thereby exposed as fantasmatic constructions that have to be invested with affect and notoriety in order to be effective and, hence, are never constructed and elevated by the president alone.

Loose Ends

What Trump's wall exposes then is the gendered imaginary of whiteness as a national charge, animating imperial nostalgia in the present and (re)producing a distinctly (settler colonial) imaginary of the United States. In this scenario the wall is most powerful as a fantasy structure or affective screen capable of magnifying Trump's celebrity persona and prop masculinity. The wall thereby invokes metaphors of an im/penetrable membrane or skin as both an affective surface (a channel) and physical boundary (a shield) to highlight the interplay between body and nation, and to negotiate impermeability in opposition to intrusion. This sense of porousness, or what Ahmed calls the nation's "softness," reveals collective construction of the homeland as a feminized body, which, in the logic of the infiltration metaphor, also runs a risk "of becoming 'less white,' by allowing those who are recognized as racially other to penetrate the surface of the body."[126] Trump's ego project, in other words, provides insights into the wall as an affective surface and projection screen on which the gendered and racialized sensibilities of the past as well as the anxieties of the present find expression and resonance.

Essentially, the wall, bespeaks an affective public sphere in which whiteness is utilized to reestablish hierarchies of protection that exclude anyone who does not fit the "right" way of being great in America. As an image (and imago) it thereby provides insight into the collective fantasies and intimate boundaries that circumscribe support for Trump across different bodies and in an effort to delimit the nation. The wall here works as a patriarchal gesture, believed to be capable of securing the feminine (frail) nation, but also promising to restore a particular relationship to the homeland which goes back all the way to the frontier fantasy of manifest conquest. More to the point, Trump's wall renews investments into imperial whiteness or an emotional attachment to being white as the crux of American dreaming or greatness. Conversely, it thereby also highlights anxieties about unstable belonging to the nation, staging a conflict about who constitutes the nation and takes ownership of its boundaries and sovereignty.

Tellingly, by the time Trump lost the office of president in January 2021, his wall had been left in pieces. Despite obsessively pushing construction to the very last day (the day of Joe Biden's inauguration) the wall's materialization remains a lost cause. Odd, partially completed segments are now scattered across the border region, leaving the current administration with an array of unresolved mess, but also revealing once again, that what is decisive about Trump's wall has always been the fantasy it articulates (rather than the physical obstruction it produces). Accordingly, these wall patches have widely been read as symbolic tokens of the Trump administration's broken promises[127]; however, visually they also convey an image of lose teeth (which Freud of course associates with a fear of castration). The unattractive structure thereby (once more) epitomizes the clandestine fragility of Trump's gendered performance as Commander and Chief, but it also works as a powerful reminder that the wall, alongside all the affects and fantasies that have been attached to it, still hovers in the present. A loose end that cannot be settled or fully put to rest, the wall produces ongoing obstacles and challenges, sustaining the imperial remnants of the American Dream.

8

Leap into Freedom: Concluding Remarks

One of the iconic images of the Cold War shows a young East German soldier defecting to the West by jumping over the freshly rolled-out barbed wire that was to become the Berlin Wall. Conrad Schumann, the nineteen-year-old renegade in the picture, had been guarding the construction of the Berlin Wall for two days when, cheered on by a crowd of West Berlin onlookers, he made the decision to escape in the late afternoon of August 15, 1961. According to eyewitnesses, Schumann had been pacing nervously for hours, chain-smoking and throwing anxious glances over to the crowd who kept encouraging him to "come on over." Then suddenly, at around 4 pm, the young soldier flicked away his cigarette, turned around, and made the jump, dropping his machine gun mid-air.[1] The moment was captured by photographer Peter Leibing and the resulting picture, *Leap into Freedom*, has since been featured in numerous reiterations (there is a graffiti, a sculpture, a mural, etc.), becoming one of the essential emblems in the narrative of (Western) liberty that pervades the memorialization of the Berlin Wall.

Looking at the image it is almost impossible not to feel the charge of the situation: the fear, the desperation, the rush and excitement, the triumph over confinement, and the thrill of defiance. A young man saves himself in a (literal) leap of faith, not knowing whether he'll make it, and not knowing what comes next. It's an impossible jump. An irreversible decision. Bold. Stunning. Cathartic. And yet, I linger. What is most striking about the image to me is not necessarily this sense of spectacular liberation, but the way in which the photograph captures him mid-air, right in the moment of crossing, and thereby reveals something about the inbetween of boundaries: a passage that not simply documents the soldier's shifting alliances but also comments on the wall's own destabilized setting.

Exchanging one side for the other, one leg is in the West, the other is still in the East, with the barbed wire unfolding underneath and the gun only halfway removed, the soldier achieves an ambivalent conjunction between the two sides. In this moment Schumann's wavering status between prison guard and prisoner, soldier and individual, executioner and excluded is dramatically captured, exposing the two crucial modes of political spatialization inscribing walled life. That is, the jump makes apparent that the wall creates a space of heightened security and profound vulnerability at the same time as it blurs their indistinction. In other words, the photograph—like the wall—(un)veils an intimate correspondence between inside and outside, presence and absence, intimacy and flight, ghosts and their manifestations, us and them, then and now.

Throughout this book I have set out to make sense of these tensions and junctures in order to argue that political walls are more than physical obstructions that give expression to a political moment and more than the two sides they so visually enforce. Instead, I have looked at the wall as a point of contact or more precisely as an affective screen, capable of revealing and shielding the various narratives, imaginaries, and fantasies that sustain its materialization. I have also read the wall as a stage, an image, a projection surface and even a membrane that tells us something about the emotional presence of political barriers—a presence which evokes and contains all kinds of stories, perceptions, attachments, and resistances that promote and exceed the spatialization of politics. In this sense, I have been interested in the ways in which political walls run through the hearts and minds of those who build them and those who have to live with them—how they are internalized, experienced, performed, and defied. What I find fascinating about a wall of brick and concrete then is the way it articulates (at times involuntarily) the messy feelings, silent barriers, personal conflicts, and haunting legacies that make up walled life as an evolving signpost in the current global border regime—a regime, which dominates politicized spaces increasingly, but also, as I hope to have shown, intimately occupies people who often push back in surprising and creative ways.

What I want to highlight then is that political walls may sooth a number of anxieties concerned with a yearning for safety, protection, and sovereignty, but they also demonstrate that a walled life cannot be maintained without also creating its "other(ed)" side/site in the form of a space of confinement, precarity, and control. Such spaces are saturated with affects and feelings, producing a visceral experience of the wall: boredom, anxiety, fear, humiliation, fatigue, and melancholy are the prevalent emotional markers of walled existences, but, as the book has demonstrated, there is also rebelliousness, enthusiasm, and a whole lot of hope. In each case, to those who become invested in walls and those who seek to tear them down, the encounter with the barrier is intimate, close, and visceral. It touches us in a certain way. It warrants a response. The wall, in other words, projects a variety of mediations that function as sensory readings of the self in relation to an "other." What these structures hence expose is that repressive topologies work in the spatial as well as in the psychological realm, creating a walled life on "both sides" that screens the circuits of its affects in the form of a series of confrontations.

Certainly, what is foregrounded in the photograph of the defecting soldier (and many of the examples I have addressed throughout my discussion) is the possibility of putting these sides into contact. While this suggests a mode of resistance to the wall and its provocations, ultimately we learn that the distinction between prison and prisoner, inside and outside is hard to maintain. The wall establishes these positions and spaces in the form of a telling symbol, mediating the drastic political and imaginary differences and divisions on which they are premised; on the other hand, these binary oppositions espouse themselves to be intimately entwined and sometimes coinciding. The concluding remarks of this book are therefore an attempt to emphasize the intimate relations between political walls and the various passages they foreclose and enable in order to highlight how the two sides are continuously put in touch. In other words, the final leap I am trying to make here is to consider the pitfalls and opportunities of the wall's "inbetween," and, perhaps, to take one last look at its troubling ambiguities.

Topographies of Feeling

I have examined how affect circumvents boundaries and walls but also creates them as we navigate national belonging through trails of feeling and public intimacies. As Sara Ahmed reminds us, emotions create "the very effect of an inside and an outside" and simultaneously introduce "the very surfaces and boundaries that allow the individual and the social to be delineated as if they are objects."[2] In this sense, walls are entities that are felt and further reproduce feelings about others. They constitute confined "affect worlds"[3] or enclosed public spheres to which people are bound through a negotiation of shared emotional investments, conflicts, and oppositions as Lauren Berlant might add. I read the wall as integral to these visceral spheres, precisely because it is through emotional experience that we come to understand that boundaries keep us apart and simultaneously put us into relationships with each other.

Put simply, walls always mediate a relationship between the inside and the outside, the self and the other, the past and the present, etc. and we come to grasp this through the visual provocation of the monument and sensory responses of our bodies. The book suggests that these affective circuits are supplemented by stories, films, and images that articulate ongoing legacies of domination on the one hand and trouble these boundaries on the other. In response, I consider political walls as thoroughly mediated and as media in their own right through which to understand the shifting conditions and interventions of fantasmatic nation building as a means of intimate negotiation. In this sense, I take Schuman's defiant jump as an opportunity to revisit the wall's meaning as a protective structure in order to approach his leap as instructive to overcome the tainted comfort it provides.

As the examples in this book assert, the walls delimiting imaginative space as topographies of feeling gratify narratives about the self (and conversely about the other) before all else, often staging a need for safekeeping through distressing ideas of cultural insularity that quickly turn into means of aggression. Exemplifying this dynamic, the Berlin Wall was designated an anti-fascist protection rampart, despite effectively working as a prison wall to the East. Today European border regimes present themselves in much the same way, staging protective strongholds, while exposing thousands of people to precarity, violence, and death. The wall in Israel makes use of a similarly defensive rhetoric, presenting the anti-terrorist security fence, which has been shown to also be a tool of ferociously controlling and destroying Palestinian territory. Finally, the impending wall in Mexico notoriously relies on anti-immigration anxieties, pitching a need for national protection and security, while reproducing the postcolonial interdependencies it works to hide. In each case, walls create the inside and the outside simultaneously, establishing the enemy/friend distinctions through affective circulation and imaginative reinforcement.

Imaginative Walls

Indeed, it is essential to examine that the walls of past, present, and future not simply occupy spaces and territories, but more pressingly manifest as barriers of the mind. Edward Said speaks of "imaginative geographies" to explain how a group of people situated within a particular territory "will set up boundaries between their land and its immediate surroundings"[4] in order to demarcate themselves from what they perceive as "the land of barbarians"[5] producing a distinction between "familiar" and "unfamiliar space."[6] According to Derek Gregory, the "other side" in Said's imaginative topography is then best understood as "a sort of negative in the photographic sense,"[7] invoking both similarity and absence (in the sense of lack) between other and self, and further reflecting the interplay between psychological and technological screenings, which is, of course, also central to the projective function of the wall.

Similarly, the three walls I examine in this book serve as media for the political context they have inscribed, creating the other by projecting the other onto the screen of the political. While, to Said, space "acquires emotional and even rational sense[8]" in this way, converting geography into interpretations about who the other is, Gregory further suggest that we consider such imaginative geographies "as fabrications" combining "'something fictionalized' and 'something made real' because they are imaginations given substance."[9] The wall as the intersection between the physical, the imaginary, the emotional, and the psychological demarcation of politicized space is hence both a means of fantasizing the inside as immediate, protected, and privileged, while projecting otherness (in the form of threat, regression, and lack) onto the land on the "other side."

Said's discussion is useful in reflecting on the psychological makeup of walled life, translating space into imaginations on the one hand, and producing a peculiar psychological blindness on the other. The walled identity dramatically "intensifies its own sense of itself,"[10] as he might put it, while simultaneously erasing the other (side). Indeed, each wall remediates a structural absence in this way, and often serves to substantiate it. For example, the Berlin Wall has been shown to invoke an affective absence that has outlived the wall's demise. Similarly, the wall in Israel inscribes a political and psychological "absence" of Palestine as the condition for realizing the dream of a nation; and the ghost-wall at the US-Mexican border helps to repress the imperial histories (and presents) of US-Mexican relations, while projecting a "forgotten" America (in order to make it great again) onto the national screen. In this way political walls lay the groundworks for establishing the two central political spaces of modernity: the fortress, as a space of protective containment meant to keep out "the barbarians" and the detention camp as a space of projective containment, designed to keep them in.

It is then not surprising that alongside the reappearance of walls all over the world, fortifications and detention spaces are seeing an extraordinary resurgence in the face of dramatic geopolitical reconfigurations of livable space. The repercussions of colonial exploitation, resource extraction, proxy wars, and climate change have put vast populations on the move in a desperate attempt to break out of their designated spaces, resulting from the imperial scattering of the earth into precarious distributions of territory and assets. Conversely, these new forms of mobility have led those in charge of the old orders to hide behind fortress walls while attempting to contain unwanted movements with the help of detention camps and other barriers.

Consider the emblematic barricading of Fortress Europe with the help of ever new walls and pop-up fences while detaining incoming refugees in transit centers or on outpost island (e.g., Lampedusa, Melilla). The same xenophobic fears underwrite the plans for a wall between the United States and Mexico and the vast detention industry that has (already) developed in its shadow.[11] Israel's production of precarious containment in Gaza or the West Bank also dramatically resonates with these examples; however, it is the Berlin Wall that reminds us of the fallibility of such ideas.

When Conrad Schumann leaped over the barbed wire of the Berlin Wall, he knew that the rhetoric of security is sometimes self-defeating, as being secure comes at the cost of being secured. As capitalism's global expansionism has dreamed the neoliberal borderless world, globalization's order of privilege has led to an excessive reterritorialization of the earth in order to prevent large parts of the world's population from participating in its "benefits." New walls create a landscape of incarceration, limits, and boundaries in an effort to keep the excluded in their place and yet what is often overlooked is that such confinement works on both "sides" of the wall. In saying this I do not wish to equate the experience of those who build walls and those that are excluded by them. Rather, I want to suggest that political walls inform the lived experiences in their reach, which creates consequences on both sides. In other words, political walls build psychological (and real) prisons, creating confined memories and limited futures, most severely for those whom they exclude but also significantly in those they secure. Put simply, walls do not offer safekeeping for either side; they build prisons.

Etat de Siege

In order to unravel this interplay between fear and containment, I want to briefly dwell on the notion of the fortress, which has gained particular momentum alongside the resurgence of political walls, primarily because it responds to a prevalent feeling of besiegement that drives fortification today. Protecting an imaginary of racial, political, religious, and/or cultural privilege, the fortress is often associated with a discourse of hypervisible border security, serving as a psychological stronghold against the decomposition of worn-out power formations in the globalized world. In this way, political walls emerge under the banner of shielding—projecting a fantasy of besiegement and security in response to the crumbling dominance of privileged nations. More to the point, the walls of present and future construct the fortress in the physical, political, and psychological sense in an attempt to reanimate an outdated or fantasized sovereignty. Such a fortress is often built on perceptions of moral, legal, and economic authority, defending the fantasy of "civilized modernity" from the dangers on the "outside" and defining a communal identity in opposition to its other. Comparing the interior to the inside of a house, Said's discussion of spatial appropriation suggests that the fortress "acquires a sense of intimacy, secrecy, security, real or imagined" in much the same way the home (or homeland) does. It is, in other words, a point of anxious belonging.

This is not to say that fears about changing geopolitical orders are not substantiated or merely the phantasms of paranoid collectives, but to intimate that like the "fabrications" that realize Said's imaginative geographies, the feeling of besiegement provides insight into how the psychology of walls informs their political evocation. Indeed, Hage explains that the fantasy of being besieged is not necessarily (just) a fiction of the xenophobic mind, but instead may point to a real unraveling of privileged geographies.[12] In this regard, the wall is a defensive symptom of a tangibly changing order in response to which the forces of antiquated power structures are amplified by means of walls. On the other hand, the politics of fear are often overstated or used to legitimize violence against those who already exist under conditions of extreme precarity and vulnerability. Pointedly the very "civilizations" who fear their values could be endangered by the inclusion of "outsiders" are prone to compromise the democratic principles, humane values, and civil conduct they hold dear in order to ward off these intruders.[13] What is interesting about this process is the way in which the *feeling* of being besieged (substantiated or not) translates into a progression of walling.

In order to interrogate this trajectory of violence it is useful to return to the fantasmatic function of walls. Like a screen, the siege narrative shields the interior from its own barbarism, projecting the threat onto the outside. The wall of the fortress enables this trick, sustaining the imaginative civility of the inside. Yet, the feeling of being besieged also returns repressed atrocities to the consciousness of the interior, albeit screening such violence in inverted, or *verdichtet*, forms. More precisely, the violence committed against the other, which has been screened out by the wall, returns as the fantasy of being violated *by* others, producing more violence in turn. Hage intimates this idea referring to a "psychological residue of a kind of primordial colonial theft, murder, and exploitation."[14] He suggests that "this act haunts the culture of all those who have consciously or unconsciously benefited from it, making them more fearful,"[15] and by extension legitimizes new forms of exclusion, allowing the aggressor to project violence as defense.

Read through this lens political walls are always both aggressive and defensive means that respond to a "structure of feeling"[16] through projection. Of course, projection is both an expression of the repressed and a refusal to recognize it—an idea which is made tangible via the screen of the wall. Like the fortresses of the past, contemporary political walls reflect the narrative of besiegement as a way to disguise the racialized hierarchization inscribed in them. In this way, political walls bring into sight and simultaneously hide the ways in which access to safety, prosperity, and citizenship is allocated according to race, culture, religion, etc. Put simply the wall as screen does not merely shield (the view), concealing what (or who) is excluded on the other(ed) side; the screen is also always projective, in the sense that it reveals (again and again) this point of erasure.

Concrete Media

In this sense, the walls I have interrogated in this book always make known the histories and wounds that underwrite them and, thereby, reveal how we deal with political scars. Engaging political walls as screens that tell us about the violent formations of political and psychological division throughout history is then also an attempt to face the traumatic legacies and silent barriers of walled life without strictly resolving them. Understanding the reappearance of walls as a traumatic repetition of divisive politics encourages us to engage with the crises and injuries they repeat. Seeing the wall in this light, in other words, begins to answer Gabriele Schwab's call for an "intercultural transference between different violent histories,"[17] which she conceptualizes out of Germany's atrocious Second World War legacies. It also resonates with Jaqueline Rose's agreement with Edward Said's appeal that we must "enter into each other's historical and ongoing pain"[18] in the context of Israel-Palestine and Gloria Anzaldúa's claim that "the struggle has always been inner" and that it is merely "played out in the outer terrains,"[19] with regard to Mexico. Making a leap between these contexts and histories (or in the case of Berlin, Palestine, and Mexico delicately interlacing a post-socialist, post-holocaust, postcolonial imaginary) then does not refuse each wall's contextual specificity but highlights moments of encounter in the past to probe the possibilities of shared futures.

In this sense, the notion of an intercultural transference between the three walls intimates a call for connective projection. Rather than externalizing repressed violence and projecting it onto (one) an/other (so as then to legitimize the exercise of further violence), such a projection allows for traumatic or haunting legacies to resurface in another context, establishing points of connections instead of obstructions. If we look more closely, each wall recalls the barriers that have come before it and will be built in the future. Hence, like the screen memories of the unconscious, walls do not simply defer relationality but also offer passages, a point of contact in the Freudian sense, creating channels of meaning-making by which the wounds, affects, and attachments of one wall are transferred onto another and so may be made legible (at least somewhat) in a different light.

Returning to the image of Conrad Schumann's astonishing flight, the many layers of the photograph's affective charge begin to unravel as they subvert and highlight the politics of containment still operative today. Halfway across the line, an escapee in uniform, Schuman appears to liberate walled life, overcoming the self and the wall in one daring moment. And, yet the photograph eternalizes a forever deferred finale, fixing the transition and marking the enduring presence of the wall that has not yet been built. Today's political walls remediate this sense of timeless ambiguity: spectacularizing strength, they disclose a feeling of besiegement. Asserting visibility, they nonetheless ensure hiding and withdrawal. Creating monuments, they disremember the past. Halfway across the line, inbetween here and there, they work both to shield and to project the ambivalent (and often contradictory) political imaginaries, fantasies, and feelings that circulate as part of an affective infrastructure of exclusion, in resonance with which various sensibilities of walled life can be performed and cultivated. The boundaries produced by these circumscriptions are (always) both physical and psychological, visible and invisible, appearing not simply as fences and walls but also demarcating affective, symbolic, and imaginary media.

I have foregrounded this medial capacity of the wall in order to highlight how art and storytelling resonate with spaces of confinement around the world, often by reclaiming expression as a form of making-conscious or as a challenge to the way in which the wall divests the other's agency to look and speak, to being seen and being heard. As artist Maddie Kramer once put it "walls aren't meant to divide us. Walls are meant for art."[20] In the same spirit, the works I have discussed engage the onlooker with the wall's "other side" in the literal and the conceptual sense. This "other" side of the wall is not a curtain, a shield, a prison, or a limit. It is a stage, a mirror, a channel, and a screen. It is this potential of critical self-reflexivity that turns the wall into a medium, making visible (rather than invisible) the encounter between other and self, and projecting, rather than shielding, the relationship the wall has come to materialize. In other words, in thinking about modes of opposition, we need to acknowledge that the wall cannot help but disclose, make visible, and even connect the sides it seeks to divide.

This is particularly important because a vast array of political entities, from Australia to India and Pakistan, South Africa and Brazil, Korea or Cyprus, remain preoccupied with complex negotiations of bordering and walling. In 2020 the United States put up fences toward Canada to curb the Covid-19 pandemic while Greece planned to build a floating water wall in the Mediterranean

Sea. These curious cases are symptomatic of the ways barriers, fences, and walls increasingly stage responses to shifting ecologies and increased global mobilities, producing escalating forms of exclusion. It appears that the wall's counter-intuitive resurgence in a crisis-ridden world provides a peculiar material setting for future battles: about climate change, health, housing, equity, etc. These newly emerging walls and barriers need to be viewed with respect to their full material, ideological, and patently racialized consequences as they draw on and feed back into the ways in which myriad physical, affective, and fantasmatic boundaries are established and channeled to defend continued investments into privileged access to well-being and safety.

The Impossible Leap

Returning, once more, to Schuman's remarkable escape with respect to contemporary politics, the image intimates a sentimental, yet claustrophobic, resonance with those who continue to live within the bounds of walls and barriers. While, Schumann's "leap into freedom" conjures up the possibility of exchanging one life for another (as so many have dreamed at the US-Mexican border) and of breaking through the structures of confinement (still holding Palestinians and refugees in place), it also suggests a notable restraint of catharsis in the walled contexts of the present. After all, could the people arriving at Europe, or those in Palestine or Mexico just jump these fences? Could they leap into freedom and begin a new life, like Schumann did? The image suggests a notable difference in possibility between the walled spaces then and now.

Despite the emblematic resonances between the Berlin Wall's barbed wire and the walls still imprisoning people today, Schuman's jump is exceptional and privileged by comparison. Cheered on by the people on the other side, the climactic escape is possible, precisely because it plays out beyond the racialized topologies containing walled life today. While Schumann "merely" has to cross a line, many people who currently live under conditions of spatial confinement, extreme precarity, and radical vulnerability have (literally and figuratively) nowhere to jump to. They are excluded by virtue of a racialized territorialization of space as well as access to safety and prosperity which continue to be affective and effective even if and when these boundaries are crossed. Rather than liberation per se, the image hence signifies a cathartic disavowal of defensive aggression.

I suggest that the extraordinary "leap" depicted in the image is then not simply the escape of the prisoner, but the change of heart in the prison guard.

LEAP INTO FREEDOM: CONCLUDING REMARKS

What makes this image significant to a discussion of contemporary division is the affective evocation of self-reflexive opposition on the part of someone in charge of "defending" the barrier. What makes this image relevant to contemporary fortresses and barriers is the refusal to build walls, to hold, enforce, and guard them. Instead, the photograph marks the traversal of a defensive imaginary and the resistance to maintain it as an act of liberation. While the soldier notably only saves himself and hence does not extend a leap of freedom to those who remain oppressed, the image does work as a powerful reminder that the walls that scatter the world, above all, must first be overcome by those who construct and secure them.

Ultimately, political walls (and the images they provoke) demonstrate how histories stay alive. How fantasies, feelings, and investments animate the present and produce orientations toward im/possible futures. Understanding such a wall as a task, we need to acknowledge the ghosts of the past and consider the conditions of one another's traumatic constitution in the present: the inner barriers, limitations, fears, and aspirations joining the detaining and creative prospects of a walled life. Who is left behind by Schumann? Who does not (ever) get to jump? Who should drop the gun mid-air? Facing the wall's legacies as an unfinished crisis involves acknowledging these questions as a form of responsibility (or ability to respond). It also means to examine the privileges and hierarchies attached to walls and to investigate the various confrontations they generate and expose. Put simply, walls mark both an opening and defense. In each case, they need to be brought into full view so that they can be seen, felt, remembered, and finally dismantled. If this sounds like an impossible leap, I am merely asking to unmake the/your world.

Notes

Chapter 1

1 Alain Badiou, "The Communist Hypothesis," *New Left Review*, vol. 49 (January–February 2008): 38.
2 Ibid.
3 Élisabeth Vallet, "State of Borderwalls in a Globalized World," in *Borders and Borderwalls: In-Securities, Symbolism, Vulnerabilities*, ed. Élisabeth Vallet and Andréanne Bissonnette (New York: Routlege, 2021).
4 Badiou, "The Communist Hypothesis." Étienne Balibar, *We, the People of Europe? – Reflections on Transnational Citizenship* (Princeton: Princeton University Press, 2004). Étienne Balibar, *Politics and the Other Scene* (London: Verso, 2002). Étienne Balibar, "Europe as Borderland," *Society and Space*, vol. 27 (2009): 190–215.
5 Wendy Brown, *Walled States: Waning Sovereignty* (New York: Zone Books, 2010).
6 Reece Jones, *Border Walls Security and the War on Terror in the United States, Israel and India* (London: ZedBooks, 2012).
7 Achille Mbembe, *Critique of Black Reason* (Durham: Duke University Press, 2017), 24.
8 Ibid.
9 Achille Mbembe, "Society of Enmity," *Radical Philosophy*, vol. 200 (2016): 24.
10 Achille Mbembe, "Necropolitics," *Public Culture*, vol. 15, no. 1 (2003): 11–40.
11 Judith Butler, *Frames of War: When Is Life Grievable?* (London: Verso, 2010).
12 Mbembe, *Critique of Black Reason*, 3.
13 David Makovsky, "How to Build a Fence," *Foreign Affairs*, vol. 83, no.2 (2004): 52. In this article, Makovsky argues that the wall provides security and encourages peace, ignoring the fact that such a wall is the literal site (and enforcement) of conflict division.
14 Sara Ahmed, *The Cultural Politics of Emotion* (Edinburgh: Edinburgh University Press, 2014), 12.
15 Lauren Berlant, *Cruel Optimism* (Durham: Duke University Press, 2011), 226.
16 Ahmed, *The Cultural Politics*, 8.
17 Ibid., 2.

18 Sigmund Freud, *The Interpretation of Dreams* (Harmondsworth: Penguin Books, 1986). Cathy Caruth, *Trauma: Explorations in Memory*, ed. Cathy Caruth (Baltimore: Johns Hopkins University Press, 1995). Jacqueline Rose, *The Question of Zion* (Princeton: Princeton University Press, 2005). Kaja Silverman, "Historical Trauma and Male Subjectivity," in *Cinema & Psychoanalysis*, ed. E. Ann Kaplan (New York: Routledge, 1990), 110–27.

19 Renata Salecl, *The Spoils of Freedom* (New York: Routledge, 1994).

20 Berlant, *Cruel Optimism*, 10.

21 Ibid., 63.

22 Brown, *Walled States*.

23 Jacob D. Lindy, "Legacy of Trauma and Loss," in *Beyond Invisible Walls, the Psychological Legacy of Soviet Trauma*, ed. Jacob D. Lindy and Robert Jay Lifton (New York: Routledge, 2001), 13.

24 Sigmund Freud and Joseph Breuer, *Studies on Hysteria* (New York: Basic Books, 2000), 6.

25 Hannah Arendt, *The Human Condition* (Chicago: University of Chicago Press, 1958). Giorgio Agamben, *Homo Sacer: Sovereign Power and Bare Life* (Stanford: Stanford University Press, 1998). Robert Cover, *Narrative Violence and the Law* (Ann Arbor: University of Michigan Press, 1993). Carl Schmitt, *The Nomos of the Earth in the International Law of the Jus Publicum Europaeum* (New York: Telos Press Publishing, 2006).

26 Ghassan Hage, *Against Paranoid Nationalism: Searching for Hope in a Shrinking Society* (London: Merlin, 2003). Ghassan Hage, "État de Siège: A Dying Domesticating Colonialism?," *American Ethnologist*, vol. 43, no. 1 (2016): 38–49. Salecl, *The Spoils of Freedom*.

27 Arendt, *The Human Condition*, 63.

28 Ibid., 64.

29 Ibid., 63.

30 Ibid.

31 Ibid., 64.

32 Ibid.

33 Achille Mbembe, "The Idea of a Borderless World," *Africa Is a Country*, https://africasacountry.com/2018/11/the-idea-of-a-borderless-world.

34 Schmitt, *The Nomos of the Earth*, 67.

35 Ibid.

36 Patrick Wolfe, "Settler Colonialism and the Elimination of the Native," *Journal of Genocide Research*, vol. 8, no. 4 (2006): 387–409.

37 Schmitt, *The Nomos of the Earth*, 70.

38 Ibid.

39 Ibid.

40 Ibid.

41 Ibid.

42 Agamben, *Homo Sacer*, 19.
43 Ibid.
44 Ibid., 7.
45 Ibid., 19.
46 Ibid., 131.
47 Giorgio Agamben, *State of Exception* (Chicago: Chicago University Press, 2005), 6.
48 Ibid.
49 Ibid., 2–3.
50 Agamben, *Homo Sacer*, 123.
51 Ibid.
52 Ibid.
53 Badiou, "The Communist Hypothesis," 38.
54 Balibar, *Politics and the Other Scene*, 93.
55 Balibar, *We, the People of Europe?*, 113.
56 Balibar, *Politics and the Other Scene*, 92.
57 Balibar, *We, the People of Europe?*, 113.
58 Ibid.
59 Ibid.
60 Ibid.
61 Brown, *Walled States*, 24.
62 Junita Sundberg, "Delimiting Democracy: Witnessing along the US-Mexico Borderlands," *Political Geography*, vol. 33 (2013): 53.
63 Ibid.
64 Brown, *Walled States*, 73.
65 Ibid., 114.
66 Ibid., 132.
67 Ibid., 114.
68 Corinne Squire, Amal Treacher and Susannah Radstone, *Public Emotions* (New York: Palgrave Macmillan, 2007), 19.
69 Paul Verhaeghe, "Trauma and Hysteria within Freud and Lacan," *The Letter: Lacanian Perspectives on Psychoanalysis*, no. 14 (Autumn 1998): 93.
70 Berlant, *Cruel Optimism*, 49.
71 Silverman, "Historical Trauma and Male Subjectivity," 115.
72 Schmitt, *The Nomos of the Earth*, 70.
73 Berlant, *Cruel Optimism*, 226.
74 Cover, *Narrative Violence and the Law*, 95.
75 Ibid., 95–6.
76 Ibid., 97.

77 Kaja Silverman, *World Spectators* (Stanford: Stanford University Press, 2000), 84.
78 Berlant, *Cruel Optimism*, 226.
79 Ibid., 15.
80 Ibid., 16.
81 Freud, *The Interpretation of Dreams*, 684–5.
82 Ibid., 67.
83 Ibid.
84 Freud discusses a "screen" which stands between the unconscious and consciousness. See, Freud, *The Interpretation of Dream*, 690.
85 Quoted in Silverman, "Historical Trauma and Male Subjectivity," 148.
86 Ibid., 145.
87 Quoted in Bettina Funke, "Displaced Struggles: On Rancière and the Art World," *Artforum* (March 2007): 341.
88 Beuys explains this in the instructions to his work: Joseph Beuys, "Beuys empfiehlt Erhöhung der Berliner Mauer um 5 cm (bessere Proportion!)," *Aktenvermerk für das Innenministerium*, July 20, 1964, http://www.josephbeuys.de/texthand.htm.
89 Ramon Resendiz, Rosalva Resendiz, and Irene J. Klaver, "Colonialism and Imperialism: Indigenous Resistance on the US/Mexico Border," *Perspectives on Global Development and Technology*, no. 16 (2017): 30.

Chapter 2

1 Joachim Schloer, "It Has to Go Away, but at the Same Time It Has to Be Kept: The Berlin Wall and the Making of an Urban Icon," *Urban History*, vol. 33 (2006): 98.
2 Andreas Huyssen, "The Voids of Berlin," *Critical Inquiry*, vol. 24, no. 1 (Autumn 1997): 64.
3 The Four Power Agreement took effect in June 1972 and allowed "unimpeded" traveling from West to East. However, traveling from the East to the West was still nearly impossible and only permitted in the case of a family emergency. See for example, Klaus Schütz, "Berlin in the Age of Détente," *The World Today*, vol. 31, no. 1 (January 1975): 29–35. Jochen Frowein, "Legal Problems of the German Ostpolitik," *International and Comparative Law Quarterly*, vol. 23, no. 1 (January 1974): 105–26.
4 Olaf Briese, "The Different Aesthetics of the Berlin Wall," in *The German Wall: Fallout in Europe*, ed. Marc Silberman (New York: Palgrave MacMillan, 2011), 49.
5 Serge Schmemann, "Upheaval in the East: Berlin, Abject and Crumbling, Berlin Wall Surrenders," *The New York Times*, January 28, 1990, http://

www.nytimes.com/1990/01/28/world/upheaval-in-the-east-berlin-abject-and-crumbling-berlin-wall-surrenders.html.

6   Briese, "The Different Aesthetics of the Berlin Wall," 55.
7   Lars Kristensen, Introduction to *Post-Communist Film: Russia, Eastern Europe and World Culture: Moving Images of Postcommunism*, ed. Lars Kristensen (New York: Routledge, 2012), 3.
8   Claudia Mesch, *Modern Art at the Berlin Wall: Demarcating Culture in the Cold War Germanys* (London: Tauris Academic Studies, 2008), 12.
9   Berlant, *Cruel Optimism*, 10.
10 Ibid., 4.
11 Ibid.
12 Jill Bennett and Rosanne Kennedy, Introduction to *World Memory*, ed. Jill Bennett and Rosanne Kennedy (New York: Palgrave Macmillan, 2002), 3.
13 Roland Barthes, *Camera Lucida: Reflections on Photography* (New York: Hill and Wang, 2010), 27.
14 RBB/Stilbruch, "Blickpunkt Ost: Detlef Matthes fotografiert die Mauer," YouTube, http://www.youtube.com/watch?v=L3pmNNySW-I.
15 Stefan Locke, "Mauerfotos: Interview mit Detlef Matthes," *Frankfurter Allgemeine Zeitung*, May 3, 2011, http://www.faz.net/aktuell/gesellschaft/mauerfotos-das-musste-immer-ganz-schnell-gehen-1624904.html.
16 Ibid.
17 RBB/Stilbruch, "Blickpunkt Ost."
18 In June 1987, during the so-called "Pfingst-holidays" David Bowie, Genesis, and the Eurhythmics were singing at "the concert for Berlin" right next to the wall in the Western part of the city. In the Eastern part, young people had gathered to catch a few sounds of the concert. Things escalated when people moved toward the Brandenburg Gate, facing up to police and NVA. During the three-day confrontation 158 people were detained (and subsequently "filed" by the Stasi). See Olaf Leitner "Rock Music in the GDR. An Epitaph," In *Rocking the State: Rock Music and Politics in Eastern Europe and Russia*, ed. Sabrina Petra Ramet (Oxford: Westview Press, 1994), 17–40. Jochen Winters "Der Ruf 'die Mauer muss weg' wird der SED noch lange in den Ohren klingen" *Frankfurter Allgemeine Zeitung*, June 10, 1987. WWS „Schallmauer" *Frankfurter Allgemeine Zeitung*, June 10, 1987.
19 For example, "Berliner Mauer: Fotos Verboten," organized by *BStU*, August 11, 2013–December 31, 2013, https://www.bstu.bund.de/SharedDocs/Ausstellungen/Region-Frankfurt/ffo_fotos_verboten.html.
20 Matthew Shaul and Nicola Freeman, *Do Not Refreeze: Photography behind the Berlin Wall* (Manchester: Cornerhouse Publications, 2007), 17. Paul Betts, *Within Walls: Private Life in the German Democratic Republic* (Oxford: Oxford University Press, 2010), 193.
21 Mesch, *Modern Art*, 11–12.
22 Betts, *Within Walls*, 222.

NOTES

23 Susan Sontag, *On Photography* (New York: Farrar, Straus and Giroux, 1977), 121.
24 See Betts, *Within Walls*, 194.
25 Ibid., 226.
26 Shaul and Freeman, *Do Not Refreeze*, 16.
27 Betts, *Within Walls*, 216.
28 Sontag, *On Photography*, 15.
29 Boris Groys, "Back from the Future," *Third Text,* vol. 17, no. 4 (2003): 327.
30 Ibid., 326.
31 Ibid.
32 Tyrus Miller, Introduction to *Given World and Time: Temporalities in Context*, ed. Tyrus Miller (Budapest: Central European University Press, 2008), 3.
33 Ibid.
34 "Berlin hatte damals etwas von einer untergegangenen Stadt" Humanistischer Pressedienst, "Interview mit Gundula Schulze Eldowy, Teil 1," *YouTube*, http://www.youtube.com/watch?v=YqYDoQEjI8A.
35 "Es ist ja nicht so, dass mit dem 9. November plötzlich mit Herrn Schabowski die Grenze aufging. Sieht man meine Bilder an, da ist ja die Agonie schon zu sehen." Humanistischer Pressedienst, "Interview mit Gundula Schulze Eldowy, Teil 3," *YouTube*, http://www.youtube.com/watch?v=M7_2s4eHkoQ.
36 Gundula Schulze Eldowy, *Berlin in einer Hundenacht*, http://www.berlin-ineinerhundenacht.de/hundenacht.html.
37 Gundula Schulze Eldowy, "Im Herbstlaub des Vergessens," *Berlin in einer Hundenacht*. http://www.berlin-ineinerhundenacht.de/hundenacht.html.
38 "Die Zerissenheit Berlins, ist die Zerissenheit seiner Bewohner" "Im Herbstlaub des Vergessens," *Berlin in einer Hundenacht,* http://www.berlin-ineinerhundenacht.de/hundenacht.html.
39 Britta Duelke, "Quoting from the Past or Dealing with Temporality," in *Given World and Time: Temporalities in Context*, ed. Tyrus Miller (Budapest: Central European University Press, 2008), 105.
40 The description was used to advertise the exhibition "Do Not Refreeze," *Cornerhouse*, http://www.cornerhouse.org/art/art-exhibitions/do-not-refreeze.
41 Ibid.
42 Eckhart Gillen, Annette Tietz, Paula Böttcher, "Blick Zurück Nach Vorne," *Galerie Pankow* 2009.
43 Unsicker speaks about "die Mauer im Kopf" (the wall in the head) or mental wall; Patrice Massenet, "Homo Ludens: Der Mensch lernt durch Spiel – Interview mit Peter Unsicker 1987," *YouTube*, http://www.youtube.com/watch?v=jMV-fcOG6ZU.
44 "Mauerkunst hat mich wirklich null interessiert." Ralf Gründer, "Das Wundpflaster: Interview mit Peter Unsicker 2009," *Youtube*, http://www.youtube.com/watch?v=wBGjNoVfN5o.

45 Serge Schmemann, "Berlin Journal: In Search of a Work of Art to Overcome the Wall," *The New York Times*, November 13, 1987, http://www.nytimes.com/1987/11/13/world/berlin-journal-in-search-of-a-work-of-art-to-overcome-the-wall.html.
46 Peter Unsicker, *Die Arbeit am Verdorbenen: Eine Dokumentation Angewandter Kunst* (Berlin: Luftfilterverlag, 2001), 25.
47 "eine ganz persönliche Betroffenheit" Quoted in Massenet, "Homo Ludens."
48 So lange ich die Mauer vor mir sehe, weiss ich, ich hab die Mauer nicht im Kopf. Ibid.
49 Kaja Silverman, *Male Subjectivity at the Margins* (New York: Routledge, 1992), 148.
50 Lacan quoted in Silverman, *Male Subjectivity*, 150.
51 Ibid.
52 Bill Niven, *Germans as Victims: Remembering the Past in Contemporary Germany* (New York: Palgrave Macmillan, 2006), 1.
53 Evelyn Preuss, "The Wall You Will Never Know," *Perspecta*, vol. 36 (2005): 19.
54 "Bauchbinde... welche die DDR vor dem 'ausbluten' beschützen sollte" Unsicker, *Die Arbeit am Verdorbenen*, 8.
55 "ein heilsames Vorgehen bezogen auf geistige Versteinerung in dieser durch die Mauer-Wunde beschädigten Stadtlandschaft" Quoted in Michael Nungesser, "Im Schatten des Monstrums," *Berliner Zeitung*, August 9, 2001.
56 Ibid.
57 Cathy Caruth, "Trauma and Experience," 5.
58 Ibid.
59 Rancière, *The Aesthetic Unconscious* (Cambridge; Malden, MA: Polity, 2009), 18.
60 Unsicker, *Die Arbeit am Verdorbenen*, 15.
61 Ibid., 21.
62 Sigrid Weigel, *Body and Image Space* (New York: Routledge, 1996), 51.
63 Ibid., 52.
64 Walter Benjamin, *Illuminations: Essays and Reflections* (New York: Schocken Books, 2007).
65 Weigel, *Body and Image Space*, 58.
66 Theordor Adorno, *Notes to Literature* (New York: Columbia University Press, 1992), 323.
67 Verhaeghe, "Trauma and Hysteria," 92.
68 Lacan characterizes the screen and the mirror stage as an imaginary mapping. See Silverman, *Male Subjectivity*, 148.
69 "Die von Anbeginn an vorhandene Spannung an diesem Platz wurde durch die soziale Kraft der Kunst aufgelöst – in Licht und Reflex transformiert." Unsicker, *Die Arbeit am Verdorbenen*, 29.

70 Peter Unsicker, "Privatkampf mit der DDR," *Spiegel Online*, February 19, 2009, http://www.spiegel.de/einestages/mauerkunst-privatkampf-mit-der-ddr-a-949740.html.

71 Even after the wall had lost its function as an enclosure and therefore no longer served a particular point, it was not immediately decided what to do with the monument or what its legal status would be. In this context, the painting on the wall was technically declared illegal, while there were not really any means to enforce this rule. Deutsches Rundfunkarchiv, "Mauermalerei und Mauerspechte," *DRA*, http://1989.dra.de/themendossiers/politik/mauer/mauermalerei-und-mauerspechte.html.

72 Berlant, *Cruel Optimism*, 63.

73 Briese, "The Different Aesthetics of the Berlin Wall," 55.

74 Ibid., 52.

75 Ibid.

76 "History of the Eastside Gallery," *Eastside Gallery*, http://www.eastsidegallery.com/historyesg.htm.

77 Ibid.

78 Lauren Berlant and Jordan Greenwald, "Affect at the End of Times: A Conversation with Lauren Berlant," *Qui Parle?*, vol. 20, no. 2 (2012): 71–89, 87.

79 Ibid.

80 Sina Najafi, David Serlin, and Lauren Berlant, "The Broken Circuit: An Interview with Lauren Berlant," *Cabinet*, no. 31 (Fall 2008), http://www.cabinetmagazine.org/issues/31/najafi_serlin.php.

81 For example: Markus Horeld and Juliane Leopold, "Berlins legitimer Mauer-Protest oder Scheinheiligkeit?," *Zeit Online*, March 4, 2013, http://www.zeit.de/gesellschaft/zeitgeschehen/2013-03/east-side-gallery-protest/komplettansicht. Sebastian Heiser, "Mauer in Geiselhaft," *TAZ*, March 3, 2013, http://www.taz.de/!112114/.

82 Deutsche Presse Agentur, "Tausende Demonstrieren Gegen Teilabriss der East Side Gallery," *Zeit Online*, March 4, 2013, http://www.zeit.de/gesellschaft/zeitgeschehen/2013-03/demo-east-side-gallery.

83 Berlant, *Cruel Optimism*, 2.

84 Earl McCabe, "Depressive Realism: An Interview with Lauren Berlant," *Hypocrite Reader*, no. 5 (June 2011): hypocritereader.com/5/depressive-realism.

85 David Hasselhoff, who had been singing at the wall in November 1989 and became an iconic figure affectively associated with these celebrations, joined the protesters for a concert. Arguably, it is not the music that drew a large audience to this concert, but precisely the affective relationship to the past explained by Berlant and here expressed in a sense of ironic, yet genuine, sentimentality for the aging pop star.

86 "Die Mauer bleibt stehen," reversal of the infamous 1989 slogan "Die Mauer muss weg" (the Wall must go). For example, see Martin Hendrichs, "Retten Eastside Gallery," *Youtube* https://www.youtube.com/watch?v=clyN6p3HRBo&NR=1&feature=endscreen.

87 "Niemand hat die Absicht eine Mauer abzureißen." For example, "Niemand hat die Absicht eine Mauer Abzureißen: Eastside Gallery wird weiter demoliert," *Soldiner Kiez Kurier,* http://soldinerkiezkurier.wordpress.com/10376-2/.

88 "Niemand hat die Absicht eine Mauer zu errichten." For example quoted in Henning Wrage, "Politics, Culture, and Media before and after the Berlin Wall," in *The German Wall: Fallout in Europe*, ed. Marc Silberman (New York: Palgrave MacMillan, 2011), 61.

89 "Bauarbeiter reißen Lücke in Eastside Gallery," *Zeit Online*, March 27, 2014, http://www.zeit.de/gesellschaft/2013-03/abriss-east-side-gallery.

90 Lars Kristensen, Introduction to *Postcommunist Film*, 8.

91 Ibid., 3.

92 Ibid., 7.

93 Sigmund Freud, "Project for a Scientific Psychology," in *The Standard Edition of the Complete Psychological Works of Sigmund Freud*, ed. James Strachey (London: Hogarth Press, 1974), 356.

94 Nikolas Kulish and Judy Dempsey, "Leaders in Berlin Retrace the Walk West," *The New York Times*, November 9, 2009, http://www.nytimes.com/2009/11/10/world/europe/10germany.html?_r=0.

95 "Fest der Freiheit."

96 The Polish President Lech Walesa was the leader of *Solidarnosc* in Poland in the 1980s. The independent trade union was majorly involved in opening the border of Poland, which enabled thousands of Germans to flee the GDR, eventually leading to the demise of the Berlin Wall.

97 ZDF, "The Domino Fall of the Berlin Wall," *YouTube*, http://www.youtube.com/watch?v=HG97uKKdwyY.

98 Charles Hawley, "Interview with Lech Walesa," *Spiegel Online International*, November 6, 2009, http://www.spiegel.de/international/europe/spiegel-online-interview-with-lech-walesa-it-s-good-that-gorbachev-was-a-weak-politician-a-659752.html.

99 Badiou, "The Communist Hypothesis," 38.

100 Ben Gook, "Being There Is Everything," *Memory Studies*, vol. 4, no. 13 (2011): 14.

101 Ibid., 16.

102 Ibid., 14.

103 Ibid., 15.

104 Ibid., 18.

105 Guy Debord, *The Society of the Spectacle* (New York: Zone Books, 1994), 10.

106 Gook, "Being There Is Everything," 19.

107 Salecl, *The Spoils of Freedom*, 6.

108 Ibid.

109 The same concert which led to the infamous Pfingstkrawalle (which also led to Detlef Matthes arrest) and which sparked a first voicing of the slogan

NOTES

"the wall must go" from the Eastern side. Kate Conolly, "New Berlin Wall Built for U2 Gig to Mark Fall of Old One," *The Guardian*, November 5, 2009, http://www.theguardian.com/world/2009/nov/05/new-berlin-wall-u2-gig.

110 Casey quoted in Gook, "Being There Is Everything," 20.
111 Sigmund Freud, "Remembering, Repeating and Working Through," in *The Standard Edition of the Complete Psychological Works of Sigmund Freud Volume XII*, ed. James Strachey (London: Hogarth Press, 1958), 151.
112 Ibid.
113 ECB, "Dominoes for Peace: Mandela Family to Participate in Symbolic Toppling of the Wall," *Spiegel Online International*, August 26, 2009, http://www.spiegel.de/international/germany/dominoes-for-peace-mandela-family-to-participate-in-symbolic-toppling-of-berlin-wall-a-645012.html.
114 Ben Gook, *Divided Subjects, Invisible Borders* (London: Rowman & Littlefield, 2015), 247.
115 Ibid., 258.
116 Derek P. McCormack, *Atmospheric Things: On the Allure of Elemental Envelopment* (Durham: Duke University Press, 2018).
117 Ibid., 58.
118 Jurgens, Jeffrey, "Invisible Migrants: Memory and Nationhood in the Shadow of the Berlin Wall," in *Walls, Borders, Boundaries: Spatial and Cultural Practices in Europe*, ed. Janet Ward, Marc Silberman and Karen E. Till (New York: Berghahn Books. 2012), 192.
119 Jurgens, "Invisible Migrants," 192.
120 Ainhoa Ruiz Benedicto and Pere Brunet, "Building Walls: Fear and Securitization in the European Union," *Transnational Institute*, November 9 2018, https://www.tni.org/en/publica-tion/building-walls.
121 "Wir kämpfen gegen jede Form der Ausgrenzung" Bert Schulz. "Schluss mit dem Mauern: Kommentar zu Berlins Mauerfall-Feiern," *TAZ*, November 8, 2019, https://taz.de/Kommentar-zu-Berlins-Mauerfall-Feiern/!5637268/.
122 Sontag, *On Photography*, 168.
123 The Berlin Wall was opened on November 9, 1989, as a result of a press conference, in which the spokesman for the East German Politbüro, Günther Schabowski to the surprise of the journalists (and also seemingly to himself) read out a statement that promised the opening of the border. When asked by a journalist when the new regulation would take effect, Schabowski (mistakenly) replied "immediately," propelling the events of the night.
124 Gook, "Being There Is Everything," 20.

Chapter 3

1 Gabriele Schwab, *Haunting Legacies, Haunting Legacies: Violent Histories and Transgenerational Trauma* (New York: Columbia University Press, 2010), 84.

2   Ibid., 8.
3   Ibid.
4   Christina Braun quoted in Marianne Hirsch, *Family Frames: Photography, Narrative and Postmemory* (Cambridge, MA: Harvard University Press, 1997), 24.
5   Walter Benjamin, "The Work of Art in the Age of Mechanical Reproduction," in *Illuminations*, ed. Hannah Arendt (New York: Schocken Books, 2007), 237.
6   Schwab, *Haunting Legacies,* 8.
7   Anthony Smith, "Images of the Nation: Cinema, Art and National Identity," in *Cinema and Nation*, ed. Mette Hjort and Scott Mackenzie (London: Routledge, 2000), 52.
8   Schwab, *Haunting Legacies,* 23.
9   Susannah Radstone, "Cinema and Memory," in *Memory: History, Theories, Debates*, ed. Susannah Radstone and Bill Schwarz (New York: Fordham University Press, 2010), 327.
10 Katharina Gerstenberger and Jana Evans Braziel, "After the Berlin Wall: Realigned Worlds, Invisible Lines, and Incalculable Remnants," in *After the Berlin Wall: Germany and beyond*, ed. Katharina Gerstenberger and Jana Evans Braziel (New York: Palgrave Macmillan, 2011), 6.
11 Silverman, "Historical Trauma," 117.
12 Radstone and Schwarz, "Mapping Memory," in *Memory: Histories, Theories, Debates*, ed. Susannah Radstone and Bill Schwarz (New York: Fordham University Press, 2010), 4.
13 *Rabbit à la Berlin*, directed by Bartozs Konopka (Germany, Poland: Deckert Distribution, 2009), DVD.
14 Thomas White, "Meet the Filmmaker: Bartek Konopka – Rabbit à la Berlin," *International Documentary Association*, August 2009, http://www.documentary.org/content/meet-filmmakers-bartek-konopka-rabbit-a-la-berlin.
15 W. J. T Mitchell, "Imperial Landscapes," in *Landscape and Power*, ed. W. J. T Mitchell (Chicago: University of Chicago Press, 1994), 5.
16 Schmitt, *The Nomos of the Earth*, 70.
17 Ibid.
18 Arendt, *The Human Condition*, 63–4.
19 Ibid., 63.
20 Ibid., 64.
21 Alexander Zinoviev, *Homo Sovieticus* (New York: The Atlantic Monthly, 1985).
22 Visions Du Reel, "Interview Bartek Konopka," *YouTube*, http://www.youtube.com/watch?v=IJA61bBRg1Q.
23 Günter Gaus cited in Betts, *Within Walls*, 10.
24 Nick Hodgin, *Screening the East: Heimat, Memory and Nostalgia in German Film since 1989* (New York: Berghahn Books, 2011), 67.
25 Paul Cooke, *Representing East Germany since Unification: From Colonization to Nostalgia* (New York: Berg, 2005), 12.

NOTES

26 Visions Du Reel, "Interview Bartek Konopka."
27 Mary O'Brien, *Post-wall German Cinema and National History: Utopianism and Dissent* (Rochester, NY: Camden House, 2012), 4.
28 Bartozs Konopka, *Rabbit à la Berlin*.
29 Katie Trumpener, "La Guerre est fini: New Waves, Historical Contingency, and the GDR 'Rabbit Film'," in *The Power of Intellectuals in Contemporary Germany*, ed. M. Geyer (Chicago: The University of Chicago Press, 2001), 115.
30 Ingeborg Ruthe, "Der Hase bin Ich," *Berliner Zeitung*, January 21, 2006, http://www.berliner-zeitung.de/archiv/beuys-hat-begeistert-und-genervt--um-die-welt-zu-bessern--was-bleibt-20-jahre-nach-seinem-tod--der-hase-bin-ich,10810590,10355472.html.
31 The forbidden "rabbit films" include Gerhard Klein *Berlin um die Ecke* (Berlin around the Corner), Juergen Boettcher's *Born in '45*, Herman Zschoche's *Karla*, Frank Vogel *Denk bloß nicht ich heule* (Just don't think I'll cry), and Frank Beyer *Spur der Steine* (The Traces of Stones).
32 Trumpener, "La Guerre est fini," 116.
33 Barton Byg, "Is There Still an East German Cinema," in *Cinemas in Transition in Central Eastern Europe after 1989*, ed. C. Portuges and P. Hames (Philadelphia: Temple University Press, 2013), 79.
34 *The Invisible Frame*, directed by Cynthia Beatts (Germany, 2009; Brooklyn, NY: Icarus Film, 2009), DVD.
35 Beatts cited in Katja Petrowskaja, "Interview with Cynthia Beatts," *Invisible-Frame* 2009, http://www.invisible-frame.com/en/the-film/interview/.
36 Anke Westphal "An Approach to the Wall," *Berliner Zeitung*, November 7, 2009, http://www.invisible-frame.com/en/the-film/reviews/2009.
37 *Cycling the Frame*, directed by Cynthia Beatts (Berlin, Germany, 1988; Brooklyn, NY: Icarus Film, 2009), DVD.
38 Kristensen, Introduction to *Postcommunist Film*, 2.
39 Ibid., 3.
40 Mila Ganeva, "No Histories Just Stories: Revisiting Traditions in Berlin Films of the 1990s," in *Berlin: The Symphony Continues: Orchestrating Architectural, Social and Artistic Change in Germany's New Capital*, ed. C.A. Costabile-Heming and R. J. Halverson (New York: Walter de Gruyter, 2004), 266.
41 Kristensen, Introduction to *Postcommunist Film*, 3.
42 Skoller cited by Kristensen, Ibid.
43 Balibar, "Europe as Borderland," 193.
44 Kristensen, Introduction to *Postcommunist Film*, 3
45 O'Brien, *Post-wall German Cinema*, 23.
46 cited in Petrowskaja, "Interview with Cynthia Beatts."
47 O'Brien, *Post-wall German Cinema*, 26.
48 Huyssen, "Trauma and Memory: A New Imaginary of Temporality," in *World Memory: Personal Trajectories in Global Time*, ed. Jill Bennett and Rosanne Kennedy (New York: Palgrave Macmillan, 2002), 16.

49 Beatts cited in Petrowskaja, "Interview with Cynthia Beatts"
50 Ibid.
51 cited in Cooke, *Representing East Germany since Unification*, 3.
52 Earlier in the film, the Cuckoo is associated with the notion of greed, hence indicating the means of capitalism's all-consuming emergence.
53 Richard Terdiman, "Taking Time: Temporal Representation and Cultural Politics," in *Given Time and World: Temporalities in Context*, ed. T. Miller (New York: Central European University Press, 2008), 132.
54 Ibid.
55 Cooke, *Representing East Germany*, 3.
56 *The Lives of Others*, directed by Florian Henckel von Donnersmarck (Germany: Sony Pictures Home Entertainment, 2006), DVD.
57 Cheryl Dueck, "The Humanization of the Stasi in "Das Leben der Anderen," *German Studies Review*, vol. 31, no. 3 (October 2008): 599.
58 Susan Stone, "DDR Living: Museum Offers 'Ostalgic' Look at East Germany," *Spiegel Online International*, July 20, 2006, http://www.spiegel.de/international/ddr-living-museum-offers-ostalgic-look-at-east-germany-a-427579.html.
59 See Dueck, "The Humanization of the Stasi," Anna Funder, "Tyranny of Terror," *The Guardian*, May 5, 2007, http://www.theguardian.com/books/2007/may/05/featuresreviews.guardianreview12.
60 Funder, "Tyranny of Terror."
61 Ibid.
62 Timothy Garton Ash, "The Stasi in Our Minds," *The New York Review of Books*, May 31, 2007, http://www.nybooks.com/articles/archives/2007/may/31/the-stasi-on-our-minds/.
63 Lauren Berlant, "Intimacy: A Special Issue," *Critical Inquiry*, vol. 24 (Winter 1998): 286.
64 Frédéric Rouvillois, "Utopia and Totalitarianism," in *Utopia: The Search for the Ideal Society in the Western World*, ed. Roland Schaer et al. (Oxford: Oxford University Press, 2000), 319.
65 Ibid.
66 Ibid.
67 O'Brien, *Post-wall German Cinema*, 137.
68 Michel Foucault, "Governmentality," in *The Foucault Effect: Studies in Governmentality*, ed. Graham Burchell, Colin Gordon, and Peter Miller (London: Harvester Wheatsheaf, 1991), 87–104.
69 Berlant, *Cruel Optimism*, 224.
70 Preuss, "The Wall You Will Never Know," 25.
71 Ewa Mazierska, *European Cinema and Intertextuality: History, Memory and Politics* (New York: Palgrave Macmillan, 2011), 216.

72 Betts, *Within Walls*, 6.
73 Ibid., 4.
74 Jacques Alain Miller, "Extimité," in *Lacanian Theory of Discourse: Subject, Structure, and Society*, ed. Mark Bracher et al. (New York: New York University Press, 1988), 76.
75 Ibid.
76 Ibid.
77 Ibid., 77.
78 Rouvillois, "Utopia and Totalitarianism," 319.
79 Jean Laplanche and J. B. Pontalis, *The Language of Psycho-Analysis* (London: Karnac Books, 1988), 205.
80 Ibid., 206.
81 Ibid., 205.
82 Ibid., 206.
83 Ibid.
84 Funder, "Tyranny of Terror."
85 Grubitz about Dreyman.
86 Jean Laplanche and J. B. Pontalis, "Fantasy and the Origins of Sexuality," in *Formations of Fantasy*, ed. Victor Burgin, James Donald, and Cora Kaplan (New York: Methuen, 1986), 6.
87 Sigmund Freud, "Creative Writers and Day-Dreaming," in *The Freud Reader*, ed. Peter Gay (London: Vintage, 1995), 438.
88 Laplanche and Pontalis, "Fantasy and the Origins of Sexuality," 14.
89 Wolf Bierman, "The Ghosts Are Leaving the Shadows," *Signandsight.com*, March 29, 2006, http://www.signandsight.com/features/682.html.
90 O'Brien, *Post-wall German Cinema*, 297.
91 Ibid., 145.
92 Quoted in Dueck, "The Humanization of the Stasi," 601.
93 Quoted in Garton Ash, "The Stasi in Our Minds."
94 Cooke, *Representing East Germany*, 81.
95 Freud, *The Interpretation of Dreams*, 596.
96 Jacqueline Rose, *The Last Resistance* (New York: Verso, 2007), 146.
97 *Kawasaki's Rose*, directed by Jan Hřebejk (Prague, Czech Republic: Madman, 2009), DVD Film Festival Screener.
98 Mazierska, *European Cinema and Intertextuality*, 241.
99 Kennedy, "Memory and the Unconscious," in *Memory: History, Theories, Debates*, ed. Susannah Radstone and Bill Schwarz (New York: Fordham University Press, 2010), 185.
100 Ibid.

101 Ibid., 186.
102 For an in-depth discussion, see Herman Westerink, *A Dark Trace: Sigmund Freud on the Sense of Guilt* (Leuven: Leuven University Press, 2009).
103 See Freud, *The Interpretation of Dreams*, 363. Westerink, *A Dark Trace*.
104 Freud and Breuer, *Studies on Hysteria*, 6.
105 Ibid.
106 Schwab, *Haunting Legacies*, 95.
107 Ibid.
108 Quoted in Schwab, *Haunting Legacies*, 96.
109 Ibid.
110 Ibid., 107.
111 Ibid., 115.
112 Ibid., 14.
113 Ibid., 100.
114 Hirsch, *Family Frames*, 22.
115 Quoted in Schwab, *Haunting Legacies*, 25.
116 Ibid.
117 Laplanche and Pontalis, *The Language of Psycho-analysis*, 457.
118 Schwab, *Haunting Legacies*, 29
119 Ibid., 34.
120 Milan Kundera, *The Book of Laughter and Forgetting* (London: Penguin Books, 1983), 3.
121 Hirsch, *Family Frames*, 13.
122 Ibid.
123 Mazierska, *European Cinema and Intertextuality*, 239.
124 Ibid., 1.
125 Ibid., 2.
126 Radstone, "Cinema and Memory," 341.

Chapter 4

1 Makovsky, "How to Build a Fence," 52.
2 Hamid Dabashi, Introduction to *Dreams of a Nation: On Palestinian Cinema*, ed. Hamid Dabashi (London: Verso, 2006), 10.
3 Ibid., 11.
4 Ella Shohat, *Israeli Cinema: East/West and the Politics of Representation* (London: I.B. Tauris, 2010), 252.
5 Lauren Berlant, "Structures of Unfeeling: Mysterious Skin," *International Journal of Politics, Culture and Society*, vol. 28, no. 3 (2015): 194.

6   Butler, *Precarious Life*, 33.
7   Rose, *The Question of Zion*, xvii.
8   "The Separation Barrier," *B'Tselem*, January 1, 2011, http://www.btselem.org/separation_barrier. B'Tselem is the Israeli Information Center for Human Rights in the Occupied Territories
9   United Nations Human Rights Council, "Annual Report of the United Nations High Commissioner for Human Rights and Reports of the Office of the High Commissioner and the Secretary-General on the Human Rights Situation in the Occupied Palestinian Territory, including East Jerusalem," *OHCHR*, January 20, 2016, http://www.ohchr.org/EN/HRBodies/HRC/RegularSessions/Session31/_layouts/15/WopiFrame.aspx?sourcedoc=/EN/HRBodies/HRC/RegularSessions/Session31/Documents/A_HRC_31_44_E.doc&action=default&DefaultItemOpen=1, 6.
10 Israel Ministry of Defense, "Operational Concept," *Israel's Security Fence*, January 31, 2007, http://www.securityfence.mod.gov.il/Pages/ENG/operational.htm.
11 The Green Line is a demarcation line which delimits the territories administered by Israel since the 1967 Six Day War.
12 Larry Abramson, "What Does Landscape Want? A Walk in W. J. T. Mitchell' Holy Landscape," in *The Pictorial Turn*, ed. Neal Curtis (London: Routledge, 2010), 182.
13 Ravitsky quoted in Rose, *The Question of Zion*, 35.
14 Annie Pfingst, "The Presence of Palestinian Absence in Narrating the Zionist Nation into Being," *Cultural Studies Review*, vol. 14, no. 1 (March 2008): 115.
15 Said, *The Question of Palestine* (London: Routledge, 1980), 9.
16 Ibid., 8.
17 Ibid.
18 Rose refers to the language of redemption quoting Ravitsky Rose, *The Question of Zion*, 35.
19 Abramson, "What Does Landscape Want?," 178.
20 Salecl, *The Spoils of Freedom*, 15.
21 Weizman, *Hollow Land: Israel's Architecture of Occupation* (London: Verso, 2007), 178.
22 Said, *The Question of Palestine*, 172–3.
23 Rose, *The Question of Zion*, 16.
24 Ibid.
25 Ibid.
26 Freud, *The Interpretation of Dreams*, 714.
27 Ibid., 682.
28 Weizman, *Hollow Land*.
29 Ibid., 12.
30 Bar-On gives the example of a banner of the Zionist Council, which said: "We shall continue to dream the dream." Modechai Bar-On, "Conflicting Narratives

or Narratives of a Conflict: Can the Zionist and Palestinian Narratives of the 1948 War Be Bridged?," in *Israeli and Palestinian Narratives of Conflict: History's Double Helix*, ed. Robert L. Rothberg (Bloomington: Indiana University Press, 2006), 163.

31 Sharon Rotbart, "Wall and Tower (Homa Umigdal): The Mold of Israeli Architecture," in *A Civilian Occupation: The Politics of Israel's Architecture*, ed. Rafi Segal and Eyal Weizman (New York: Verso, 2003), 40.
32 Amira Hass, "You Can Drive along and Never See an Arab," *Ha'aretz*, January 22, 2003, http://www.haaretz.com/print-edition/opinion/you-can-drive-along-and-never-see-an-arab-1.21522.
33 Weizman, *Hollow Land*, 11–12.
34 Shohat, *Israeli Cinema*, 250.
35 Ibid.
36 Auguste and Louis Lumière, "Palestine 1896," *YouTube*, http://www.youtube.com/watch?v=1vaIK8wlAI0. Louis Lumière, "Leaving Jerusalem by Railway 1897," *YouTube*, http://www.youtube.com/watch?v=Ctp1IVef9Yo.
37 Anat Y. Zanger, *Place, Memory and Myth in Contemporary Israeli Cinema* (Edgware: Vallentine Mitchell, 2012), xviii.
38 Salecl, *The Spoils of Freedom*.
39 Shohat, *Israeli Cinema*, 289.
40 Ibid., 251.
41 Ibid.
42 Elia Suleiman's complaint about the burden of national cinema, as having "to tell the story of Palestine." See Elia Suleiman, "A Cinema of Nowhere," *Journal of Palestine Studies*, vol 29, no. 2 (Winter 2000): 98.
43 Said, *The Question of Palestine*, 25.
44 Edward Said, "Preface: Keynote Speech for the Dreams of a Nation," in *Dreams of a Nation: On Palestinian Cinema*, ed. Hamid Dabashi (London: Verso, 2006), 3.
45 Butler, *Precarious Life*, 147.
46 Ibid.
47 Shohat, *Israeli Cinema*, 273.
48 Dabashi, Introduction to *Dreams of a Nation*, 11.
49 Ibid.
50 Schmitt, *The Nomos of the Earth*.
51 Zanger, *Place, Memory and Myth*, 138.
52 Schmitt, *The Nomos of the Earth*, 67.
53 David Theo Goldberg, *The Threat of Race: Reflections on Racial Neoliberalism* (Malden MA: Wiley-Blackwell, 2009), 111.
54 Said, *The Question of Palestine*, 8
55 Ibid.
56 Ibid., 25.

NOTES

57 Zanger, *Place, Memory and Myth*, 46.
58 Sundberg, "Delimiting Democracy," 53.
59 Agamben, *Homo Sacer*, 8.
60 Miri Talmon and Yaron Peleg, *Israeli Cinema: Identities in Motion* (Austin: University of Texas Press, 2011), 284.
61 Ibid., 285.
62 Ibid., 284.
63 Israel Ministry of Foreign Affairs, "Suicide and Other Bombing Attacks on Israel since the Declaration of Principles (Sept 1993)," *Terrorism*, https://mfa.gov.il/MFA/ForeignPolicy/Terrorism/Palestinian/Pages/Suicide%20and%20Other%20Bombing%20Attacks%20in%20Israel%20Since.aspx.
64 *Paradise Now*, directed by Hany Abu-Assad (Palestine, 2005; United States: Augustus Film, 2008), DVD. The film won the Golden Globe for best foreign movie and was also nominated for an Oscar, marking the first official recognition of Palestine by the Academy.
65 Warner Independent Pictures, "Q and A with Hany Abu-Assad," in *Paradise Now Press Kit* (2005), 7.
66 Ibid.
67 James Bowman, "Humanized without Honor," *The American Spectator* (April 2006), 58.
68 Ibid.
69 see Edward Said, "Permission to Narrate," *Journal of Palestine Studies*, vol. 13, no. 2 (Spring 1984): 27–48.
70 Butler, *Precarious Life*, xvii
71 Ibid.
72 Ibid., 144.
73 Joseph A. Massad, *The Persistence of the Question of Palestine: Essays on Zionism and the Palestinians* (New York: Routledge, 2006), 1.
74 Massad, *The Persistence of the Question*, 8.
75 Said, *The Question of Palestine*, 20.
76 Shohat, *Israeli Cinema*, 294.
77 Hage, *Against Paranoid Nationalism*, 137–8.
78 Ibid., 134.
79 Ibid., 138.
80 Mbembe, "Necropolitics."
81 Ibid., 40.
82 Ibid., 27.
83 Hage, *Against Paranoid Nationalism*, 129.
84 Ibid., 134.
85 Ibid., 131.

86 Ibid., 134.
87 Simone Britton and Elia Suleiman, "Wall-Mur," *The European Graduate School*, May 7, 2005, http://www.egs.edu/faculty/elia-suleiman/videos/wall-mur/.
88 *Chronicle of a Disappearance*, directed by Elia Suleiman (1996; Jerusalem, Israel: Kino International 2005), DVD.
89 Berlant, "Structures of Unfeeling."
90 *Divine Intervention*, directed by Elia Suleiman (Palestine/Israel, 2002; New York: Artificial Eye, 2003), DVD.
91 *The Time That Remains*, directed by Elia Suleiman (Palestine/Israel, 2009; United States: IFC Films, 2012), DVD.
92 Gertz and Khleifi, *Palestinian Cinema: Landscape, Memory and Trauma* (Bloomington: Indiana University Press, 2008), 41.
93 Hamid Dabashi, "In Praise of Frivolity: On the Cinema of Elia Suleiman," in *Dreams of a Nation: On Palestinian Cinema*, ed. Hamid Dabashi (London: Verso, 2006), 136.
94 Sabah Haider, "Palestine Already Exists on Film," *Le Monde Diplomatique*, March 2010, http://mondediplo.com/2010/03/16palestinecinema.
95 Berlant, "Structures of Unfeeling," 191.
96 Ibid.
97 Ibid., 194.
98 Ibid.
99 Ibid., 198.
100 Ibid., 203.
101 Ibid., 197.
102 Gertz and Khleifi, *Palestinian Cinema*, 175–6.
103 Dabashi, "In Praise of Frivolity," 158.
104 Suleiman, "The Occupation (and Life) through an Absurdist Lens," *Journal of Palestine Studies*, vol. 32, no. 2 (Winter 2003): 68.
105 Also see Haim Bresheeth, "A Symphony of Absence: Borders and Liminality in Elia Suleiman's 'Chronicle of a Disappearance,'" *The Journal of Cinema and Media*, vol. 43, no. 2 (Fall 2002): 81.
106 Said, *The Question of Palestine*, 180.
107 Kristin Ross, "Introduction on Jacques Rancière," *Art Forum* (March 2007): 254–5.
108 Carnevale and Kelsey, "Art of the Possible," An Interview with Jacques Rancière." *Art Forum* (March 2007): 263.
109 Elia Suleiman, "Interview with Elia Suleiman," *Divine Intervention* DVD (France/Palestine: Artificial Eye, 2002).
110 Dabashi, "In Praise of Frivolity," 135.
111 Ibid.
112 Jacqueline Rose, *Proust among the Nations: From Dreyfus to the Middle East* (Chicago: The University of Chicago Press, 2011), 180.
113 Said, *The Question of Palestine*, 5.

114 For example, Suleiman, "The Cinema of Nowhere," 96.
115 Ibid., 175.
116 Bresheeth, "A Symphony of Absence," 74.
117 Linda Mokdad, "The Reluctance to Narrate: Elia Suleiman's Chronicle of a Disappearance and Divine Intervention," in *Storytelling in World Cinema Volume One: Forms*, ed. Lina Khatib (London: Wallflower press, 2012), 199.
118 Berlant, "Structures of Unfeeling," 195.
119 Refqua Abu-Remaileh, "Palestinian Anti-Narratives in the Films of Elia Suleiman," *Arab Media and Society*, no. 5 (Spring 2008): 2.
120 Sabah Haider, "A Different Kind of Occupation: An Interview with Elia Suleiman," *Electronic Intifada*, February 1, 2010, http://electronicintifada.net/content/different-kind-occupation-interview-elia-suleiman/8654.
121 Suleiman, "Interview with Elia Suleiman."
122 Lina Khatib, *Filming the Modern Middle East* (New York: Palgrave MacMillan, 2006), 131.
123 Rose, *The Last Resistance*, 62.
124 Butler, *Giving an Account of Oneself* (New York: Fordham University Press, 2005), 89.
125 Suleiman, "The Occupation (and Life)," 65.
126 Bennett and Kennedy, Introduction to *World Memory*, 14.

Chapter 5

1 Weizman, *Hollow Land*, 162.
2 Ibid., 171.
3 Ibid.
4 Ibid.
5 Hage, "État de Siège," 40.
6 Carnevale and Kelsey, "Art of the Possible," 259.
7 Anna Waclawek, *Graffiti and Street Art* (New York: Thames & Hudson, 2011), 43.
8 Ibid., 54.
9 Penelope J. Craw et al., "The Mural of Graffiti Deterrence," *Environment and Behaviour*, vol. 38, no. 3 (May 2006): 423.
10 Waclawek, *Graffiti and Street Art*, 10.
11 Ibid.
12 For a detailed discussion see Waclawek, *Graffiti and Street Art*, 58–62.
13 Julie Peteet, "The Writing on the Walls: The Graffiti of the Intifada," *Cultural Anthropology*, vol. 11, no. 2 (1996): 139–59.
14 Said, *The Question of Palestine*, 39.

15 Ibid., 103.
16 Edward Said, "Invention Memory and Place," in *Landscape and Power*, ed. W. J. T Mitchell (Chicago: University of Chicago Press, c2002), 250.
17 Ibid.
18 Robert R Sauders, "Whose Place Is This Anyway: The Israeli Separation Barrier, International Activists and Graffiti," *Anthropology News* (March 2011): 16.
19 Ibid., 16.
20 For a detailed discussion see Peteet, "The Writing on the Walls," 139–59.
21 Sauders, "Whose Place Is This," 16.
22 Peteet, "The Writing on the Walls," 143.
23 Emily Hanssen Arent, "Searching for Banksy on the West Bank Wall," *Matador Network*, May 14, 2012, http://matadornetwork.com/abroad/searching-for-banksy-on-the-west-bank-Wall/.
24 Badiou, "The Communist Hypothesis," 38.
25 Hillel Halkin quoted in Ronen Eidelmann, "The Separation Wall in Palestine: Artists Love to Hate It," in *Cultural Activism: Practices Dilemmas and Possibilities*, ed. Begüm Özden Firat and Aylin Kuryel (New York: Rodopi, 2011), 107.
26 Sauders, "Whose Place Is This," 16.
27 Sigmund Freud, "A Note upon the Mystic Writing Pad," in *Collected Papers Volume V*, ed. James Strachey (London: Hogarth Press, 1950).
28 Ibid., 179.
29 Ibid., 178.
30 Ibid., 179.
31 Ibid., 180.
32 Ibid., 179.
33 Ibid.
34 William Parry, "Donald Trump Is Wrong about Israel's Security Wall," *Aljazeera*, January 31, 2017, https://www.aljazeera.com/indepth/opinion/2017/01/donald-trump-wrong-israel-security-wall-170129075510513.html.
35 In 2017, during a news conference with Colombian president Juan Manuek Santos, Donald Trump stated "walls work, just ask Israel." Washington Post. "Trump: Walls work, just ask Israel," *Youtube*, May 18, 2017, https://www.youtube.com/watch?v=9PbtEAJ2d64.
36 Saeb Erekat, "Response to Jason Greenblatt/ The Trump Administration, Peddling Israeli Extremism, Is Killing the Peace Process, Not Me," *Haaretz*, June 10, 2018, https://www.haaretz.com/middle-east-news/.premium-trump-envoys-peddling-israeli-extremism-are-killing-peace-not-me-1.6159732.
37 Banksy, *Wall and Piece* (London: Random House Group, 2006), 136.
38 Ibid., 139, 143–4.

39 Nigel Parry, "Well-known UK Graffiti Artist Banksy Hacks the Wall," *Electronic Intifada*, September 2, 2012, http://electronicintifada.net/content/well-known-uk-graffiti-artist-banksy-hacks-Wall/5733.
40 Ibid.
41 Banksy, *Wall and Piece*, 136.
42 Ibid.
43 Banksy, http://walledoffhotel.com/. 2018.
44 Emma Graham-Harrison, "'Worst View in the World': Banksy Opens Hotel Overlooking Bethlehem Wall," *The Guardian*, March 3, 2017, https://www.theguardian.com/world/2017/mar/03/banksy-opens-bethlehem-barrier-wall-hotel.
45 Graham-Harrison, "'Worst View in the World."
46 Mbembe, "Necropolitics," 25.
47 Hage, "État de Siège."
48 Said, *Orientalism* (London: Penguin Books, 2003), 7.
49 Ian Fischer, "Banksy Hotel in the West Bank: Small but Plenty of Wall Space," *New York Times*, April 16, 2017, https://www.nytimes.com/2017/04/16/world/middleeast/banksy-hotel-bethlehem-west-bank-wall.html.
50 Adrian Margaret Brune, "Banksy in the West Bank," *Huffpost*, November 7, 2011, http://www.huffingtonpost.com/adrian-margaret-brune/banksy-in-the-west-bank_b_895037.html.
51 Fischer, " Banksy Hotel."
52 Banksy, *Wall and Piece*, 142.
53 The Wall in Gilo was built in 2000 during the second Intifada and eventually removed in 2010, because it was thought that "the security situation in the area is stable." While Gilo residents expressed sadness to part with the painted slaps, the Jerusalem municipality deemed them no longer necessary. Although this can be read in support of the IDF's argument that the wall is a security measurement only (and not, as has been proposed, an architectural extension of power and a mode of destruction targeting Palestinian communities), it needs to be pointed out that since the wall's inception, the Israeli authorities have been careful to not define the construction as a border and thereby an acknowledgment of territorial limitation. It is therefore politically necessary, as Weizman points out, to keep the wall "dynamic" and "constantly shifting." This creates an "irresolvable geography" on the one hand and secures the territorial "openness" of Israel on the other. See Nir Hasson, "IDF Engineers Begin Removal of Gilo Barrier Built during Second Intifada," *Haaretz*, August 16, 2010, http://www.haaretz.com/print-edition/news/idf-engineers-begin-removal-of-gilo-barrier-built-during-second-intifada-1.308237. Weizman, *Hollow Land*, 6–8.
54 Rose, *The Last Resistance*, 197.
55 Ibid., 198.
56 Ibid.

57. Rose, *The Question of Zion*, 67.
58. Ibid.
59. Richard Flemming "Paint Your Troubles Away" *Cabinet Magazine*, no. 9 (Winter 2002/2003), http://cabinetmagazine.org/issues/9/fleming.php.
60. Ibid.
61. Weizman, *Hollow Land,* 161.
62. Harlap's speech at the 2004 annual convention of Israel's Architect Association in Weizman, *Hollow Land,* 161. It is worth noting how the sentiment is repeated in the wall design competition initiated by Trump in the US context. See Chapter 7.
63. Weizman, *Hollow Land,* 169.
64. Ibid., 170.
65. Brosh quoted in Flemming "Paint Your Troubles Away."
66. Ibid.
67. Salecl, *The Spoils of Freedom*, 15.
68. Ibid.
69. Rose, *The Question of Zion*, xiii.
70. Rose, *The Last Resistance*, 197.
71. Ibid.
72. Said, *The Question of Palestine*, 49.
73. Rose, *The Last Resistance*, 198.
74. Said, *The Question of Palestine*, 232.
75. Ibid., 238.
76. Ibid.
77. Terry Boulatta "The Spirit of Activism," in *Against the Wall: Israel's Barrier to Peace*, ed. Michael Sorkin (New York: New Press, 2005), 257.
78. Artists without Walls "Separation Mentality," *Osaarchivum*, April 1, 2004, http://osaarchivum.org/galeria/the_divide/chapter12.html.
79. Ibid.
80. Berlant, *Cruel Optimism*, 226.
81. Boulatta "The Spirit of Activism," 257.
82. Lauren Berlant "Affect, Noise, Silence, Protest: Ambient Citizenships," *Social Science Research Counsel*, http://publicsphere.ssrc.org/berlant-affect-noise-silence-protest-ambientcitizenship/.
83. Boulatta "The Spirit of Activism," 257.
84. Berlant "Affect, Noise, Silence, Protest."
85. Ibid.
86. Ibid.
87. Rose, *The Question of Zion*, 68.

88 In *The Interpretation of Dreams*, Freud explains that psychoanalysis "recognizes the affect as being... justified" in the disguised fantasy of the dream. Freud, *The Interpretation of Dreams*, 597.
89 Gregory J. Seigworth and Melissa Gregg, Introduction to *The Affect Theory Reader*, ed. Gregory J. Seigworth and Melissa Gregg (Durham: Duke University Press, 2010), 2.
90 Emmanuel Lévinas, *Totality and Infinity: An Essay on Exteriority* (Pittsburgh: Duquesne University Press, 2000).
91 Roland Barthes, *Camera Lucida*, 11.
92 Butler, *Precarious Life*, 20.
93 Sontag, *On Photography*, 15.
94 JR and Marco, *Face2Face* (Paris: Édition Alternative, 2007), 16–17.
95 Ibid., 120.
96 Ibid., 16.
97 Barthes, *Camera Lucida*, 12.
98 Emmanuel Lévinas, "Reality and Its Shadows," in *Collected Papers*, trans. Alphonso Lingis (Pittsburgh: Duquesne University Press, 1998), 1.
99 Ibid., 3.
100 Sontag, *On Photography*, 59.
101 Lévinas articulates this idea in more detail in Lévinas, "Reality and Its Shadows," 6.
102 Ibid.
103 Barthes, *Camera Lucida*, 34.
104 Ibid.
105 Ibid.
106 Berlant "Intimacy: A Special Issue," 286.
107 Sontag, *On Photography*, 167.
108 JR and Marco, *Face2Face*.
109 Ibid.
110 JR, "My Wish: Use Art to Turn the World Inside Out," *TED*, March 2011, https://www.ted.com/talks/jr_s_ted_prize_wish_use_art_to_turn_the_world_inside_out.
111 Berlant "Intimacy: A Special Issue," 281.
112 Ibid., 283.
113 Ibid.
114 Ibid., 285.
115 Barthes, *Camera Lucida*, 6.
116 Ibid., 55.
117 Sontag, *On Photography*, 23.
118 Gregory, *The Colonial Present*.

Chapter 6

1. Mike Davis quoted in Said Sadiki, *World of Walls* (Cambridge: Open Book Publisher, 2017), 4.
2. Brown, *Walled States*, 24.
3. Sundberg, "Delimiting Democracy," 53.
4. Trump quoted in Michael Finnegan, "It's Going to Be a Big Fat Beautiful Wall: Trump's Words Make His California Climb an Even Steeper Trek," *LA Times*, June 3, 2016, http://www.latimes.com/politics/la-na-pol-trump-california-campaign-20160602-snap-story.html.
5. Roger Batra, Introduction to *Warrior for Gringostroika*, ed. Guillermo Gómez-Peña (St. Paul: Graywolf Press, 1993), 11.
6. Brown, *Walled States*, 114.
7. Eve Tuck and C. Ree. "A Glossary of Haunting," in *Handbook of Autoethnography*, ed. Stacey Holman Jones, Tony E. Adams, and Carolyn Ellis (Walnut Creek: Left Coast Press, 2013), 642.
8. Avery Gordon, *Ghostly Matters: Haunting and the Sociological Imagination* (Minneapolis: Minnesota University Press, 1997), xvi.
9. Del Pilar Blanco, Maria. *Ghost-Watching American Modernity* (New York: Fordham University Press, 2012),
10. Del Pilar Blanco, *Ghost-Watching*, 15.
11. Edward Casey and Mary Watkins, *Up against the Wall: Re-imagining the US-Mexican Border* (Houston: University of Texas Press, 2014), 226.
12. Del Pilar Blanco, *Ghost-Watching*, 26.
13. Ibid.
14. Gloria Anzaldúa, *Borderlands/ LA Frontera* (San Francisco: Aunt Lute Books, 1987), 25.
15. Ibid., 108.
16. Ibid.
17. Resendiz, Resendiz and Klaver, "Colonialism and Imperialism."
18. Evelyn Nakano Glenn, "Settler Colonialism as Structure: A Framework for Comparative Studies of US Race and Gender Formation," *Sociology of Race and Ethnicity*, vol. 1, no. 1 (2015): 55.
19. Mbembe, *Critique of Black Reason*, 37.
20. Resendiz, Resendiz and Klaver, "Colonialism and Imperialism," 22–3.
21. Reece Jones, *Violent Border: Refugees and the Right to Move* (New York: Verso, 2016), 85.
22. Mohammed Chaichian, *Empires and Walls: Globalization, Migration and Colonial Domination* (Leiden: Brill, 2014), 195.
23. Juanita Sundberg, "The State of Exception and the Imperial Way of Life in the United States-Mexico Borderlands," *Environment and Planning D: Society and Space*, vol. 33 (2015): 214.

24 Ibid.
25 Chaichian, *Empires and Walls,* 179.
26 Resendiz, Resendiz and Klaver, "Colonialism and Imperialism," 30.
27 See Wolfe, "Settler Colonialism," 388.
28 Quoted in Resendiz, Resendiz and Klaver, "Colonialism and Imperialism," 23.
29 It is not surprising that the sentiment is often echoed by people who share this experience of settler colonialism. See for example Ella Shohat who expresses a similar idea in relation to the Palestinian context or Leonie Pihama, who also used the expression to qualify Maori experiences of colonial walls in the context of Aotearoa/ New Zealand. Shohat, *Israeli Cinema*, 288. Leonie Pihama, "Colonisation and Systemic Violence in Aotearoa," conference paper at *Space, Race, Bodies: Walls*, Otago University, Dunedin 2018.
30 Casey and Watkins, *Up against the Wall,* 142.
31 David Lloyd and Laura Pulipo, "In the Long Shadow of the Settler: On Israeli and US Colonialism," *American Quarterly*, vol. 62, no. 4 (2010): 802.
32 Wolfe, "Settler Colonialism," 387.
33 Resendiz, Resendiz and Klaver, "Colonialism and Imperialism," 30.
34 Ibid., 17.
35 Ibid., 29.
36 Glenn, "Settler Colonialism as Structure," 67.
37 Ibid., 59.
38 Ibid., 67–8.
39 Alexander Weheliye, *Habeas Viscus: Racializing Assemblages, Biopolitics, and Black Feminist Theories of the Human* (Durham: Duke University Press, 2014).
40 Jones, *Violent Borders*, 96.
41 See Resendiz, Resendiz, and Klaver, "Colonialism and Imperialism"; Sundberg, "The State of Exception."
42 Sundberg, "The State of Exception," 209.
43 See Todd Miller, "Creating a Military-Industrial-Immigration Complex," *Aljazeera*, August 4, 2013, https://www.aljazeera.com/indepth/opinion/2013/07/2013714154732351793.html.
44 Agamben, *State of Exception*, 1.
45 Aimé Césaire, *Discourse on Colonialism* (New York: NYU Press, Monthly Review Press, 2000), 39.
46 Ibid., 35.
47 Ibid., 68.
48 Brown, *Walled States*, 117.
49 Ibid., 122.
50 Michel Foucault, *Discipline and Punish: The Birth of the Prison* (New York: Vintage Books, 1979), 200.

51 Jacques Rancière, *Dissenting Words: Interviews with Jacques Rancière* (London: Bloomsbury, 2017), 5.
52 Ibid.
53 Ibid.
54 Ibid.
55 Deborah Shaw, '"You are Alright, But…": Individual and Collective Representations of Mexicans, Latinos, Anglo Americans and Africans in Steen Soderbergh's Traffic," *Quarterly Review of Film and Video*, vol. 25, no. 3 (2005): 217.
56 Leslie Berestein, "An Openness to Border Fence: Divider Boundless as Visual Forum for Political Expression," *The Border Wall in the News*, November 30, 2009, http://borderwallinthenews.blogspot.co.nz/2009/12/openness-to-border-fence-divider.html.
57 Marion Schmid, *Chantal Akerman* (Manchester: Manchester University Press, 2010), 114.
58 Thomas Torrans, *The Magic Curtain: The Mexican-American Border in Fiction, Film, and Song* (Fort Worth: Texas Christian University Press, 2002).
59 Lauro Zavala, "Towards a Dialogical Theory of Cultural Liminality: Contemporary Writing and Cultural Identity in Mexico," *Arizona Journal of Hispanic Cultural Studies*, vol. 1 (1997): 9.
60 Paul Stenner, *Liminality and Experience: A Transdisciplinary Approach to the Psychosocial* (London: Palgrave MacMillan, 2017), 14.
61 Del Pilar Blanco, *Ghost-Watching*, 14.
62 Jonathan Rutherford, "The Third Space: Interview with Homi Babha," in *Identity: Community, Culture, Difference*, ed. Jonathan Rutherford (London: Lawrence and Wishart, 1990), 209.
63 Ibid.
64 Guillermo Gómez-Peña, *Conversations across the Border: A Performance Artist Converses with Theorists, Curators, Activists and Fellow Artists*, ed. Laura Levin (London: Seagull Books, 2011), 322.
65 Patricia Zavella, *I'm Neither Here Nor There: Mexican Quotidian Struggles with Migration and Poverty* (Durham: Duke University Press, 2011), 192.
66 Coco Fusco, "The Border Art Workshop/Taller de Arte Fronterizo: Interview with Guillermo Gómez-Peña and Emily Hicks," *Third Text*, vol. 3, no. 7 (1989): 53.
67 Ibid., 57.
68 Andrea Noble, *Mexican National Cinema* (New York: Routledge, 2005), 166.
69 Claire F. Fox, "The Portable Border: Site Specificity, Art and the US–Mexico Frontier," *Social Text*, no. 41 (Winter, 1994): 63.
70 Guillermo Gómez-Peña, *Warrior for Gringostroika* (St Paul, MN: Graywolf Press, 1993), 75–96. "Estracto: Guillermo Gomez - Peña / Museo de Arte Moderno 2011," *Vimeo*, http://www.frequency.com/video/border-brujo-19/34601261.

NOTES

71 Fox, "The Portable Border," 63.
72 Gómez-Peña, *Conversations across the Border*, 324.
73 Ibid.
74 Coco Fusco, "The Border Art Workshop," 57.
75 Ibid.
76 Guillermo Gómez-Peña, "Philosophical Tantrum," *YouTube*, http://www.youtube.com/watch?v=74ajLA7MFDw.
77 Fox, "The Portable Border," 63.
78 Pamela Maria Smorkaloff, "Shifting Borders, Free Trade, and Frontier Narrative US, Canada and Mexico," *American Literary History*, vol. 6, no. 1 (Spring 1994): 90.
79 Fusco, "The Border Art Workshop," 59.
80 Ibid.
81 Guillermo Gómez-Peña, *Essential Works*, https://www.guillermogomezpena.com/works/.
82 Gómez-Peña, *Warrior for Gringostroika*, 75.
83 Ibid.
84 Del Pilar Blanco, *Ghost-Watching*, 7.
85 Gómez-Peña, *Warrior for Gringostroika*, 87.
86 Ibid., 88.
87 Ibid., 76–83.
88 Quoted in Del Pilar Blanco, *Ghost-Watching*, 7.
89 Gómez-Peña, *Warrior for Gringostroika*, 38.
90 Ibid., 78.
91 Ibid., 82.
92 Fusco, "The Border Art Workshop," 70.
93 Ibid.
94 Gómez-Peña, *Warrior for Gringostroika*, 39.
95 Fusco, "The Border Art Workshop," 59.
96 Ibid., 16.
97 Noble, *Mexican National Cinema*, 164.
98 Gómez-Peña, *Warrior for Gringostroika*, 43.
99 Ibid.
100 John Kraniauska, "Border Dialogue: Talking to Guillermo Gómez-Peña," *Traversia*, vol. 3, no. 1 (1994): 159.
101 Ibid.
102 Fusco, "The Border Art Workshop," 57.
103 Gómez-Peña, *Warrior for Gringostroika*, 12.
104 Kraniauska, "Border Dialogue," 170.

105 Gómez-Peña, *Warrior for Gringostroika*, 76.
106 Balibar, *We, the People of Europe?*, 62.
107 Fusco, "The Border Art Workshop," 66.
108 Ibid.
109 Kraniauska, "Border Dialogue," 161.
110 Ibid.
111 Gómez-Peña, *Warrior for Gringostroika*, 75.
112 Ibid., 82.
113 Ibid.
114 Ibid.
115 Fusco, "The Border Art Workshop," 66.
116 Ibid.
117 Gómez-Peña, *Conversations across the Border*, 23.
118 Kraniauska, "Border Dialogue," 161.
119 Fusco, "The Border Art Workshop," 54.
120 Tuck and Ree, "A Glossary of Haunting," 642.
121 Gómez-Peña, "Philosophical Tantrum."
122 *From the Other Side*, directed by Chantal Akerman (USA/Mexico, 2002; Brooklyn, NY: Icarus Films, 2012), DVD.
123 Schmid, *Chantal Akerman*, 2–3.
124 Ibid., 119.
125 Ibid., 2.
126 Philip Rosen, "Border Times and Geopolitical Frames," The Martin Walsh Memorial Lecture 2006," *Canadian Journal of Film Studies* (Fall 2006): 15.
127 Rob Nixon, *Slow Violence and the Environmentalism of the Poor* (Cambridge, MA: Harvard University Press, 2011), 150.
128 Ibid., 151.
129 Ibid.
130 Terri Ginsberg, "Bordering on Disaster—Toward an Epistemology of Divided Cinematic Space," *Spectator*, vol. 29, no. 1 (Spring 2009): 33.
131 Ibid.
132 Ibid.
133 See Hage, "Etat de Siege."
134 Schmid, *Chantal Akerman*, 116.
135 Brown, *Walled States*, 40.
136 Torrans, *Magic Curtain*, 24.
137 Ibid., 9.
138 Ibid.
139 Gómez-Peña, *Warrior for Gringostroika*, 11.

140 Klaus Ottman, "From the Other Side (De l'Autre Côté)," in *Chantal Akerman: Moving through Time and Space*, ed. Terrie Sultan (Houston: Blaffer Gallery, the Art Museum of the University of Houston, 2008), 33.

141 Kaira Marie Cabanas, "What the Map Cuts Up, the Story Cuts across: Chantal Akerman's De L'autre Cote," *Parachute* (1 October 2005): 26.

142 Scott Macdonald, "Chantal Akerman," in *A Critical Cinema 4: Interviews with Independent Filmmakers* (Berkeley: University of California Press, 2005), 267.

143 Ibid.

144 Ibid.

145 Ibid.

146 Ibid., 268.

147 Bryan Barcena, "Chantal Akerman: Macro to Micro," *artpulse*, November 29, 2008, http://artpulsemagazine.com/chantal-akerman-macro-to-micro.

148 Schmid, *Chantal Akerman*, 120.

149 Del Pilar Blanco, *Ghost-Watching*, 180.

150 Anne McClintock, "Imperial Ghosting and National Tragedy: Revenants from Hiroshima and Indian Country in the War on Terror," *PMLA Publications of the Modern Language Associations of America*, vol. 129, no. 4 (2014): 821.

151 Ibid., 820.

152 Ibid., 821.

Chapter 7

1 Trump stated the memorable line at rally in Phoenix, Arizona in 2016.

2 Chaichian, *Empires and Walls*, 243.

3 Salecl, *The Spoils of Freedom*, 15.

4 Glenn, "Settler Colonialism as Structure," 59.

5 Sara Ahmed, "The Organisation of Hate," *Law and Critique*, vol. 12, no. 3 (2001): 345.

6 Salecl, *The Spoils of Freedom*, 30.

7 Kevin Bruyneel, "*Happy Days* (of the White Settler Imaginary) Are Here Again," *Theory & Event*, vol. 20, no. 1 (2017): 47.

8 Bruyneel, "*Happy Days*," 48.

9 Salecl, *The Spoils of Freedom*, 30.

10 Bruyneel, "*Happy Days*," 46.

11 Ibid., 45.

12 Emily Nussbaum, "The TV That Created Donald Trump," *The New Yorker*, July 31, 2017, https://www.newyorker.com/magazine/2017/07/31/the-tv-that-created-donald-trump.

13. Jodi A. Byrd, Alyosha Goldstein, Jodi Melamed and Chandan Reddy, "Predatory Value: Economies of Dispossession and Disturbed Relationalities," *Social Text*, vol. 36, no. 2 (2018): 4.
14. Camilla Pastor, "President Trump's Moving Targets: Walls, Expulsions and Prisoner States," *Journal of Middle East Women's Studies*, vol. 13, no. 3 (2017): 492.
15. Gregory, *The Colonial Present*.
16. Cornel West, "The Trump Era: Hope in a Time of Escalating Despair," *Transition*, no. 122 (2017): 27.
17. "einen neuen affektiven Autoritarismus" Misha Kavka, "Trump, Fernsehen und Das Neue Camp," *Zeitschrift für Medienwissenschaften*, vol. 10, no. 1 (2018): 154.
18. McClintock, "Imperial Ghosting."
19. *The New York Times* reported that "dynamite crews were still blasting hillsides on [Joe Biden's] Inauguration Day" to move construction forward. Sabrina Rodriguez, "Trump's Partially Built 'Big Beautiful' Wall," *Politco*, January 12, 2021, https://www.politico.com/news/2021/01/12/trump-border-wall-partially-built-458255.
20. Fay Hipsman and Doris Meissner, "Trump Executive Order and His DHS Implementation Memo on Border Enforcement: A Brief Review," *Migration Policy Institute*, April 2017, https://www.migrationpolicy.org/research/trump-executive-order-and-dhs-implementation-memo-border-enforcement-brief-review.
21. Saddiki, *World of Walls*, 87.
22. quoted in Ron Nixon, "Trump Seeks Proposal for 'Physically Imposing' Wall with Mexico," *The New York Times*, March 18, 2017, https://www.nytimes.com/2017/03/18/us/politics/trump-seeks-proposals-for-physically-imposing-wall-with-mexico.html.
23. Ibid.
24. Ibid.
25. Ibid.
26. Brown, *Walled States*, 24.
27. Ibid., 39.
28. Julia Carrie Wong, "The Beauty Pageant to Build Trump's Border Wall Is Beginning," *The Guardian*, March 29, 2017, https://www.theguardian.com/us-news/2017/mar/29/trump-border-wall-mexico-construction-proposals.
29. This is Trump's estimation. According to an estimation by the Washington Post the cost will be much higher at about $25 billion dollars AFP/dpa, "US selects shortlist for Mexican Wall Builders," *DW*, September 7, 2017, https://www.dw.com/en/us-selects-shortlist-for-mexican-wall-builders/a-40408343.
30. Ibid.
31. Saddiki, *World of Walls*, 92.

32 Enrique Penã Nieto posted a video on Twitter in early 2017, responding to Trump's claims that Mexico will pay for the Wall, stating that he does not believe in walls and that he will never pay for it. CNN, "Mexico's President: We Will Not Pay for the Wall," *CNN*, January 26, 2017, https://edition.cnn.com/videos/world/2017/01/26/mexico-president-will-not-pay-for-wall-santiago-ctn.cnn.

33 Todd Miller, "Beyond Trump's Big Beautiful Wall," *NCLA Report on the Americas*; New York, vol. 49 no. 2 (2017), 145.

34 Tom McCarthy, "Trump Tweets Misleading Photos Suggesting Border Wall under Way," *The Guardian*, March 29, 2018, https://www.theguardian.com/us-news/2018/mar/28/trump-border-wall-construction-photo-tweet.

35 The New York Times, "Full Transcripts: Trump's Speech on Immigration and the Democratic Response," *The New York Times*, 8 January 2019, https://www.nytimes.com/2019/01/08/us/politics/trump-speech-transcript.html.

36 Rodriguez, "Trump's Partially Built 'Big Beautiful' Wall."

37 Ibid.

38 Curtis Marez, "Of Walls and Robots: The Future of Immigration," *University of Minnesota Pressblog*, June 30, 2016, http://www.uminnpressblog.com/2016/06/of-walls-and-robots-future-of.html.

39 Wong, "The Beauty Pageant to Build Trump's Border Wall Is Beginning."

40 Ibid.

41 Nadja Sayej "Should Donald Trump's Border Wall Prototypes Be Considered Art" *The Guardian*, January 12, 2018, https://www.theguardian.com/artanddesign/2018/jan/12/should-donald-trumps-border-wall-prototypes-be-considered-art.

42 Ibid.

43 Ibid.

44 Kate Morrissey, "Border Wall Prototypes Become Canvas for Light Graffiti," *The San Diego Union Tribune*, November 22, 2017, http://www.sandiegouniontribune.com/news/california/la-me-border-wall-project-20171122-story.html.

45 Gregory, *The Colonial Present*.

46 Matthew Flisfeder, "'Trump' —What Does the Name Signify? Or, Protofascism and the Alt Right," *Cultural Politics*, vol. 14, no. 2 (2018): 2.

47 Wolfe, "Settler Colonialism," 394.

48 Sigmund Freud, "Screen Memory (1899)." In *The Freud Reader*, ed, Peter Gay (London: Vintage, 1995), 117–226.

49 McClintock, "Imperial Ghosting."

50 Ibid., 821.

51 Ibid.

52 Ibid., 826.

53 Bruyneel, "*Happy Days*," 52.

54 Jodi Kim, "Settler Modernity, Debt Imperialism, and The Necropolitics of the Promise," *Social Text*, vol. 36, no. 2 (2018): 43.
55 McClintock, "Imperial Ghosting," 821.
56 Lloyd and Pulido, "In the Long Shadow," 799.
57 Mbembe, *Critique of Black Reason*, 24.
58 Yinon Cohen and Neve Gordon, "Israel's Biospatial Politics: Territory, Demography and Effective Control," *Public Culture*, vol. 30, no. 2 (2018): 200.
59 Ibid.
60 quoted in Glenn, "Settler Colonialism as Structure," 59.
61 Adam Gomez, "Deus Vult: John L. O' Sullivan, Manifest Destiny and American Democratic Messianism," *American Political Thought*, vol. 1, no. 2 (2012): 237.
62 Ibid., 249.
63 Ibid., 244.
64 During his 2016 election campaign Trump famously stated that "the system is rigged," winning enthusiasm from his supporters.
65 Sundberg, "The State of Exception," 211.
66 Sam Levin, "'Over My Dead Body: Tribe Aims to Block Trump's Border Wall on Arizona Lands," *The Guardian*, January 26, 2017, https://www.theguardian.com/us-news/2017/jan/26/donald-trump-border-wall-tohono-oodham-arizona-tribe.
67 Resendiz, Residenz and Klaver, "Colonialism and Imperialism," 30.
68 Ted Widmer, "Draining the Swamp," *The New Yorker*, January 19, 2017, https://www.newyorker.com/news/news-desk/draining-the-swamp.
69 Nira Yuval-Davis, *Gender and Nation* (London: Sage, 1997); Anne McClintock, *Imperial Leather: Race, Gender and Sexuality in the Colonial Contest* (New York: Routledge, 1995); Hage, *Against Paranoid Nationalism*; Ahmed, *The Cultural Politics*.
70 Amy Kaplan, "Manifest Domesticity," *American Literature*, vol. 70, no. 3 (1998): 582.
71 Berlant, *Cruel Optimism*, 226.
72 Maureen Sioh, "The Wound of Whiteness: Conceptualizing Economic Convergence as Trauma in the 2016 United States Presidential Election," *Geoforum*, vol. 95 (July 2018): 112–21.
73 Hage, *Against Paranoid Nationalism*, 31.
74 Ibid. 32.
75 Ibid. 33.
76 Ibid.
77 Benedict Anderson, *Imagined Communities: Reflections on the Origin and Spread of Nationalism* (New York: Verso, 2006).

NOTES

78. Salecl, *The Spoils of Freedom*, 15.
79. Kaplan, "Manifest Domesticity," 582.
80. Hage, *Against Paranoid Nationalism*, 38.
81. Lefort quoted in Hage, *Against Paranoid Nationalism*, 40
82. Ibid.
83. Ibid., 37.
84. Danielle Parquette, "Trump's Travel Ban on 'Bad Dudes' Actually Keeps Out Women and Children," *The Washington Post*, January 30, 2017, https://www.washingtonpost.com/news/wonk/wp/2017/01/30/president-trump-wanted-to-ban-bad-dudes-he-could-block-more-women-and-children/?noredirect=on&utm_term=.5f28680eafc5.
85. Ibid.
86. Steve Holland and Ginger Gibson, "After Florida Shooting Trump Hardens Stance on Muslims," *Reuters*, June 14, 2016, https://www.reuters.com/article/us-usa-election-clinton-idUSKCN0YZ1GE.
87. Hage, *Against Paranoid Nationalism*, 38.
88. "negativen Affekt" Kavka, "Trump, Fernsehen und Das Neue Camp," 160.
89. Ahmed, *The Cultural Politics*, 2.
90. Ibid.
91. Hage makes a similar point about the rise of nationalism in Australia in *Against Paranoid Nationalism*, 42.
92. Hage, *Against Paranoid Nationalism*, 37.
93. Ibid., 41.
94. Sioh, "The Wound of Whiteness," 113.
95. Ibid.
96. Mike DeBonis, "It's Like a Manhood Thing for Him: Pelosi's Power Play with Trump Serves as Message for Opponents," *The Washington Post*, December 11, 2018, https://www.washingtonpost.com/powerpost/pelosi-questions-trumps-manhood-after-confrontational-white-house-meeting/2018/12/11/2b2111be-fd79-11e8-862a-b6a6f3ce8199_story.html?noredirect=on&utm_term=.fe1fbb785d65.
97. Jane Junn, "The Trump Majority: White Womanhood and the Making of Female Voters in the US," *Politics, Groups and Identities* vol. 5, no. 2 (2017): 343–52. Emma Blackett, "Sexism Defeated: Women for Trump and the Binding Energy of Political Hope," *Women's Studies Journal*, vol. 31, no. 2 (2017): 18–26.
98. Ibid.
99. Roxane Gay, "Feminist Author Roxane Gay Says Racism Got Trump Elected," *CBC Radio*, November 11, 2016, https://www.cbc.ca/radio/asithappens/as-it-happens-friday-edition-1.3847360/feminist-author-roxane-gay-says-racism-got-trump-elected-1.3847797.
100. June, "The Trump Majority," 348.

101 Lauren Gambino, "Truly the Year of the Woman: Female Candidates Win in Record Numbers," *The Guardian*, November 7, 2018, https://www.theguardian.com/us-news/2018/nov/07/women-candidates-midterms-wins.

102 Illma Gore, "If Anyone Is Going to Be Threatened by a Small Penis, It's Going to Be Trump," *The Guardian*, May 7, 2016, https://www.theguardian.com/us-news/2016/may/07/donald-trump-penis-painting-ilma-gore.

103 Jacqueline Rose, "Who Do You Think You Are," *London Review of Books*, vol. 38, no. 9 (May 5, 2016): 11.

104 Ibid.

105 Gore, "If Anyone."

106 Ibid.

107 News, "New York's Knockdown Center Raises More Than $50,000 for Community Health and Reproductive Justice Organizations," *Artforum*, January 17, 2017, https://www.artforum.com/news/new-york-s-knockdown-center-raises-more-than-50-000-for-community-health-and-reproductive-justice-organizations-65923.

108 Ibid.

109 Erica L. Green, Katie Benner and Robert Pear, "Transgender Could Be Defined out of Existence under Trump Administration," *The New York Times*, October 21, 2018, https://www.nytimes.com/2018/10/21/us/politics/transgender-trump-administration-sex-definition.html.

110 Becky Strum and Danika Fears, "Trump: Megyn Kelly Had 'Blood Coming out of Her Wherever'," *The New York Post*, August 8, 2015, https://nypost.com/2015/08/08/trump-megyn-kelly-had-blood-coming-out-of-her-wherever/.

111 Julia Kristeva, *Powers of Horror: An Essay on Abjection* (New York: Columbia University Press, 1982), 15.

112 Ibid., 3.

113 Ibid., 4.

114 Ibid.

115 Ibid., 15.

116 Ibid., 47.

117 Ibid.

118 Kavka, "Trump, Fernsehen und Das Neue Camp" John Street, "What Is Donald Trump? Forms of 'Celebrity' in Celebrity Politics," *Political Studies Review* (2018): 1–11. Emily Nussbaum, "The TV That Created Donald Trump."

119 J. Westen Phippen, "Trump's Wall Goes Up (In Miniature)," *The Atlantic*, July 20, 2016, https://www.theatlantic.com/news/archive/2016/07/plastic-jesus-trump-wall/492179/.

120 Mark Wheeler, *Celebrity Politics* (Cambridge: Polity, 2013), 7.

121 Ibid., 3.

122 Street, "What Is Donald Trump?," 1.

123 Nussbaum, "The TV That Created Donald Trump."

124 Ibid.
125 Plastic Jesus, "Stop Making Stupid People Famous," http://www.plasticjesus.net/.
126 Ahmed, *The Cultural Politics*, 3.
127 Rodriguez, "Trump's Partially Built 'Big Beautiful' Wall."

Chapter 8

1 Rare Historical Photos. https://rarehistoricalphotos.com/conrad-schumann-defects-west-berlin-1961/ (accessed November 28, 2018).
2 Ahmed, *The Cultural Politics*, 10.
3 Berlant, *Cruel Optimism*, 226.
4 Edward Said, "Imaginative Geographies and Its Representation: Orientalizing the Orient," in *Orientalism* (London: Penguin, 2003), 54.
5 Ibid.
6 Ibid.
7 Gregory, *The Colonial Present*, 17.
8 Said, "Imaginative Geographies," 55.
9 Gregory, *The Colonial Present*, 17.
10 Said, "Imaginative Geographies," 55.
11 See Casey and Watkins, *Up against the Wall* for a detailed discussion of US detention systems.
12 Hage "État de Siège," 45.
13 Agamben *State of Exception*.
14 Hage, "État de Siège," 44.
15 Ibid.
16 Raymond Williams quoted in Hage, "État de Siège," 39.
17 Schwab, *Haunting Legacies*, 29.
18 Rose, *The Last Resistance*, 10.
19 Anzaldúa, *Borderlands/ LA Frontera*, 109.
20 Maddy Kramer, "The Most Beautiful Wall," http://themostbeautifulwall.com/.

Bibliography

Abramson, Larry. "What Does Landscape Want? A Walk in W. J. T. Mitchell's Holy Landscape." In *The Pictorial Turn*, edited by Neal Curtis, 178–91. London: Routledge, 2010.
Abu-Remaileh, Refqua. "Palestinian Anti-Narratives in the Films of Elia Suleiman." *Arab Media and Society* no. 5 (Spring 2008): 1–29.
Adorno, Theordor. *Notes to Literature*. New York: Columbia University Press, 1992.
AFP/dpa. "US Selects Shortlist for Mexican Wall Builders." *DW*, September 7, 2017. https://www.dw.com/en/us-selects-shortlist-for-mexican-wall-builders/a-40408843.
Agamben, Giorgio. *Homo Sacer: Sovereign Power and Bare Life*. Stanford: Stanford University Press, 1998.
Agamben, Giorgio. *State of Exception*. Chicago: Chicago University Press, 2005.
Ahmed, Sara. *The Cultural Politics of Emotion*. Edinburgh: Edinburgh University Press, 2014.
Ahmed, Sara. "The Organisation of Hate." *Law and Critique* 12, no. 3 (2001): 345–65.
Anderson, Benedict. *Imagined Communities: Reflections on the Origin and Spread of Nationalism*. New York: Verso, 2006.
Anzaldúa, Gloria. *Borderlands/ LA Frontera*. San Francisco: Aunt Lute Books, 1987.
Arendt, Hannah. *The Human Condition*. Chicago: University of Chicago Press, 1958.
Artists without Walls. "Separation Mentality." *Osaarchivum*. April 1, 2004. http://osaarchivum.org/galeria/the_divide/chapter12.html.
Badiou, Alain. "The Communist Hypothesis." *New Left Review* 49 (January–February 2008): 29–42.
Balibar, Étienne. "Europe as Borderland." *Society and Space* 27 (2009): 190–215.
Balibar, Étienne. *Politics and the Other Scene*. London: Verso, 2002.
Balibar, Étienne. *We, the People of Europe?—Reflections on Transnational Citizenship*. Princeton: Princeton University Press, 2004.
Banksy. *Wall and Piece*. London: Random House Group, 2006.
Barcena, Bryan. "Chantal Akerman: Macro to Micro." *Artpulse*, November 29, 2008. http://artpulsemagazine.com/chantal-akerman-macro-to-micro.
Bar-On, Modechai. "Conflicting Narratives or Narratives of a Conflict: Can the Zionist and Palestinian Narratives of the 1948 War Be Bridged?" In *Israeli and Palestinian Narratives of Conflict: History's Double Helix*, edited by Robert L. Rothberg, 142–73. Bloomington: Indiana University Press, 2006.

BIBLIOGRAPHY

Barthes, Roland. *Camera Lucida: Reflections on Photography.* New York: Hill and Wang, 2010.

Batra, Roger. Introduction to *Warrior for Gringostroika*, by Guillermo Gómez-Peña. St. Paul: Graywolf Press, 1993.

"Bauarbeiter reißen Lücke in Eastside Gallery." *Zeit Online*, March 27, 2014. http://www.zeit.de/gesellschaft/2013-03/abriss-east-side-gallery.

Benedicto, Ainhoa Ruiz and Pere Brunet. "Building Walls: Fear and Securitization in the European Union." *Transnational Institute*, November 9, 2018. https://www.tni.org/en/publication/building-walls.

Benjamin, Walter. *Illuminations: Essays and Reflections.* New York: Schocken Books, 2007.

Benjamin, Walter. "The Work of Art in the Age of Mechanical Reproduction." In *Illuminations*, translated by Harry Zohn, 217–52. New York: Schocken Books, 2007.

Bennett, Jill and Rosanne Kennedy. Introduction to *World Memory: Personal Trajectories in Global Time*, edited by Jill Bennett and Rosanne Kennedy, 1–15. New York: Palgrave Macmillan, 2002.

Berestein, Leslie. "An Openness to Border Fence: Divider Boundless as Visual Forum for Political Expression." *The Border Wall in the News*, November 30, 2009. http://borderwallinthenews.blogspot.co.nz/2009/12/openness-to-border-fence-divider.html

Berlant, Lauren. "Affect, Noise, Silence, Protest: Ambient Citizenship." *Social Science Research Counsel.* http://publicsphere.ssrc.org/berlant-affect-noise-silence-protest-ambientcitizenship/.

Berlant, Lauren and Jordan Greenwald. "Affect at the End of Times: A Conversation with Lauren Berlant." *Qui Parle?* 20, no. 2 (2012): 71–89.

Berlant, Lauren. *Cruel Optimism.* Durham: Duke University Press, 2011.

Berlant, Lauren. "Intimacy: A Special Issue." *Critical Inquiry* 24 (Winter 1998): 281–8.

Berlant, Lauren. "Structures of Unfeeling: Mysterious Skin," *International Journal of Politics, Culture and Society* 28, no. 3 (2015): 191–213.

"Berliner Mauer: Fotos Verboten." organized by *BStU*, August 11, 2013 – December 31, 2013. https://www.bstu.bund.de/SharedDocs/Ausstellungen/Region-Frankfurt/ffo_fotos_verboten.html.

Betts, Paul. *Within Walls: Private Life in the German Democratic Republic.* Oxford: Oxford University Press, 2010.

Beuys, Joseph. "Beuys empfiehlt Erhöhung der Berliner Mauer um 5 cm (bessere Proportion!)." *Aktenvermerk für das Innenministerium*, July 20, 1964. http://www.josephbeuys.de/texthand.htm.

Bierman, Wolf. "The Ghosts Are Leaving the Shadows." *Signandsight*, March 29, 2006. http://www.signandsight.com/features/682.html.

Blackett, Emma. "Sexism Defeated: Women for Trump and the Binding Energy of Political Hope." *Women's Studies Journal* 31, no. 2 (2017): 18–26.

Boulatta, Terry. "The Spirit of Activism." In *Against the Wall: Israel's Barrier to Peace*, edited by Michael Sorkin, 254–59. New York: New Press, 2005.

Bowman, James. "Humanized without Honor." *The American Spectator* (April 2006): 58–9.

Bresheeth, Haim. "A Symphony of Absence: Borders and Liminality in Elia Suleiman's 'Chronicle of a Disappearance'." *The Journal of Cinema and Media* 43, no. 2 (Fall 2002): 71–84.

Briese, Olaf. "The Different Aesthetics of the Berlin Wall." In *The German Wall: Fallout in Europe*, edited by Marc Silberman, 37–58. New York: Palgrave MacMillan, 2011.

Britton, Simone and Elia Suleiman. "Wall-Mur." *The European Graduate School*, May 7, 2005. http://www.egs.edu/faculty/elia-suleiman/videos/wall-mur/.

Brown, Wendy. *Walled States: Waning Sovereignty*. New York: Zone Books, 2010.

Brune, Adrian Margaret. "Banksy in the West Bank." *Huffingtonpost*, November 7, 2011. http://www.huffingtonpost.com/adrian-margaret-brune/banksy-in-the-west-bank_b_895037.html.

Bruyneel, Kevin. "*Happy Days* (of the White Settler Imaginary) Are here Again." *Theory & Event* 20, no. 1 (2017): 44–54.

Butler, Judith. *Giving an Account of Oneself*. New York: Fordham University Press, 2005.

Butler, Judith. *Precarious Life: The Power of Mourning and Violence*. New York: Verso, 2004.

Byg, Barton. "Is There Still an East German Cinema?" In *Cinemas in Transition in Central Eastern Europe after 1989*, edited by Catherine Portuges and Peter Hames, 75–103. Philadelphia: Temple University Press, 2013.

Byrd, Jodi A., Alyosha Goldstein, Jodi Melamed and Chandan Reddy. "Predatory Value: Economies of Dispossession and Disturbed Relationalities." *Social Text* 36, no. 2 (2018): 1–18.

Cabanas, Kaira Marie. "What the Map Cuts Up, the Story Cuts across: Chantal Akerman's De L'Autre Côté." *Parachute* (October 1, 2005): 12–27.

Carnevale, Fulvia and John Kelsey. "Art of the Possible: An Interview with Jacques Rancière." *Art Forum* (March 2007): 256–69.

Caruth, Cathy. Introduction to *Trauma: Explorations in Memory*, edited by Cathy Caruth. Baltimore: Johns Hopkins University Press, 1995.

Casey, Edward and Mary Watkins. *Up against the Wall: Re-imagining the U.S.-Mexican Border*. Houston: University of Texas Press, 2014.

Césaire, Aimé. *Discourse on Colonialism*. New York: NYU, Monthly Review Press, 2000.

Chaichian, Mohammed. *Empires and Walls: Globalization, Migration and Colonial Domination*. Leiden: Brill, 2014.

Chronicle of a Disappearance. Directed by Elia Suleiman. 1996. Jerusalem, Israel: Kino International 2005. DVD.

CNN. "Mexico's President: We Will Not Pay for the Wall." *CNN*, January 26, 2017. https://edition.cnn.com/videos/world/2017/01/26/mexico-president-will-not-pay-for-wall-santiago-ctn.cnn.

Cohen, Yinon and Neve Gordon, "Israel's Biospatial Politics: Territory, Demography and Effective Control." *Public Culture* 30, no. 2 (2018): 199–220.

Conolly, Kate. "New Berlin Wall Built for U2 Gig to Mark Fall of Old One." *The Guardian*, November 5, 2009. http://www.theguardian.com/world/2009/nov/05/new-berlin-wall-u2-gig.

Cooke, Paul. *Representing East Germany since Unification: From Colonization to Nostalgia*. New York: Berg, 2005.

Cover, Robert. *Narrative Violence and the Law*. Ann Arbor: University of Michigan Press, 1993.
Craw, Penelope J. et al. "The Mural of Graffiti Deterrence." *Environment and Behaviour* 38, no. 3 (May 2006): 422–34.
Cycling the Frame. Directed by Cynthia Beatts. Berlin, Germany, 1988. Brooklyn, NY: Icarus Film, 2009. DVD.
Dabashi, Hamid. "In Praise of Frivolity: On the Cinema of Elia Suleiman." In *Dreams of a Nation: On Palestinian Cinema*, edited by Hamid Dabashi, 131–62. London: Verso, 2006.
Dabashi, Hamid. Introduction to *Dreams of a Nation: On Palestinian Cinema*, edited by Hamid Dabashi. London: Verso, 2006.
DeBonis, Mike. "It's like a Manhood Thing for Him: Pelosi's Power Play with Trump Serves as Message for Opponents." *The Washington Post*, December 11, 2018. https://www.washingtonpost.com/powerpost/pelosi-questions-trumps-manhood-after-confrontational-white-house-meeting/2018/12/11/2b2111be-fd79-11e8-862a-b6a6f3ce8199_story.html?noredirect=on
Debord, Guy. *The Society of the Spectacle*. New York: Zone Books, 1994.
Del Pilar Blanco, Maria. *Ghost-Watching American Modernity*. New York: Fordham University Press, 2012.
Deutsche Presse Agentur. "Tausende demonstrieren gegen Teilabriss der East Side Gallery." *Zeit Online*, March 4, 2013. http://www.zeit.de/gesellschaft/zeitgeschehen/2013-03/demo-east-side-gallery.
Deutsches Rundfunkarchiv. "Mauermalerei und Mauerspechte." *DRA*. http://1989.dra.de/themendossiers/politik/mauer/mauermalerei-und-mauerspechte.html.
Divine Intervention: A Chronicle of Love and Pain. Directed by Elia Suleiman. Palestine/ Israel, 2002. New York: Artificial Eye, 2003. DVD.
"Do Not Refreeze." *Cornerhouse*. http://www.cornerhouse.org/art/art-exhibitions/do-not-refreeze.
Dueck, Cheryl. "The Humanization of the Stasi in 'Das Leben der Anderen'." *German Studies Review* 31, no. 3 (October 2008): 599–609.
Duelke, Britta. "Quoting from the Past or Dealing with Temporality." In *Given World and Time: Temporalities in Context*, edited by Tyrus Miller, 105–29. Budapest: Central European University Press, 2008.
ECB. "Dominoes for Peace: Mandela Family to Participate in Symbolic Toppling of the Wall." *Spiegel Online International*, August 26, 2009. http://www.spiegel.de/international/germany/dominoes-for-peace-mandela-family-to-participate-in-symbolic-toppling-of-berlin-wall-a-645012.html.
Eidelmann, Ronen. "The Separation Wall in Palestine: Artists Love to Hate It." In *Cultural Activism: Practices Dilemmas and Possibilities*, edited by Begüm Özden Firat and Aylin Kuryel, 95–113. New York: Rodopi, 2011.
Erekat, Saeb. "Response to Jason Greenblatt/ The Trump Administration, Peddling Israeli Extremism, Is Killing the Peace Process, Not Me." *Haaretz*, June 10, 2018. https://www.haaretz.com/middle-east-news/.premium-trump-envoys-peddling-israeli-extremism-are-killing-peace-not-me-1.6159732.
"Estracto: Guillermo Gomez—Peña/Museo de Arte Moderno 2011." *Vimeo*. http://www.frequency.com/video/border-brujo-19/34601261.

Finnegan, Michael. "It's Going to Be a Big Fat Beautiful Wall: Trump's Words Make His California Climb an Even Steeper Trek." *LA Times*, June 3, 2016. http://www.latimes.com/politics/la-na-pol-trump-california-campaign-20160602-snap-story.html.

Fischer, Ian. "Banksy Hotel in the West Bank: Small but Plenty of Wall Space." *New York Times*, April 16, 2017. https://www.nytimes.com/2017/04/16/world/middleeast/banksy-hotel-bethlehem-west-bank-wall.html.

Flemming, Richard. "Paint Your Troubles Away." *Cabinet Magazine* no. 9 (Winter 2002/2003). http://cabinetmagazine.org/issues/9/fleming.php.

Flisfeder, Matthew. "'Trump'—What Does the Name Signify? Or, Protofascism and the Alt Right." *Cultural Politics* 14, no. 2 (2018): 1–19.

Foucault, Michel. *Discipline and Punish: The Birth of the Prison*. New York: Vintage Books, 1979.

Foucault, Michel. "Governmentality." In *The Foucault Effect: Studies in Governmentality*, edited by Graham Burchell, Colin Gordon and Peter Miller, 87–104. London: Harvester Wheatsheaf, 1991.

Fox, Claire F. "The Portable Border: Site Specificity, Art and the U.S.-Mexico Frontier." *Social Text*, no. 41 (Winter 1994): 61–82.

Freud, Sigmund. "A Note upon the Mystic Writing Pad." In *Collected Papers Volume V*, edited by James Strachey, 227–32. London: Hogarth Press, 1950.

Freud, Sigmund. "Creative Writers and Day-Dreaming." In *The Freud Reader*, edited by Peter Gay, 436–42. London: Vintage, 1995.

Freud, Sigmund. *The Interpretation of Dreams*. Harmondsworth: Penguin Books, 1986.

Freud, Sigmund. "Project for a Scientific Psychology." In *The Standard Edition of the Complete Psychological Works of Sigmund Freud*, edited by James Strachey, 283–398. London: Hogarth Press, 1974.

Freud, Sigmund. "Remembering, Repeating and Working Through." In *The Standard Edition of the Complete Psychological Works of Sigmund Freud Volume XII*, edited by James Strachey, 145–56. London: Hogarth Press, 1958.

Freud, Sigmund. "Screen Memory (1899)." In *The Freud Reader*, edited by Peter Gay, 117–226. London: Vintage, 1995.

Freud, Sigmund and Joseph Breuer. *Studies on Hysteria*. New York: Basic Books, 2000.

From the Other Side. Directed by Chantal Akerman. USA/Mexico, 2002. Brooklyn, NY: Icarus Films, 2012. DVD.

Frowein, Jochen. "Legal Problems of the German Ostpolitik." *International and Comparative Law Quarterly* 23, no.1 (January 1974): 105–26.

Funder, Anna. "Tyranny of Terror." *The Guardian*, May 5, 2007. http://www.theguardian.com/books/2007/may/05/featuresreviews.guardianreview12.

Funke, Bettina. "Displaced Struggles: On Rancière and the Art World." *Artforum* (March 2007): 282–5.

Fusco, Coco. "The Border Art Workshop/ Taller de Arte Fronterizo: Interview with Guillermo Gómez-Peña and Emily Hicks." *Third Text* 3, no. 7 (1989): 53–76.

Gambino, Lauren. "Truly the Year of the Woman: Female Candidates Win in Record Numbers." *The Guardian*, November 7, 2018. https://www.theguardian.com/us-news/2018/nov/07/women-candidates-midterms-wins.

Ganeva, Mila. "No Histories just Stories: Revisiting Traditions in Berlin Films of the 1990s." In *Berlin: The Symphony Continues: Orchestrating Architectural, Social and Artistic Change in Germany's New Capital*, edited by C. A. Costabile-Heming and R. J. Halverson, 261–78. New York: Walter de Gruyter, 2004.

Garton Ash, Timothy. "The Stasi in Our Minds." *The New York Review of Books*, May 31, 2007. http://www.nybooks.com/articles/archives/2007/may/31/the-stasi-on-our-minds/.

Gay, Roxane. "Feminist Author Roxane Gay Says Racism Got Trump Elected," *CBC Radio*, November 11, 2016. https://www.cbc.ca/radio/asithappens/as-it-happens-friday-edition-1.3847360/feminist-author-roxane-gay-says-racism-got-trump-elected-1.3847797.

Gerstenberger, Katharina and Jana Evans Braziel. "After the Berlin Wall: Realigned Worlds, Invisible Lines, and Incalculable Remnants." In *After the Berlin Wall: Germany and beyond*, edited by Katharina Gerstenberger and Jana Evans Braziel, 1–18. New York: Palgrave Macmillan, 2011.

Gertz, Nurith and George Khleifi. *Palestinian Cinema: Landscape, Memory and Trauma*. Bloomington: Indiana University Press, 2008.

Gillen, Eckhart, Annette Tietz, and Paula Böttcher. "Blick Zurück Nach Vorne." *Galerie Pankow*. 2009.

Ginsberg, Terri. "Bordering on Disaster—Toward an Epistemology of Divided Cinematic Space." *Spectator* 29, no. 1 (Spring 2009): 30–6.

Goldberg, David Theo. *The Threat of Race: Reflections on Racial Neoliberalism*. Malden MA: Wiley-Blackwell, 2009.

Gomez, Adam. "Deus Vult: John L. O' Sullivan, Manifest Destiny and American Democratic Messianism." *American Political Thought* 1, no. 2 (2012): 236–62.

Gómez-Peña, Guillermo. *Conversations across the Border: A Performance Artist Converses with Theorists, Curators, Activists and Fellow Artists*, edited by Laura Levin. London: Seagull Books, 2011.

Gómez-Peña, Guillermo. "Philosophical Tantrum." *Youtube*. http://www.youtube.com/watch?v=74ajLA7MFDw.

Gómez-Peña, Guillermo *Warrior for Gringostroika*. St Paul Minnesota: Graywolf Press, 1993.

Gook, Ben. "Being There Is Everything." *Memory Studies* 4, no. 13 (2011): 13–22.

Gook, Ben. *Divided Subjects, Invisible Borders*. London: Rowman & Littlefield, 2015.

Gordon, Avery. *Ghostly Matters: Haunting and the Sociological Imagination*. Minneapolis: Minnesota University Press, 1997.

Gore, Illma. "If Anyone Is Going to Be Threatened by a Small Penis, It's Going to Be Trump." *The Guardian*, May 7, 2016. https://www.theguardian.com/us-news/2016/may/07/donald-trump-penis-painting-ilma-gore.

Graham-Harrison, Emma. "'Worst View in the World': Banksy Opens Hotel Overlooking Bethlehem Wall." *The Guardian*, March 3, 2017. https://www.theguardian.com/world/2017/mar/03/banksy-opens-bethlehem-barrier-wall-hotel.

Green, Erica L., Katie Benner and Robert Pear. "'Transgender' Could Be Defined Out of Existence under Trump Administration." *The New York Times*, October

21, 2018. https://www.nytimes.com/2018/10/21/us/politics/transgender-trump-administration-sex-definition.html.

Gregory, Derek. *The Colonial Present: Afghanistan, Palestine, Iraq*. Malden, MA: Blackwell, 2004.

Groys, Boris. "Back from the Future." *Third Text* 17, no. 4 (2003): 323–31.

Gründer, Ralf. "Das Wundpflaster: Interview mit Peter Unsicker 2009." *Youtube*. http://www.youtube.com/watch?v=wBGjNoVfN5o.

Hage, Ghassan. *Against Paranoid Nationalism: Searching for Hope in a Shrinking Society*. London: Merlin, 2003.

Hage, Ghassan. "État de Siège: A Dying Domesticating Colonialism?" *American Ethnologist* 43, no. 1 (2016): 38–49.

Haider, Sabah. "A Different Kind of Occupation: An Interview with Elia Suleiman." *Electronic Intifada*, February 1, 2010. http://electronicintifada.net/content/different-kind-occupation-interview-elia-suleiman/8654.

Haider, Sabah. "Palestine Already Exists on Film." *Le Monde Diplomatique*, March 2010. http://mondediplo.com/2010/03/16palestinecinema.

Hanssen Arent, Emily. "Searching for Banksy on the West Bank Wall." *Matador Network*, May 14, 2012. http://matadornetwork.com/abroad/searching-for-banksy-on-the-west-bank-wall/.

Hass, Amira. "You Can Drive along and Never See an Arab." *Ha'aretz*, January 22, 2003. http://www.haaretz.com/print-edition/opinion/you-can-drive-along-and-never-see-an-arab-1.21522.

Hasson, Nir. "IDF Engineers Begin Removal of Gilo Barrier Built during Second Intifada." *Ha'aretz*, August 16, 2010. http://www.haaretz.com/print-edition/news/idf-engineers-begin-removal-of-gilo-barrier-built-during-second-intifada-1.308237.

Hawley, Charles. "Interview with Lech Walesa." *Spiegel Online International*, November 6, 2009. http://www.spiegel.de/international/europe/spiegel-online-interview-with-lech-walesa-it-s-good-that-gorbachev-was-a-weak-politician-a-659752.html.

Heiser, Sebastian. "Mauer in Geiselhaft." *TAZ*, March 3, 2013. http://www.taz.de/!112114/.

Hendrichs, Martin. "Retten Eastside Gallery." *Youtube* https://www.youtube.com/watch?v=clyN6p3HRBo&NR=1&feature=endscreen.

Hipsman, Fay and Doris Meissner. "Trump Executive Order and His DHS Implementation Memo on Border Enforcement: A Brief Review." *Migration Policy Institute*, April 2017. https://www.migrationpolicy.org/research/trump-executive-order-and-dhs-implementation-memo-border-enforcement-brief-review.

Hirsch, Marianne. *Family Frames: Photography, Narrative and Postmemory*. Cambridge, MA: Harvard University Press, 1997.

"History of the Eastside Gallery." *Eastside Gallery*. http://www.eastsidegallery.com/historyesg.htm.

Hodgin, Nick. *Screening the East: Heimat, Memory and Nostalgia in German Film since 1989*. New York: Berghahn Books, 2011.

Holland, Steve and Ginger Gibson, "After Florida Shooting Trump Hardens Stance on Muslims." *Reuters*, June 14, 2016. https://www.reuters.com/article/us-usa-election-clinton-idUSKCN0YZ1GE.

Horeld, Markus and Juliane Leopold. "Berlins legitimer Mauer-Protest oder Scheinheiligkeit?" *Zeit Online*, March 4, 2013. http://www.zeit.de/gesellschaft/zeitgeschehen/2013-03/east-side-gallery-protest/komplettansicht.

Humanistischer Pressedienst. "Interview mit Gundula Schulze Eldowy, Teil 1." *YouTube*. http://www.youtube.com/watch?v=YqYDoQEjI8A.

Humanistischer Pressedienst. "Interview mit Gundula Schulze Eldowy, Teil 3." *YouTube*. http://www.youtube.com/watch?v=YqYDoQEjI8A.

Huyssen, Andreas. "The Voids of Berlin." *Critical Inquiry* 24, no. 1 (Autumn 1997): 57–81.

Huyssen, Andreas. "Trauma and Memory: A New Imaginary of Temporality." In *World Memory: Personal Trajectories in Global Time*, edited by Jill Bennett and Rosanne Kennedy, 16–29. New York: Palgrave Macmillan, 2002.

The Invisible Frame. Directed by Cynthia Beatts. Berlin, Germany, 2009. Brooklyn, NY: Icarus Film, 2009. DVD.

Israel Ministry of Defense. "Operational Concept." *Israel's Security Fence*, January 31, 2007. http://www.securityfence.mod.gov.il/Pages/ENG/operational.htm.

Israel Ministry of Foreign Affairs. "Suicide and Other Bombing Attacks on Israel since the Declaration of Principles (Sept 1993)." *Terrorism*, September 1993. https://mfa.gov.il/MFA/ForeignPolicy/Terrorism/Palestinian/Pages/Suicide%20and%20Other%20Bombing%20Attacks%20in%20Israel%20Since.aspx.

Jones, Reece. *Border Walls Security and the War on Terror in the United States, Israel and India*. London: ZedBooks, 2012.

Jones, Reece. *Violent Border: Refugees and the Right to Move*. New York: Verso, 2016.

JR and Marco. *Face2Face*. Paris: Édition Alternative, 2007.

JR. "My Wish: Use Art to Turn the world Inside Out." *TED*, March 2011. https://www.ted.com/talks/jr_s_ted_prize_wish_use_art_to_turn_the_world_inside_out.

Junn, Jane. "The Trump Majority: White Womanhood and the Making of Female Voters in the U.S." *Politics, Groups and Identities* 5, no. 2 (2017): 343–52.

Jurgens, Jeffrey. "Invisible Migrants: Memory and Nationhood in the Shadow of the Berlin Wall." In *Walls, Borders, Boundaries: Spatial and Cultural Practices in Europe*, edited by Janet Ward, Marc Silberman and Karen E. Till, 191–210. New York: Berghahn Books, 2012.

Kaplan, Amy. "Manifest Domesticity," *American Literature* 70, no. 3 (1998): 581–606

Kavka, Misha. "Trump, Fernsehen und Das Neue Camp." *Zeitschrift für Medienwissenschaften* 10, no. 1 (2018): 149–68.

Kawasaki's Rose. Film Festival Screener. Directed by Jan Hřebejk. Prague, Czech Republic: Madman, 2009. DVD.

Kennedy, Roger. "Memory and the Unconscious." In *Memory: History, Theories, Debates*, edited by Susannah Radstone and Bill Schwarz, 179–97. New York: Fordham University Press, 2010.

Khatib, Lina. *Filming the Modern Middle East*. New York: Palgrave MacMillan, 2006.

Kim, Jodi. "Settler Modernity, Debt Imperialism, and the Necropolitics of the Promise." *Social Text* 36, no.2 (2018): 41–61.

Kramer, Maddy. "The Most Beautiful Wall." http://themostbeautifulwall.com/.

Kraniauska, John. "Border Dialogue: Talking to Guillermo Gómez-Peña." *Traversia* 3, no. 1 (2009): 152–78.
Kristensen, Lars. Introduction to *Post-Communist Film: Russia, Eastern Europe and World Culture: Moving Images of Postcommunism*, edited by Lars Kristensen, 1–10. New York: Routledge, 2012.
Kristeva, Julia. *Powers of Horror: An Essay on Abjection*. New York: Columbia University Press, 1982.
Kulish, Nikolas and Judy Dempsey. "Leaders in Berlin Retrace the Walk West." *New York Times*, November 9, 2009. http://www.nytimes.com/2009/11/10/world/europe/10germany.html?_r=0 (accessed: February 2, 2013).
Kundera, Milan. *The Book of Laughter and Forgetting*. London: Penguin Books, 1983.
Laplanche, Jean and J. B. Pontalis. "Fantasy and the Origins of Sexuality." In *Formations of Fantasy*, edited by Victor Burgin, James Donald and Cora Kaplan, 5–34. New York: Methuen, 1986.
Laplanche, Jean and Jean-Bertrand Pontalis. *The Language of Psychoanalysis*. London: Karnac Books, 1988.
Leitner, Olaf. "Rock Music in the GDR. An Epitaph." In *Rocking the State: Rock Music and Politics in Eastern Europe and Russia*, edited by Sabrina Petra Ramet, 17–40. Oxford: Westview Press, 1994.
Lemon Tree. Directed by Eran Riklis. Palestine/ Israel, 2008. Collingwood: Madman, 2009. DVD.
Lévinas, Emmanuel. "Reality and Its Shadows." In *Collected Papers*, translated by Alphonso Lingis, 1–14. Pittsburgh: Duquesne University Press, 1998.
Lévinas, Emmanuel. *Totality and Infinity: An Essay on Exteriority*. Pittsburgh: Duquesne University Press, 2000.
Levin, Sam. "'Over My Dead Body': Tribe Aims to Block Trump's Border Wall on Arizona Lands." *The Guardian*, January 26, 2017. https://www.theguardian.com/us-news/2017/jan/26/donald-trump-border-wall-tohono-oodham-arizona-tribe.
Lindy, Jacob D. "Legacy of Trauma and Loss." In *Beyond Invisible Walls, the Psychological Legacy of Soviet Trauma*, edited by Jacob D. Lindy and Robert Jay Lifton, 13–32. New York: Routledge, 2001.
The Lives of Others. Directed by Florian Henckel von Donnersmarck. Germany: Sony Pictures Home Entertainment, 2006. DVD.
Lloyd, David and Laura Pulipo. "In the Long Shadow of the Settler: On Israeli and U.S. Colonialism." *American Quarterly* 62, no. 4 (2010): 795–809.
Locke, Stefan. "Mauerfotos: Interview mit Detlev Matthes." *Frankfurter Allgemeine Zeitung*, May 3, 2011. http://www.faz.net/aktuell/gesellschaft/mauerfotos-das-musste-immer-ganz-schnell-gehen-1624904.html.
Lumière, Auguste and Louis. "Palestine 1896." *YouTube*. http://www.youtube.com/watch?v=1valK8wlAl0.
Lumière, Louis. "Leaving Jerusalem by Railway 1897." *YouTube*. http://www.youtube.com/watch?v=Ctp1IVef9Yo.
Macdonald, Scott. "Chantal Akerman." In *A Critical Cinema 4: Interviews with Independent Filmmakers*, 258–73. Berkeley: University of California Press, 2005.
Makovsky, David. "How to Build a Fence." *Foreign Affairs* 83, no.2 (2004): 50–64.
Marez, Curtis. "Of Walls and Robots: The Future of Immigration." *University of Minnesota Pressblog*. http://www.uminnpressblog.com/2016/06/of-walls-and-robots-future-of.html.

Massad, Joseph A. *The Persistence of the Question of Palestine: Essays on Zionism and the Palestinians*. New York: Routledge, 2006.
Massenet, Patrice. "Homo Ludens: Der Mensch lernt durch Spiel—Interview mit Peter Unsicker 1987." *YouTube*. http://www.youtube.com/watch?v=jMVfcOG6ZU.
Mazierska, Ewa. *European Cinema and Intertextuality: History, Memory and Politics*. New York: Palgrave Macmillan, 2011.
Mbembe, Achille. *Critique of Black Reason*. Durham: Duke University Press, 2017.
Mbembe, Achille. "Necropolitics." *Public Culture* 15, no. 1 (2003): 11–40.
Mbembe, Achille. "Society of Enmity." *Radical Philosophy* 200 (2016): 23–35.
Mbembe, Achille. "The Idea of a Borderless World." *Africa Is a Country*, https://africasacountry.com/2018/11/the-idea-of-a-borderless-world.
McCabe, Earl. "Depressive Realism: An Interview with Lauren Berlant." *Hypocrite Reader* no. 4, June 2011. hypocritereader.com/5/depressive-realism.
McCarthy, Tom. "Trump Tweets Misleading Photos Suggesting Border Wall under Way." *The Guardian*, March 29, 2018. https://www.theguardian.com/us-news/2018/mar/28/trump-border-wall-construction-photo-tweet.
McClintock, Anne. "Imperial Ghosting and National Tragedy: Revenants from Hiroshima and Indian Country in the War on Terror." *PMLA Publications of the Modern Language Associations of America* 129, no. 4 (2014): 819–29.
McClintock, Anne. *Imperial Leather: Race, Gender and Sexuality in the Colonial Contest*. New York: Routledge, 1995.
McCormack, Derek P. *Atmospheric Things: On the Allure of Elemental Envelopment*. Durham: Duke University Press, 2018.
Mesch, Claudia. *Modern Art at the Berlin Wall: Demarcating Culture in the Cold War Germanys*. London: Tauris Academic Studies, 2008.
Miller, Jacques-Alain. "Extimate." In *Lacanian Theory and Discourse: Subject, Structure and Society*, edited by Mark Bracher et al., 74–87. New York: New York University Press, 1994.
Miller, Todd. "Beyond Trump's Big Beautiful Wall." *NCLA Report On the Americas* 49, no. 2 (2017): 145–51.
Miller, Todd. "Creating a Military Industrial Immigration Complex." *Aljazeera*, August 3, 2013. http://www.aljazeera.com/indepth/opinion/2013/07/2013714154732351793.html.
Miller, Tyrus. Introduction to *Given World and Time: Temporalities in Context*, edited by Tyrus Miller. Budapest: Central European University Press, 2008.
Mitchell, W. J. T. "Imperial Landscapes." In *Landscape and Power*, edited by W. J. T. Mitchell, 5–34. Chicago: University of Chicago Press, 1994.
Mokdad, Linda. "The Reluctance to Narrate: Elia Suleiman's Chronicle of a Disappearance and Divine Intervention." In *Storytelling in World Cinema Volume One: Forms*, edited by Lina Khatib, 192–204. London: Wallflower Press, 2012.
Morrissey, Kate. "Border Wall Prototypes Become Canvas for Light Graffitti." *The San Diego Union Tribune*, November 22, 2017. http://www.sandiegouniontribune.com/news/california/la-me-border-wall-project-20171122-story.html.

Najafi, Sina, David Serlin and Lauren Berlant. "The Broken Circuit: An Interview with Lauren Berlant." *Cabinet* no. 31 (Fall 2008). http://www.cabinetmagazine.org/issues/31/najafi_serlin.php.

Nakano Glenn, Evelyn. "Settler Colonialism as Structure: A Framework for Comparative Studies of U.S. Race and Gender Formation." *Sociology of Race and Ethnicity* 1, no. 1 (2015): 52–72.

The New York Times. "Full Transcripts: Trump's Speech on Immigration and the Democratic Response." *The New York Times*, January 8, 2019. https://www.nytimes.com/2019/01/08/us/politics/trump-speech-transcript.html.

News, "New York's Knockdown Center Raises More than $50,000 for Community Health and Reproductive Justice Organizations." *Artforum*, January 17, 2017. https://www.artforum.com/news/new-york-s-knockdown-center-raises-more-than-50-000-for-community-health-and-reproductive-justice-organizations-65923.

"Niemand hat die Absicht eine Mauer Abzureißen: Eastside Gallery wird weiter demoliert." *Soldiner Kiez Kurier*. http://soldinerkiezkurier.wordpress.com/10376-2/.

Niven, Bill. *Germans as Victims: Remembering the Past in Contemporary Germany*. New York: Palgrave Macmillan, 2006.

Nixon, Rob. *Slow Violence and the Environmentalism of the Poor*. Cambridge, MA: Harvard University Press, 2011.

Nixon, Ron. "Trump Seeks Proposal for 'Physically Imposing' Wall with Mexico." *The New York Times*, March 18, 2017. https://www.nytimes.com/2017/03/18/us/politics/trump-seeks-proposals-for-physically-imposing-wall-with-mexico.html.

Noble, Andrea. *Mexican National Cinema*. New York: Routledge, 2005.

Nungesser, Michael. "Im Schatten des Monstrums." *Berliner Zeitung*, August 9, 2001.

Nussbaum, Emily. "The TV That Created Donald Trump." *The New Yorker*, July 31, 2017. https://www.newyorker.com/magazine/2017/07/31/the-tv-that-created-donald-trump.

O'Brien, Mary. *Post-wall German Cinema and National History: Utopianism and Dissent*. Rochester, NY: Camden House, 2012.

Ottman, Klaus. "From the Other Side (De l'Autre Côté)." In *Chantal Akerman: Moving through Time and Space*, edited by Terrie Sultan, 28–39. Houston: Blaffer Gallery, the Art Museum of the University of Houston, 2008.

Paradise Now. Directed by Hany Abu-Assad. Palestine, 2005. United States: Augustus Film, 2008. DVD.

Parquette, Danielle. "Trump's Travel Ban on 'Bad Dudes' Actually Keeps out Women and Children." *The Washington Post*, January 30, 2017. https://www.washingtonpost.com/news/wonk/wp/2017/01/30/president-trump-wanted-to-ban-bad-dudes-he-could-block-more-women-and-children/?noredirect=on&utm_term=.5f28680eafc5.

Parry, Nigel. "Well-known UK Graffiti Artist Banksy Hacks the Wall." *Electronic Intifada*, September 2, 2012. http://electronicintifada.net/content/well-known-uk-graffiti-artist-banksy-hacks-wall/5733.

Parry, William. "Donald Trump Is Wrong about Israel's Security Wall." *Aljazeera*, January 31, 2017. https://www.aljazeera.com/indepth/opinion/2017/01/donald-trump-wrong-israel-security-wall-170129075510513.html.

Pastor, Camilla. "President Trump's Moving Targets: Walls, Expulsions and Prisoner States." *Journal of Middle East Women's Studies* 13, no. 3 (2017): 491–3.
Peteet, Julie. "The Writing on the Walls: The Graffiti of the Intifada." *Cultural Anthropology* 11, no. 2 (1996): 139–59.
Petrowskaja, Katja. "Interview with Cynthia Beatts." *Inivisible-frame*, 2009. http://www.invisible-frame.com/en/the-film/interview/.
Pfingst, Annie. "The Presence of Palestinian Absence in Narrating the Zionist Nation into Being." *Cultural Studies Review* 14, no. 1 (March 2008): 111–23.
Phippen, J. Westen. "Trump's Wall Goes Up (In Miniature)," *The Atlantic*, July 20, 2016. https://www.theatlantic.com/news/archive/2016/07/plastic-jesus-trump-wall/492179/.
Pihama, Leonie. "Colonisation and Systemic Violence in Aotearoa." Conference paper at *Space, Race, Bodies: Walls*, Otago University, Dunedin 2018.
Plastic Jesus, "Stop Making Stupid People Famous." http://www.plasticjesus.net/.
Preuss, Evelyn. "The Wall You Will Never Know." *Perspecta* 36 (2005): 19–31.
Rabbit à la Berlin. Directed by Bartozs Konopka. Germany, Poland: Deckert Distribution, 2009. DVD.
Radstone, Susannah. "Cinema and Memory." In *Memory: History, Theories, Debates*, edited by Susannah Radstone and Bill Schwarz, 325–42. New York: Fordham University Press, 2010.
Radstone, Susannah and Bill Schwarz. "Mapping Memory." In *Memory: Histories, Theories, Debates*, edited by Susannah Radstone and Bill Schwarz, 1–9. New York: Fordham University Press, 2010.
Rancière, Jacques. *Dissenting Words: Interviews with Jacques Rancière*. London: Bloomsbury, 2017.
Rancière, Jacques. *The Aesthetic Unconscious*. Cambridge; Malden, MA: Polity, 2009.
Rare Historical Photos. https://rarehistoricalphotos.com/conrad-schumann-defects-west-berlin-1961/.
RBB/Stilbruch. "Blickpunkt Ost: Detlev Matthes fotografiert die Mauer." *YouTube*. http://www.youtube.com/watch?v=L3pmNNySW-I.
Resendiz, Ramon, Rosalva Resendiz and Irene J. Klaver. "Colonialism and Imperialism: Indigenous Resistance on the US/Mexico Border." *Perspectives on Global Development and Technology*, no. 16 (2017): 15–33.
Rodriguez, Sabrina. "Trump's Partially Built 'Big Beautiful' Wall." *Politco*, January 12, 2021. https://www.politico.com/news/2021/01/12/trump-border-wall-partially-built-458255.
Rose, Jacqueline. *The Last Resistance*. New York: Verso, 2007.
Rose, Jacqueline. *Proust among the Nations: From Dreyfus to the Middle East*. Chicago: The University of Chicago Press, 2011.
Rose, Jacqueline. *The Question of Zion*. Princeton: Princeton University Press, 2005.
Rose, Jacqueline. "Who Do You Think You Are," *London Review of Books*, 38 no. 9 (May 5, 2016). https://www.lrb.co.uk/the-paper/v38/n09/jacqueline-rose/who-do-you-think-you-are.
Rosen, Philip. "Border Times and Geopolitical Frames: The Martin Walsh Memorial Lecture 2006." *Canadian Journal of Film Studies* (Fall 2006): 2–19.
Ross, Kristin. "Introduction on Jacques Rancière." *Art Forum* (March 2007): 254–5.

Rotbart, Sharon. "Wall and Tower (Homa Umigdal): The Mold of Israeli Architecture." In *A Civilian Occupation: The Politics of Israel's Architecture*, edited by Rafi Segal and Eyal Weizman, 39–58. New York: Verso, 2003.

Rouvillois, Frédéric. "Utopia and Totalitarianism." In *Utopia: The Search for the Ideal Society in the Western World*, edited by Roland Schaer et. al, 316–32. Oxford: Oxford University Press, 2000.

Ruthe, Ingeborg. "Der Hase bin Ich." *Berliner Zeitung*, January 21, 2006. http://www.berliner-zeitung.de/archiv/beuys-hat-begeistert-und-genervt--um-die-welt-zu-bessern--was-bleibt-20-jahre-nach-seinem-tod--der-hase-bin-ich,10810590,10355472.html.

Rutherford, Jonathan. "The Third Space: Interview with Homi Bhabha." In *Identity: Community, Culture, Difference*, edited by Jonathan Rutherford, 207–21. London: Lawrence and Wishart, 1990.

Sadiki, Said. *World of Walls*. Cambridge: Open Book Publisher, 2017.

Said, Edward. "Imaginative Geographies and Its Representation: Orientalizing the Orient." In *Orientalism*. London: Penguin, 2003.

Said, Edward. "Invention Memory and Place." In *Landscape and Power*, edited by W. J. T. Mitchell, 241–60. Chicago: University of Chicago Press, 2002.

Said, Edward. "Orientalism." *The Georgia Review* 31, no. 1 (Spring 1977): 162–206.

Said, Edward. "Permission to Narrate." *Journal of Palestine Studies* 13, no. 2 (Spring, 1984): 27–48.

Said, Edward. "Preface: Keynote Speech for the Dreams of a Nation." In *Dreams of a Nation: On Palestinian Cinema*, edited by Hamid Dabashi, 1–6. London: Verso, 2006.

Said, Edward. *The Question of Palestine*. London: Routledge, 1980.

Salecl, Renata. *The Spoils of Freedom*. New York: Routledge, 1994.

Sauders, Robert. "Whose Place Is This Anyway: The Israeli Separation Barrier, International Activists and Graffiti." *Anthropology News* (March 2011): 16.

Sayej, Nadja. "Should Donald Trump's Border Wall Prototypes Be Considered Art." *The Guardian*, January 12, 2018. https://www.theguardian.com/artanddesign/2018/jan/12/should-donald-trumps-border-wall-prototypes-be-considered-art.

Schloer, Joachim. "It Has to Go away, but at the Same Time It Has to Be Kept: The Berlin Wall and the Making of an Urban Icon." *Urban History* 33 (2006): 85–205.

Schmemann, Serge. "Berlin Journal: In Search of a Work of Art to Overcome the Wall." *New York Times*, November 13, 1987. http://www.nytimes.com/1987/11/13/world/berlin-journal-in-search-of-a-work-of-art-to-overcome-the-wall.html.

Schmemann, Serge. "Upheaval in the East: Berlin, Abject and Crumbling, Berlin Wall Surrenders." *New York Times*, January 28, 1990. http://www.nytimes.com/1990/01/28/world/upheaval-in-the-east-berlin-abject-and-crumbling-berlin-wall-surrenders.html.

Schmid, Marion. *Chantal Akerman*. Manchester: Manchester University Press, 2010.

Schmitt, Carl. *The Nomos of the Earth in the International Law of the Jus Publicum Europaeum*. New York: Telos Press, 2003.

Schulz, Bert. "Schluss mit dem Mauern: Kommentar zu Berlins Mauerfall-Feiern," *TAZ*, 8, November 2019.
Schulze Eldowy, Gundula. *Berlin in einer Hundenacht*. http://www.berlin-ineinerhundenacht.de/hundenacht.html.
Schulze Eldowy, Gundula. "Im Herbstlaub des Vergessens." *Berlin in einer Hundenacht*. http://www.berlin-ineinerhundenacht.de/hundenacht.html.
Schütz, Klaus. "Berlin in the Age of Détente." *The World Today* 31, no. 1 (January 1975): 29–35.
Schwab, Gabriele. *Haunting Legacies: Violent Histories and Transgenerational Trauma*. New York: Columbia University Press, 2010.
Seigworth, Gregory J. and Melissa Gregg (ed.). *The Affect Theory Reader*. Durham: Duke University Press, 2010.
"The Separation Barrier." *B'Tselem*. January 1, 2011. http://www.btselem.org/separation_barrier.
Shaul, Matthew and Nicola Freeman. *Do Not Refreeze: Photography behind the Berlin Wall*. Manchester: Cornerhouse Publications, 2007.
Shaw, Deborah. "'You Are Alright, But...': Individual and Collective Representations of Mexicans, Lations, Anglo-Amerians and Africans in Steen Soderbergh's Traffic." *Quarterly Review of Film and Video* 25, no. 3 (2005): 211–23.
Shohat, Ella. *Israeli Cinema: East/West and the Politics of Representation*. London: I. B. Tauris, 2010.
Silverman, Kaja. "Historical Trauma and Male Subjectivity." In *Cinema & Psychoanalysis*, edited by E. Ann Kaplan, 110–27. New York: Routlege, 1990.
Silverman, Kaja. *Male Subjectivity at the Margins*. New York: Routledge, 1992.
Silverman, Kaja. *World Spectators*. Stanford: Stanford University Press, 2000.
Sioh, Maureen. "The Wound of Whiteness: Conceptualizing Economic Convergence as Trauma in the 2016 United States Presidential Election." *Geoforum* 95 (July 2018): 112–21.
Smith, Anthony. "Images of the Nation: Cinema, Art and National Identity." In *Cinema and Nation*, edited by Mette Hjort and Scott Mackenzie, 45–59. London: Routledge, 2000.
Sontag, Susan. *On Photography*. New York: Farrar, Straus and Giroux, 1977.
Squire, Corinne, Amal Treacher and Susannah Radstone. *Public Emotions*. New York: Palgrave Macmillan, 2007.
Stenner, Paul. *Liminality and Experience: A Transdisciplinary Approach to the Psychosocial*. London: Palgrave MacMillan, 2017.
Stone, Susan. "DDR Living: Museum Offers 'Ostalgic' Look at East Germany." *Spiegel Online International*, July 20, 2006. http://www.spiegel.de/international/ddr-living-museum-offers-ostalgic-look-at-east-germany-a-427579.html.
Street, John. "What Is Donald Trump? Forms of 'Celebrity' in Celebrity Politics." *Political Studies Review* (2018): 1–11.
Strum, Becky and Danika Fears. "Trump: Megyn Kelly Had 'Blood Coming out of Her Wherever'." *The New York Post*, August 8, 2015. https://nypost.com/2015/08/08/trump-megyn-kelly-had-blood-coming-out-of-her-wherever/.
Stümer, Jenny. "The Berlin Wall Revisited: Reframing Historical Space between East and West in Cynthia Beatts's Cycling the Frame (2009) and Bartosz

Konopka's Rabbit à la Berlin (2009)." In *East West and The Center: Reframing Post-1989 European Cinema*, edited by Michael Gott and Todd Herzog, 23–36. Edinburgh: Edinburgh University Press, 2015.

Stümer, Jenny. "Imperial Whiteness: Fantasy, Colonialism and New Walls." *New Global Studies* 13, no. 3 (2019): 301–20.

Suleiman, Elia. "A Cinema of Nowhere." *Journal of Palestine Studies* 29, no. 2 (Winter 2000): 95–101.

Suleiman, Elia. "The Occupation (and Life) through an Absurdist Lens." *Journal of Palestine Studies* 32, no. 2 (Winter 2003): 63–73.

Sundberg, Juanita. "Delimiting Democracy: Witnessing along the US-Mexico Borderlands." *Political Geography* 33 (2013): 53–5.

Sundberg, Juanita. "The State of Exception and the Imperial Way of Life in the United States-Mexico Borderlands." *Environment and Planning D: Society and Space* 33 (2015): 209–28.

Talmon, Miri and Yaron Peleg. *Israeli Cinema: Identities in Motion*. Austin: University of Texas Press, 2011.

Terdiman, Richard. "Taking Time: Temporal Representations and Cultural Politics." In *Given World and Time: Temporalities in Context*, edited by Tyrus Miller, 131–44. Budapest: Central European University Press, 2008.

The Time That Remains: Chronicle of a Present Absentee. Directed by Elia Suleiman. Palestine/ Israel, 2009. United States: IFC Films, 2012. DVD.

Torrans, Thomas. *The Magic Curtain: The Mexican-American Border in Fiction, Film, and Song*. Fort Worth: Texas Christian University Press, 2002.

Trumpener, Katie. "La Guerre est fini: New Waves, Historical Contingency, and the GDR 'Rabbit Film'." In *The Power of Intellectuals in Contemporary Germany*, edited by M. Geyer, 113–37. Chicago: The University of Chicago Press, 2001.

Tuck, Eve and C. Ree. "A Glossary of Haunting." In *Handbook of Autoethnography*, edited by Stacey Holman Jones, Tony E. Adams and Carolyn Ellis, 639–58. Walnut Creek: Left Coast Press, 2013.

United Nations Human Rights Council. "Annual Report of the United Nations High Commissioner for Human Rights and Reports of the Office of the High Commissioner and the Secretary-General on the human rights situation in the Occupied Palestinian Territory, including East Jerusalem." *OHCHR*, January 20, 2016. http://www.ohchr.org/EN/HRBodies/HRC/RegularSessions/Session31/_layouts/15/WopiFrame.aspx?sourcedoc=/EN/HRBodies/HRC/RegularSessions/Session31/Documents/A_HRC_31_44_E.doc&action=default&DefaultItemOpen=1.

Unsicker, Peter. *Die Arbeit am Verdorbenen: Eine Dokumentation Angewandter Kunst*. Berlin: Luftfilterverlag, 2001.

Unsicker, Peter. "Privatkampf mit der DDR. " *Spiegel Online*, February 19, 2009. http://www.spiegel.de/einestages/mauerkunst-privatkampf-mit-der-ddr-a-949740.html.

Vallet, Élisabeth. "State of Borderwalls in a Globalized World." In *Borders and Borderwalls: In-Securities, Symbolism, Vulnerabilities*, edited by Élisabeth Vallet and Andréanne Bissonnette, 7–25. New York: Routlege, 2021.

Verhaeghe, Paul. "Trauma and Hysteria within Freud and Lacan." *The Letter: Lacanian Perspectives on Psychoanalysis*, no. 14 (Autumn 1998): 87–106.

Visions Du Reel. "Interview Bartek Konopka." *YouTube*. http://www.youtube.com/watch?v=IJA61bBRg1Q.
Waclawek, Anna. *Graffiti and Street Art*. New York: Thames & Hudson, 2011.
Warner Independent Pictures. "Q and A with Hany Abu-Assad." *Paradise Now Press Kit* (2005).
Washington Post. "Trump: Walls Work, Just Ask Israel." *Youtube*, May 18, 2017. https://www.youtube.com/watch?v=9PbtEAJ2d64.
Weheliye, Alexander. *Habeas Viscus: Racializing Assemblages, Biopolitics, and Black Feminist Theories of the Human*. Durham: Duke University Press, 2014.
Weigel, Sigrid. *Body and Image Space*. New York: Routledge, 1996.
Weizman, Eyal. *Hollow Land: Israel's Architecture of Occupation*. London: Verso, 2007.
West, Cornel. "The Trump Era: Hope in a Time of Escalating Despair." *Transition*, no. 122 (2017): 22–41.
Westerink, Herman. *A Dark Trace: Sigmund Freud on the Sense of Guilt*. Leuven: Leuven University Press, 2009.
Westphal, Anke. "An Approach to the Wall." *Berliner Zeitung*, November 7, 2009. http://www.invisible-frame.com/en/the-film/reviews/2009.
Wheeler, Mark. *Celebrity Politics*, Cambridge: Polity, 2013.
White, Thomas. "Meet the Filmmaker: Bartek Konopka—Rabbit à la Berlin." *International Documentary Association*, August 2009. http://www.documentary.org/content/meet-filmmakers-bartek-konopka-rabbit-a-la-berlin.
Widmer, Ted. "Draining the Swamp." *The New Yorker*, January 19, 2017. https://www.newyorker.com/news/news-desk/draining-the-swamp.
Winters, Jochen. "Der Ruf 'die Mauer muss weg' wird der SED noch lange in den Ohren klingen." *Frankfurter Allgemeine Zeitung*, June 10, 1987.
Wolfe, Patrick. "Settler Colonialism and the Elimination of the Native." *Journal of Genocide Research* 8, no. 4 (2006): 387–409.
Wong, Julia Carrie. "The Beauty Pageant to Build Trump's Border Wall Is Beginning." *The Guardian*, March 29, 2017. https://www.theguardian.com/us-news/2017/mar/29/trump-border-wall-mexico-construction-proposals.
Wrage, Henning. "Politics, Culture, and Media before and after the Berlin Wall." In *The German Wall: Fallout in Europe*, edited by Marc Silberman, 59–76. New York: Palgrave MacMillan, 2011.
WWS. Schallmauer. *Frankfurter Allgemeine Zeitung*, June 10, 1987.
Yuval-Davis, Nira. *Gender and Nation*. London: Sage, 1997.
Zanger, Anat Y. *Place, Memory and Myth in Contemporary Israeli Cinema*. Edgware: Vallentine Mitchell, 2012.
Zavala, Lauro. "Towards a Dialogical Theory of Cultural Liminality: Contemporary Writing and Cultural Identity in Mexico." *Arizona Journal of Hispanic Cultural Studies* 1 (1997): 9–22.
Zavella, Patricia. *I'm neither Here nor There: Mexican Quotidian Struggles with Migration and Poverty*. Durham: Duke University Press, 2011.
ZDF. "The Domino Fall of the Berlin Wall." *YouTube*. http://www.youtube.com/watch?v=HG97uKKdwyY.
Zinoviev, Alexander. *Homo Sovieticus*. New York: The Atlantic Monthly, 1985.

Index

abject 182–4
absence 12, 16–17, 21–9, 44–6, 58–60, 79, 83
   aesthetic of 23, 24, 25, 79
   of Palestine 99, 101–2, 121
   and presence 7, 34–6, 49, 188
   psychological 39, 42, 191
absurdity 16, 31–3, 56, 98–105, 149, 162, 167
aestheticization 16, 17, 63, 107–11, 120, 122, 165
affect of walling 165
affective fascism 164
Agamben, Giorgio
   bare life 88
   camp 9
   state of exception 8, 10, 141
Ahmed, Sara
   affective economy 4, 15, 162
   boundaries 189
   gendered nation 173
   skin 4–5, 13
   soft nation 178, 186
Akerman, Chantal 138, 150–8
alienation 43, 71
   affective 89
   cultural 5
   narrative of 121
   political 46, 57, 150, 178
   psychological 52, 145
Al-Nabka 85, 100
American empire 142, 162–4, 169, 170–3
American exceptionality 169–71
American greatness 18, 161–3, 169–73, 186
amnesia 59, 152
another scene 32, 47

anxiety 49, 157, 188
   creative 136, 138
   imperial 178–84
   xenophobic 153
Anzaldúa, Gloria 137, 148, 194
archive 44, 112–15
Arendt, Hannah
   banality of evil 64
   nomos 6–8, 54
Artists without Walls 125–7
atmosphere 1, 6, 13, 36, 80, 96, 119
   atmospheric poetics 43–6
   collective atmospheres 49

Badiou, Alain 3, 9
   the world's wall 2, 112
Balibar, Étienne 3, 9, 59
Banksy 117–20, 122
Barthes, Roland 25, 128–31
beautification 108, 118, 120–2, 165
Beit Jalla 121–2
Benjamin, Walter
   thought-image 34
   transmitting the past 29
   unconscious optics 50–1
Berlant, Lauren 4–5, 13, 24
   affective togetherness 65, 126–7
   affect worlds 4, 37, 127, 189
   cruel optimism 38
   fantasy 11, 63
   flat affect 99–103
   intimacy 130–1, 63
   intimate public 12, 125
   negative attachments 12
   sentimentality 37–8
   structure of un/feeling 80, 100, 113
Beuys, Joseph 16, 57, 167
biopolitics 88, 143

INDEX

biospatiality 171
Birth of A Nation 142
body 10–11, 64, 95, 103, 127–8
    nation as 142, 173–8, 186
Brecht, Bertolt 67–9, 76
Brown, Wendy 3, 10–11, 135, 141, 154, 165
Butler, Judith
    face 85, 93
    grief 4
    violence 80
    vulnerability 104, 128

caricature 129, 179
cartoons 176
castration 96–7, 181, 183, 186
catharsis 33, 46, 72, 98, 99, 101–2, 104–5, 115, 149, 187, 196
celebrity 43, 161, 166, 167, 184–5
Césaire, Aimé 141
Chronicle of a Disappearance 99, 101, 103–5
Clinton, Hillary 40, 172, 179, 182
commemoration 39–46, 70, 74
communal 100, 158
    affect 72, 74
    identity 193
    liberation 105
    memory 40
community 4, 7, 10, 27, 54, 109–11, 119, 149–50
    artistic 35, 125–7, 146
    imagined 10, 173, 175
    LGBTQ 177
    Mexican 154
    Palestinian 85, 98
    political 54
    transnational 3, 146
    unimagined 152–3
colonialism 4, 8, 18, 46, 87, 119–20, 133, 136–40, 144–6, 150, 169, 171–3, 185, 191
    colonial affect 96–8
    colonial boundary 45, 108, 139, 168
    colonial expansion 139, 175
    colonial fantasy 119–23, 163, 173, 193

colonial ghost 136, 141, 144, 159, 170
colonial histories 141, 170
colonial humiliation 96
colonial legacy 4, 108
colonial modernity 162
colonial narrative 133, 193
colonial present 133, 164, 168
colonial stereotypes 147
colonial structure 139–40, 155, 158, 169
colonial subjectivity 158
colonial violence 79, 120, 136–7, 145, 158
colonial walls 18, 115, 117, 153, 168
Conrad Schumann 187–8, 192, 195–7
Counter-narrative 53, 75, 95, 144, 146, 148–50
Cycling the Frame 57–8, 62

Das Kaninchen Bin Ich 57
death 55, 87, 95, 97, 136–8, 143, 154, 156, 190
    political death 97
    social death 91, 97
death strip 22–3, 52, 54–6
death-worlds 97
déjà vu 32, 170
displacement 44, 71–3, 93, 99, 111, 121, 137
dispossession 90, 99, 138–40
Divine Intervention: A Chronicle of Love and Pain 99, 102–5
Do Not Refreeze: Photography Behind the Iron Curtain 29
documentary 6, 52–62, 70, 76, 150–7
dominant fiction 12, 43, 142–3, 145–50, 158
doppelgänger 137
doubling 35, 129, 137–8
dream 60, 96, 105, 192, 196
    American Dream 157, 178–9, 186
    dreamwork 17, 51, 68–69, 79, 83, 104
    national dream 82–3, 84, 85, 121–4, 127, 176, 191

Eastside Gallery 23, 36–8, 45
effacement 3, 82–3, 85, 9, 105, 109, 121, 128
El Día De La Raza 148
encounter 6, 12, 13, 35, 58, 80–1, 86, 90, 108–9, 137, 140, 145–6, 189, 194
   affective 2, 44
   artistic 18, 25, 26, 34, 125–7, 127–32
   and emotion 3
   with the other 66, 150, 195
   with the past 37–8, 49, 168
   traumatic 33, 106, 124, 151, 158
executive order 165
extimacy 66

face 27–30, 31, 32, 37, 85, 92–6, 100, 105, 109, 127–32, 155
face-to-face 18, 91, 102, 127–32
Face2Face 127–32
faceless 26, 27, 64
family 27–8, 69–76, 90, 94–5, 99–103, 142, 152
fantasy 4, 6, 18, 62–3, 68, 74, 82–4, 97, 104–5, 132, 136, 148, 157, 181–3, 186
   landscape 121–4
   national fantasy 17, 51, 52–3, 105, 115, 142, 158, 162–7, 171–7, 183
   political fantasy 5, 11–12, 133, 162–7, 172
   and screen 13
   siege fantasy 153, 192–3
   structure 18, 162, 177–8, 181, 183, 185
fascism 162–64, 185
feminine monstrosity 182–3
femininity
   and the nation 173–7, 179
   transgressive 180–4
   white femininity 175–6
forgetting 25, 29, 40, 44, 50, 52–3, 59–60, 70, 73, 75, 113, 118, 152–3, 159, 164, 168–9, 191
fortress 46, 164–5, 174, 183, 191–4, 197
Foucault, Michel 64, 97, 171, 147

Freud, Sigmund 5, 6, 11, 42, 148, 153, 186
   affect 69, 106, 127, 162
   dream 17, 51, 68–69, 79, 83, 104
   foreign body 71, 73, 104
   joke 101–2
   mystic writing pad 113–4
   Nachträglichkeit 39, 70
   psychical screen 14, 50–1, 69
   Schauplatz 12, 123, 163
   screen memory 168–9, 194–5
   working through 31–4
From the Other Side 150–7
frontier 136, 162, 171–3, 175, 180, 186

Gast, John
   American Progress 175
Gay, Roxane 180
Gaza 3, 81, 116, 192
ghosts 59, 60, 100, 136, 137, 138, 140–3, 144, 145, 147, 150–7, 170, 197
   imperial ghosting 159, 164
Gilo 120–4
globalization 9, 178, 192
Gómez-Peña, Guillermo 138, 144–50, 157
   Border Art Workshop/Taller de Arte Fronterizo (BAW/TAW) 145–6, 148
   Border Brujo 145–6, 147–8, 149
Gore, Illma 180–2
   Make America Great Again
governmentality 64
government shut down 166
graffiti 2, 6, 35–7, 21–3, 56, 107, 109–13, 115–17, 117–20, 167–8, 187
Gregory, Derek 133, 164, 168, 190–1

Hage, Ghassan 6, 173
   paranoid nationalism 174–7
   state of siege 108, 193
   suicide bombing 96–7
haunting 2, 29, 50, 52, 61, 136–6, 138, 142, 146–7, 150–1, 155, 158–9, 170, 194
Hirsch, Marianne 72, 75
   "post-memory" 72, 151

INDEX

Holocaust 45, 79, 82, 90, 151, 156, 158, 194
homeland 52, 81–3, 85–6, 89–90, 100, 121–4, 162, 173–5, 186, 193
humor 16, 30, 73, 94, 98–102, 129, 148, 167, 180
hybridity 144–8

identification 37, 51, 63–4, 67, 68, 74, 85, 89–90, 99, 130–2, 162–3, 166, 171, 178
identity 52–5, 57–8, 65–6, 75, 93, 94, 111–12, 138, 183, 193
   border identity 140, 143–9
   national identity 6, 44, 46, 70, 74, 80–5, 121–5, 135, 154, 171
   rabbit-identity 54–5
   walled identity 5, 14, 52–3, 75, 191
imaginary 6, 35, 36, 95, 113, 116, 136, 163–4, 192, 194, 197
   collective 19, 22, 45, 85–7, 101
   gendered 173–7, 178–9, 181–3
   national 10, 40, 51, 79–80, 81–4, 121–4, 127, 140–3, 149–50, 153, 168, 171–2, 185
   political 4, 106, 157–9, 165–7
imaginative geographies 190–3
imperialism 136, 163–4, 168–73, 174–5, 177–9, 185–6
   imperial structure 18, 139–40, 172
   imperial violence 138–40, 159, 191
imprisonment 2, 6, 12, 22, 26, 50, 53, 62, 70, 71–4, 80, 83–4, 90, 96, 103, 108, 111, 118, 133, 136, 137, 155–6, 190, 192, 196–7
indigenous rights 3, 140–1, 166
Intifada 91, 112, 122
intimacy 14, 27–8, 51, 63–9, 73, 81, 86, 93, 102–4, 124, 127–32, 154–5, 177, 193
intimate public 12, 13, 24, 37, 125, 127, 174
Israel Defense Forces (IDF) 80, 91

Jerusalem 84, 116, 121–4
Jones, Reece 3–4, 139
JR and Marco 127–32

Kaplan, Amy 176
Kavka, Misha 164, 177
Kawasaki's Rose 52–3, 69–76
Kelly, Megyn 183
Kristeva, Julia 183–4
Kundera, Milan 75

Lacan, Jacques 15, 31, 34–5, 66, 111–12, 166, 174
   imaginary mapping 15, 31, 34
land 7–8, 82–4, 86–91, 111, 138, 139–41, 166, 168–75, 190–1
landscape 14, 38–9, 53–4, 58–62, 84–5, 110–11, 119, 121–4, 126, 143, 152, 172–3
   haunted 135–7, 157, 159
   political 5, 16–18, 80–91, 107, 130–3
Laplanche, Jean and Jean-Bertrand Pontalis 67–8
law 7, 10, 24, 54, 57, 68, 86–8, 135, 141, 172, 177
Leibing, Peter 187
Lemon Tree 86–91, 105
Lévinas, Emmanuel 128–9
Levy, Sarah 182–4
liminality 138, 144, 146, 150, 152, 158
Lumière brothers 84
Lushux 115–17

manifest destiny 169–73, 175, 178–9
manifest domesticity 176
masculinity 97–8, 102, 116, 162–3, 169, 173, 174, 176–7, 178–85
mask 31–2, 85, 129–30
Matthes, Detlef 25–6
Mazierska, Ewa 64–5, 75
Mbembe, Achille 1, 4, 8, 97, 139
McClintock, Anne 159, 164, 169–70, 173
McCormack, Derek P. 43–4
McNaughton, John 173
melancholy 27, 30, 36, 44, 60, 188
migrant 44, 46, 137, 139, 141, 149, 154–6, 161, 165, 169, 177, 182
Miller, Jacques-Alain 66
mirror 6, 17, 18, 34, 45, 59, 89–90, 94, 108, 109–12, 117, 123–4, 127–32, 142, 150, 152, 155, 166, 174, 195

mirror stage 15
Mitchell, W. J. T. 53
Muslim ban 165
myth 3, 31, 87, 95, 154, 162, 169–70
mythology 162, 164, 168–75, 181–2

Nakano Glenn, Evelyn 140, 162
Nasty Women 182
nationalism 18, 99, 102, 141, 153–4, 159, 162, 163, 185
  and gender 174–83
  nationalist fantasy 18, 153, 162, 175–8
  and paranoia 167, 174–8
necropolitics 4, 97
9/11 91, 93, 140
Nixon, Rob 152–3
Noir Thierry 30, 35, 36, 56
nomos 6, 7–9, 12, 54, 86–7, 177
nostalgia 43, 45, 57–59
Nussbaum, Emily 185

Obama, Barack 116, 141
occupation 7–8, 17, 19, 49, 80–4, 95–8, 99–105, 110–12, 120, 123, 127, 135
Ostalgie 63
Overpass Light Brigade San Diego 167

palimpsest 45, 112
Paradise Now 91–8, 105
Patriotic Europeans Against the Islamization of the Occident (PEGIDA) 45
Pelosi, Nancy 175
People over Profits San Diego 176
phallic woman 181–2
phallus 116, 161, 179, 181–2, 184
phantom 142, 155, 162
photography 25–30, 46, 72, 93–4, 127–32, 187–9, 190, 195–7
Plastic Jesus 184–5
post-colonial 6, 45, 140, 144–50, 152–3, 158, 163–4, 190, 194
post-communism 6, 39, 45, 55, 60, 163, 194
precarity 8, 79, 139, 188, 190, 191–3, 196

preservation 23, 36–7, 58, 69, 75
privilege 3, 8, 10, 18, 89, 98, 138, 142, 159, 170, 174, 177–80, 191–3, 196–7
projection 6, 9, 14–15, 17–18, 31, 35, 50, 59, 80, 108, 123–4, 125–7, 137, 140, 142, 157, 162, 167–8, 193, 194
prop 120, 162, 166, 174, 179, 181, 184–5
Proustian Madeleine 43

Rabbit à la Berlin 52–7
race 45, 79, 137–43, 145–50, 151, 153, 156, 158–9, 162–6, 168–71, 174–80, 186, 191–4, 196
Rancière, Jacques 33, 101, 108, 142
recognition 12, 18, 67, 87–91, 103, 107, 111, 116, 124, 125, 127–9, 150, 193
reconciliation 40, 53, 67–8, 74, 90, 125–7
redemption 44, 63, 67, 82–4, 87, 95, 98
re-enactment 5, 40, 42, 43, 46–7, 145–50
remediation 40, 46
repetition 39, 40, 42, 46, 50, 61–2, 98, 100, 103, 106, 117, 138, 140, 142, 151, 157, 159, 170, 194
repression 14, 31, 38, 42, 50–2, 71, 73, 82–5, 87, 103–6, 109, 122–4, 126–7, 130, 136–8, 149, 151–4, 156, 157–9, 170, 183, 189, 191, 193–4
  return of the repressed 71–3, 100, 151, 155–6, 157–8, 164, 168, 170, 193
responsibility 31, 74, 90, 131–2, 156, 197
Rose, Jacqueline 5, 6, 11, 69, 82–3, 104, 121–4, 127, 181, 194

Salecl, Renata 5, 6, 11, 42, 83–4, 123, 162–3, 169, 174–5
Said, Edward 82–3, 85, 87, 101, 102, 111, 120, 124, 191–3, 194
Schauplatz 12, 123, 163
Schmitt, Carl 6–8, 54, 86–7

INDEX

Schulze-Eldowy, Gundula 27–30
  Berlin in a Dog's Night
  Look back forward
  Nude
Schwab, Gabriele 50–1, 71–4, 194
screen 1, 2, 5–7, 13–15, 16, 19, 56, 59,
    85, 109, 110–13, 115–17, 131–3,
    141–2, 145, 151, 154, 164,
    174–6, 185, 191, 193–5
  affective 13, 18, 83, 106, 114, 125,
    132, 155, 178, 188
  cinema 17, 50–1, 76, 96, 153
  ideological 15, 30–1, 35, 41, 83,
    121, 142
  Lacanian 15, 31, 34, 174
  media 41, 104, 108, 156–7, 163
  national 76, 79, 84, 176
  projective 45, 56, 59, 79–80, 137,
    109, 120, 126, 137, 167, 171, 174,
    178, 186
  psychical 14, 50, 146, 168
screening through 33
Second World War 3, 31, 37, 67, 82,
    158, 194
sentimentality 37–9, 45, 59, 94, 196
Shohat, Ella 79–80, 84, 96
siege 100, 104, 142, 153, 162, 177,
    178, 192–5
Silverman, Kaja 5, 12, 13, 31, 52
socialism 6, 8, 22–3, 27–30, 45, 67,
    194
Sontag, Susan 27, 28, 46, 128–30
sovereignty 3–4, 7–9, 10, 88, 96, 135,
    162–6, 168, 170–4, 186, 188,
    192
spectacle 10, 19, 25, 40–6, 47, 177,
    181, 185
State Security (Stasi) 26, 51, 62, 64–6,
    69
stereotypes 85, 91, 137, 147, 150
Street, John 184–5
structure of feeling 80, 105–6, 109,
    113, 125–7, 132–3, 193
  structure of unfeeling 100, 105–6,
    109, 113
Suleiman Elia 85, 98–105
surveillance 9, 10, 22, 28, 52, 54–5,
    63–9, 111, 120, 141, 155–6, 166

temporality 28, 39, 46–7, 61, 76,
    136–7, 159
terror 55, 62–3, 65, 69, 72, 75, 91–8
terrorism 17, 80, 85, 88, 91–8, 177,
    190
  War on Terror 3, 91
The Apprentice 163, 184, 185
The Invisible Frame 52, 57–62, 77
The Lives of Others 52, 62–9, 74,
    75–6
The Time That Remains 99, 103–4, 105
The Walled Off Hotel 119–20
Tiny Wall 184–5
tourism 23, 58, 107, 112–13, 118–19
transference 19, 47, 51, 73–4, 103,
    114, 116–7, 156, 194
trauma 5, 6, 12, 13, 17–19, 30–6,
    36–9, 44, 50, 55, 60, 72–3, 85,
    90, 99–105, 106, 109, 114, 117,
    121–4, 125, 127, 132–3, 136–9,
    151–7, 158–9, 179, 194, 197
Trump, Donald 18, 108, 115–17, 135–6,
    158–9, 161–86
Trump, Melania 173, 175–6
Tuck, Eve 136, 150

Unsicker, Peter 30–6, 56
  Crack in the Mirror
  The Ice Cold War
  MuSehum fuer Unbewaeltigtes
  Wood against Concrete
  The Work on Ruination
  Wound Plaster

Vallet, Élisabeth 3
Verdichtung 68–9, 76, 193
viscerality 2, 5, 11, 13, 23, 30, 80, 96,
    98, 103–5, 127, 155, 188–9
vulnerability 2, 10, 11, 17, 27, 28, 74,
    75, 89–90, 91, 96, 120, 123–4,
    127, 128, 135, 139, 147, 158,
    176–8, 188, 193, 196

Waclawek, Anna 110
War of Independence 85, 103
Weizman, Eyal 83–4, 108, 122
West, Cornel 164
white supremacy 162, 163–4, 178

whiteness 18, 45, 138–40, 142, 159, 162–5, 169–73, 173–7, 178–9, 180–4, 185–6
Wolfe, Patrick 8, 139, 169
woman-as-nation 142, 173–7
working through 31–4, 40, 133, 150
wound 25, 32, 74, 85, 136, 137, 143, 148, 157, 174, 179, 183, 195

xenophobia 45, 46, 115, 153, 157, 171, 174, 177, 184, 192, 193

Yuval-Davis, Nira 173–4

Zionism 82–5, 95, 99, 101, 105, 121–4

www.ingramcontent.com/pod-product-compliance
Lightning Source LLC
Chambersburg PA
CBHW062126300426
44115CB00012BA/1824